THE STANDARD BOOK OF BRITISH AND AMERICAN VERSE

THE STANDARD BOOK OF BRITISH AND AMERICAN VERSE

Selected by NELLA BRADDY

Preface by
CHRISTOPHER MORLEY

Granger Index Reprint Series

BOOKS FOR LIBRARIES PRESS
FREEPORT, NEW YORK

Reprinted 1972 by arrangement.

INTERNATIONAL STANDARD BOOK NUMBER:
0-8369-6326-1

LIBRARY OF CONGRESS CATALOG CARD NUMBER:
72-38594

PRINTED IN THE UNITED STATES OF AMERICA
BY
NEW WORLD BOOK MANUFACTURING CO., INC.
HALLANDALE, FLORIDA 33009

ACKNOWLEDGMENTS

PERMISSION has been secured from the authors or from the authorized publishers or agents for the use of all copyrighted material reprinted in this volume, and special arrangements have been made for the use of various poems, both English and American, on which the copyright no longer holds. The publishers' thanks are due to the following for permission to reprint:

THE CENTURY COMPANY and Mr. Cale Young Rice for *New Dreams for Old* from "Selected Plays and Poems," by Cale Young Rice, copyright, 1915, by the Century Company.

COVICI, FRIEDE, INC., for *After Two Years* by Richard Aldington, from "The Collected Poems of Richard Aldington," published by Covici, Friede, Inc.

THE BOBBS-MERRILL COMPANY for *When the Frost Is on the Punkin* from "Neighborly Poems" by James Whitcomb Riley, copyrighted 1891 and 1919. This poem is used by special permission of the publishers, The Bobbs-Merrill Company.

DODD, MEAD AND COMPANY, INC. The poems by Laurence Binyon, Rupert Brooke, Bliss Carman, Ernest Dowson, Richard Hovey, Henry Newbolt, John Davidson, and Arthur Symons are used by permission of Dodd, Mead and Company, Inc.

E. P. DUTTON AND COMPANY, INC., for *The White Rose* from "Moondyne" by John Boyle O'Reilly, published by E. P. Dutton and Company, Inc.

FARRAR AND RINEHART, INC., for *Tears* from "Selected Poems" by Lizette Woodworth Reese.

HARCOURT, BRACE AND COMPANY, INC. The poems from "Challenge" by Louis Untermeyer are used by permission of Harcourt, Brace and Company, Inc., holders of the copyright.

HARPER AND BROTHERS for the poems by Algernon Charles Swinburne from "Poems and Ballads," First Series.

WILLIAM HEINEMANN, LTD., and Mr. Siegfried Sassoon for the latter's poem, *Everyone Sang,* from "The Picture Show."

HENRY HOLT AND COMPANY for the poems by Walter de la Mare from "The Listeners and Other Poems," 1916; by Carl Sandburg from "Chicago Poems," 1916, and "Cornhuskers," 1918; and by Robert Frost from "North of Boston," 1915, and "New Hampshire," 1923.

HOUGHTON MIFFLIN COMPANY. The poems by Amy Lowell, Louise Imogen Guiney, William Vaughan Moody, Edward Rowland Sill, Thomas Bailey Aldrich, John Burroughs, Ralph Waldo Emerson, Oliver Wendell Holmes, Henry Wadsworth Longfellow, James Russell Lowell, and John Greenleaf Whittier are used by permission of, and special arrangement with, the Houghton Mifflin Company.

ALFRED A. KNOPF, INC. *War Is Kind* is reprinted from the "Collected Poems" of Stephen Crane and *Song* from "Verse" by Adelaide Crapsey, by permission of, and special arrangement with, Alfred A. Knopf, Inc., authorized publishers.

JOHN LANE THE BODLEY HEAD, LTD., and the author for *Full Moon* from "Orchard and Vineyard" by V. Sackville-West.

LITTLE, BROWN AND COMPANY. The selections from "The Poems of Emily Dickinson," Centenary Edition, edited by Martha Dickinson Bianchi and Alfred Leete, are reprinted by permission of Little, Brown and Company, to whom the publishers are also indebted for the use of *High Tide on the Coast of Lincolnshire* by Jean Ingelow and *Light* by Francis William Bourdillon.

HORACE LIVERIGHT, INC., and Mr. Sheamus O'Sheel for the latter's poem, *He Whom a Dream Hath Possessed* from "Jealous of Dead Leaves," 1928.

LONGMANS, GREEN AND COMPANY for *The Waves of Breffny* from "Poems" by Eva Gore-Booth.

THE MACMILLAN COMPANY. The poems by Matthew Arnold from "Lyric and Elegiac Poems" and "Early Poems, Narrative Poems and Sonnets"; the poem by Padraic Colum from "Wild Earth"; the poems by Thomas Hardy from "Collected Poems" and "Late Lyrics and Earlier"; the poems by Wilfrid Wilson Gibson from "Collected Poems"; the poems by Vachel Lindsay from "Collected Poems"; by John Masefield from "Collected Poems"; by John Neihardt from "The Quest"; by Edwin Arlington Robinson from "Collected Poems"; by James Stephens from "Songs from the Clay" and "A Poetry Recital"; by Sara Teasdale from "Dark of the Moon"; by William Butler Yeats from "Early Poems and Stories"; by Thomas Brown from "Poems"; by Ralph Hodgson from "Poems"; by Moira O'Neill from "Songs of the

Glens of Antrim"; by Wilfrid Scawen Blunt from "Poems"; by W. S. Gilbert from "Bab Ballads"; and the selections from the collected poems of Christina Rossetti and Alfred Tennyson are used by permission of The Macmillan Company, publishers.

METHUEN AND COMPANY, LTD., for *Love Is a Keeper of Swans* from "The Unknown Goddess" by Humbert Wolfe.

THE OXFORD UNIVERSITY PRESS for the poems by Austin Dobson, and The Clarendon Press, Oxford, England, for the selections from the "Shorter Poems of Robert Bridges," Clarendon Press, 1931.

CHARLES SCRIBNER'S SONS for the poems by Conrad Aiken from "Selected Poems"; by Max Eastman from "Kinds of Love"; and for the selections from the poetical works of Eugene Field, William Ernest Henley, Sidney Lanier, George Meredith ("Love in the Valley"), Edwin Arlington Robinson ("Dionysius in Doubt"), Alice Meynell, Alan Seeger, Robert Louis Stevenson, Henry van Dyke, Francis Thompson, and George Santayana.

MARTIN SECKER, LTD., for the selections from "The Collected Poems of James Elroy Flecker."

FREDERICK A. STOKES AND COMPANY for the selections from "Collected Poems," Volume I, by Alfred Noyes.

THE SOUTHWEST PRESS for *Let Me Grow Lovely* from "Dreamers on Horseback" by Karle Wilson Baker.

YALE UNIVERSITY PRESS for the selections from "The Poems of Arthur O'Shaughnessy," selected and edited by William Alexander Percy, and for *Merchants from Cathay* from the volume of the same name by William Rose Benét.

BRANDT AND BRANDT and Miss Edna St. Vincent Millay for the latter's poem, *God's World,* which is taken from "Renascence," published by Harper Bros. Copyright, 1917, by Edna St. Vincent Millay.

THE PAGET LITERARY AGENCY. *Leisure* from "Songs of Joy" by W. H. Davies is used by permission of Jonathan Cape, Ltd.

A. P. WATT AND SON for *Recessional* from "The Five Nations," by Rudyard Kipling, copyright, 1905.

MRS. GEORGE SARGENT BURGESS, executrix, for *America the Beautiful* by Katherine Lee Bates.

MR. GELETT BURGESS for *The Purple Cow* from the "Burgess Book of Nonsense," Boni and Liveright, publishers, N. Y.

MRS. CARL H. ELMORE (AMELIA JOSEPHINE BURR) for *A Song*

of Living from "Selected Lyrics" by Amelia Josephine Burr, copyright, 1927, by Doubleday, Doran and Company, Inc.

MRS. CHARLOTTE P. S. GILMAN for her poem, *The Conservative.*

MR. GERALD GURNEY and the Oxford University Press for *God's Garden* by Dorothy Frances Gurney.

MR. HERMANN HAGEDORN for *Song Is So Old* from "A Troop of the Guard."

MRS. JOYCE KILMER (ALINE KILMER) for her husband's poem, *Trees.*

MR. LOUIS LOVEMAN for *April Rain* by Robert Loveman.

DR. THOMAS MCCRAE for *In Flanders Fields* by John McCrae.

MR. EDWIN MARKHAM for *The Man with the Hoe* which is copyrighted by him.

MR. EDGAR LEE MASTERS for *Herbert Marshall* from the "Spoon River Anthology."

MR. CHRISTOPHER MORLEY for the selections from the "Poems" of Christopher Morley.

CONTENTS

PREFACE

For various reasons I had been immersed in prose. But I was sharply aware that it was a long time since I had read much poetry. It was like that feeling one has in early summer before the first swim: a hankering, after months mostly indoors, for the open freedom and shock of chill salt water. Then by chance I was handed a big bundle of galley sheets, the proofs of this book. One whole morning my mind plunged and sunned itself in these deep clear waters. (I read the book, as anthologies should be read, from the last page backward, so that you begin with the contemporary mood and gradually swim toward older words and manners.) And I realized again what poverty we live in when we deny ourselves the Gold Standard of verse. How rich, how frank, how full of truth are those outcries of human song. Yes, I am mixing my metaphors. But how clumsy and evasive is the strongest novelist by comparison: like a longshoreman in rubber boots plodding along the beach, while the poet, bare athletic swimmer, is diving from the end of the pier.

There are innumerable anthologies, but perhaps there can never be too many. Every time a new one is published it reminds me of a traveller who once more shoulders his pack after a wayside halt. So humanity goes on, bundling up anew the things it has found precious. This collection is conservative; it sticks to the standard things, but in poetry familiarity breeds no contempt. The familiar poems come to us fresh and with new-washed color every time we meet them.

A generous anthology of verse is a household necessity: it is the pantry-cupboard of the spirit on whose shelves are nourishment for any emergency. Unexpected guests come to dinner in the mind as well as in the household: the poets have stored wine and meat and spices for every requirement. With what queerly mingled joy (mixed of old recollection and new surprise) the well-loved lines come back to us. After a few hours reading, how delightful a jumble of honored memories fills us. We sing them to ourselves to tunes of our own:—

"When I have fears that I may cease to be, My name is Ozymandias, King of Kings, To think such breasts must suckle slaves, Say I'm growing old, but add—Jenny kissed me, Aye, tear her tattered ensign down,

The fever called Living is conquered at last, A chieftain to the Highlands bound cries, 'Boatman, do not tarry,' Wheneas in silks my Julia goes, 'Tis the middle of night by the castle clock, O world be nobler for her sake, Thine alabaster cities gleam undimmed by human tears, And what can ail the mastiff bitch? Her paps are centres of delight, Heigh-ho, would she were mine, Thou straggler into loving arms, young climber-up of knees. . . ."

And each of the familiar miracles strengthens us when we find it still imperishably right. The years tremble and reel beneath us, as Walt Whitman said; kingdoms crumble and old buildings are wrecked in dust and splinters, but no one tears down old poems. They have the life beyond life. They deal not with shams and brokerages, not with paper values and stage tears, but with the real joys and horrors every person knows. There is a sign I have sometimes seen on main roads—ARTERIAL HIGHWAY. A book like this preserves the circulation of bright human blood. It is an Arterial Highway. Not to know what joy and sadness is to be had in reading poetry is not to have begun to live. James Elroy Flecker gracefully expressed the mood in which our older brothers greet us here:—

O friend unseen, unborn, unknown,
Student of our sweet English tongue,
Read out my words at night, alone:
I was a poet, I was young.

Since I can never see your face,
And never shake you by the hand,
I send my soul through time and space
To greet you. You will understand.

The world cried out "for madder music and for stronger wine." But the maddest and strongest was always waiting for us in these pages.

CHRISTOPHER MORLEY.

THE STANDARD BOOK OF BRITISH AND AMERICAN VERSE

ANONYMOUS

Carol

I SING of a maiden
  That is mateless
King of all kinges
  To her son she chose.

He came all so stille
  There his mother was
As dew in Aprille
  That falleth on grass.

He came all so stille
  To his mother's bower,
As dew in Aprille
  That falleth on the flower.

He came all so stille
  There his mother lay,
As dew in Aprille
  That falleth on the spray.

Mother and maiden
  Was never none but she;
Well may such a lady
  Godes mother be.

GEOFFREY CHAUCER

(c. 1340–1400)

To Rosemounde. A Balade

Madame, ye ben of al beauté shryne
As fer as cercled is the mappemounde;
For as the cristal glorious ye shyne,
And lyke ruby ben your chekes rounde.
Therwith ye ben so mery and so jocounde,
That at a revel whan that I see you daunce,
It is an oynement unto my wounde,
Thogh ye to me ne do no daliaunce.

For though I wepe of teres ful a tyne,
Yet may that wo myn herte nat confounde;
Your seemly voys that ye so smal out-twyne
Maketh my thoght in joye and blis habounde.
So curteisly I go, with lovë bounde,
That to my-self I sey, in my penaunce,
Suffyseth me to love you, Rosemounde,
Thogh ye to me do no daliaunce.

Nas never pyk walwed in galauntyne
As I love am walwed and y-wounde;
For which ful ofte I of my-self divyne
That I am trewe Tristam the secounde.
My love may not refreyd be nor afounde;
I brenne ay in an amorous pleasaunce.
Do what you list, I wil your thral be founde,
Thogh ye to me do no daliaunce.

Morning in May

The busy larke, messager of daye,
Salueth in hire song the morwe graye;

And fyry Phebus ryseth up so brighte,
That al the orient laugheth of the lighte,
And with his stremes dryeth in the greves
The silver dropes, hongyng on the leeves.
And Arcite, that is in the court ryal
With Theseus, his squyer principal,
Is risen, and loketh on the merye day.
And for to doon his observaunce to May,
Remembryng on the poynt of his desir,
He on his courser, stertyng as the fir,
Is riden, into the feeldes him to pleye,
Out of the court, were it a myle or tweye.
And to the grove, of which that I yow tolde,
By aventure his wey he gan to holde,
To maken him a garland of the greves,
Were it of woodebynde or hawethorn leves,
And lowde he song ayens the sonne scheene:
"May, with alle thy floures and thy greene,
Welcome be thou, wel faire, fressche May,
I hope that I som grene gete may."

From THE KNIGHTES TALE.

Nowel

AND this was, as the bokes me remembre,
The colde frosty seson of Decembre.
Phebus wex old, and hewed lyk latoun,
That in his hote declinacioun
Shoon as the burned gold with stremes brighte;
But now in Capricorn adoun he lighte,
Wher-as he shoon ful pale, I dar wel seyn.
The bittre frostes, with the sleet and reyn,
Destroyed hath the grene in every yerd.
Janus sit by the fyr, with double berd,
And drinketh of his bugle-horn the wyn.
Biforn him stant braun of the tusked swyn,
And "Nowel" cryeth every lusty man.

From THE FRANKELEYNS TALE.

The Compleint of Chaucer to His Empty Purse

To you, my purse, and to non other wight
Compleyne I, for ye be my lady dere!
I am so sory, now that ye be light;
For certes, but ye make me hevy chere,
Me were as leef be leyd up-on my bere;
For whiche un-to your mercy thus I crye:
Beth hevy ageyn, or elles mot I dye!

Now voucheth sauf this day, or hit be night,
That I of you the blisful soun may here,
Or see your colour lyk the sonne bright,
That of yelownesse hadde never pere.
Ye be my lyf, ye be myn hertes stere,
Quene of comfort and of good companye:
Beth hevy ageyn, or elles mot I dye!

Now purs, that be to me my lyves light,
And saveour, as doun in this worlde here,
Out of this toune help me through your might,
Sin that ye wole nat been my tresorere;
For I am shave as nye as any frere.
But yit I pray un-to your curtesye:
Beth hevy ageyn, or elles mot I dye!

L'ENVOY DE CHAUCER

O conquerour of Brutes Albioun!
Which that by lyne and free eleccioun
Ben verray king, this song to you I sende;
And ye, that mowen al our harm amende,
Have minde up-on my supplicacioun!

BALLADS

(Authors unknown)

Sir Patrick Spens

THE King sits in Dunfermline town,
  Drinking the blude-red wine:
"O whaur will I get a skeely skipper
  To sail this new ship o' mine?"

O up and spake an eldern knight,
  Sat at the King's right knee:
"Sir Patrick Spens is the best sailor
  That ever sailed the sea."

Our King has written a braid letter
  And sealed it wi' his hand,
And sent it to Sir Patrick Spens,
  Was walking on the strand.

"To Noroway, to Noroway,
  To Noroway o'er the faem;
The King's daughter to Noroway,
  'Tis thou maun bring her hame."

The first word that Sir Patrick read,
  Sae loud, loud lauchèd he;
The neist word that Sir Patrick read,
  The tear blinded his ee.

"O wha is this has done this deed,
  And tauld the King of me,
To send us out at this time o' year
  To sail upon the sea?

Be it wind, be it weet, be it hail, be it sleet,
  Our ship must sail the faem;
The King's daughter to Noroway,
  'Tis we must bring her hame."

They hoysed their sails on Monday morn
  Wi' a' the speed they may;
They hae landed in Noroway
  Upon a Wodensday.

They hadna been a week, a week,
  In Noroway but twae,
When that the lords o' Noroway
  Began aloud to say:

"Ye Scottishmen spend a' our King's goud
  And a' our Queenis fee."
"Ye lie, ye lie, ye liars loud,
  Fu' loud I hear ye lie!

For I brought as mickle white monie
  As gane my men and me,
And I brought a half-fou o' gude red goud
  Out-o'er the sea wi' me.

Mak' ready, mak' ready, my merry men a'!
  Our gude ship sails the morn."
"Now, ever alake, my master dear,
  I fear a deadly storm.

I saw the new moon late yestreen
  Wi' the auld moon in her arm;
And, if we gang to sea, master,
  I fear we'll come to harm."

They hadna sailed a league, a league,
  A league but barely three,
When the lift grew dark, and the wind blew loud,
  And gurly grew the sea.

"O where will I get a gude sailor
  To tak' my helm in hand,
Till I gae up to the tall topmast
  To see if I can spy land?"

"O here am I, a sailor gude,
  To tak' the helm in hand,
Till you gae up to the tall topmast;
  But I fear you'll ne'er spy land."

He hadna gane a step, a step,
  A step but barely ane,
When a bolt flew out o' our goodly ship,
  And the salt sea it came in.

"Gae fetch a web o' the silken claith,
  Anither o' the twine,
And wap them into our ship's side,
  And letna the sea come in."

They fetched a web o' the silken claith,
  Anither o' the twine,
And they wapped them round that gude ship's side,
  But still the sea cam' in.

O laith, laith were our gude Scots lords
  To weet their milk-white hands;
But lang ere a' the play was ower
  They wat their gowden bands.

O laith, laith were our gude Scots lords
  To weet their cork-heeled shoon;
But lang ere a' the play was played
  They wat their hats aboon.

O lang, lang may the ladies sit
  Wi' their fans intill their hand,
Before they see Sir Patrick Spens
  Come sailing to the strand!

And lang, lang may the maidens sit
  Wi' their goud kaims in their hair,
A' waiting for their ain dear loves!
  For them they'll see nae mair.

Half ower, half ower to Aberdour,
It's fifty fathoms deep,
And there lies gude Sir Patrick Spens
Wi' the Scots lords at his feet.

Edward, Edward

"Why does your brand sae drop wi' blude,
Edward, Edward?
Why does your brand sae drop wi' blude,
And why sae sad gang ye, O?"—
"O I hae kill'd my hawk sae gude,
Mither, mither;
O I hae kill'd my hawk sae gude,
And I had nae mair but he, O."

"Your hawk's blude was never sae red,
Edward, Edward;
Your hawk's blude was never sae red,
My dear son, I tell thee, O."—
"O I hae kill'd my red-roan steed,
Mither, mither;
O I hae kill'd my red-roan steed
That erst was sae fair and free, O."

"Your steed was auld, and ye hae got mair,
Edward, Edward;
Your steed was auld, and ye hae got mair;
Some other dule[1] ye dree,[2] O."
"O I hae kill'd my father dear,
Mither, mither;
O I hae kill'd my father dear,
Alas, and wae is me, O!"

[1]Dole, woe. [2]Suffer.

"And whatten penance will ye dree for that,
Edward, Edward?
Whatten penance will ye dree for that?
My dear son, now tell me, O."—
"I'll set my feet in yonder boat,
Mither, mither;
I'll set my feet in yonder boat,
And I'll fare over the sea, O."

"And what will ye do wi' your tow'rs and your ha',
Edward, Edward?
And what will ye do wi' your tow'rs and your ha',
That were sae fair to see, O?"—
"I'll let them stand till they doun fa',
Mither, mither;
I'll let them stand till they doun fa',
For here never mair maun I be, O."

"And what will ye leave to your bairns and your wife,
Edward, Edward?
"And what will ye leave to your bairns and your wife,
When ye gang owre the sea, O?"—
"The warld's room: let them beg through life,
Mither, mither;
The warld's room: let them beg through life;
For them never mair will I see, O."

"And what will ye leave to your ain mither dear,
Edward, Edward?
And what will ye leave to your ain mither dear,
My dear son, now tell me, O?"—
"The curse of hell frae me sall ye bear,
Mither, mither;
The curse of hell frae me sall ye bear:
Sic counsels ye gave to me, O!"

Lord Randal

"O WHERE ha'e ye been, Lord Randal, my son?
O where ha'e ye been, my handsome young man?"
"I ha'e been to the wild wood; mother make my bed soon;
For I'm weary wi' hunting, and fain wald lie down."

"Where gat ye your dinner, Lord Randal, my son?
Where gat ye your dinner, my handsome young man?"
"I dined wi' my true-love; mother, make my bed soon;
For I'm weary wi' hunting, and fain wald lie down."

"What gat ye to your dinner, Lord Randal, my son?
What gat ye to your dinner, my handsome young man?"
"I gat eels boiled in broo'; mother, make my bed soon;
For I'm weary wi' hunting, and fain wald lie down."

"What became of your bloodhounds, Lord Randal, my son?
What became of your bloodhounds, my handsome young man?"
"O they swelled and they died; mother, make my bed soon;
For I'm weary wi' hunting, and fain wald lie down."

"O I fear ye are poisoned, Lord Randal, my son!
I fear ye are poisoned, my handsome young man!"
"Oh yes! I am poisoned; mother, make my bed soon;
For I'm sick at the heart, and I fain wald lie down."

Waly, Waly, But Love Be Bonny

O, WALY, waly up the bank,
  And waly, waly down the brae,
And waly, waly yon burn side,
  Where I and my love wont to gae.

I leaned my back unto an aik,
  I thought it was a trusty tree;
But first it bowed, and syne it brak—
  Sae my true love did lightly me!

O, waly, waly, but love be bonny,
  A little time while it is new;
But when 't is auld it waxeth cauld,
  And fades away like the morning dew.

O, wherefore should I busk my head?
  Or wherefore should I kame my hair?
For my true love has me forsook,
  And says he'll never love me mair.

Now Arthur-Seat shall be my bed;
  The sheets shall ne'er be fyled by me;
Saint Anton's well shall be my drink,
  Since my true love has forsaken me.

Martinmas wind, when wilt thou blaw,
  And shake the green leaves off the tree?
O gentle death, when wilt thou come?
  For of my life I'm weary.

'T is not the frost that freezes fell,
  Nor blawing snaw's inclemency;
'T is not sic cauld that makes me cry,
  But my love's heart grown cauld to me.

When we came in by Glasgow town,
  We were a comely sight to see;
My love was clad in the black velvet,
  And I mysell in cramasie.

But had I wist, before I kissed,
  That love had been sae ill to win,
I'd locked my heart in a case of gold,
  And pinned it with a silver pin.

Oh, oh, if my young babe were born,
  And set upon the nurse's knee,
And I mysell were dead and gane,
  And the green grass growin' over me!

Binnorie

Also called "The Twa Sisters"

THERE were twa sisters sat in a bour;
  Binnorie, O Binnorie!
There cam a knight to be their wooer,
  By the bonnie milldams o' Binnorie.

He courted the eldest with glove and ring,
But he lo'ed the youngest abune[1] a' thing.

The eldest she was vexèd sair,
And sair enviėd her sister fair.

Upon a morning fair and clear,
She cried upon her sister dear:

"O sister, sister, tak my hand,
And we'll see our father's ships to land."

She's ta'en her by the lily hand,
And led her down to the river-strand.

The youngest stood upon a stane,
The eldest cam and push'd her in.

"O sister, sister, reach your hand!
And ye sall be heir o' half my land:

"O sister, reach me but your glove!
And sweet William sall be your love."—

[1]Above.

"Foul fa' the hand that I should take;
It twin'd[1] me o' my warldis make.[2]

"Your cherry cheeks and your yellow hair
Gar'd me gang maiden evermair."

Sometimes she sank, sometimes she swam.
Until she cam to the miller's dam.

Out then cam the miller's son,
And saw the fair maid soummin'[3] in.

"O father, father, draw your dam!
There's either a mermaid or a milk-white swan."

The miller hasted and drew his dam,
And there he found a drown'd womàn.

You couldna see her middle sma',
Her gowden girdle was sae braw.

You couldna see her lily feet,
Her gowden fringes were sae deep.

You couldna see her yellow hair
For the strings o' pearls was twisted there.

You couldna see her fingers sma',
Wi' diamond rings they were cover'd a'.

And by there cam a harper fine,
That harpit to the king at dine.

And when he look'd that lady on,
He sigh'd and made a heavy moan.

He's made a harp of her breast-bane,
Whose sound wad melt a heart of stane.

[1]Robbed. [2]My one mate in the world. [3]Swimming.

He's ta'en three locks o' her yellow hair,
And wi' them strung his harp sae rare.

He went into her father's hall,
And there was the court assembled all.

He laid his harp upon a stane,
And straight it began to play by lane.[1]

"O yonder sits my father, the King,
And yonder sits my mother, the Queen;

"And yonder stands my brother Hugh,
And by him my William, sweet and true."

But the last tune that the harp play'd then—
Binnorie, O Binnorie!
Was, "Woe to my sister, false Helèn!"
By the bonnie milldams o' Binnorie.

The Wife of Usher's Well

THERE lived a wife at Usher's Well,
And a wealthy wife was she;
She had three stout and stalwart sons,
And sent them o'er the sea.

They hadna been a week from her,
A week but barely ane,
Whan word came to the carline wife,
That her three sons were gane.

They hadna been a week from her,
A week but barely three,
Whan word came to the carline wife,
That her sons she'd never see.

[1] By itself.

"I wish the wind may never cease,
  Nor fishes in the flood,
Till my three sons come hame to me,
  In earthly flesh and blood!"

It fell about the Martinmas,
  When nights are lang and mirk,
The carline wife's three sons came hame,
  And their hats were o' the birk.

It neither grew in syke nor ditch,
  Nor yet in ony sheugh;
But at the gates o' Paradise,
  That birk grew fair eneugh.

"Blow up the fire, my maidens!
  Bring water from the well!
For a' my house shall feast this night,
  Since my three sons are well."

And she has made to them a bed,
  She's made it large and wide;
And she's ta'en her mantle her about,
  Sat down at the bed-side.

Up then crew the red, red cock,
  And up and crew the grey;
The eldest to the youngest said,
  " 'Tis time we were awa'."

The cock he hadna crawed but once,
  And clapped his wings at a'
Whan the youngest to the eldest said,
  "Brother, we must awa'.

"The cock doth craw, the day doth daw',
  The channerin' worm doth chide;
Gin we be missed out o' our place,
  A sair pain we maun bide."

"Lie still, lie still, a little wee while,
  Lie still but if we may;
Gin my mother should miss us when she wakes,
  She'll go mad ere it be day."

O they've ta'en up their mother's mantle
  And they've hinged it on the pin:
"O lang may ye hing, my mother's mantle,
  Ere ye hap us again!

"Fare-ye-weel, my mother dear!
  Fareweel to barn and byre!
And fare-ye-weel, the bonny lass
  That kindles my mother's fire."

The Twa Corbies

As I was walking all alane,
I heard twa corbies making a mane:
The tane unto the tither say,
"Where sall we gang and dine the day?"

"In behint yon auld fail dyke
I wot there lies a new-slain knight;
And naebody kens that he lies there
But his hawk, his hound, and his lady fair.

His hound is to the hunting gane,
His hawk to fetch the wild-fowl hame,
His lady's ta'en another mate,
Sae we may mak' our dinner sweet.

Ye'll sit on his white hause-bane,
And I'll pike out his bonny blue e'en:
Wi' ae lock o' his gowden hair
We'll theek our nest when it grows bare.

Mony a one for him makes mane,
But nane sall ken where he is gane:
O'er his white banes, when they are bare,
The wind sall blaw for evermair."

Bonnie George Campbell

HIE upon Hielands
And low upon Tay
Bonnie George Campbell
Rade out on a day.

Saddled and bridled
And gallant rade he;
Hame came his gude horse
But never cam he!

Out cam his auld mither
Greeting fu' sair,
And out cam his bonnie bride
Rivin' her hair.

Saddled and bridled
And booted rade he;
Toom[1] hame cam the saddle,
But never cam he!

"My meadow lies green,
And my corn is unshorn;
My barn is to big,
And my babie's unborn."

Saddled and bridled
And booted rode he,
A plume in his helmet,
A sword at his knee.

[1] Empty.

But toom cam his saddle
All bluidy to see;
Oh, hame cam his guid horse,
But never cam he.

Barbara Allen's Cruelty

In scarlet town, where I was born,
There was a fair maid dwellin',
Made every youth cry *Well-a-way!*
Her name was Barbara Allen.

All in the merry month of May
When green buds they were swellin',
Young Jemmy Grove on his death-bed lay,
For love of Barbara Allen.

He sent his man in to her then,
To the town where she was dwellin',
"O haste and come to my master dear,
If your name be Barbara Allen."

So slowly, slowly rase she up,
And slowly she came nigh him,
And when she drew the curtain by—
"Young man, I think you're dyin'."

"O it's I'm sick and very very sick,
And it's all for Barbara Allen."
"O the better for me ye'se never be,
Tho' your heart's blood were a-spillin'!

"O dinna ye mind, young man," says she,
When the red wine ye were fillin',
That ye made the healths go round and round,
And slighted Barbara Allen?"

He turn'd his face unto the wall,
  And death was with him dealin':
"Adieu, adieu, my dear friends all,
  And be kind to Barbara Allen!"

As she was walking o'er the fields,
  She heard the dead-bell knellin';
And every jow the dead-bell gave
  Cried "Woe to Barbara Allen."

"O mother, mother, make my bed,
  O make it saft and narrow:
My love has died for me to-day,
  I'll die for him to-morrow.

"Farewell," she said, "ye virgins all,
  And shun the fault I fell in:
Henceforth take warning by the fall
  Of cruel Barbara Allen."

Fine Flowers in the Valley

SHE sat down below a thorn,
  Fine flowers in the valley;
And there she has her sweet babe born,
  And the green leaves they grow rarely.

"Smile na sae sweet, my bonny babe,
  Fine flowers in the valley,
And ye smile sae sweet, ye'll smile me dead,"
  And the green leaves they grow rarely.

She's ta'en out her little penknife,
  Fine flowers in the valley,
And twinn'd the sweet babe o' its life,
  And the green leaves they grow rarely.

She's howket a grave by the light o' the moon,
Fine flowers in the valley,
And there she's buried her sweet babe in,
And the green leaves they grow rarely.

As she was going to the church,
Fine flowers in the valley,
She saw a sweet babe in the porch,
And the green leaves they grow rarely.

"O sweet babe, and thou were mine,
Fine flowers in the valley,
I wad clead thee in the silk so fine,"
And the green leaves they grow rarely.

"O mother dear, when I was thine,
Fine flowers in the valley,
Ye did na prove to me sae kind,"
And the green leaves they grow rarely.

Fair Helen

I WISH I were where Helen lies;
Night and day on me she cries;
O that I were where Helen lies
On fair Kirconnell lea!

Curst be the heart that thought the thought,
And curst the hand that fired the shot,
When in my arms burd Helen dropt,
And died to succour me!

O think na but my heart was sair
When my Love dropt down and spak nae mair!
I laid her down wi' meikle care,
On fair Kirconnell lea.

As I went down the water-side,
None but my foe to be my guide,
None but my foe to be my guide,
On fair Kirconnell lea;

I lighted down my sword to draw,
I hackèd him in pieces sma',
I hackèd him in pieces sma',
For her sake that died for me.

O Helen fair, beyond compare!
I'll make a garland of thy hair,
Shall bind my heart for evermair,
Until the day I die.

O that I were where Helen lies!
Night and day on me she cries;
Out of my bed she bids me rise,
Says, "Haste and come to me!"

O Helen fair! O Helen chaste!
If I were with thee, I were blest,
Where thou lies low and takes thy rest
On fair Kirconnell lea.

I wish my grave were growing green,
A winding-sheet drawn ower my een,
And I in Helen's arms lying,
On fair Kirconnell lea.

I wish I were where Helen lies!
Night and day on me she cries;
And I am weary of the skies,
Since my Love died for me.

JOHN SKELTON

(c. 1460–1529)

To Mistress Margaret Hussey

MERRY Margaret,
As midsummer flower,
Gentle as falcon,
Or hawk of the tower;
With solace and gladness,
Much mirth and no madness,
All good and no badness;
So joyously,
So maidenly,
So womanly
Her demeaning,
In everything
Far, far passing
That I can indite,
Or suffice to write,
Of merry Margaret,
As midsummer flower,
Gentle as falcon
Or hawk of the tower;
As patient and as still,
And as full of good-will,
As fair Isiphil,
Coliander,
Sweet Pomander,
Good Cassander;
Stedfast of thought,
Well made, well wrought;
Far may be sought
Ere you can find
So courteous, so kind,
As merry Margaret,
This midsummer flower,
Gentle as falcon,
Or hawk of the tower.

STEPHEN HAWES

(d. 1523)

An Epitaph

O MORTAL folk, you may behold and see
How I lie here, sometime a mighty knight;
The end of joy and all prosperitee
Is death at last, thorough his course and might:
After the day there cometh the dark night,
For though the day be never so long,
At last the bells ringeth to evensong.

ANONYMOUS

Hey Nonny No!

HEY nonny no!
Men are fools that wish to die!
Is't not fine to dance and sing
When the bells of death do ring?
Is't not fine to swim in wine,
And turn upon the toe,
And sing hey nonny no!
When the winds blow and the seas flow?
Hey nonny no!

Joly Joly Wat

THE shepherd upon a hill he sat;
He had on him his tabard and his hat,
His tarbox, his pipe, and his flagat;
His name was called Joly Joly Wat,
For he was a good herdes boy
Ut hoy!
For in his pipe he made so much joy.

The shepherd upon a hill was laid;
His dog to his girdle was tied;
He had not slept but a little braid,
But "Gloria in excelsis" was to him said.
Ut hoy!
For in his pipe he made so much joy.

The shepherd on a hill he stood;
Round about him his sheep they yode;
He put his hand under his hood,
He saw a star as red as blood.
Ut hoy!
For in his pipe he made so much joy.

The shepherd said anon right,
"I will go see yon farly sight,
Whereas the angel singeth on height,
And the star that shineth so bright."
Ut hoy!
For in his pipe he made so much joy.

"Now farewell, Moll, and also Will!
For my love go ye all still
Unto I come again you till,
And evermore, Will, ring well thy bell."
Ut hoy!
For in his pipe he made so much joy.

"Now must I go there Christ was born;
Farewell! I come again to morn.
Dog, keep well my sheep from the corn,
And warn well 'Warroke' when I blow my horn!"
Ut hoy!
For in his pipe he made so much joy.

When Wat to Bethlehem come was,
He sweat, he had gone faster than a pace;
He found Jesu in a simple place,
Between an ox and an ass.
Ut hoy!
For in his pipe he made so much joy.

"Jesu, I offer thee here my pipe,
My skirt, my tarbox, and my scrip;
Home to my fellows now will I skip,
And also look unto my sheep."
Ut hoy!
For in his pipe he made so much joy.

"Now farewell, mine own herdsman Wat!"
"Yea, for God, lady, even so I hight;
Lull well Jesu in thy lap,
And farewell, Joseph, with thy round cape!"
Ut hoy!
For in his pipe he made so much joy.

"Now may I well both hope and sing,
For I have been at Christ's bearing;
Home to my fellows now will I fling,
Christ of Heaven to his bliss us bring!"
Ut hoy!
For in his pipe he made so much joy.

There Is a Lady Sweet and Kind

THERE is a Lady sweet and kind,
Was never face so pleased my mind;
I did but see her passing by,
And yet I love her till I die.

Her gesture, motion, and her smiles,
Her wit, her voice my heart beguiles,
Beguiles my heart, I know not why,
And yet I love her till I die.

Cupid is wingèd and doth range,
Her country so my love doth change:
But change she earth, or change she sky,
Yet will I love her till I die.

Love Not Me for Comely Grace

Love not me for comely grace,
For my pleasing eye or face,
Nor for any outward part,
No, nor for my constant heart;
For those may fail or turn to ill,
So thou and I shall sever;
Keep therefore a true woman's eye,
And love me still, but know not why.
So hast thou the same reason still
To dote upon me ever.

I Saw My Lady Weep

I saw my Lady weep,
And Sorrow proud to be advancèd so
In those fair eyes where all perfections keep.
Her face was full of woe;
But such a woe (believe me) as wins more hearts
Than Mirth can do with her enticing parts.

Sorrow was there made fair,
And Passion wise; Tears a delightful thing;
Silence beyond all speech, a wisdom rare:
She made her sighs to sing,
And all things with so sweet a sadness move
As made my heart at once both grieve and love.

O fairer than aught else
The world can show, leave off in time to grieve!
Enough, enough: your joyful look excels:
Tears kill the heart, believe.
O strive not to be excellent in woe,
Which only breeds your beauty's overthrow.

Weep You No More, Sad Fountains

Weep you no more, sad fountains;
  What need you flow so fast?
Look how the snowy mountains
  Heaven's sun doth gently waste!
But my Sun's heavenly eyes
    View not your weeping,
    That now lies sleeping
Softly, now softly lies
      Sleeping.

Sleep is a reconciling,
  A rest that peace begets;
Doth not the sun rise smiling
  When fair at even he sets?
Rest you then, rest, sad eyes!
    Melt not in weeping,
    While she lies sleeping
Softly, now softly lies
      Sleeping.

SIR THOMAS WYATT

(1503–1542)

Forget Not Yet

Forget not yet the tried intent
Of such a truth as I have meant;
My great travail so gladly spent,
          Forget not yet!

Forget not yet when first began
The weary life ye know, since whan
The suit, the service, none tell can;
          Forget not yet!

Forget not yet the great assays,
The cruel wrong, the scornful ways,
The painful patience in delays,
Forget not yet!

Forget not! O, forget not this!—
How long ago hath been, and is
The mind that never meant amiss—
Forget not yet!

Forget not then thine own approved,
The which so long hath thee so loved,
Whose steadfast faith yet never moved:
Forget not this!

An Earnest Suit,

To His Unkind Mistress Not to Forsake Him.

AND wilt thou leave me thus?
Say nay! say nay! for shame!
To save thee from the blame
Of all my grief and grame.
And wilt thou leave me thus?
Say nay! say nay!

And wilt thou leave me thus,
That hath loved thee so long,
In wealth and woe among?
And is thy heart so strong
As for to leave me thus?
Say nay! say nay!

And wilt thou leave me thus,
That hath given thee my heart,
Never for to depart,
Neither for pain nor smart?
And wilt thou leave me thus?
Say nay! say nay!

And wilt thou leave me thus,
And have no more pity
Of him that loveth thee?
Alas! thy cruelty!
And wilt thou leave me thus?
Say nay! say nay!

HENRY HOWARD, EARL OF SURREY

(1516–1547)

Give Place, Ye Lovers

GIVE place, ye lovers, here before
That spent your boasts and brags in vain;
My lady's beauty passeth more
The best of yours, I dare well sayen,
Than doth the sun the candle-light,
Or brightest day the darkest night.

And thereto hath a troth as just
As had Penelope the fair;
For what she saith, ye may it trust,
As it by writing sealed were:
And virtues hath she many mo'
Than I with pen have skill to show.

I could rehearse, if that I would,
The whole effect of Nature's plaint,
When she had lost the perfect mould,
The like to whom she could not paint:
With wringing hands, how she did cry,
And what she said, I know it aye.

I know she swore with raging mind,
Her kingdom only set apart,
There was no loss by law of kind
That could have gone so near her heart;

And this was chiefly all her pain;
She could not make the like again.

Sith Nature thus gave her the praise,
  To be the chiefest work she wrought,
In faith, methink, some better ways
  On your behalf might well be sought,
Than to compare, as ye have done,
To match the candle with the sun.

JOHN STILL

(1543–1608)

Good Ale

I CANNOT eat but little meat,—
  My stomach is not good;
But, sure, I think that I can drink
  With him that wears a hood.
Though I go bare, take ye no care;
  I nothing am a-cold,—
I stuff my skin so full within
  Of jolly good ale and old.
    Back and side go bare, go bare;
      Both foot and hand go cold;
    But, belly, God send thee good ale enough,
      Whether it be new or old!

I love no roast but a nut-brown toast,
  And a crab laid in the fire;
A little bread shall do me stead,—
  Much bread I not desire.
No frost, nor snow, nor wind, I trow,
  Can hurt me if I wold,—
I am so wrapt, and thorowly lapt
  Of jolly good ale and old.
    Back and side, etc.

And Tyb, my wife, that as her life
  Loveth well good ale to seek,
Full oft drinks she, till you may see
  The tears run down her cheek;
Then doth she trowl to me the bowl,
  Even as a malt-worm should;
And saith, "Sweetheart, I took my part
  Of this jolly good ale and old."
    Back and side, etc.

Now let them drink till they nod and wink,
  Even as good fellows should do;
They shall not miss to have the bliss
  Good ale doth bring men to;
And all poor souls that have scoured bowls,
  Or have them lustily trowled,
God save the lives of them and their wives,
  Whether they be young or old!
    Back and side, etc.

ANONYMOUS

The Vicar of Bray

IN GOOD King Charles's golden days,
  When loyalty no harm meant,
A zealous high-churchman was I,
  And so I got preferment.
To teach my flock I never missed:
  Kings were by God appointed,
And lost are those that dare resist
  Or touch the Lord's anointed.
    And this is law that I'll maintain
      Until my dying day, sir,
    That whatsoever king shall reign,
      Still I'll be the Vicar of Bray, sir.

When royal James possessed the crown,
  And popery came in fashion,
The penal laws I hooted down,
  And read the Declaration;
The Church of Rome I found would fit
  Full well my constitution;
And I had been a Jesuit
  But for the Revolution.
    And this is law, etc.

When William was our king declared,
  To ease the nation's grievance;
With this new wind about I steered,
  And swore to him allegiance;
Old principles I did revoke,
  Set conscience at a distance;
Passive obedience was a joke,
  A jest was non-resistance.
    And this is law, etc.

When royal Anne became our queen,
  The Church of England's glory,
Another face of things was seen,
  And I became a Tory;
Occasional conformists base,
  I blamed their moderation;
And thought the Church in danger was,
  By such prevarication.
    And this is law, etc.

When George in pudding-time came o'er,
  And moderate men looked big, sir,
My principles I changed once more,
  And so became a Whig, sir;
And thus preferment I procured
  From our new faith's-defender,
And almost every day abjured
  The Pope and the Pretender.
    And this is law, etc.

The illustrious house of Hanover,
  And Protestant succession,
To these I do allegiance swear—
  While they can keep possession:
For in my faith and loyalty
  I nevermore will falter,
And George my lawful king shall be—
  Until the times do alter.
    And this is law, etc.

NICHOLAS BRETON
(1545–1626)

Phillida and Corydon

In the merry month of May,
In a morn by break of day,
With a troop of damsels playing
Forth I rode, forsooth, a-maying,
When anon by a woodside,
Where as May was in his pride,
I espièd, all alone,
Phillida and Corydon.

Much ado there was, God wot!
He would love and she would not:
She said, "Never man was true:"
He says, "None was false to you."
He said he had loved her long:
She says, "Love should have no wrong."

Corydon he would kiss her then.
She says, "Maids must kiss no men
Till they do for good and all."
Then she made the shepherd call
All the heavens to witness, truth
Never loved a truer youth.

Thus, with many a pretty oath,
Yea and nay, and faith and troth,—
Such as silly shepherds use
When they will not love abuse,—
Love, which had been long deluded,
Was with kisses sweet concluded;
And Phillida, with garlands gay,
Was made the lady of the May.

A Cradle Song

Come little babe, come silly soul,
Thy father's shame, thy mother's grief,
Born as I doubt to all our dole,
And to thy self unhappy chief:
    Sing lullaby and lap it warm,
    Poor soul that thinks no creature harm.

Thou little think'st and less dost know
The cause of this thy mother's moan;
Thou want'st the wit to wail her woe,
And I myself am all alone:
    Why dost thou weep? why dost thou wail?
    And knowest not yet what thou dost ail.

Come little wretch—ah silly heart!
Mine only joy, what can I more?
If there be any wrong thy smart
That may the destinies implore:
    'Twas I, I say, against my will,
    I wail the time, but be thou still.

And dost thou smile? O, thy sweet face!
Would God Himself He might thee see!—
No doubt thou wouldst soon purchase grace,
I know right well, for thee and me:
    But come to mother, babe, and play,
    For father false is fled away.

Sweet boy, if it by fortune chance,
Thy father home again to send,
If death do strike me with his lance,
Yet mayst thou me to him commend:
    If any ask thy mother's name,
    Tell how by love she purchased blame.

Then will his gentle heart soon yield:
I know him of a noble mind:
Although a lion in the field,
A lamb in town thou shalt him find:
    Ask blessing, babe, be not afraid,
    His sugar'd words hath me betray'd.

Then mayst thou joy and be right glad,
Although in woe I seem to moan,
Thy father is no rascal lad,
A noble youth of blood and bone:
    His glancing looks, if he once smile,
    Right honest women may beguile.

Come, little boy, and rock asleep;
Sing lullaby and be thou still,
I that can do nought else but weep,
Will sit by thee and wail my fill:
    God bless my babe, and lullaby
    From this thy father's quality.

SIR EDWARD DYER

(1550–1607)

My Mind to Me a Kingdom Is

MY MIND to me a kingdom is,
  Such present joys therein I find,
That it excels all other bliss
  That earth affords or grows by kind:

Though much I want which most would have,
Yet still my mind forbids to crave.

No princely pomp, no wealthy store,
  No force to win the victory,
No wily wit to salve a sore,
  No shape to feed a loving eye;
To none of these I yield as thrall:
For why? My mind doth serve for all.

I see how plenty [surfeits] oft,
  And hasty climbers soon do fall;
I see that those which are aloft
  Mishap doth threaten most of all;
They get with toil, they keep with fear:
Such cares my mind could never bear.

Content to live, this is my stay;
  I seek no more than may suffice;
I press to bear no haughty sway;
  Look, what I lack my mind supplies:
Lo, thus I triumph like a king,
Content with that my mind doth bring.

Some have too much, yet still do crave;
  I little have, and seek no more.
They are but poor, though much they have,
  And I am rich with little store:
They poor, I rich; they beg, I give;
They lack, I leave; they pine, I live.

I laugh not at another's loss;
  I grudge not at another's gain;
No wordly waves my mind can toss;
  My state at one doth still remain:
I fear no foe, I fawn no friend;
I loathe not life, nor dread my end.

Some weigh their pleasure by their lust,
  Their wisdom by their rage of will;
Their treasure is their only trust;
  A cloakèd craft their store of skill:

But all the pleasure that I find
Is to maintain a quiet mind.

My wealth is health and perfect ease;
  My conscience clear my chief defense;
I neither seek by bribes to please,
  Nor by deceit to breed offense:
Thus do I live; thus will I die;
Would all did so as well as I!

SIR WALTER RALEIGH

(1552–1618)

The Nymph's Reply[1]

IF ALL the world and love were young,
And truth in every shepherd's tongue,
These pretty pleasures might me move
To live with thee, and be thy love.

Time drives the flocks from field to fold,
When rivers rage and rocks grow cold;
And Philomel becometh dumb,
The rest complain of cares to come.

The flowers do fade, and wanton fields
To wayward winter reckoning yields;
A honey tongue, a heart of gall,
Is fancy's spring, but sorrow's fall.

Thy gowns, thy shoes, thy beds of roses,
Thy cap, thy kirtle, and thy posies,
Soon break, soon wither, soon forgotten,
In folly ripe, in reason rotten.

[1]See page 60.

Thy belt of straw and ivy buds,
Thy coral clasps and amber studs;
All these in me no means can move
To come to thee and be thy love.

But could youth last, and love still breed,
Had joys no date, nor age no need,
Then these delights my mind might move
To live with thee and be thy love.

His Pilgrimage

GIVE me my scallop-shell of quiet,
  My staff of faith to walk upon,
My scrip of joy, immortal diet,
  My bottle of salvation,
My gown of glory, hope's true gage;
And thus I'll make my pilgrimage.

Blood must be my body's balmer;
  No other balm will there be given:
Whilst my soul, like quiet palmer,
  Travelleth towards the land of heaven;
Over the silver mountains,
Where spring the nectar fountains;
  There will I kiss
  The bowl of bliss;
  And drink mine everlasting fill
  Upon every milken hill.
  My soul will be a-dry before;
  But, after, it will thirst no more.

The Conclusion

Even such is Time, that takes in trust
Our youth, our joys, our all we have,
And pays us but with earth and dust;
Who in the dark and silent grave,
When we have wander'd all our ways,
Shuts up the story of our days;
But from this earth, this grave, this dust,
My God shall raise me up, I trust.

EDMUND SPENSER

(1552–1599)

Prothalamion

Calm was the day, and through the trembling air
Sweet-breathing Zephyrus did softly play
A gentle spirit, that lightly did delay
Hot Titan's beams, which then did glister fair;
When I, (whom sullen care,
Through discontent of my long fruitless stay
In princes' court, and expectation vain
Of idle hopes, which still do fly away
Like empty shadows, did afflict my brain,)
Walked forth to ease my pain
Along the shore of silver-streaming Thames;
Whose rutty bank, the which his river hems,
Was painted all with variable flowers,
And all the meads adorned with dainty gems
Fit to deck maidens' bowers,
And crown their paramours
Against the bridal day, which is not long:
Sweet Thames! run softly, till I end my song.

There in a meadow by the river's side
A flock of nymphs I chancèd to espy,
All lovely daughters of the flood thereby,
With goodly greenish locks all loose untied
As each had been a bride;
And each one had a little wicker basket
Made of fine twigs entrailèd curiously,
In which they gathered flowers to fill their flasket,
And with fine fingers cropped full feateously
The tender stalks on high.
Of every sort which in that meadow grew
They gathered some; the violet, pallid blue,
The little daisy that at evening closes,
The virgin lily and the primrose true,
With store of vermeil roses,
To deck their bridegrooms' posies
Against the bridal day, which was not long:
Sweet Thames! run softly, till I end my song.

With that I saw two swans of goodly hue
Come softly swimming down along the Lee;
Two fairer birds I yet did never see;
The snow which doth the top of Pindus strew
Did never whiter shew,
Nor Jove himself, when he a swan would be
For love of Leda, whiter did appear;
Yet Leda was, they say, as white as he,
Yet not so white as these, nor nothing near;
So purely white they were
That even the gentle stream, the which them bare,
Seemed foul to them, and bade his billows spare
To wet their silken feathers, lest they might
Soil their fair plumes with water not so fair,
And mar their beauties bright
That shone as Heaven's light
Against their bridal day, which was not long;
Sweet Thames! run softly, till I end my song.

Eftsoons the nymphs, which now had flowers their fill,
Ran all in haste to see that silver brood

As they came floating on the crystal flood;
Whom when they saw, they stood amazèd still
Their wondering eyes to fill;
Them seem'd they never saw a sight so fair
Of fowls, so lovely, that they sure did deem
Them heavenly born, or to be that same pair
Which through the sky draw Venus' silver team;
For sure they did not seem
To be begot of any earthly seed,
But rather angels, or of angels' breed;
Yet were they bred of summer's heat, they say,
In sweetest season, when each flower and weed
The earth did fresh array;
So fresh they seem'd as day.
Even as their bridal day, which was not long:
  Sweet Thames! run softly, till I end my song.

Then forth they all out of their baskets drew
Great store of flowers, the honour of the field,
That to the sense did fragrant odours yield,
All which upon those goodly birds they threw
And all the waves did strew,
That like old Peneus' waters they did seem
When down along by pleasant Tempe's shore
Scatter'd with flowers, through Thessaly they stream,
That they appear, through lilies' plenteous store,
Like a bride's chamber-floor.
Two of those nymphs meanwhile two garlands bound
Of freshest flowers which in that mead they found,
The which presenting all in trim array,
Their snowy foreheads therewithal they crowned,
Whilst one did sing this lay
Prepared against that day,
Against their bridal day, which was not long:
  Sweet Thames! run softly, till I end my song.

"Ye gentle birds! the world's fair ornament,
And heaven's glory, whom this happy hour
Doth lead unto your lovers' blissful bower,
Joy may you have, and gentle heart's content
Of your love's complement;

And let fair Venus, that is queen of love,
With her heart-quelling son upon you smile,
Whose smile, they say, hath virtue to remove
All love's dislike, and friendship's faulty guile
For ever to assoil.
Let endless peace your steadfast hearts accord,
And blessèd plenty wait upon your board;
And let your bed with pleasures chaste abound,
That fruitful issue may to you afford,
Which may your foes confound,
And make your joys rebound
Upon your bridal day, which is not long:
  Sweet Thames! run softly, till I end my song."

So ended she; and all the rest around
To her redoubled that her undersong,
Which said their bridal day should not be long:
And gentle Echo from the neighbour ground
Their accents did resound.
So forth those joyous birds did pass along,
Adown the Lee that to them murmured low,
As he would speak but that he lacked a tongue,
Yet did by signs his glad affection show,
Making his stream run slow.
And all the fowl which in his flood did dwell
'Gan flock about these twain, that did excel
The rest, so far as Cynthia doth shend
The lesser stars. So they, enrangèd well,
Did on those two attend,
And their best service lend
Against their wedding day, which was not long:
  Sweet Thames! run softly, till I end my song.

At length they all to merry London came,
To merry London, my most kindly nurse,
That to me gave this life's first native source,
Though from another place I take my name,
An house of ancient fame:
There when they came whereas those bricky towers
The which on Thames' broad aged back do ride,

Where now the studious lawyers have their bowers,
There whilome wont the Templar-Knights to bide,
Till they decay'd through pride;
Next whereunto there stands a stately place,
Where oft I gainèd gifts and goodly grace
Of that great lord, which therein wont to dwell,
Whose want too well now feels my friendless case;
But ah! here fits not well
Old woes, but joys to tell
Against the bridal day, which is not long:
  Sweet Thames! run softly, till I end my song.

Yet therein now doth lodge a noble peer,
Great England's glory and the world's wide wonder,
Whose dreadful name late thro' all Spain did thunder
And Hercules' two pillars standing near
Did make to quake and fear:
Fair branch of honour, flower of chivalry!
That fillest England with thy triumphs' fame,
Joy have thou of thy noble victory,
And endless happiness of thine own name
That promiseth the same;
That through thy prowess and victorious arms
Thy country may be freed from foreign harms,
And great Eliza's glorious name may ring
Through all the world, filled with thy wide alarms,
Which some brave Muse may sing
To ages following,
Upon the bridal day, which is not long:
  Sweet Thames! run softly, till I end my song.

From those high towers this noble lord issùing,
Like radiant Hesper when his golden hair
In the ocean billows he hath bathèd fair,
Descended to the river's open viewing,
With a great train ensuing.
Above the rest were goodly to be seen
Two gentle knights of lovely face and feature,
Beseeming well the bower of any queen,
With gifts of wit and ornaments of nature
Fit for so goodly stature,

That like the twins of Jove they seemed in sight
Which deck the baldric of the heavens bright;
They two, forth pacing to the river's side,
Received those two fair brides, their love's delight;
Which, at the appointed tide,
Each one did make his bride
Against their bridal day, which is not long:
  Sweet Thames! run softly, till I end my song.

ANTHONY MUNDAY

(1553–1633)

Beauty Sat Bathing

BEAUTY sat bathing by a spring,
  Where fairest shades did hide her;
The winds blew calm, the birds did sing,
  The cool streams ran beside her.
My wanton thoughts enticed mine eye
  To see what was forbidden:
But better memory said, Fie;
  So vain desire was chidden—
          Hey nonny nonny O!
          Hey nonny nonny!

Into a slumber then I fell,
  When fond imagination
Seemèd to see, but could not tell
  Her feature or her fashion.
But ev'n as babes in dreams do smile,
  And sometimes fall a-weeping,
So I awaked as wise that while
  As when I fell a-sleeping—
          Hey nonny nonny O!
          Hey nonny nonny!

JOHN LYLY
(c.1553–1606)

Cupid and Campaspe

CUPID and my Campaspe played
At cards for kisses—Cupid paid:
He stakes his quiver, bow and arrows,
His mother's doves, and team of sparrows;
Loses them too; then down he throws
The coral of his lip, the rose
Growing on's cheek (but none knows how);
With these, the crystal of his brow,
And then the dimple of his chin:
All these did my Campaspe win.
At last he set her both his eyes,
She won, and Cupid blind did rise.
O Love! has she done this to thee?
What shall, alas, become of me?

SIR PHILIP SIDNEY
(1554–1586)

My True-Love Hath My Heart

MY TRUE-LOVE hath my heart, and I have his,
By just exchange one to the other given:
I hold his dear, and mine he cannot miss,
There never was a better bargain driven:
My true-love hath my heart, and I have his.

His heart in me keeps him and me in one;
My heart in him his thoughts and senses guides:
He loves my heart, for once it was his own;
I cherish his because in me it bides:
My true-love hath my heart, and I have his.

The Nightingale, as Soon as April Bringeth

THE nightingale, as soon as April bringeth
  Unto her rested sense a perfect waking,
While late-bare earth, proud of new clothing, springeth,
  Sings out her woes, a thorn her song-book making:
    And mournfully bewailing,
    Her throat in tunes expresseth
    What grief her breast oppresseth
For Tereus' force on her chaste will prevailing.

O Philomela fair, O take some gladness,
That here is juster cause of plaintful sadness:
      Thine earth now springs, mine fadeth;
    Thy thorn without, my thorn my heart invadeth.

Alas, she hath no other cause of anguish
  But Tereus' love, on her by strong hand wroken.
Wherein she suffering, all her spirits languish,
  Full womanlike complains her will was broken.
    But I, who, daily craving,
    Cannot have to content me,
    Have more cause to lament me,
Since wanting is more woe than too much having.

O Philomela fair, O take some gladness
That here is juster cause of plaintful sadness:
      Thine earth now springs, mine fadeth;
Thy thorn without, my thorn my heart invadeth.

With How Sad Steps, O Moon

WITH how sad steps, O Moon! thou climb'st the skies,
How silently, and with how wan a face!
What may it be, that even in heavenly place
That busy Archer his sharp arrows tries?

Sure, if that long with love acquainted eyes
Can judge of love, thou feel'st a lover's case;
I read it in thy looks, thy languished grace
To me that feel the like thy state descries.
Then, even of fellowship, O Moon, tell me,
Is constant love deemed there but want of wit?
Are beauties there as proud as here they be?
Do they above love to be loved, and yet
Those lovers scorn whom that love doth possess?
Do they call virtue there ungratefulness?

Come, Sleep! O Sleep

COME, Sleep! O Sleep, the certain knot of peace,
The baiting-place of wit, the balm of woe,
The poor man's wealth, the prisoner's release,
The indifferent judge between the high and low,
With shield of proof shield me from out the prease
Of those fierce darts Despair at me doth throw:
Oh, make in me those civil wars to cease;
I will good tribute pay, if thou do so.
Take thou of me smooth pillows, sweetest bed,
A chamber deaf to noise and blind to light,
A rosy garland and a weary head:
And if these things, as being thine in right,
  Move not thy heavy grace, thou shalt in me,
  Livelier than elsewhere, Stella's image see.

GEORGE PEELE

(c.1558–c.1597)

His Golden Locks Time Hath to Silver Turned

HIS golden locks time hath to silver turned;
  O time too swift, O swiftness never ceasing,
His youth 'gainst time and age hath ever spurned,
  But spurned in vain; youth waneth by increasing:

Beauty, strength, youth, are flowers but fading seen;
Duty, faith, love, are roots, and ever green.

His helmet now shall make a hive for bees;
And, lovers' sonnets turned to holy psalms,
A man-at-arms must now serve on his knees,
And feed on prayèrs, which are age his alms:
But though from court to cottage he depart,
His saint is sure of his unspotted heart.

And when he saddest sits in homely cell,
He'll teach his swains this carol for a song,—
"Blest be the hearts that wish my sovereign well,
Curst be the souls that think her any wrong."
Goddess, allow this agèd man his right,
To be your beadsman now that was your knight.

THOMAS LODGE

(c. 1558–1625)

Rosalind's Complaint

Love in my bosom, like a bee,
Doth suck his sweet;
Now with his wings he plays with me,
Now with his feet;
Within mine eyes he makes his nest,
His bed amidst my tender breast,
My kisses are his daily feast,
And yet he robs me of my rest:
Ah! wanton, will ye?

And if I sleep, then percheth he
With pretty flight,
And makes his pillow of my knee,
The livelong night.

Strike I the lute, he tunes the string;
He music plays, if so I sing;
He lends me every lovely thing,
Yet, cruel, he my heart doth sting:
  Whist! wanton, still ye!

Else I with roses every day
  Will whip you hence,
And bind you when you long to play,
  For your offence;
I'll shut my eyes to keep you in,
I'll make you fast it for your sin,
I'll count your power not worth a pin:
Alas! what hereby shall I win
  If he gainsay me!

What if I beat the wanton boy
  With many a rod?
He will repay me with annoy,
  Because a god;
Then sit thou safely on my knee,
And let thy bower my bosom be;
Lurk in my eyes, I like of thee,
O Cupid! so thou pity me;
  Spare not, but play thee!

Rosaline

LIKE to the clear in highest sphere
Where all imperial glory shines:
Of selfsame colour is her hair,
Whether unfolded, or in twines:
  Heigh-ho, fair Rosaline!
Her eyes are sapphires set in snow,
Resembling heaven by every wink;
The gods do fear whenas they glow,
And I do tremble when I think
  Heigh-ho, would she were mine!

Her cheeks are like the blushing cloud
That beautifies Aurora's face,
Or like the silver crimson shroud
That Phœbus' smiling looks doth grace:
  Heigh-ho, fair Rosaline!
Her lips are like two budded roses
Whom ranks of lilies neighbor nigh,
Within which bounds she balm encloses
Apt to entice a deity:
  Heigh-ho, would she were mine!

Her neck is like a stately tower
Where Love himself imprisoned lies
To watch for glances every hour
From her divine and sacred eyes;
  Heigh-ho, fair Rosaline!
Her paps are centres of delight,
Her breasts are orbs of heavenly frame,
Where Nature moulds the dew of light
To feed perfection with the same:
  Heigh-ho, would she were mine!

With orient pearl, with ruby red,
With marble white, with sapphire blue,
Her body every way is fed,
Yet soft in touch and sweet in view:
  Heigh-ho, fair Rosaline!
Nature herself her shape admires;
The gods are wounded in her sight;
And Love forsakes his heavenly fires
And at her eyes his brand doth light:
  Heigh-ho, would she were mine!

Then muse not, Nymphs, though I bemoan
The absence of fair Rosaline,
Since for a fair there's fairer none,
Nor for her virtues so divine:
  Heigh-ho, fair Rosaline!
Heigh-ho, my heart! would God that she were mine!

ROBERT GREENE

(1560–1592)

Sephestia's Lullaby

WEEP not, my wanton, smile upon my knee;
When thou art old there's grief enough for thee.
Mother's wag, pretty boy,
Father's sorrow, father's joy;
When thy father first did see
Such a boy by him and me,
He was glad, I was woe;
Fortune changèd made him so,
When he left his pretty boy,
Last his sorrow, first his joy.

Weep not, my wanton, smile upon my knee;
When thou art old there's grief enough for thee.
Streaming tears that never stint,
Like pearl drops from a flint,
Fell by course from his eyes,
That one another's place supplies;
Thus he grieved in every part,
Tears of blood fell from his heart,
When he left his pretty boy,
Father's sorrow, father's joy.

Weep not, my wanton, smile upon my knee,
When thou art old there's grief enough for thee.
The wanton smiled, father wept,
Mother cried, baby leapt;
More he crow'd, more we cried,
Nature could not sorrow hide:
He must go, he must kiss
Child and mother, baby bliss,
For he left his pretty boy,
Father's sorrow, father's joy.
Weep not, my wanton, smile upon my knee,
When thou art old there's grief enough for thee.

Sweet Are the Thoughts That Savor of Content

SWEET are the thoughts that savor of content;
The quiet mind is richer than a crown;
Sweet are the nights in careless slumber spent,—
The poor estate scorns Fortune's angry frown:
Such sweet content, such minds, such sleep, such bliss,
Beggars enjoy, when princes oft do miss.

The homely house that harbors quiet rest,
The cottage that affords no pride or care,
The mean, that 'grees with country music best,
The sweet consort of mirth's and music's fare.
Obscurèd life sets down a type of bliss;
A mind content both crown and kingdom is.

ALEXANDER HUME

(1560–1609)

O Happie Death

O HAPPIE death, to life the readie way,
The end of greefe, and salve of sorrowes all;
O pleasant sleepe, thy pains they are bot play;
Thy cup is sweete, although it taste of gall.
Thou brings the bound and wretched out of thrall
Within the port sure from the stormie blast,
For after death na mischiefe may befall,
But wo, wan-chance, and perrels all are past.
Of kindelie death nane suld affraied be
But sich as hope for na felicitie.

FRANCIS BACON, BARON VERULAM

(1561–1626)

The World's a Bubble

THE world's a bubble, and the life of man
        Less than a span:
In his conception wretched, from the womb
        So to the tomb:
Curst from his cradle, and brought up to years
        With cares and fears.
Who then to frail mortality shall trust,
But limns on water, or but writes in dust.

Yet whilst with sorrow here we live opprest,
        What life is best?
Courts are but only superficial schools
        To dandle fools:
The rural parts are turn'd into a den
        Of savage men:
And where's a city from foul vice so free,
But may be term'd the worst of all the three?

Domestic cares afflict the husband's bed,
        Or pains his head:
Those that live single, take it for a curse,
        Or do things worse:
Some would have children; those that have them, moan
        Or wish them gone:
What is it, then, to have, or have no wife,
But single thraldom, or a double strife?

Our own affections still at home to please
        Is a disease:
To cross the seas to any foreign soil
        Peril and toil;
Wars with their noise affright us; when they cease,
        We're worse in peace;
What then remains, but that we still should cry
Not to be born, or, being born, to die?

SAMUEL DANIEL

(1562–1619)

Love Is a Sickness

Love is a sickness full of woes,
All remedies refusing;
A plant that most with cutting grows,
Most barren with best using.
Why so?
More we enjoy it, more it dies;
If not enjoyed, it sighing cries
Heigh-ho!

Love is a torment of the mind,
A tempest everlasting;
And Jove hath made it of a kind,
Not well, nor full, nor fasting.
Why so?
More we enjoy it, more it dies;
If not enjoyed, it sighing cries
Heigh-ho!

MICHAEL DRAYTON

(1563–1631)

Since There's No Help, Come Let Us Kiss and Part

Since there's no help, come let us kiss and part—
Nay, I have done, you get no more of me;
And I am glad, yea, glad with all my heart,
That thus so cleanly I myself can free.
Shake hands for ever, cancel all our vows
And when we meet at any time again,
Be it not seen in either of our brows
That we one jot of former love retain.

Now at the last gasp of Love's latest breath,
When his pulse failing, Passion speechless lies,
When Faith is kneeling by his bed of death,
And Innocence is closing up his eyes,
—Now if thou would'st, when all have given him over,
From death to life thou might'st him yet recover.

Letters and Lines

LETTERS and lines we see are soon defaced,
Metals do waste and fret with canker's rust,
The diamond shall once consume to dust,
And freshest colours with foul stains disgraced;
Paper and ink can paint but naked words,
To write with blood of force offends the sight,
And, if with tears, I find them all too light,
And sighs and signs a silly hope affords:
O sweetest Shadow, how thou serv'st my turn!
Which still shalt be, as long as there is sun,
Nor, whilst the world is, never shall be done,
Whilst moon shall shine, or any fire shall burn:
That everything whence shadow doth proceed,
May in his shadow my love's story read.

Agincourt

FAIR stood the wind for France
When we our sails advance,
Nor now to prove our chance
Longer will tarry;
But putting to the main,
At Caux, the mouth of Seine,
With all his martial train
Landed King Harry.

And taking many a fort,
Furnished in warlike sort,
Marcheth towards Agincourt
In happy hour;
Skirmishing day by day
With those that stopped his way,
Where the French general lay
With all his power;

Which, in his height of pride,
King Henry to deride,
His ransom to provide
To the king sending;
Which he neglects the while
As from a nation vile,
Yet with an angry smile
Their fall portending.

And turning to his men,
Quoth our brave Henry then,
"Though they to one be ten,
Be not amazèd;
Yet have we well begun,
Battles so bravely won
Have ever to the sun
By fame been raisèd.

"And for myself," quoth he,
"This my full rest shall be:
England ne'er mourn for me,
Nor more esteem me;
Victor I will remain
Or on this earth lie slain,
Never shall she sustain
Loss to redeem me.

"Poitiers and Cressy tell,
When most their pride did swell,
Under our swords they fell;
No less our skill is

Than when our grandsire great,
Claiming the regal seat,
By many a warlike feat
    Lopped the French lilies."

The Duke of York so dread
The eager vanward led;
With the main Henry sped,
    Amongst his henchmen.
Exeter had the rear,
A braver man not there;
O Lord, how hot they were
    On the false Frenchman!

They now to fight are gone,
Armour on armour shone,
Drum now to drum did groan,
    To hear was wonder:
That with the cries they make
The very earth did shake;
Trumpet to trumpet spake,
    Thunder to thunder.

Well it thine age became,
O noble Erpingham,
Which didst the signal aim
    To our hid forces!
When, from a meadow by,
Like a storm suddenly
The English archery
    Struck the French horses:

With Spanish yew so strong,
Arrows a cloth-yard long,
That like to serpents stung,
    Piercing the weather;
None from his fellow starts,
But, playing manly parts,
And like true English hearts,
    Stuck close together.

When down their bows they threw,
And forth their bilbos drew,
And on the French they flew,
    Not one was tardy;
Arms were from shoulders sent,
Scalps to the teeth were rent,
Down the French peasants went:
    Our men were hardy.

This while our noble King,
His broad sword brandishing,
Down the French host did ding
    As to o'erwhelm it;
And many a deep wound lent,
His arms with blood besprent,
And many a cruel dent
    Bruisèd his helmet.

Gloucester, that duke so good,
Next of the royal blood,
For famous England stood
    With his brave brother;
Clarence, in steel so bright,
Though but a maiden knight,
Yet in that furious fight
    Scarce such another.

Warwick in blood did wade,
Oxford the foe invade,
And cruel slaughter made
    Still as they ran up;
Suffolk his axe did ply,
Beaumont and Willoughby
Bare them right doughtily,
    Ferrers and Fanhope.

Upon Saint Crispin's day
Fought was this noble fray,
Which fame did not delay
    To England to carry;

Oh, when shall English men
With such acts fill a pen?
Or England breed again
  Such a King Harry?

JOSHUA SYLVESTER

(1563–1618)

Love's Omnipresence

WERE I as base as is the lowly plain,
And you, my Love, as high as heaven above,
Yet should the thoughts of me your humble swain,
Ascend to heaven, in honor of my Love.
Were I as high as heaven above the plain,
And you, my Love, as humble and as low
As are the deepest bottoms of the main,
Whereso'er you were, with you my love should go.
Were you the earth, dear Love, and I the skies,
My love should shine on you like to the sun,
And look upon you with ten thousand eyes,
Till heaven wax'd blind, and till the world were done.
  Whereso'er I am, below,—or else above you,—
  Whereso'er you are, my heart shall truly love you.

CHRISTOPHER MARLOWE

(1564–1593)

The Passionate Shepherd to His Love[1]

COME live with me and be my Love,
And we will all the pleasures prove

[1]See page 37.

That hills and valleys, dale and field,
And all the craggy mountains yield.

There will we sit upon the rocks
And see the shepherds feed their flocks
By shallow rivers, to whose falls
Melodious birds sing madrigals.

There will I make thee beds of roses
And a thousand fragrant posies;
A cap of flowers, and a kirtle
Embroider'd all with leaves of myrtle.

A gown made of the finest wool
Which from our pretty lambs we pull;
Fair linèd slippers for the cold,
With buckles of the purest gold.

A belt of straw and ivory-buds
With coral clasps and amber studs:
And if these pleasures may thee move,
Come live with me and by my Love.

Thy silver dishes for thy meat
As precious as the gods do eat,
Shall on an ivory table be
Prepared each day for thee and me.

The shepherd swains shall dance and sing
For thy delight each May morning:
If these delights thy mind may move,
Then live with me and be my Love.

WILLIAM SHAKESPEARE
(1564-1616)

Who Is Silvia?

Who is Silvia? What is she,
 That all our swains commend her?
Holy, fair, and wise is she;
 The heaven such grace did lend her,
That she might admirèd be.

Is she kind as she is fair?
 For beauty lives with kindness:
Love doth to her eyes repair,
 To help him of his blindness;
And, being helped, inhabits there.

Then to Silvia let us sing,
 That Silvia is excelling;
She excels each mortal thing
 Upon the dull earth dwelling;
To her let us garlands bring.

When Icicles Hang by the Wall

When icicles hang by the wall,
 And Dick the shepherd blows his nail,
And Tom bears logs into the hall,
 And milk comes frozen home in pail,
When blood is nipped, and ways be foul,
Then nightly sings the staring owl,
   To-who;
To-whit, to-who, a merry note,
While greasy Joan doth keel the pot.

When all aloud the wind doth blow,
  And coughing drowns the parson's saw,
And birds sit brooding in the snow,
  And Marian's nose looks red and raw,
When roasted crabs hiss in the bowl,
Then nightly sings the staring owl,
    To-who;
To-whit, to-who, a merry note,
While greasy Joan doth keel the pot.

Under the Greenwood Tree

UNDER the greenwood tree,
Who loves to lie with me,
And turn his merry note
Unto the sweet bird's throat,
Come hither, come hither, come hither;
  Here shall he see
  No enemy
But winter and rough weather.

Who doth ambition shun,
And loves to live i' the sun,
Seeking the food he eats,
And pleased with what he gets,
Come hither, come hither, come hither;
  Here shall he see
  No enemy
But winter and rough weather.

Blow, Blow, Thou Winter Wind

BLOW, blow, thou winter wind,
Thou art not so unkind

As man's ingratitude;
Thy tooth is not so keen,
Because thou art not seen,
Although thy breath be rude.
Heigh ho! sing, heigh ho! unto the green holly:
Most friendship is feigning, most loving mere folly:
Then, heigh ho! the holly!
This life is most jolly.

Freeze, freeze, thou bitter sky,
Thou dost not bite so nigh
As benefits forgot:
Though thou the waters warp,
Thy sting is not so sharp
As friend remember'd not.
Heigh ho! sing, heigh ho! unto the green holly:
Most friendship is feigning, most loving mere folly:
Then, heigh ho! the holly!
This life is most jolly.

O Mistress Mine

O MISTRESS mine, where are you roaming?
O, stay and hear! your true-love's coming
That can sing both high and low;
Trip no further, pretty sweeting,
Journeys end in lovers' meeting,—
Every wise man's son doth know.

What is love? 't is not hereafter;
Present mirth hath present laughter;
What's to come is still unsure:
In delay there lies no plenty,—
Then come kiss me, Sweet-and-twenty,
Youth's a stuff will not endure.

Take, O, Take Those Lips Away

Take, O, take those lips away,
That so sweetly were forsworn;
And those eyes, the break of day,
Lights that do mislead the morn:
But my kisses bring again,
        Bring again;
Seals of love, but seal'd in vain,
        Seal'd in vain.

Hark, Hark! the Lark

Hark, hark! the lark at heaven's gate sings,
    And Phœbus 'gins arise,
His steeds to water at those springs
    On chaliced flowers that lies;
And winking Mary-buds begin
    To ope their golden eyes;
With everything that pretty bin,
    My lady sweet, arise;
        Arise, arise!

Fear No More the Heat o' the Sun

Fear no more the heat o' the sun,
  Nor the furious winter's rages;
Thou thy worldly task hast done,
  Home art gone, and ta'en thy wages:
Golden lads and girls all must,
As chimney-sweepers, come to dust.

Fear no more the frown o' the great;
  Thou art past the tyrant's stroke:
Care no more to clothe and eat;
  To thee the reed is as the oak:
The sceptre, learning, physic, must
All follow this, and come to dust.

Fear no more the lightning-flash,
  Nor the all-dreaded thunder-stone;
Fear not slander, censure rash;
  Thou hast finished joy and moan:
All lovers young, all lovers must
Consign to thee, and come to dust.

No exorciser harm thee!
  Nor no witchcraft charm thee!
Ghost unlaid forbear thee!
  Nothing ill come near thee!
Quiet consummation have;
And renownèd be thy grave!

Come Away, Come Away, Death

  COME away, come away, death,
And in sad cypress let me be laid;
  Fly away, fly away, breath;
I am slain by a fair cruel maid.
My shroud of white, stuck all with yew,
    Oh, prepare it!
My part of death, no one so true
    Did share it.

  Not a flower, not a flower sweet,
On my black coffin let there be strown;
  Not a friend, not a friend greet
My poor corpse, where my bones shall be thrown:
A thousand thousand sighs to save,
    Lay me, oh, where
Sad true lover never find my grave,
    To weep there!

Where the Bee Sucks

WHERE the bee sucks, there suck I;
In a cowslip's bell I lie;
There I couch when owls do cry;
On the bat's back I do fly
After summer merrily:
Merrily, merrily, shall I live now
Under the blossom that hangs on the bough.

Come unto These Yellow Sands

COME unto these yellow sands,
    And then take hands:
Court'sied when you have, and kiss'd
    The wild waves whist,
Foot it featly here and there;
And, sweet sprites, the burthen bear.
        Hark, hark!
            Bow-wow.
        The watch-dogs bark:
            Bow-wow.
        Hark, hark! I hear
The strain of strutting chanticleer
        Cry, Cock-a-diddle-dow!

Shall I Compare Thee to a Summer's Day?

SHALL I compare thee to a summer's day?
Thou art more lovely and more temperate:
Rough winds do shake the darling buds of May,
And summer's lease hath all too short a date:

Sometime too hot the eye of heaven shines,
And often is his gold complexion dimmed:
And every fair from fair sometime declines,
By chance, or nature's changing course, untrimmed.
But thy eternal summer shall not fade,
Nor lose possession of that fair thou ow'st,
Nor shall death brag thou wander'st in his shade,
When in eternal lines to time thou grow'st;
So long as men can breathe, or eyes can see,
So long lives this, and this gives life to thee.

Devouring Time, Blunt Thou the Lion's Paws

DEVOURING Time, blunt thou the lion's paws,
And make the earth devour her own sweet brood;
Pluck the keen teeth from the fierce tiger's jaws,
And burn the long-liv'd phoenix in her blood;
Make glad and sorry seasons as thou fleets,
And do whate'er thou wilt, swift-footed Time,
To the wide world and all her fading sweets;
But I forbid thee one most heinous crime:
O! carve not with thy hours my love's fair brow,
Nor draw no lines there with thine antique pen;
Him in thy course untainted do allow
For beauty's pattern to succeeding men.
Yet, do thy worst, old Time: despite thy wrong,
My love shall in my verse ever live young.

When, in Disgrace with Fortune and Men's Eyes

WHEN, in disgrace with fortune and men's eyes,
I all alone beweep my outcast state,
And trouble deaf heaven with my bootless cries,
And look upon myself, and curse my fate,

Wishing me like to one more rich in hope,
Featured like him, like him with friends possessed,
Desiring this man's art, and that man's scope,
With what I most enjoy contented least;
Yet in these thoughts myself almost despising,
Haply I think on thee, and then my state,
Like to the lark at break of day arising
From sullen earth, sings hymns at heaven's gate;
  For thy sweet love remembered such wealth brings
  That then I scorn to change my state with kings.

When to the Sessions of Sweet Silent Thought

When to the sessions of sweet silent thought
I summon up remembrance of things past,
I sigh the lack of many a thing I sought,
And with old woes new wail my dear time's waste;
Then can I drown an eye, unused to flow,
For precious friends hid in death's dateless night,
And weep afresh love's long-since-cancell'd woe,
And moan the expense of many a vanish'd sight.
Then can I grieve at grievances foregone,
And heavily from woe to woe tell o'er
The sad account of fore-bemoanèd moan,
Which I new pay as if not paid before:
  —But if the while I think on thee, dear friend,
  All losses are restored, and sorrows end.

Being Your Slave

Being your slave, what should I do but tend
Upon the hours and times of your desire?
I have no precious time at all to spend,
Nor services to do, till you require.

Nor dare I chide the world-without-end hour
Whilst I, my sovereign, watch the clock for you,
Nor think the bitterness of absence sour
When you have bid your servant once adieu;
Nor dare I question with my jealous thought
Where you may be, or your affairs suppose,
But like a sad slave, stay and think of nought
Save, where you are, how happy you make those.
    So true a fool is love, that in your will
    Though you do anything, he thinks no ill.

Like as the Waves Make Towards the Pebbled Shore

LIKE as the waves make towards the pebbled shore,
So do our minutes hasten to their end;
Each changing place with that which goes before,
In sequent toil all forwards do contend,
Nativity, once in the main of light,
Crawls to maturity, wherewith being crown'd,
Crooked eclipses 'gainst his glory fight,
And Time that gave, doth now his gift confound.
Time doth transfix the flourish set on youth
And delves the parallels in beauty's brow,
Feeds on the rarities of nature's truth,
And nothing stands but for his scythe to mow;
    And yet, to times in hope, my verse shall stand,
    Praising Thy worth, despite his cruel hand.

Tir'd with All These, for Restful Death I Cry

TIR'D with all these, for restful death I cry
As to behold desert a beggar born,
And needy nothing trimm'd in jollity,
And purest faith unhappily forsworn,

And gilded honour shamefully misplac'd,
And maiden virtue rudely strumpeted,
And right perfection wrongfully disgraced,
And strength by limping sway disabled,
And art made tongue-tied by authority,
And folly—doctor-like—controlling skill,
And simple truth miscall'd simplicity,
And captive good attending captain ill:
  Tir'd with all these, from these would I be gone,
  Save that, to die, I leave my love alone.

No Longer Mourn for Me, when I Am Dead

No LONGER mourn for me, when I am dead,
Than you shall hear the surly sullen bell
Give warning to the world that I am fled
From this vile world, with vilest worms to dwell;
Nay, if you read this line, remember not
The hand that writ it, for I love you so
That I in your sweet thoughts would be forgot,
If thinking on me then should make you woe.
Oh, if, I say, you look upon this verse
When I perhaps compounded am with clay,
Do not so much as my poor name rehearse,
But let your love even with my life decay;
  Lest the wise world should look into your moan,
  And mock you with me after I am gone.

That Time of Year Thou May'st in Me Behold

THAT time of year thou may'st in me behold
When yellow leaves, or none, or few, do hang
Upon those boughs which shake against the cold,
Bare ruined choirs, where late the sweet birds sang.

In me thou see'st the twilight of such day
As after sunset fadeth in the west;
Which by and by black night doth take away,
Death's second self, that seals up all the rest.
In me thou see'st the glowing of such fire,
That on the ashes of his youth doth lie,
As the death-bed whereon it must expire,
Consumed with that which it was nourished by.
  This thou perceiv'st, which makes thy love more strong,
  To love that well which thou must leave ere long.

Farewell! Thou Art too Dear

FAREWELL! thou art too dear for my possessing,
And like enough thou know'st thy estimate
The charter of thy worth gives thee releasing;
My bonds in thee are all determinate.
For how do I hold thee but by thy granting?
And for that riches where is my deserving?
The cause of this fair gift in me is wanting,
And so my patent back again is swerving.
Thyself thou gav'st, thy own worth then not knowing,
Or me, to whom thou gav'st it, else mistaking;
So thy great gift, upon misprision growing,
Comes home again, on better judgment making.
  Thus have I had thee, as a dream doth flatter;
  In sleep a king, but, waking, no such matter.

Then Hate Me when Thou Wilt

THEN hate me when thou wilt; if ever, now;
Now, while the world is bent my deeds to cross,
Join with the spite of fortune, make me bow,
And do not drop in for an after-loss:

Ah! do not, when my heart hath 'scaped this sorrow,
Come in the rearward of a conquered woe;
Give not a windy night a rainy morrow,
To linger out a purposed overthrow.
If thou wilt leave me, do not leave me last,
When other petty griefs have done their spite,
But in the onset come; so shall I taste
At first the very worst of fortune's might;
And other strains of woe, which now seem woe,
Compared with loss of thee will not seem so.

They That Have Power to Hurt, and Will Do None

THEY that have power to hurt, and will do none,
That do not do the things they most do show,
Who, moving others, are themselves as stone,
Unmovèd, cold, and to temptation slow,
They rightly do inherit heaven's graces
And husband nature's riches from expense;
They are the lords and owners of their faces,
Others, but stewards of their excellence.
The summer's flower is to the summer sweet,
Though to itself it only live and die,
But if that flower with base infection meet,
The basest weed outbraves his dignity:
For sweetest things turn sourest by their deeds;
Lilies that fester smell far worse than weeds.

How Like a Winter Hath My Absence Been

How like a winter hath my absence been
From thee, the pleasure of the fleeting year!
What freezings have I felt, what dark days seen,
What old December's bareness everywhere!

And yet this time remov'd was summer's time;
The teeming autumn, big with rich increase,
Bearing the wanton burden of the prime,
Like widow'd wombs after their lords' decease:
Yet this abundant issue seem'd to me
But hope of orphans, and unfather'd fruit;
For summer and his pleasures wait on thee,
And, thou away, the very birds are mute;
  Or if they sing, 'tis with so dull a cheer
  That leaves look pale, dreading the winter's near.

Let Me Not to the Marriage of True Minds

LET me not to the marriage of true minds
Admit impediments: love is not love
Which alters when it alteration finds,
Or bends with the remover to remove.
Oh, no! it is a never-fixèd mark
That looks on tempests, and is never shaken;
It is the star to every wandering bark,
Whose worth's unknown, although his height be taken.
Love's not Time's fool, though rosy lips and cheeks
Within his bending sickle's compass come;
Love alters not with his brief hours and weeks,
But bears it out even to the edge of doom:
  If this be error, and upon me proved,
  I never writ, nor no man ever loved.

To Me, Fair Friend, You Never Can Be Old

TO ME, fair friend, you never can be old,
For as you were when first your eye I eyed,
Such seems your beauty still. Three winters cold
Have from the forests shook three summers' pride.

Three beauteous springs to yellow autumn turn'd
In process of the seasons have I seen,
Three April perfumes in three hot Junes burn'd,
Since first I saw you fresh, which yet are green.
Ah! yet doth beauty, like a dial-hand,
Steal from his figure, and no pace perceived;
So your sweet hue, which methinks still doth stand,
Hath motion, and mine eye may be deceived:
  For fear of which, hear this, thou age unbred:
  Ere you were born, was beauty's summer dead.

The Expense of Spirit in a Waste of Shame

The expense of spirit in a waste of shame
Is lust in action, and till action, lust
Is perjur'd, murderous, bloody, full of blame,
Savage, extreme, rude, cruel, not to trust;
Enjoy'd no sooner but despised straight;
Past reason hunted; and no sooner had,
Past reason hated, as a swallow'd bait,
On purpose laid to make the taker mad:
Mad in pursuit, and in possession so;
Had, having, and in quest to have, extreme;
A bliss in proof,—and prov'd, a very woe;
Before, a joy propos'd; behind, a dream.
  All this the world well knows; yet none knows well
  To shun the heaven that leads men to this hell.

When in the Chronicle of Wasted Time

When in the chronicle of wasted time
I see descriptions of the fairest wights,
And beauty making beautiful old rhyme
In praise of ladies dead and lovely knights,

Then, in the blazon of sweet beauty's best,
Of hand, of foot, of lip, of eye, of brow,
I see their antique pen would have expressed
Even such a beauty as you master now.
So all their praises are but prophecies
Of this our time, all you prefiguring;
And, for they looked but with divining eyes,
They had not skill enough your worth to sing:
  For we, which now behold these present days,
  Have eyes to wonder, but lack tongues to praise.

THOMAS NASH

(1567–1601)

Spring

SPRING, the sweet spring, is the year's pleasant king;
Then blooms each thing, then maids dance in a ring,
Cold doth not sting, the pretty birds do sing,
  Cuckoo, jug-jug, pu-we, to-witta-woo!

The palm and may make country-houses gay,
Lambs frisk and play, the shepherds pipe all day,
And we hear aye birds tune this merry lay,
  Cuckoo, jug-jug, pu-we, to-witta-woo!

The fields breathe sweet, the daisies kiss our feet,
Young lovers meet, old wives a sunning sit,
In every street these tunes our ears do greet,
  Cuckoo, jug-jug, pu-we, to-witta-woo!
    Spring! the sweet spring!

THOMAS CAMPION

(c. 1567–1619)

Cherry-Ripe

THERE is a garden in her face
  Where roses and white lilies blow;
A heavenly paradise is that place,
  Wherein all pleasant fruits do flow;
There cherries grow that none may buy
Till "Cherry-Ripe" themselves do cry.

Those cherries fairly do enclose
  Of orient pearl, a double row,
Which when her lovely laughter shows,
  They look like rose-buds fill'd with snow;
Yet them nor peer nor prince may buy,
Till "Cherry-Ripe" themselves do cry.

Her eyes like angels watch them still;
  Her brows like bended bows do stand,
Threat'ning with piercing frowns to kill
  All that attempt with eye or hand
These sacred cherries to come nigh,
Till "Cherry-Ripe" themselves do cry!

Kind Are Her Answers

  KIND are her answers,
  But her performance keeps no day;
Breaks time, as dancers
  From their own music when they stray:
  All her free favors and smooth words,
Wing my hopes in vain.
O did ever voice so sweet but only fain?
  Can true love yield such delay,
  Converting joy to pain?

Lost is our freedom
When we submit to women so:
Why do we need them,
When in their best they work our woe?
There is no wisdom
Can alter ends, by Fate prefixed.
O why is the good of man with evil mixed?
Never were days yet call'd two,
But one night went betwixt.

Follow Your Saint

Follow your saint, follow with accents sweet!
Haste you, sad notes, fall at her flying feet!
There, wrapt in cloud of sorrow, pity move,
And tell the ravisher of my soul I perish for her love:
But if she scorns my never-ceasing pain,
Then burst with sighing in her sight, and ne'er return again!

All that I sung still to her praise did tend;
Still she was first, still she my songs did end;
Yet she my love and music both doth fly,
The music that her echo is and beauty's sympathy:
Then let my notes pursue her scornful flight!
It shall suffice that they were breathed and died for her delight.

A Hymn in Praise of Neptune

Of neptune's empire let us sing,
At whose command the waves obey;
To whom the rivers tribute pay,
Down the high mountains sliding:

To whom the scaly nation yields
Homage for the crystal fields
Wherein they dwell:
And every sea-god pays a gem
Yearly out of his watery cell
To deck great Neptune's diadem.

The Tritons dancing in a ring
Before his palace gates do make
The water with their echoes quake,
Like the great thunder sounding:
The sea-nymphs chant their accents shrill,
And the Syrens taught to kill
With their sweet voice,
Make every echoing rock reply
Unto their gentle murmuring noise
The praise of Neptune's empery.

Integer Vitae

THE man of life upright,
Whose guiltless heart is free
From all dishonest deeds,
Or thought of vanity;

The man whose silent days
In harmless joys are spent,
Whom hopes cannot delude,
Nor sorrow discontent;

That man needs neither towers
Nor armour for defence,
Nor secret vaults to fly
From thunder's violence:

He only can behold
With unaffrighted eyes
The horrors of the deep
And terrors of the skies.

Thus scorning all the cares
That fate or fortune brings,
He makes the heaven his book,
His wisdom heavenly things;

Good thoughts his only friends,
His wealth a well-spent age,
The earth his sober inn
And quiet pilgrimage.

My Sweetest Lesbia

My sweetest Lesbia, let us live and love,
And though the sager sort our deeds reprove,
Let us not weigh them; heaven's great lamps do dive
Into their west, and straight again revive;
But, soon as once is set our little light,
Then must we sleep one ever-during night.

If all would lead their lives in love like me,
Then bloody swords and armour should not be,
No drum nor trumpet peaceful sleeps should move,
Unless alarm came from the camp of love.
But fools do live, and waste their little light,
And seek with pain their ever-during night.

When timely death my life and fortune ends,
Let not my hearse be vexed with mourning friends;
But let all lovers rich in triumph come,
And with sweet pastimes grace my happy tomb;
And, Lesbia, close up thou my little light,
And crown with love my ever-during night.

SIR HENRY WOTTON
(1568–1639)

Elizabeth of Bohemia

You meaner beauties of the night,
  That poorly satisfy our eyes
More by your number than your light,
  You common people of the skies;
What are you, when the Moon shall rise?

You curious chanters of the wood,
  That warble forth dame Nature's lays,
Thinking your passions understood
  By your weak accents; what's your praise
When Philomel her voice doth raise?

You violets that first appear,
  By your pure purple mantles known
Like the proud virgins of the year,
  As if the spring were all your own;
What are you, when the rose is blown?

So when my Mistress shall be seen
  In form and beauty of her mind,
By virtue first, then choice, a Queen,
  Tell me, if she were not design'd
Th' eclipse and glory of her kind?

Character of a Happy Life

How happy is he born and taught
That serveth not another's will;
Whose armour is his honest thought,
And simple truth his utmost skill!

Whose passions not his masters are,
Whose soul is still prepared for death;
Untied unto the world by care
Of public fame, or private breath;

Who envies none that chance doth raise,
Nor vice; Who never understood
How deepest wounds are given by praise;
Nor rules of state, but rules of good;

Who hath his life from rumours freed,
Whose conscience is his strong retreat;
Whose state can neither flatterers feed,
Nor ruin make oppressors great;

Who God doth late and early pray
More of His grace than gifts to lend;
And entertains the harmless day
With a religious book or friend;

—This man is freed from servile bands
Of hope to rise, or fear to fall;
Lord of himself, though not of lands;
And having nothing, yet hath all.

SIR JOHN DAVIES

(1569–1626)

Which Is a Proud, and Yet a Wretched Thing

I KNOW my body's of so frail a kind,
  As force without, fevers within, can kill;
I know the heavenly nature of my mind,
  But 'tis corrupted both in wit and will.

I know my soul hath power to know all things
   Yet is she blind and ignorant in all;
I know I am one of nature's little kings,
   Yet to the least and vilest things am thrall.

I know my life's a pain, and but a span;
   I know my sense is mocked with everything;
And to conclude, I know myself a man,
   Which is a proud, and yet a wretched thing.

THOMAS DEKKER

(c. 1570–c. 1641)

The Happy Heart

ART thou poor, yet hast thou golden slumbers?
      O sweet content!
Art thou rich, yet is thy mind perplexed?
      O punishment!
Dost thou laugh to see how fools are vexed
To add to golden numbers, golden numbers?
O sweet content! O sweet, O sweet content!
   Work apace, apace, apace, apace;
   Honest labor bears a lovely face;
Then hey nonny nonny, hey nonny nonny!

Canst drink the waters of the crispèd spring?
      O sweet content!
Swimm'st thou in wealth, yet sink'st in thine own tears?
      O punishment!
Then he that patiently want's burden bears
No burden bears, but is a king, a king!
O sweet content! O sweet, O sweet content!
   Work apace, apace, apace, apace;
   Honest labor bears a lovely face;
Then hey nonny nonny, hey nonny nonny!

SIR ROBERT AYTON

(1570–1638)

Inconstancy Reproved

I DO confess thou'rt smooth and fair,
And I might have gone near to love thee,
Had I not found the slightest pray'r
That lips could speak, had pow'r to move thee;
But I can let thee now alone,
As worthy to be loved by none.

I do confess thou'rt sweet; yet find
Thee such an unthrift of thy sweets,
Thy favors are but like the wind,
Which kisseth everything it meets:
And since thou canst love more than one,
Thou'rt worthy to be kiss'd by none.

The morning rose that untouch'd stands,
Arm'd with her briars, how sweet she smells!
But pluck'd, and strain'd through ruder hands,
Her sweets no longer with her dwells;
But scent and beauty both are gone,
And leaves fall from her, one by one.

Such fate, ere long, will thee betide,
When thou hast handled been awhile,
Like fair flow'rs to be thrown aside;
And thou shalt sigh, when I shall smile
To see thy love to every one
Hath brought thee to be lov'd by none.

I Loved Thee Once

I LOVED thee once, I'll love no more,
  Thine be the grief as is the blame;
Thou art not what thou wast before,
  What reason I should be the same?
    He that can love unloved again,
    Hath better store of love than brain:
  God sends me love my debts to pay,
  While unthrifts fool their love away.

Nothing could have my love o'erthrown,
  If thou hadst still continued mine;
Yea, if thou hadst remained thy own,
  I might perchance have yet been thine.
    But thou thy freedom didst recall,
    That if thou might elsewhere inthrall;
  And then how could I but disdain
  A captive's captive to remain?

When new desires had conquered thee,
  And changed the object of thy will,
It had been lethargy in me,
  Not constancy, to love thee still.
    Yea, it had been a sin to go
    And prostitute affection so,
  Since we are taught no prayers to say
  To such as must to others pray.

Yet do thou glory in thy choice,
  Thy choice of his good fortune boast;
I'll neither grieve nor yet rejoice,
  To see him gain what I have lost;
    The height of my disdain shall be,
    To laugh at him, to blush for thee;
  To love thee still, but go no more
  A begging to a beggar's door.

THOMAS HEYWOOD
(c. 1570–1650)

Pack Clouds Away

PACK clouds away, and welcome day,
  With night we banish sorrow;
Sweet air, blow soft; mount, lark, aloft,
  To give my love good morrow.
Wings from the wind to please her mind,
  Notes from the lark I'll borrow:
Bird, prune thy wing; nightingale, sing,
  To give my love good morrow.
  To give my love good morrow,
  Notes from them all I'll borrow.

Wake from thy nest, robin redbreast,
  Sing, birds, in every furrow;
And from each hill let music shrill
  Give my fair love good morrow.
Blackbird and thrush in every bush,
  Stare, linnet, and cock-sparrow,
You petty elves, amongst yourselves,
  Sing my fair love good morrow.
  To give my love good morrow,
  Sing, birds, in every furrow.

BEN JONSON
(1573–1637)

Hymn to Diana

QUEEN and Huntress, chaste and fair,
  Now the sun is laid to sleep,
Seated in thy silver chair,
  State in wonted manner keep:

Hesperus entreats thy light,
Goddess excellently bright.

Earth, let not thy envious shade
Dare itself to interpose;
Cynthia's shining orb was made
Heaven to clear when day did close:
Bless us then with wishèd sight,
Goddess excellently bright.

Lay thy bow of pearl apart
And thy crystal-shining quiver;
Give unto the flying hart
Space to breathe, how short soever:
Thou that mak'st a day of night,
Goddess excellently bright!

Drink to Me only with Thine Eyes

(TO CELIA)

DRINK to me only with thine eyes,
And I will pledge with mine;
Or leave a kiss but in the cup,
And I'll not look for wine.
The thirst that from the soul doth rise
Doth ask a drink divine;
But might I of Jove's nectar sup,
I would not change for thine.

I sent thee late a rosy wreath,
Not so much honouring thee
As giving it a hope that there
It could not withered be;
But thou thereon didst only breathe
And sent'st it back to me;
Since when it grows, and smells, I swear,
Not of itself but thee!

O, Do Not Wanton with Those Eyes

O, DO not wanton with those eyes,
  Lest I be sick with seeing;
Nor cast them down, but let them rise,
  Lest shame destroy their being.

O, be not angry with those fires,
  For then their threats will kill me;
Nor look too kind on my desires,
  For then my hopes will spill me.

O, do not steep them in thy tears,
  For so will sorrow slay me;
Nor spread them as distract with fears:
  Mine own enough betray me.

Simplex Munditiis

STILL to be neat, still to be dressed,
As you were going to a feast;
Still to be powdered, still perfumed:
Lady, it is to be presumed,
Though art's hid causes are not found,
All is not sweet, all is not sound.

Give me a look, give me a face,
That makes simplicity a grace;
Robes loosely flowing, hair as free:
Such sweet neglect more taketh me
Then all the adulteries of art;
They strike mine eyes, but not my heart.

Good Life, Long Life

It is not growing like a tree
In bulk, doth make man better be;
Or standing long an oak, three hundred year,
To fall a log at last, dry, bald, and sear:
A lily of a day
Is fairer far in May,
Although it fall and die that night,—
It was the plant and flower of Light.
In small proportions we just beauties see,
And in short measures life may perfect be.

JOHN DONNE

(1573-1631)

Go and Catch a Falling Star

Go and catch a falling star,
Get with child a mandrake root,
Tell me where all times past are,
Or who cleft the devil's foot;
Teach me to hear mermaids singing,
Or to keep off envy's stinging,
And find
What wind
Serves to advance an honest mind.

If thou be'st born to strange sights,
Things invisible go see,
Ride ten thousand days and nights
Till age snow white hairs on thee;

Thou, when thou return'st, wilt tell me
All strange wonders that befell thee,
And swear
No where
Lives a woman true and fair.

If thou find'st one let me know,
Such a pilgrimage were sweet;
Yet do not; I would not go,
Though at next door we might meet.
Though she were true when you met her,
And last till you write your letter,
Yet she
Will be
False, ere I come, to two or three.

The Message

SEND home my long-strayed eyes to me,
Which, oh! too long have dwelt on thee;
Yet since there they have learned such ill,
Such forced fashions
And false passions,
That they be
Made by thee
Fit for no good sight, keep them still.

Send home my harmless heart again,
Which no unworthy thought could stain;
But if it be taught by thine
To make jestings
Of protestings,
And break both
Word and oath,
Keep it, for then 'tis none of mine.

Yet send me back my heart and eyes,
That I may know and see thy lies,

And may laugh and joy, when thou
Art in anguish
And dost languish
For some one
That will none,
Or prove as false as thou art now.

Sweetest Love

Sweetest love, I do not go,
For weariness of thee,
Nor in hope the world can show
A fitter Love for me;
But since that I
Must die at last, 'tis best,
To use myself in jest
Thus by fain'd deaths to die.

Yesternight the Sun went hence,
And yet is here to-day,
He hath no desire nor sense,
Nor half so short a way:
Then fear not me,
But believe that I shall make
Speedier journeys, since I take
More wings and spurs than he.

O how feeble is man's power,
That if good fortune fall,
Cannot add another hour
Nor a lost hour recall!
But come bad chance,
And we join to 'it our strength,
And we teach it art and length,
Itself o'er us to 'advance.

When thou sigh'st, thou sigh'st not wind,
  But sigh'st my soul away,
When thou weep'st, unkindly kind,
  My life's blood doth decay.
    It cannot be
That thou lov'st me, as thou say'st,
If in thine my life thou waste,
  That art the best of me.

Let not thy divining heart
  Forethink me any ill,
Destiny may take thy part,
  And may thy fears fulfill;
    But think that we
Are but turned aside to sleep;
They who one another keep
  Alive, ne'er parted be.

The Good-Morrow

I WONDER, by my troth, what thou and I
Did, till we loved? were we not wean'd till then?
But suck'd on country pleasures, childishly?
Or snorted we in the Seven Sleepers' den?
'Twas so; but this, all pleasures fancies be;
If ever any beauty I did see,
Which I desired, and got, 'twas but a dream of thee.

And now good-morrow to our waking souls,
Which watch not one another out of fear;
For love all love of other sights controls,
And makes one little room an everywhere.
Let sea-discovers to new worlds have gone;
Let maps to other, worlds on worlds have shown;
Let us possess one world; each hath one, and is one.

My face in thine eye, thine in mine appears,
And true plain hearts do in the faces rest;
Where can we find two better hemispheres
Without sharp north, without declining west?
Whatever dies, was not mix'd equally;
If our two loves be one, or thou and I
Love so alike that none can slacken, none can die.

The Dream

Dear love, for nothing less than thee
Would I have broke this happy dream;
It was a theme
For reason, much too strong for fantasy.
Therefore thou waked'st me wisely; yet
My dream thou brok'st not, but continued'st it.
Thou art so true that thoughts of thee suffice
To make dreams truths and fables histories;
Enter these arms, for since thou thought'st it best
Not to dream all my dream, let's act the rest.

As lightning, or a taper's light,
Thine eyes, and not thy noise, waked me;
Yet I thought thee—
For thou lov'st truth—an angel, at first sight;
But when I saw thou saw'st my heart,
And knew'st my thoughts beyond an angel's art,
When thou knew'st what I dreamt, when thou knew'st when
Excess of joy would wake me, and cam'st then,
I must confess it could not choose but be
Profane to think thee anything but thee.

Coming and staying show'd thee thee,
But rising makes me doubt that now
That art not thou.
That Love is weak where Fear's as strong as he;
'Tis not all spirit pure and brave
If mixture it of Fear, Shame, Honor have.

Perchance as torches, which must ready be,
Men light and put out, so thou deal'st with me.
Thou cam'st to kindle, go'st to come; then I
Will dream that hope again, but else would die.

The Sun Rising

BUSY old fool, unruly Sun,
Why dost thou thus,
Through windows, and through curtains, call on us?
Must to thy motions lovers' seasons run?
Saucy pedantic wretch, go chide
Late school-boys and sour prentices,
Go tell court-huntsmen that the king will ride,
Call country ants to harvest offices;
Love, all alike, no season knows nor clime,
Nor hours, days, months, which are the rags of time.

Thy beams so reverend and strong
Why shouldst thou think?
I could eclipse and cloud them with a wink,
But that I would not lose her sight so long.
If her eyes have not blinded thine,
Look, and to-morrow late tell me,
Whether both th' Indias of spice and mine
Be where thou left'st them, or lie here with me.
Ask for those kings whom thou saw'st yesterday,
And thou shalt hear, "All here in one bed lay."

She's all states, and all princes I;
Nothing else is;
Princes do but play us; compared to this,
All honour's mimic, all wealth alchemy.
Thou? Sun, art half as happy as we,
In that the world's contracted thus;
Thine age asks ease, and since thy duties be
To warm the world, that's done in warming us.
Shine here to us, and thou art everywhere;
This bed thy center is, these walls thy sphere.

The Curse

WHOEVER guesses, thinks, or dreams he knows
Who is my mistress, wither by this curse;
His only, and only his purse
May some dull heart to love dispose,
And she yield then to all that are his foes;
May he be scorn'd by one, whom all else scorn,
Forswear to others, what to her he 'hath sworn,
With fear of missing, shame of getting, torn;

Madness his sorrow, gout his cramp, may he
Make, by but thinking, who hath made him such;
And may he feel no touch
Of conscience, but of fame, and be
Anguished, not that 'twas sin, but that 'twas she;
In early and long scarceness may he rot,
For land which had been his, if he had not
Himself incestuously an heir begot:

May he dream Treason, and believe, that he
Meant to perform it, and confess and die,
And no record tell why:
His sons, which none of his may be,
Inherit nothing but his infamy:
Or may he so long Parasites have fed
That he would fain be theirs, whom he hath bred,
And at the last be circumcised for bread:

The venom of all stepdames, gamster's gall,
What Tyrants, and their subjects interwish,
What Plants, Mind, Beasts, Fowl, Fish,
Can contribute, all ill which all
Prophets, or Poets spake; And all which shall
Be annex'd in schedules until this by me,
Fall on that man; for if it be a she
Nature beforehand hath out-cursed me.

The Will

BEFORE I sigh my last gasp, let me breathe,
Great Love, some legacies: here I bequeathe
Mine eyes to Argus, if mine eyes can see;
If they be blind, then, Love, I give them thee;
My tongue to Fame; to embassadors mine ears;
To women or the sea, my tears;
Thou, Love, hast taught me heretofore
By making me serve her who had twenty more
That I should give to none, but such as had too much before.

My constancy I to the planets give;
My truth to them who at the court do live;
Mine ingenuity and openness,
To Jesuits; to buffoons my pensiveness;
My silence to any, who abroad have been;
My money to a Capuchin:
Thou, Love, taught'st me, by appointing me
To love there, where no love received can be,
Only to give to such as have an incapacity.

My faith I give to Roman Catholics;
All my good works unto the schismatics
Of Amsterdam; my best civility
And courtship to an University;
My modesty I give to shoulders bare;
My patience let gamesters share:
Thou, Love, taught'st me, by making me
Love her that holds my love disparity,
Only to give to those that count my gifts indignity.

I give my reputation to those
Which were my friends; mine industry to foes;
To schoolmen I bequeathe my doubtfulness;
My sickness to physicians, or excess;
To Nature all that I in rhyme have writ;
And to my company my wit:

Thou, Love, by making me adore
Her, who begot this love in me before,
Taught'st me to make, as though I gave, when I do but restore.

To him, for whom the passing-bell next tolls,
I give my physic-books; my written rolls
Of moral counsels I to Bedlam give;
My brazen medals unto them which live
In want of bread; to them which pass among
All foreigners, mine English tongue:
Thou, Love, by making me love one
Who thinks her friendship a fit portion
For younger lovers, dost my gifts thus disproportion.

Therefore I'll give no more, but I'll undo
The world by dying; because Love dies too.
Then all your beauties will be no more worth
Than gold in mines, where none doth draw it forth;
And all your graces no more use shall have,
Than a sun-dial in a grave:
Thou, Love, taught'st me, by making me
Love her, who doth neglect both me and thee,
To invent and practise this one way to annihilate all three.

Present in Absence

ABSENCE, hear thou this protestation
Against thy strength,
Distance, and length:
Do what thou canst for alteration,
For hearts of truest mettle
Absence doth join, and Time doth settle.

Who loves a mistress of such quality,
His mind hath found
Affection's ground
Beyond time, place, and all mortality.
To hearts that cannot vary
Absence is present, Time doth tarry.

By absence this good means I gain,
That I can catch her
Where none can watch her,
In some close corner of my brain:
There I embrace and kiss her,
And so enjoy her and none miss her.

Death, Be Not Proud

DEATH, be not proud, though some have callèd thee
Mighty and dreadful, for thou art not so:
For those, whom thou think'st thou dost overthrow,
Die not, poor Death; nor yet canst thou kill me.
From rest and sleep, which but thy pictures be,
Much pleasure, then from thee much more must flow;
And soonest our best men with thee do go,
Rest of their bones, and souls' delivery.
Thou art slave to fate, chance, kings, and desperate men,
And doth with poison, war, and sickness dwell;
And poppy or charms can make us sleep as well
And better than thy stroke; why swell'st thou then?
One short sleep past, we wake eternally,
And Death shall be no more: Death, thou shalt die.

RICHARD BARNEFIELD

(1574–1627)

To the Nightingale

AS IT fell upon a day,
In the merry month of May,
Sitting in a pleasant shade
Which a grove of myrtles made,

Beasts did leap, and birds did sing,
Trees did grow, and plants did spring;
Everything did banish moan,
Save the nightingale alone.
She, poor bird, as all forlorn,
Leaned her breast up-till a thorn;
And there sung the doleful'st ditty
That to hear it was great pity.
Fie, fie, fie! now would she cry;
Teru, teru, by and by;
That, to hear her so complain,
Scarce I could from tears refrain;
For her griefs, so lively shown,
Made me think upon mine own.
Ah! (thought I) thou mourn'st in vain;
None takes pity on thy pain;
Senseless trees, they cannot hear thee;
Ruthless bears, they will not cheer thee;
King Pandion, he is dead;
All thy friends are lapped in lead:
All thy fellow-birds do sing,
Careless of thy sorrowing!
Whilst as fickle Fortune smiled,
Thou and I were both beguiled,
Every one that flatters thee
Is no friend in misery.
Words are easy, like the wind;
Faithful friends are hard to find.
Every man will be thy friend
Whilst thou hast wherewith to spend;
But, if stores of crowns be scant,
No man will supply thy want.
If that one be prodigal,
Bountiful they will him call;
And, with such-like flattering,
"Pity but he were a king."
If he be addict to vice,
Quickly him they will entice;
But if Fortune once do frown,
Then farewell his great renown:
They that fawned on him before,

Use his company no more.
He that is thy friend indeed,
He will help thee in thy need;
If thou sorrow, he will weep,
If thou wake, he cannot sleep.
Thus, of every grief in heart,
He with thee doth bear a part.
These are certain signs to know
Faithful friend from flattering foe.

JOHN FLETCHER

(1579–1625)

Lay a Garland on My Hearse

LAY a garland on my hearse
  Of the dismal yew;
Maidens, willow branches bear,
  Say I dièd true.

My Love was false, but I was firm
  From my hour of birth.
Upon my buried body lay
  Lightly, gently, earth.

Spring

Now the lusty Spring is seen;
    Golden yellow, gaudy blue,
    Daintily invite the view.
Everywhere, on every green,

Roses blushing as they blow,
    And enticing men to pull;
Lilies whiter than the snow;
    Woodbines of sweet honey full—
All love's emblems, and all cry:
"Ladies, if not plucked, we die!"

Yet the lusty spring hath stayed;
    Blushing red and purest white
    Daintily to love invite
Every woman, every maid:
Cherries kissing as they grow,
    And inviting men to taste,
Apples even ripe below,
    Winding gently to the waist:
All love's emblems, and all cry,
"Ladies, if not plucked, we die!"

Melancholy

Hence, all you vain delights,
As short as are the nights
Wherein you spend your folly!
There's nought in this life sweet,
If man were wise to see't,
But only melancholy—
O sweetest Melancholy!
Welcome, folded arms, and fixèd eyes,
A sigh that piercing mortifies,
A look that's fasten'd to the ground,
A tongue chain'd up without a sound!
Fountain-heads and pathless groves,
Places which pale passion loves!
Moonlight walks, when all the fowls
Are warmly housed, save bats and owls!
A midnight bell, a parting groan—
These are the sounds we feed upon;
Then stretch our bones in a still gloomy valley;
Nothing's so dainty sweet as lovely melancholy.

JOHN WEBSTER

(1580–c.1625)

A Land Dirge

Call for the robin-redbreast and the wren,
Since o'er shady groves they hover,
And with leaves and flowers do cover
The friendless bodies of unburied men.
Call unto his funeral dole
The ant, the field-mouse, and the mole,
To rear him hillocks that shall keep him warm,
And (when gay tombs are robb'd) sustain no harm;
But keep the wolf far thence, that's foe to men,
For with his nails he'll dig them up again.

The Shrouding of the Duchess of Malfi

Hark! Now everything is still,
The screech-owl and the whistler shrill,
Call upon our dame aloud,
And bid her quickly don her shroud!

Much you had of land and rent;
Your length in clay's now competent:
A long war disturb'd your mind;
Here your perfect peace is sign'd.

Of what is 't fools make such vain keeping?
Sin their conception, their birth weeping,
Their life a general mist of error,

Their death a hideous storm of terror.
Strew your hair with powders sweet,
Don clean linen, bathe your feet,

And—the foul end more to check—
A crucifix let bless your neck:
'T is now full tide 'tween night and day;
End your groan and come away.

WILLIAM ALEXANDER, EARL OF STIRLING

(c. 1580–1640)

Aurora

O HAPPY Tithon! if thou know'st thy hap,
And valuest thy wealth, as I my want,
Then need'st thou not—which ah! I grieve to grant—
Repine at Jove, lull'd in his leman's lap:
That golden shower in which he did repose—
    One dewy drop it stains
    Which thy Aurora rains
    Upon the rural plains,
When from thy bed she passionately goes.

Then, waken'd with the music of the merles,
She not remembers Memnon when she mourns:
That faithful flame which in her bosom burns
From crystal conduits throws those liquid pearls:
Sad from thy sight so soon to be removed,
    She so her grief delates.
    O favour'd by the fates
    Above the happiest states,
Who art of one so worthy well-beloved!

FRANCIS BEAUMONT

(1584–1616)

On the Tombs in Westminster Abbey

MORTALITY, behold and fear
What a change of flesh is here!
Think how many royal bones
Sleep within these heaps of stones:
Here they lie, had realms and lands,
Who now want strength to stir their hands:

Where from their pulpits seal'd with dust
They preach, "In greatness is no trust."
Here's an acre sown indeed
With the richest, royallest seed
That the earth did e'er suck in
Since the first man died for sin:
Here the bones of birth have cried
"Though gods they were, as men they died!"
Here are sands, ignoble things,
Dropt from the ruin'd sides of kings;
Here's a world of pomp and state
Buried in dust, once dead by fate.

WILLIAM DRUMMOND, OF HAWTHORNDEN

(1585-1649)

A Lament

MY THOUGHTS hold mortal strife;
I do detest my life,
And with lamenting cries
Peace to my soul to bring
Oft call that prince which here doth monarchise:
—But he, grim-grinning King,
Who caitiffs scorns, and doth the blest surprise,
Late having deck'd with beauty's rose his tomb,
Disdains to crop a weed, and will not come.

The Book of the World

OF THIS fair volume which we World do name
If we the sheets and leaves could turn with care,
Of Him who it corrects and did it frame,
We clear might read the art and wisdom rare:

Find out His power which wildest powers doth tame,
His providence extending everywhere,
His justice which proud rebels doth not spare,
In every page, no period of the same.
But silly we, like foolish children, rest
Well pleased with colored vellum, leaves of gold,
Fair dangling ribbands, leaving what is best,
On the great Writer's sense ne'er taking hold;
Or, if by chance we stay our minds on aught,
It is some picture on the margin wrought.

JOHN FORD
(1586–1639)

Dawn

FLY hence, shadows, that do keep
Watchful sorrows charm'd in sleep!
Tho' the eyes be overtaken,
Yet the heart doth ever waken
Thoughts chain'd up in busy snares
Of continual woes and cares:
Love and griefs are so exprest
As they rather sigh than rest.
Fly hence, shadows, that do keep
Watchful sorrows charm'd in sleep!

GEORGE WITHER
(1588–1667)

The Shepherd's Resolution

SHALL I, wasting in despair,
Die because a woman's fair?
Or make pale my cheeks with care
'Cause another's rosy are?

Be she fairer than the day,
Or the flowery meads in May,—
  If she be not so to me,
  What care I how fair she be?

Shall my foolish heart be pined
'Cause I see a woman kind?
Or a well-disposèd nature
Joinèd with a lovely feature?
Be she meeker, kinder than
The turtle-dove or pelican,—
  If she be not so to me,
  What care I how kind she be?

Shall a woman's virtues move
Me to perish for her love?
Or, her well deservings known,
Make me quite forget mine own?
Be she with that goodness blest,—
Which may merit name of best
  If she be not such to me,
  What care I how good she be?

'Cause her fortune seems too high,
Shall I play the fool and die?
Those that bear a noble mind
Where they want of riches find,
Think what with them they would do
That without them dare to woo:
  And unless that mind I see,
  What care I how great she be?

Great, or good, or kind, or fair,
I will ne'er the more despair:
If she love me, this believe,—
I will die ere she shall grieve.
If she slight me when I woo,
I can scorn and let her go;—
  For if she be not for me,
  What care I for whom she be?

WILLIAM BROWNE, OF TAVISTOCK

(c. 1591–1643)

Epitaph on the Countess of Pembroke

UNDERNEATH this sable hearse
Lies the subject of all verse,
Sydney's sister,—Pembroke's mother.
Death, ere thou hast slain another
Fair and wise and good as she,
Time shall throw a dart at thee!

Marble piles let no man raise
To her name in after days;
Some kind woman, born as she,
Reading this, like Niobe
Shall turn marble, and become
Both her mourner and her tomb.

ROBERT HERRICK

(1591–1674)

Delight in Disorder

A SWEET disorder in the dress
Kindles in clothes a wantonness;
A lawn about the shoulders thrown
Into a fine distraction;
An erring lace, which here and there
Inthralls the crimson stomacher;
A cuff neglectful, and thereby
Ribbons to flow confusedly;
A winning wave, deserving note,
In the tempestuous petticoat;

A careless shoestring, in whose tie
I see a wild civility;—
Do more bewitch me than when art
Is too precise in every part.

To Electra

I DARE not ask a kiss,
  I dare not beg a smile,
Lest having that, or this,
  I might grow proud the while.

No, no, the utmost share
  Of my desire shall be
Only to kiss that air
  That lately kissèd thee.

To Dianeme

SWEET, be not proud of those two eyes
Which starlike sparkle in their skies;
Nor be you proud, that you can see
All hearts your captives, yours yet free;
Be you not proud of that rich hair
Which wantons with the lovesick air;
Whenas that ruby which you wear,
Sunk from the tip of your soft ear,
Will last to be a precious stone
When all your world of beauty's gone.

Corinna's Going A-Maying

GET up, get up for shame, the blooming morn
Upon her wings presents the god unshorn.

See how Aurora throws her fair
Fresh-quilted colors through the air:
Get up, sweet slug-a-bed, and see
The dew bespangling herb and tree.
Each flower has wept and bowéd toward the east
Above an hour since: yet you not dressed;
Nay! not so much as out of bed?
When all the birds have matins said
And sung their thankful hymns, 'tis sin,
Nay, profanation, to keep in,
Whenas a thousand virgins on this day
Spring, sooner than the lark, to fetch in May.

Rise, and put on your foliage, and be seen
To come forth, like the spring-time, fresh and green,
And sweet as Flora. Take no care
For jewels for your gown or hair:
Fear not; the leaves will strew
Gems in abundance upon you:
Besides, the childhood of the day has kept,
Against you come, some orient pearls unwept;
Come and receive them while the light
Hangs on the dew-locks of the night:
And Titan on the eastern hill
Retires himself, or else stands still
Till you come forth. Wash, dress, be brief in praying:
Few beads are best when once we go a-Maying.

Come, my Corinna, come; and, coming mark
How each field turns a street, each street a park
Made green and trimmed with trees; see how
Devotion gives each house a bough
Or branch: each porch, each door ere this
An ark, a tabernacle is,
Made up of white-thorn, neatly interwove;
As if here were those cooler shades of love.
Can such delights be in the street
And open fields and we not see 't?
Come, we'll abroad; and let's obey
The proclamation made for May:

And sin no more, as we have done, by staying;
But, my Corinna, come, let's go a-Maying.

There's not a budding boy or girl this day
But is got up, and gone to bring in May.
  A deal of youth, ere this, is come
  Back, and with white-thorn laden home.
  Some have despatched their cakes and cream
  Before that we have left to dream:
And some have wept, and wooed, and plighted troth,
And chose their priest, ere we can cast off sloth:
  Many a green-gown has been given;
  Many a kiss, both odd and even:
  Many a glance too has been sent
  From out the eye, love's firmament;
Many a jest told of the keys betraying
This night, and locks picked, yet we're not a-Maying.

Come, let us go while we are in our prime;
And take the harmless folly of the time.
  We shall grow old apace, and die
  Before we know our liberty.
  Our life is short, and our days run
  As fast away as does the sun;
And, as a vapor or a drop of rain,
Once lost, can ne'er be found again,
  So when or you or I are made
  A fable, song, or fleeting shade,
  All love, all liking, all delight
  Lies drowned with us in endless night.
Then while time serves, and we are but decaying,
Come, my Corinna, come let's go a-Maying.

To the Virgins

GATHER ye rosebuds while ye may,
  Old Time is still a flying;
And this same flower that smiles to-day
  To-morrow will be dying.

The glorious lamp of Heaven, the sun,
  The higher he's a getting,
The sooner will his race be run,
  And nearer he's to setting.

The age is best which is the first,
  When youth and blood are warmer;
But being spent, the worse and worst
  Times still succeed the former.

Then be not coy, but use your time,
  And, while ye may, go marry;
For having lost but once your prime,
  You may forever tarry.

To Anthea

Who May Command Him Any Thing

Bid me to live, and I will live
  Thy Protestant to be:
Or bid me love, and I will give
  A loving heart to thee.

A heart as soft, a heart as kind,
  A heart as sound and free
As in the whole world thou canst find,
  That heart I'll give to thee.

Bid that heart stay, and it will stay
  To honour thy decree:
Or bid it languish quite away,
  And 't shall do so for thee.

Bid me to weep, and I will weep
  While I have eyes to see:
And, having none, yet I will keep
  A heart to weep for thee.

Bid me despair, and I'll despair
  Under that cypress tree:
Or bid me die, and I will dare
  E'en death to die for thee.

Thou art my life, my love, my heart,
  The very eyes of me,
And hast command of every part,
  To live and die for thee.

To Daffodils

Fair Daffodils, we weep to see
    You haste away so soon;
As yet the early-rising Sun
    Has not attain'd his noon.
        Stay, stay
    Until the hasting day
        Has run
    But to the even-song;
And, having pray'd together, we
    Will go with you along.

We have short time to stay, as you,
    We have as short a Spring;
As quick a growth to meet decay
    As you, or any thing.
        We die,
    As your hours do, and dry
        Away
    Like to the Summer's rain;
Or as the pearls of morning's dew,
    Ne'er to be found again.

To Blossoms

FAIR pledges of a fruitful tree,
Why do ye fall so fast?
Your date is not so past
But you may stay yet here awhile
To blush and gently smile,
And go at last.

What! were ye born to be
An hour or half's delight,
And so to bid good-night?
'T is pity Nature brought ye forth,
Merely to show your worth,
And lose you quite.

But you are lovely leaves, where we
May read how soon things have
Their end, though ne'er so brave;
And after they have shown their pride
Like you awhile, they glide
Into the grave.

Whenas in Silks My Julia Goes

WHENAS in silks my Julia goes,
Then, then, me thinks, how sweetly flowes
That liquefaction of her clothes.

Next, when I cast mine eyes and see
That brave vibration each way free,
O how that glittering taketh me!

IZAAK WALTON
(1593–1683)

The Angler's Wish

I IN these flowery meads would be,
These crystal streams should solace me;
To whose harmonious bubbling noise
I, with my angle, would rejoice,
    Sit here, and see the turtle-dove
    Court his chaste mate to acts of love;

Or, on that bank, feel the west-wind
Breathe health and plenty; please my mind,
To see sweet dew-drops kiss these flowers,
And then washed off by April showers;
    Here, hear my Kenna sing a song:
    There, see a blackbird feed her young,

Or a laverock build her nest;
Here, give my weary spirits rest,
And raise my low-pitched thoughts above
Earth, or what poor mortals love.
    Thus, free from lawsuits, and the noise
    Of princes' courts, I would rejoice;

Or, with my Bryan and a book,
Loiter long days near Shawford brook;
There sit by him, and eat my meat;
There see the sun both rise and set;
There bid good morning to next day;
There meditate my time away;
    And angle on; and beg to have
    A quiet passage to a welcome grave.

GEORGE HERBERT
(1593-1633)

Virtue

SWEET day, so cool, so calm, so bright,
The bridal of the earth and sky,
The dew shall weep thy fall to-night,
For thou must die.

Sweet rose, whose hue, angry and brave,
Bids the rash gazer wipe his eye,
Thy root is ever in its grave,
And thou must die.

Sweet spring, full of sweet days and roses,
A box where sweets compacted lie,
My music shows ye have your closes,
And all must die.

Only a sweet and virtuous soul,
Like seasoned timber, never gives;
But though the whole world turn to coal,
Then chiefly lives.

The Collar

I STRUCK the board, and cried, "No more;
I will abroad.
What! shall I ever sigh and pine?
My lines and life are free; free as the road,
Loose as the wind, as large as store.
Shall I be still in suit?
Have I no harvest but a thorn

To let me blood, and not restore
What I have lost with cordial fruit?
        Sure there was wine
Before my sighs did dry it: there was corn
  Before my tears did drown it.
Is the year only lost to me?
  Have I no bays to crown it?
No flowers, no garlands gay? All blasted?
        All wasted?
Not so, my heart; but there is fruit,
        And thou hast hands.
Recover all thy sigh-blown age
On double pleasures: leave thy cold dispute
Of what is fit and not; forsake thy cage,
        Thy rope of sands,
Which petty thoughts have made, and made to thee
Good cable, to enforce and draw
        And be thy law,
While thou didst wink and wouldst not see.
        Away; take heed:
        I will abroad.
Call in thy death's head there: tie up thy fears.
        He that forbears
To suit and serve his need,
        Deserves his load."
But as I raved and grew more fierce and wild
        At every word,
Methought I heard one calling, "Child":
  And I replied, "My Lord."

The Pulley

        WHEN God at first made man,
Having a glass of blessings standing by,
Let us (said he) pour on him all we can:
Let the world's riches, which dispersèd lie,
        Contract into a span.

So strength first made a way;
Then beauty flowed, then wisdom, honour, pleasure:
When almost all was out, God made a stay,
Perceiving that, alone, of all his treasure,
Rest in the bottom lay.

For if I should (said he)
Bestow this jewel also on my creature,
He would adore my gifts instead of me,
And rest in Nature, not the God of Nature:
So both should losers be.

Yet let him keep the rest,
But keep them with repining restlessness:
Let him be rich and weary, that, at least,
If goodness lead him not, yet weariness
May toss him to my breast.

THOMAS CAREW

(c. 1595–c. 1645)

Ask Me No More

Ask me no more where Jove bestows,
When June is past, the fading rose;
For in your beauties, orient deep,
These flowers, as in their causes, sleep.

Ask me no more whither do stray
The golden atoms of the day;
For in pure love heaven did prepare
Those powders to enrich your hair.

Ask me no more whither doth haste
The nightingale, when May is past;
For in your sweet dividing throat
She winters, and keeps warm her note.

Ask me no more where those stars light,
That downwards fall in dead of night;
For in your eyes they sit, and there
Fixèd become, as in their sphere.

Ask me no more if east or west
The phoenix builds her spicy nest;
For unto you at last she flies,
And in your fragrant bosom dies.

Disdain Returned

He that loves a rosy cheek,
  Or a coral lip admires,
Or from starlike eyes doth seek
  Fuel to maintain his fires;
As old Time makes these decay,
So his flames must waste away.

But a smooth and steadfast mind,
  Gentle thoughts, and calm desires,
Hearts with equal love combined,
  Kindle never-dying fires:—
Where these are not, I despise
Lovely cheeks or lips or eyes.

JAMES SHIRLEY

(1596–1666)

Death the Leveller

The glories of our blood and state
  Are shadows, not substantial things;
There is no armor against fate;
  Death lays his icy hand on kings:

Sceptre and Crown
Must tumble down,
And in the dust be equal made
With the poor crooked scythe and spade.

Some men with swords may reap the field,
And plant fresh laurels where they kill:
But their strong nerves at last must yield;
They tame but one another still:
Early or late
They stoop to fate,
And must give up their murmuring breath
When they, pale captives, creep to death.

The garlands wither on your brow;
Then boast no more your mighty deeds!
Upon Death's purple altar now
See where the victor-victim bleeds.
Your heads must come
To the cold tomb:
Only the actions of the just
Smell sweet and blossom in their dust.

WILLIAM HABINGTON

(1605–1654)

Nox Nocti Indicat Scientiam

When I survey the bright
Celestial sphere;
So rich with jewels hung, that night
Doth like an Ethiop bride appear:

My soul her wings doth spread
And heaven-ward flies,
The Almighty's mysteries to read
In the large volumes of the skies.

For the bright firmament
Shoots forth no flame
So silent, but is eloquent
In speaking the Creator's name.

No unregarded star
Contracts its light
Into so small a character,
Removed far from our human sight,

But if we steadfast look,
We shall discern
In it, as in some holy book,
How man may heavenly knowledge learn.

It tells the Conqueror
That far-stretch'd power,
Which his proud dangers traffic for,
Is but the triumph of an hour:

That from the farthest North,
Some nation may,
Yet undiscover'd, issue forth,
And o'er his new-got conquest sway.

Some nation yet shut in
With hills of ice,
May be let out to scourge his sin,
Till they shall equal him in vice.

And then they likewise shall
Their ruin have;
For as yourselves your Empires fall,
And every Kingdom hath a grave.

Thus those celestial fires,
Though seeming mute,
The fallacy of our desires
And all the pride of life, confute:—

For they have watch'd since first
The World had birth:
And found sin in itself accursed,
And nothing permanent on earth.

SIR WILLIAM DAVENANT

(1606–1668)

The Lark Now Leaves His Watery Nest

THE lark now leaves his watery nest
And climbing shakes his dewy wings.
He takes this window for the east,
And to implore your light he sings,
Awake, awake! the morn will never rise
Till she can dress her beauty at your eyes.

The merchant bows unto the seaman's star,
The ploughman from the sun his season takes;
But still the lover wonders what they are
Who look for day before his mistress wakes.
Awake, awake! break through your veils of lawn;
Then draw your curtains, and begin the dawn.

EDMUND WALLER

(1606–1687)

On a Girdle

THAT which her slender waist confined
Shall now my joyful temples bind;
No monarch but would give his crown,
His arms might do what this hath done.

It was my heaven's extremest sphere,
The pale which held that lovely deer:
My joy, my grief, my hope, my love,
Did all within this circle move.

A narrow compass! and yet there
Dwelt all that's good, and all that's fair.
Give me but what this ribbon bound,
Take all the rest the sun goes round!

Go, Lovely Rose

Go, LOVELY rose!
Tell her that wastes her time and me,
That now she knows,
When I resemble her to thee,
How sweet and fair she seems to be.

Tell her that's young,
And shuns to have her graces spied,
That hadst thou sprung
In deserts, where no men abide,
Thou must have uncommended died.

Small is the worth
Of beauty from the light retired;
Bid her come forth,
Suffer herself to be desired,
And not blush so to be admired.

Then die, that she
The common fate of all things rare
May read in thee;
How small a part of time they share,
That are so wondrous sweet and fair.

To the Younger Lady Lucy Sydney

Why came I so untimely forth
Into a world which, wanting thee,
Could entertain us with no worth,
Or shadow of felicity?
That time should me so far remove
From that which I was born to love.

Yet, fairest Blossom! do not slight
That eye which you may know so soon;
The rosy morn resigns her light
And milder splendours to the noon:
If such thy drawing beauty's power
Who shall abide its noon-tide hour?

Hope waits upon the flowery prime;
And summer though it be less gay,
Yet is not looked on as a time
Of declination or decay;
For with a full hand she doth bring
All that was promised by the spring.

JOHN MILTON

(1608–1674)

On His Being Arrived at the Age of Twenty-three

How soon hath Time, the subtle thief of youth,
  Stolen on his wing my three-and-twentieth year!
  My hasting days fly on with full career,
But my late spring no bud or blossom sheweth.
Perhaps my semblance might deceive the truth,
  That I to manhood am arrived so near;
  And inward ripeness doth much less appear,
That some more timely-happy spirits indu'th.

Yet be it less or more, or soon or slow,
  It shall be in strictest measure even
  To that same lot, however mean or high,
Towards which time leads me and the will of Heaven.
  All is, if I have grace to use it so,
  As ever in my great Task-master's eye.

On Shakespeare

WHAT needs my Shakespeare for his honoured bones,
The labour of an age in pilèd stones,
Or that his hallowed reliques should be hid
Under a star-ypointing pyramid?
Dear son of memory, great heir of fame,
What need'st thou such weak witness of thy name?
Thou in our wonder and astonishment
Hast built thyself a live-long monument.
For whilst to the shame of slow-endeavouring art
Thy easy numbers flow, and that each heart
Hath from the leaves of thy unvalued book
Those Delphic lines with deep impression took,
Then thou our fancy of itself bereaving
Dost make us marble with too much conceiving;
  And so sepùlchered in such pomp dost lie,
  That kings for such a tomb would wish to die.

l'Allegro

HENCE, loathéd Melancholy,
  Of Cerberus and blackest Midnight born
In Stygian cave forlorn
  'Mongst horrid shapes, and shrieks, and sights unholy!

Find out some uncouth cell,
  Where brooding Darkness spreads his jealous wings,
And the night-raven sings;
  There, under ebon shades and low-browed rocks,
As ragged as thy locks,
  In dark Cimmerian desert ever dwell.
But come, thou Goddess fair and free,
In heaven yclept Euphrosyne,
And by men heart-easing Mirth;
Whom lovely Venus, at a birth,
With two sister Graces more,
To ivy-crownéd Bacchus bore:
Or whether (as some sager sing)
The frolic wind that breathes the spring,
Zephyr, with Aurora playing,
As he met her once a-Maying,
There, on beds of violets blue,
And fresh-blown roses washed in dew,
Filled her with thee, a daughter fair,
So buxom, blithe, and debonair.
Haste thee, Nymph, and bring with thee
Jest, and youthful Jollity,
Quips and cranks and wanton wiles,
Nods and becks and wreathéd smiles,
Such as hang on Hebe's cheek,
And love to live in dimple sleek;
Sport that wrinkled Care derides,
And Laughter holding both his sides.
Come, and trip it, as you go,
On the light fantastic toe;
And in thy right hand lead with thee
The mountain-nymph, sweet Liberty;
And, if I give thee honour due,
Mirth, admit me of thy crew,
To live with her, and live with thee,
In unreprovéd pleasures free;
To hear the lark begin his flight,
And, singing, startle the dull night,
From his watch-tower in the skies,
Till the dappled dawn doth rise;
Then to come, in spite of sorrow,

And at my window bid good-morrow,
Through the sweet-briar or the vine,
Or the twisted eglantine;
While the cock, with lively din,
Scatters the rear of darkness thin;
And to the stack, or the barn-door,
Stoutly struts his dames before:
Oft listening how the hounds and horn
Cheerly rouse the slumbering morn,
From the side of some hoar hill,
Through the high wood echoing shrill:
Sometime walking, not unseen,
By hedgerow elms, on hillocks green,
Right against the eastern gate
Where the great Sun begins his state,
Robed in flames and amber light,
The clouds in thousand liveries dight;
While the ploughman, near at hand,
Whistles o'er the furrowed land,
And the milkmaid singeth blithe,
And the mower whets his scythe,
And every shepherd tells his tale
Under the hawthorn in the dale.
Straight mine eye hath caught new pleasures
Whilst the landscape round it measures:
Russet lawns, and fallows gray,
Where the nibbling flocks do stray,
Mountains on whose barren breast
The laboring clouds do often rest;
Meadows trim, with daisies pied;
Shallow brooks, and rivers wide;
Towers and battlements it sees
Bosomed high in tufted trees,
Where perhaps some beauty lies,
The cynosure of neighboring eyes.
Hard by a cottage chimney smokes
From betwixt two agéd oaks,
Where Corydon and Thyrsis met
Are at their savory dinner set
Of herbs and other country messes,
Which the neat-handed Phyllis dresses;

And then in haste her bower she leaves,
With Thestylis to bind the sheaves;
Or, if the earlier season lead,
To the tanned haycock in the mead.
Sometimes, with secure delight,
The upland hamlets will invite,
When the merry bells ring round,
And the jocund rebecks sound
To many a youth and many a maid
Dancing in the checkered shade,
And young and old come forth to play
On a sunshine holiday,
Till the livelong daylight fail:
Then to a spicy nut-brown ale,
With stories told of many a feat,
How Faery Mab the junkets eat.
She was pinched and pulled, she said;
And he, by Friar's lantern led,
Tells how the drudging goblin sweat
To earn his cream-bowl duly set,
When in one night, ere glimpse of morn,
His shadowy flail hath threshed the corn
That ten day-laborers could not end;
Then lies him down, the lubber fiend,
And, stretched out all the chimney's length,
Basks at the fire his hairy strength,
And crop-full out of doors he flings,
Ere the first cock his matin rings.
Thus done the tales, to bed they creep,
By whispering winds soon lulled asleep.
Towered cities please us then,
And the busy hum of men,
Where throngs of knights and barons bold,
In weeds of peace, high triumphs hold,
With store of ladies, whose bright eyes
Rain influence, and judge the prize
Of wit or arms, while both contend
To win her grace whom all commend.
There let Hymen oft appear
In saffron robe, with taper clear,
And pomp, and feast, and revelry,

With mask and antique pageantry;
Such sights as youthful poets dream
On summer eves by haunted stream.
Then to the well-trod stage anon,
If Jonson's learnéd sock be on,
Or sweetest Shakespeare, Fancy's child,
Warble his native wood-notes wild.
And ever, against eating cares,
Lap me in soft Lydian airs,
Married to immortal verse,
Such as the meeting soul may pierce,
In notes with many a winding bout
Of linkéd sweetness long drawn out
With wanton heed and giddy cunning,
The melting voice through mazes running,
Untwisting all the chains that tie
The hidden soul of harmony;
That Orpheus' self may heave his head
From golden slumber on a bed
Of heaped Elysian flowers, and hear
Such strains as would have won the ear
Of Pluto to have quite set free
His half-regained Eurydice.
These delights if thou canst give,
Mirth, with thee I mean to live.

Il Penseroso

HENCE, vain deluding Joys,
  The brood of Folly without father bred!
How little you bested,
  Or fill the fixéd mind with all your toys!
Dwell in some idle brain,
  And fancies fond with gaudy shapes possess,
As thick and numberless
  As the gay motes that people the sunbeam,
Or likest hovering dreams,
  The fickle pensioners of Morpheus' train.

But, hail! thou Goddess sage and holy!
Hail, divinest Melancholy!
Whose saintly visage is too bright
To hit the sense of human sight,
And therefore to our weaker view
O'erlaid with black, staid Wisdom's hue;
Black, but such as in esteem
Prince Memnon's sister might beseem,
Or that starred Ethiop queen that strove
To set her beauty's praise above
The Sea-Nymphs, and their powers offended.
Yet thou art higher far descended:
Thee bright-haired Vesta long of yore
To solitary Saturn bore;
His daughter she; in Saturn's reign
Such mixture was not held a stain.
Oft in glimmering bowers and glades
He met her, and in secret shades
Of woody Ida's inmost grove,
Whilst yet there was no fear of Jove.
Come, pensive Nun, devout and pure,
Sober, steadfast, and demure,
All in a robe of darkest grain,
Flowing with majestic train,
And sable stole of cypress lawn
Over thy decent shoulders drawn.
Come; but keep thy wonted state,
With even step, and musing gait,
And looks commercing with the skies,
Thy rapt soul sitting in thine eyes:
There, held in holy passion still,
Forget thyself to marble, till
With a sad leaden downward cast
Thou fix them on the earth as fast.
And join with thee calm Peace and Quiet,
Spare Fast, that oft with gods doth diet,
And hears the Muses in a ring
Aye round about Jove's altar sing;
And add to these retiréd Leisure,
That in trim gardens takes his pleasure;
But, first and chiefest, with thee bring

Him that yon soars on golden wing,
Guiding the fiery-wheeléd throne,
The Cherub Contemplation;
And the mute Silence hist along,
'Less Philomel will deign a song,
In her sweetest saddest plight,
Smoothing the rugged brow of Night,
While Cynthia checks her dragon yoke
Gently o'er the accustomed oak.
Sweet bird, that shunn'st the noise of folly,
Most musical, most melancholy!
Thee, chauntress, oft the woods among
I woo, to hear thy even-song;
And, missing thee, I walk unseen
On the dry smooth-shaven green
To behold the wandering moon,
Riding near her highest noon,
Like one that had been led astray
Through the heaven's wide pathless way,
And oft, as if her head she bowed,
Stooping through a fleecy cloud.
Oft, on a plat of rising ground,
I hear the far-off curfew sound,
Over some wide-watered shore,
Swinging slow with sullen roar;
Or, if the air will not permit,
Some still removéd place will fit,
Where glowing embers through the room
Teach light to counterfeit a gloom,
Far from all resort of mirth,
Save the cricket on the hearth,
Or the bellman's drowsy charm
To bless the doors from nightly harm.
Or let my lamp, at midnight hour,
Be seen in some high lonely tower,
Where I may oft outwatch the Bear,
With thrice great Hermes, or unsphere
The spirit of Plato, to unfold
What worlds or what past regions hold
The immortal mind that hath forsook
Her mansion in this fleshly nook;

And of those demons that are found
In fire, air, flood, or underground,
Whose power hath a true consent
With planet or with element.
Sometimes let gorgeous Tragedy
In sceptered pall come sweeping by,
Presenting Thebes, or Pelops' line,
Or the tale of Troy divine,
Or what (though rare) of later age
Ennobled hath the buskined stage.
But, O sad Virgin! that thy power
Might raise Musæus from his bower;
Or bid the soul of Orpheus sing
Such notes as, warbled to the string,
Drew iron tears down Pluto's cheek,
And made Hell grant what love did seek;
Or call up him that left half-told
The story of Cambuscan bold,
Of Camball, and of Algarsife,
And who had Canace to wife,
That owned the virtuous ring and glass,
And of the wondrous horse of brass
On which the Tartar king did ride;
And if aught else great bards beside
In sage and solemn tunes have sung,
Of turneys, and of trophies hung,
Of forests, and enchantments drear,
Where more is meant than meets the ear.
Thus, Night, oft see me in thy pale career,
Till civil-suited Morn appear,
Not tricked and frounced, as she was wont
With the Attic boy to hunt,
But kerchiefed in a comely cloud,
While rocking winds are piping loud,
Or ushered with a shower still,
When the gust hath blown his fill,
Ending on the rustling leaves,
With minute-drops from off the eaves.
And, when the sun begins to fling
His flaring beams, me, Goddess, bring
To archéd walks of twilight groves,

And shadows brown, that Sylvan loves,
Of pine, or monumental oak,
Where the rude axe with heavéd stroke
Was never heard the nymphs to daunt,
Or fright them from their hallowed haunt.
There, in close covert, by some brook,
Where no profaner eye may look,
Hide me from day's garish eye,
While the bee with honeyed thigh,
That at her flowery work doth sing,
And the waters murmuring,
With such consort as they keep,
Entice the dewy-feathered Sleep.
And let some strange mysterious dream
Wave at his wings, in airy stream
Of lively portraiture displayed,
Softly on my eyelids laid;
And, as I wake, sweet music breathe
Above, about, or underneath,
Sent by some Spirit to mortals good,
Or the unseen Genius of the wood.
But let my due feet never fail
To walk the studious cloister's pale,
And love the high embowéd roof,
With antique pillars massy-proof,
And storied windows richly dight,
Casting a dim religious light.
There let the pealing organ blow,
To the full-voiced quire below,
In service high and anthems clear,
As may with sweetness, through mine ear,
Dissolve me into ecstasies,
And bring all Heaven before mine eyes.
And may at last my weary age
Find out the peaceful hermitage,
The hairy gown and mossy cell,
Where I may sit and rightly spell
Of every star that heaven doth shew,
And every herb that sips the dew,
Till old experience do attain
To something like prophetic strain.

These pleasures, Melancholy, give;
And I with thee will choose to live.

Lycidas

Elegy on a Friend drowned in the Irish Channel

YET once more, O ye laurels, and once more
Ye myrtles brown, with ivy never sere,
I come to pluck your berries harsh and crude,
And with forced fingers rude
Shatter your leaves before the mellowing year.
Bitter constraint and sad occasion dear,
Compels me to disturb your season due:
For Lycidas is dead, dead ere his prime,
Young Lycidas, and hath not left his peer:
Who would not sing for Lycidas? he knew
Himself to sing, and build the lofty rhyme.
He must not float upon his watery bier
Unwept, and welter to the parching wind,
Without the meed of some melodious tear.

Begin then, Sisters of the sacred well,
That from beneath the seat of Jove doth spring,
Begin, and somewhat loudly sweep the string.
Hence with denial vain and coy excuse,
So may some gentle Muse
With lucky words favour my destined urn,
And as he passes, turn,
And bid fair peace be to my sable shroud.

For we were nursed upon the self-same hill,
Fed the same flock by fountain, shade, and rill.
Together both, ere the high lawns appear'd
Under the opening eye-lids of the morn,
We drove a-field, and both together heard
What time the gray-fly winds her sultry horn,
Battening our flocks with the fresh dews of night,
Oft till the star that rose at evening, bright

Toward heaven's descent had sloped his westering wheel.
Meanwhile the rural ditties were not mute,
Temper'd to the oaten flute;
Rough Satyrs danced, and Fauns with cloven heel
From the glad sound would not be absent long,
And old Damoetas loved to hear our song.

But, O! the heavy change, now thou art gone,
Now thou art gone, and never must return!
Thee, Shepherd, thee the woods and desert caves,
With wild thyme and the gadding vine o'ergrown,
And all their echoes, mourn.
The willows and the hazel copses green,
Shall now no more be seen
Fanning their joyous leaves to thy soft lays.
As killing as the canker to the rose,
Or taint-worm to the weanling herds that graze,
Or frost to flowers, that their gay wardrobe wear
When first the white-thorn blows;
Such, Lycidas, thy loss to shepherd's ear.

Where were ye, Nymphs, when the remorseless deep
Closed o'er the head of your loved Lycidas?
For neither were ye playing on the steep
Where your old bards, the famous Druids, lie,
Nor on the shaggy top of Mona high,
Nor yet where Deva spreads her wizard stream:
Ay me! I fondly dream—
Had ye been there—for what could that have done?
What could the Muse herself that Orpheus bore,
The Muse herself, for her enchanting son,
Whom universal nature did lament,
When by the rout that made the hideous roar,
His gory visage down the stream was sent,
Down the swift Hebrus to the Lesbian shore?

Alas! what boots it with uncessant care
To tend the homely, slighted, shepherd's trade,
And strictly meditate the thankless Muse?
Were it not better done, as others use,
To sport with Amaryllis in the shade,

Or with the tangles of Neæra's hair?
Fame is the spur that the clear spirit doth raise
(That last infirmity of noble mind)
To scorn delights, and live laborious days;
But the fair guerdon when we hope to find,
And think to burst out into sudden blaze,
Comes the blind Fury with the abhorrèd shears
And slits the thin-spun life. "But not the praise"
Phoebus replied, and touch'd my trembling ears;
"Fame is no plant that grows on mortal soil,
Nor in the glistering foil
Set off to the world, nor in broad rumour lies:
But lives and spreads aloft by those pure eyes
And perfect witness of all-judging Jove;
As he pronounces lastly on each deed,
Of so much fame in heaven expect thy meed."

O fountain Arethuse, and thou honour'd flood,
Smooth-sliding Mincius, crown'd with vocal reeds,
That strain I heard was of a higher mood;
But now my oat proceeds,
And listens to the herald of the sea
That came in Neptune's plea;
He ask'd the waves, and ask'd the felon winds,
What hard mishap hath doom'd this gentle swain?
And question'd every gust of rugged wings
That blows from off each beakèd promontory:
They knew not of his story;
And sage Hippotades their answer brings,
That not a blast was from his dungeon stray'd;
The air was calm, and on the level brine
Sleek Panope with all her sisters play'd.
It was that fatal and perfidious bark
Built in th' eclipse, and rigg'd with curses dark,
That sunk so low that sacred head of thine.

Next Camus, reverend sire, went footing slow,
His mantle hairy, and his bonnet sedge,
Inwrought with figures dim, and on the edge
Like to that sanguine flower inscribed with woe.
"Ah! who hath reft," quoth he, "my dearest pledge?"

Last came, and last did go,
The Pilot of the Galilean lake;
Two massy keys he bore of metals twain,
(The golden opes, the iron shuts amain);
He shook his mitred locks, and stern bespake:
"How well could I have spared for thee, young swain,
Enow of such, as for their bellies' sake,
Creep and intrude and climb into the fold!
Of other care they little reckoning make,
Than how to scramble at the shearers' feast,
And shove away the worthy bidden guest.
Blind mouths! that scarce themselves know how to hold
A sheep-hook, or have learn'd aught else the least
That to the faithful herdman's art belongs!
What recks it them? What need they? They are sped;
And when they list, their lean and flashy songs
Grate on their scrannel pipes of wretched straw;
The hungry sheep look up, and are not fed,
But swoln with wind and the rank mist they draw
Rot inwardly, and foul contagion spread:
Besides what the grim wolf with privy paw
Daily devours apace, and nothing said;
But that two-handed engine at the door
Stands ready to smite once, and smite no more."

Return, Alpheus; the dread voice is past
That shrunk thy streams; return, Sicilian Muse,
And call the vales, and bid them hither cast
Their bells and flowerets of a thousand hues.
Ye valleys low where the mild whispers use,
Of shades, and wanton winds, and gushing brooks,
On whose fresh lap the swart star sparely looks,
Throw hither all your quaint enamell'd eyes
That on the green turf suck the honey'd showers,
And purple all the ground with vernal flowers.
Bring the rathe primrose that forsaken dies,
The tufted crow-toe, and pale jessamine,
The white pink, and the pansy freak'd with jet,
The glowing violet,
The musk-rose, and the well-attired woodbine,

With cowslips wan that hang the pensive head,
And every flower that sad embroidery wears:
Bid amarantus all his beauty shed,
And daffadillies fill their cups with tears,
To strew the laureat hearse where Lycid lies.
For so to interpose a little ease,
Let our frail thoughts dally with false surmise.
Ay me! whilst thee the shores and sounding seas
Wash far away,—where'er thy bones are hurl'd,
Whether beyond the stormy Hebrides,
Where thou perhaps, under the whelming tide,
Visitest the bottom of the monstrous world;
Or whether thou, to our moist vows denied,
Sleep'st by the fable of Bellerus old,
Where the great Vision of the guarded mount
Looks toward Namancos and Bayona's hold;
Look homeward, Angel, now, and melt with ruth,
And, O ye dolphins, waft the hapless youth!

Weep no more, woeful shepherds, weep no more,
For Lycidas, your sorrow, is not dead,
Sunk though he be beneath the watery floor;
So sinks the day-star in the ocean-bed,
And yet anon repairs his drooping head
And tricks his beams, and with new-spangled ore
Flames in the forehead of the morning sky:
So Lycidas sunk low, but mounted high
Through the dear might of Him that walk'd the waves;
Where, other groves and other streams along,
With nectar pure his oozy locks he laves,
And hears the unexpressive nuptial song,
In the blest kingdoms meek of joy and love.
There entertain him all the Saints above
In solemn troops, and sweet societies,
That sing, and singing, in their glory move,
And wipe the tears forever from his eyes.
Now, Lycidas, the shepherds weep no more;
Henceforth thou art the Genius of the shore
In thy large recompense, and shalt be good
To all that wander in that perilous flood.

Thus sang the uncouth swain to the oaks and rills,
While the still morn went out with sandals gray,
He touch'd the tender stops of various quills,
With eager thought warbling his Doric lay:
And now the sun had stretch'd out all the hills,
And now was dropt into the western bay:
At last he rose, and twitch'd his mantle blue:
To-morrow to fresh woods, and pastures new.

To the Lord-General Cromwell

CROMWELL, our chief of men, who through a cloud,
Not of war only, but detractions rude,
Guided by faith and matchless fortitude,
To peace and truth thy glorious way hast ploughed,
And on the neck of crownéd fortune proud
Hast reared God's trophies, and his work pursued,
While Darwen stream, with blood of Scots imbued,
And Dunbar field resounds thy praises loud,
And Worcester's laureate wreath. Yet much remains
To conquer still; Peace hath her victories
No less renowned than War: new foes arise,
Threatening to bind our souls with secular chains:
Help us to save free conscience from the paw
Of hireling wolves, whose gospel is their maw.

On His Blindness

WHEN I consider how my light is spent
Ere half my days, in this dark world and wide,
And that one talent, which is death to hide,
Lodged with me useless, though my soul more bent
To serve therewith my Maker, and present
My true account, lest he returning chide;
"Doth God exact day-labor, light denied?"
I fondly ask. But Patience, to prevent

That murmur, soon replies, "God doth not need
Either man's work or his own gifts; who best
Bear his mild yoke, they serve him best: his state
Is kingly; thousands at his bidding speed,
And post o'er land and ocean without rest;
They also serve who only stand and wait."

On the Late Massacre in Piedmont

AVENGE, O Lord, Thy slaughter'd saints, whose bones
Lie scatter'd on the Alpine mountains cold;
Even them who kept Thy truth so pure of old,
When all our fathers worshipt stocks and stones,
Forget not: In Thy book record their groans
Who were Thy sheep, and in their ancient fold
Slain by the bloody Piemontese, that roll'd
Mother with infant down the rocks. Their moans
The vales redoubled to the hills, and they
To Heaven. Their martyr'd blood and ashes sow
O'er all the Italian fields, where still doth sway
The triple Tyrant; that from these may grow
A hundred-fold, who, having learnt Thy way,
Early may fly the Babylonian woe.

To Cyriack Skinner

CYRIACK, this three years' day, these eyes, though clear,
To outward view, of blemish or of spot,
Bereft of light, their seeing have forgot:
Nor to their idle orbs doth sight appear
Of sun, or moon, or star, throughout the year,
Or man or woman, yet I argue not
Against Heaven's hand or will, nor bate a jot
Of heart or hope; but still bear up and steer

Right onward. What supports me, dost thou ask?
The conscience, friend, to have lost them overplied
In Liberty's defence, my noble task,
Of which all Europe rings from side to side.
This thought might lead me through the world's vain mask,
Content, though blind, had I no better guide.

SIR JOHN SUCKLING

(1609–1642)

Constancy

Out upon it. I have loved
  Three whole days together;
And am like to love three more.
  If it prove fair weather.

Time shall moult away his wings,
  Ere he shall discover
In the whole wide world again
  Such a constant lover.

But the spite on 't is, no praise
  Is due at all to me;
Love with me had made no stays,
  Had it any been but she.

Had it any been but she,
  And that very face,
There had been at least ere this
  A dozen in her place.

I Prithee Send Me Back My Heart

I PRITHEE send me back my heart,
 Since I cannot have thine;
For if from yours you will not part,
 Why then shouldst thou have mine?

Yet, now I think on 't, let it lie;
 To find it were in vain;
For thou 'st a thief in either eye
 Would steal it back again.

Why should two hearts in one breast lie,
 And yet not lodge together?
O Love! where is thy sympathy
 If thus our breasts thou sever?

But love is such a mystery,
 I cannot find it out;
For when I think I'm best resolved
 I then am most in doubt.

Then farewell care, and farewell woe;
 I will no longer pine;
For I'll believe I have her heart
 As much as she has mine.

Why So Pale and Wan?

WHY so pale and wan, fond lover?
 Pr'y thee, why so pale?
Will, when looking well can't move her,
 Looking ill prevail?
 Pr'y thee, why so pale?

Why so dull and mute, young sinner?
  Pr'y thee, why so mute?
Will, when speaking well can't win her,
  Saying nothing do 't?
  Pr'y thee, why so mute?

Quit, quit, for shame! this will not move,
  This cannot take her:
If of herself she will not love,
  Nothing can make her:
  The devil take her!

WILLIAM CARTWRIGHT
(1611–1643)

To Chloe

WHO FOR HIS SAKE WISHED HERSELF YOUNGER

THERE are two births; the one when light
  First strikes the new awaken'd sense:
The other when two souls unite,
  And we must count our life from thence:
When you loved me and I loved you
Then both of us were born anew.

Love then to us new souls did give
  And in those souls did plant new powers;
Since when another life we live,
  The breath we breathe is his, not ours:
Love makes those young whom age doth chill,
And whom he finds young keeps young still.

JAMES GRAHAM, MARQUIS OF MONTROSE
(1612–1650)

I'll Never Love Thee More

MY DEAR and only Love, I pray
  That little world of thee
Be govern'd by no other sway
  Than purest monarchy;
For if confusion have a part
  (Which virtuous souls abhor),
And hold a synod in thine heart,
  I'll never love thee more.

Like Alexander I will reign,
  And I will reign alone;
My thoughts did evermore disdain
  A rival on my throne.
He either fears his fate too much,
  Or his deserts are small,
That dares not put it to the touch,
  To gain or lose it all.

And in the empire of thine heart,
  Where I should solely be,
If others do pretend a part
  Or dare to vie with me,
Or if committees thou erect,
  And go on such a score,
I'll laugh and sing at thy neglect,
  And never love thee more.

But if thou wilt prove faithful then,
  And constant of thy word,
I'll make thee glorious by my pen
  And famous by my sword;
I'll serve thee in such noble ways
  Was never heard before;
I'll crown and deck thee all with bays,
  And love thee more and more.

RICHARD CRASHAW
(1613–1649)

Wishes

TO HIS (SUPPOSED) MISTRESS

WHOE'ER she be
That not impossible she
That shall command my heart and me;

Where'er she lie,
Locked up from mortal eye,
In shady leaves of destiny;

Till that ripe birth
Of studied fate stand forth
And teach her fair steps tread our earth;

Till that divine
Idea take a shrine
Of crystal flesh, through which to shine;

Meet you her, my wishes,
Bespeak her to my blisses,
And be ye called my absent kisses.

I wish her beauty,
That owes not all its duty
To gaudy tire, or glistering shoo-ty;

Something more than
Taffeta or tissue can,
Or rampant feather, or rich fan;

More than the spoil
Of shop, or silkworm's toil,
Or a bought blush, or a set smile;

A face that's best
By its own beauty dressed,
And can alone command the rest;

A face made up
Out of no other shop
Than what Nature's white hand sets ope;

A cheek where youth
And blood, with pen of truth
Write what the reader sweetly ru'th;

A cheek where grows
More than a morning rose,
Which to no box its being owes;

Lips where all day
A lover's kiss may play,
Yet carry nothing thence away;

Looks that oppress
Their richest tires, but dress
And clothe their simplest nakedness;

Eyes that displace
The neighbour diamond and outface
That sun-shine by their own sweet grace;

Tresses that wear
Jewels, but to declare
How much themselves more precious are.

Whose native ray
Can tame the wanton day
Of gems that in their bright shades play;

Each ruby there
Or pearl that dares appear,
Be its own blush, be its own tear;

A well-tamed heart,
For whose more noble smart
Love may be long choosing a dart;

Eyes that bestow
Full quivers on Love's bow,
Yet pay less arrows than they owe;

Smiles that can warm
The blood, yet teach a charm
That chastity shall take no harm;

Blushes that bin
The burnish of no sin,
Nor flames of aught too hot within;

Joys that confess
Virtue their mistress,
And have no other head to dress;

Fears fond and slight
As the coy bride's, when night
First does the longing lover right;

Tears quickly fled
And vain, as those are shed
For a dying maidenhead;

Days that need borrow
No part of their good morrow
From a fore-spent night of sorrow;

I wish her store
Of worth may leave her poor
Of wishes; and I wish—no more.

Her that dares be
What these lines wish to see:
I seek no further, it is she.

'Tis she: and here
Lo! I unclothe and clear
My wishes' cloudy character.

May she enjoy it
Whose merit dares apply it
But modesty dares still deny it.

Such worth as this is
Shall fix my flying wishes,
And determine them to kisses.

Let her full glory,
My fancies! fly before ye;
Be ye my fictions, but her story.

RICHARD LOVELACE

(1618–1658)

To Lucasta, Going to the Wars

TELL me not, Sweet, I am unkind,
  That from the nunnery
Of thy chaste breast and quiet mind
  To war and arms I fly.

True, a new mistress now I chase,
  The first foe in the field;
And with a stronger faith embrace
  A sword, a horse, a shield.

Yet this inconstancy is such
  That thou too shalt adore;
I could not love thee, Dear, so much,
  Loved I not honour more.

To Lucasta, Going Beyond the Seas

If to be absent were to be
Away from thee;
Or that, when I am gone,
You or I were alone;
Then, my Lucasta, might I crave
Pity from blustering wind or swallowing wave.

But I'll not sigh one blast or gale
To swell my sail,
Or pay a tear to 'suage
The foaming blue-god's rage;
For, whether he will let me pass
Or no, I'm still as happy as I was.

Though seas and lands be 'twixt us both,
Our faith and troth,
Like separated souls,
All time and space controls:
Above the highest sphere we meet,
Unseen, unknown; and greet as angels greet.

So, then, we do anticipate
Our after-fate,
And are alive i' th' skies,
If thus our lips and eyes
Can speak like spirits unconfined
In heaven,—their earthly bodies left behind.

To Althea from Prison

When Love with unconfinèd wings
Hovers within my gates,
And my divine Althea brings
To whisper at the grates;

When I lie tangled in her hair
  And fetter'd to her eye,
The Gods that wanton in the air
  Know no such liberty.

When flowing cups run swiftly round
  With no allaying Thames,
Our careless heads with roses bound,
  Our hearts with loyal flames;
When thirsty grief in wine we steep,
  When healths and draughts go free—
Fishes that tipple in the deep
  Know no such liberty.

When, like committed linnets, I
  With shriller throat shall sing
The sweetness, mercy, majesty,
  And glories of my King;
When I shall voice aloud how good
  He is, how great should be,
Enlargèd winds, that curl the flood,
  Know no such liberty.

Stone walls do not a prison make,
  Nor iron bars a cage;
Minds innocent and quiet take
  That for an hermitage;
If I have freedom in my love
  And in my soul am free,
Angels alone, that soar above,
  Enjoy such liberty.

To Amarantha

That She Would Dishevel Her Hair

Amarantha sweet and fair,
Ah, braid no more that shining hair!
As my curious hand or eye
Hovering round thee, let it fly!

Let it fly as unconfined
As its calm ravisher the wind,
Who hath left his darling, th' East,
To wanton o'er that spicy nest.

Every tress must be confest,
But neatly tangled at the best;
Like a clew of golden thread
Most excellently ravellèd.

Do not then wind up that light
In ribbands, and o'ercloud in night,
Like the Sun in 's early ray;
But shake your head, and scatter day!

ABRAHAM COWLEY
(1618–1667)

On the Death of Mr. William Hervey

IT WAS a dismal and a fearful night:
Scarce could the Morn drive on th' unwilling light,
When sleep, death's image, left my troubled breast
  By something liker death possest.
My eyes with tears did uncommanded flow,
  And on my soul hung the dull weight
  Of some intolerable fate.
What bell was that? Ah me! too much I know!

My sweet companion, and my gentle peer,
Why hast thou left me thus unkindly here,
Thy end for ever, and my life, to moan?
  O thou hast left me all alone!
Thy soul and body, when death's agony
  Besieged around thy noble heart,
  Did not with more reluctance part
Than I, my dearest friend, do part from thee.

Ye fields of Cambridge, our dear Cambridge, say,
Have ye not seen us walking every day?
Was there a tree about which did not know
    The love betwixt us two?
Henceforth, ye gentle trees, for ever fade;
    Or your sad branches thicker join
    And into darksome shades combine,
Dark as the grave wherein my friend is laid.

Large was his soul: as large a soul as e'er
Submitted to inform a body here;
High as the place 'twas shortly in Heaven to have,
    But low and humble as his grave;
So high that all the virtues there did come
    As to the chiefest seat
    Conspicuous, and great;
So low that for me too it made a room.

Knowledge he only sought, and so soon caught.
As if for him knowledge had rather sought;
Nor did more learning ever crowded lie
    In such a short mortality.
Whene'er the skilful youth discoursed or writ,
    Still did the notions throng
    About his eloquent tongue;
Nor could his ink flow faster than his wit.

His mirth was the pure spirits of various wit,
Yet never did his God or friends forget;
And when deep talk and wisdom came in view,
    Retired, and gave to them their due.
For the rich help of books he always took,
    Though his own searching mind before
    Was so with notions written o'er,
As if wise Nature had made that her book.

With as much zeal, devotion, piety,
He always lived, as other saints do die.
Still with his soul severe account he kept,
    Weeping all debts out ere he slept.

Then down in peace and innocence he lay,
  Like the sun's laborious light,
  Which still in water sets at night,
Unsullied with his journey of the day.

The Wish

WELL then; I now do plainly see
This busy world and I shall ne'er agree.
The very honey of all earthly joy
Does, of all meats, the soonest cloy;
  And they, methinks, deserve my pity
Who for it can endure the stings,
The crowd, and buzz, and murmurings
  Of this great hive, the city.

Ah yet, ere I descend to the grave,
May I a small house and large garden have;
And a few friends, and many books, both true,
Both wise, and both delightful too!
  And since love ne'er will from me flee,
A mistress moderately fair,
And good as guardian angels are,
  Only beloved, and loving me!

O fountains! when in you shall I
Myself eased of unpeaceful thoughts espy?
O fields! O woods! when, when shall I be made
The happy tenant of your shade?
  Here's the spring-head of pleasure's flood;
Here's wealthy Nature's treasury,
Where all the riches lie that she
  Has coined and stamped for good.

Pride and ambition here
Only in far-fetched metaphors appear;
Here nought but winds can hurtful murmurs scatter,
And nought but echo flatter.

The gods, when they descended, hither
From heaven did always choose their way;
And therefore we may boldly say
That 'tis the way too thither.

How happy here should I
And one dear she live, and embracing die!
She who is all the world, and can exclude
In deserts solitude.
I should have then this only fear;
Lest men, when they my pleasures see,
Should hither throng to live like me,
And so make a city here.

ALEXANDER BROME

(1620–1666)

The Resolve

TELL me not of a face that's fair,
Nor lip and cheek that's red,
Nor of the tresses of her hair,
Nor curls in order laid,
Nor of a rare seraphic voice
That like an angel sings;
Though if I were to take my choice
I would have all these things:
But if that thou wilt have me love,
And it must be a she,
The only argument can move
Is that she will love me.

The glories of your ladies be
But metaphors of things,
And but resemble what we see
Each common object brings.

Roses out-red their lips and cheeks,
  Lilies their whiteness stain;
What fool is he that shadows seeks
  And may the substance gain?
Then if thou'lt have me love a lass,
  Let it be one that's kind:
Else I'm a servant to the glass
  That's with Canary lined.

ANDREW MARVELL

(1621–1678)

The Definition of Love

My love is of a birth as rare
  As 'tis for object strange and high:
It was begotten by Despair
  Upon Impossibility.

Magnanimous Despair alone
  Could show me so divine a thing,
Where feeble Hope could ne'er have flown
  But vainly flapped its tinsel wing.

And yet I quickly might arrive
  Where my extended soul is fixed;
But Fate does iron wedges drive,
  And always crowds itself betwixt.

For Fate with jealous eye doth see
  Two perfect loves; nor lets them close:
Their union would her ruin be
  And her tyrannic power depose.

And therefore her decrees of steel
  Us as the distant poles have placed,
(Though Love's whole world on us doth wheel)
  Not by themselves to be embraced:

Unless the giddy heaven fall,
And earth some new convulsion tear,
And, us to join, the world should all
Be cramped into a planisphere.

As lines, so loves oblique may well
Themselves in every angle greet:
But ours, so truly parallel,
Though infinite can never meet.

Therefore the love which us doth bind,
But Fate so enviously debars,
Is the conjunction of the mind,
And opposition of the stars.

The Garden

How vainly men themselves amaze
To win the palm, the oak, or bays,
And their incessant labors see
Crowned from some single herb or tree,
Whose short and narrow-vergèd shade
Does prudently their toils upbraid;
While all the flowers and trees do close
To weave the garlands of repose!

Fair Quiet, have I found thee here,
And Innocence, thy sister dear?
Mistaken long, I sought you then
In busy companies of men:
Your sacred plants, if here below,
Only among the plants will grow;
Society is all but rude
To this delicious solitude.

No white nor red was ever seen
So amorous as this lovely green.
Fond lovers, cruel as their flame,
Cut in these trees their mistress' name:

Little, alas! they know or heed
How far these beauties hers exceed!
Fair trees! where'er your barks I wound,
No name shall but your own be found.

When we have run our passions' heat,
Love hither makes his best retreat:
The gods, that mortal beauty chase,
Still in a tree did end their race;
Apollo hunted Daphne so
Only that she might laurel grow;
And Pan did after Syrinx speed,
Not as a nymph, but for a reed.

What wondrous life is this I lead!
Ripe apples drop about my head;
The luscious clusters of the vine
Upon my mouth do crush their wine;
The nectarine and curious peach
Into my hands themselves do reach;
Stumbling on melons, as I pass,
Ensnared with flowers, I fall on grass.

Meanwhile the mind, from pleasure less,
Withdraws into its happiness;
The mind, that ocean where each kind
Does straight its own resemblance find;
Yet it creates, transcending these,
Far other worlds, and other seas;
Annihilating all that's made
To a green thought in a green shade.

Here at the fountain's sliding foot,
Or at some fruit-tree's mossy root,
Casting the body's vest aside,
My soul into the boughs does glide;
There, like a bird, it sits and sings,
Then whets and combs its silver wings,
And, till prepared for longer flight,
Waves in its plumes the various light.

Such was that happy Garden-state
While man there walk'd without a mate:
After a place so pure and sweet,
What other help could yet be meet!
But 'twas beyond a mortal's share
To wander solitary there:
Two paradises 'twere in one,
To live in Paradise alone.

How well the skilful gardener drew
Of flowers and herbs this dial new!
Where, from above, the milder sun
Does through a fragrant zodiac run:
And, as it works, th' industrious bee
Computes its time as well as we.
How could such sweet and wholesome hours
Be reckon'd, but with herbs and flowers!

Song of the Emigrants in Bermuda

WHERE the remote Bermudas ride
In the ocean's bosom unespied,
From a small boat that rowed along
The listening winds received this song:

"What should we do but sing His praise
That led us through the watery maze
Where he the huge sea monsters wracks,
That lift the deep upon their backs,
Unto an isle so long unknown,
And yet far kinder than our own?
He lands us on a grassy stage,
Safe from the storms, and prelate's rage;
He gave us this eternal spring
Which here enamels everything,
And sends the fowls to us in care
On daily visits through the air.

He hangs in shades the orange bright
Like golden lamps in a green night.
And does in the pomegranates close
Jewels more rich than Ormus shows:
He makes the figs our mouths to meet,
And throws the melons at our feet;
But apples, plants of such a price,
No tree could ever bear them twice.
With cedars chosen by his hand
From Lebanon he stores the land;
And makes the hollow seas that roar
Proclaim the ambergris on shore.
He cast (of which we rather boast)
The gospel's pearl upon our coast;
And in these rocks for us did frame
A temple where to sound his name.
O, let our voice his praise exalt
Till it arrive at heaven's vault,
Which then perhaps rebounding may
Echo beyond the Mexique bay!"—
Thus sung they in the English boat
A holy and a cheerful note;
And all the way, to guide their chime,
With falling oars they kept the time.

HENRY VAUGHAN

(1622–1695)

The Retreat

HAPPY those early days, when I
Shined in my Angel-infancy!
Before I understood this place
Appointed for my second race,
Or taught my soul to fancy aught
But a white, celestial thought;

When yet I had not walk'd above
A mile or two from my first Love,
And looking back, at that short space
Could see a glimpse of his bright face;
When on some gilded cloud or flower
My gazing soul would dwell an hour,
And in those weaker glories spy
Some shadows of eternity;
Before I taught my tongue to wound
My conscience with a sinful sound,
Or had the black art to dispense
A several sin to every sense,
But felt through all this fleshly dress
Bright shoots of everlastingness.

O how I long to travel back,
And tread again that ancient track!
That I might once more reach that plain,
Where first I left my glorious train;
From whence th' enlighten'd spirit sees
That shady City of Palm trees!
But ah! my soul with too much stay
Is drunk, and staggers in the way:—
Some men a forward motion love,
But I by backward steps would move;
And when this dust falls to the urn,
In that state I came, return.

The World

I SAW Eternity the other night,
Like a great Ring of pure and endless light,
All calm, as it was bright;
And round beneath it, Time in hours, days, years,
Driven by the spheres
Like a vast shadow moved; in which the world
And all her train were hurled.

The doting lover in his quaintest strain
    Did there complain;
Near him, his lute, his fancy, and his flights,
    Wit's sour delights,
With gloves, and knots, the silly snares of pleasure,
    Yet his dear treasure,
All scattered lay, while his eyes did pour
    Upon a flower.

The darksome statesman, hung with weights and woe,
Like a thick mid-night fog, moved there so slow,
    He did not stay, nor go;
Condemning thoughts—like sad eclipses—scowl
    Upon his soul,
And clouds of crying witnesses without
    Pursu'd him with one shout.
Yet digg'd the mole, and lest his ways be found,
    Worked under ground,
Where he did clutch his prey; (But one did see
    That policy);
Churches and altars fed him; perjuries
    Were gnats and flies;
It rained about him blood and tears; but he
    Drank them as free.

The fearful miser on a heap of rust
Sate pining all his life there, did scarce trust
    His own hands with the dust,
Yet would not place one piece above, but lives
    In fear of thieves.
Thousands there were as frantic as himself
    And hugged each one his pelf,
The downright epicure placed heaven in sense
    And scorn'd pretence,
While others, slipp'd into a wide excess,
    Said little less;
The weaker sort slight, trivial wares enslave,
    Who think them brave;
And poor, despised Truth sate counting by
    Their victory.

Yet some, who all this while did weep and sing,
And sing, and weep, soared up into the Ring;
  But most would use no wing.
O fools (said I) thus to prefer dark night
  Before true light!
To live in grots and caves, and hate the day
  Because it shows the way,
The way, which from this dead and dark abode
  Leads up to God,
A way where you might tread the sun, and be
  More bright than he.
But as I did their madness so discuss,
  One whisper'd thus,
This Ring the Bridegroom did for none provide
  But for his bride.

They Are All Gone

THEY are all gone into the world of light,
  And I alone sit lingering here;
Their very memory is fair and bright,
    And my sad thoughts doth clear.

It glows and glitters in my cloudy breast,
  Like stars upon some gloomy grove,
Or those faint beams in which this hill is dressed
    After the sun's remove.

I see them walking in an air of glory,
  Whose light doth trample on my days:
My days, which are at best but dull and hoary,
    Mere glimmering and decays.

O holy hope, and high humility!
  High as the heavens above!
These are your walks, and you have showed them me,
    To kindle my cold love.

Dear, beauteous death! the jewel of the just,
Shining no where but in the dark;
What mysteries do lie beyond thy dusk,
Could man outlook that mark!

He that hath found some fledged bird's nest may know,
At first sight, if the bird be flown;
But what fair well or grove he sings in now,
That is to him unknown.

And yet, as angels in some brighter dreams
Call to the soul when man doth sleep,
So some strange thoughts transcend our wonted themes,
And into glory peep.

If a star were confined into a tomb,
Her captive flames must needs burn there;
But when the hand that locked her up gives room,
She'll shine through all the sphere.

O Father of eternal life, and all
Created glories under thee!
Resume thy spirit from this world of thrall
Into true liberty.

Either disperse these mists, which blot and fill
My pèrspective still as they pass,
Or else remove me hence unto that hill,
Where I shall need no glass.

JOHN DRYDEN

(1631–1700)

A Song for St. Cecilia's Day, 1687

FROM harmony, from heavenly harmony,
This universal frame began;
When Nature underneath a heap
Of jarring atoms lay,

And could not heave her head,
The tuneful voice was heard from high,
Arise, ye more than dead!
Then cold and hot, and moist and dry,
In order to their stations leap,
And Music's power obey.
From harmony, from heavenly harmony,
This universal frame began:
From harmony to harmony,
Through all the compass of the notes it ran,
The diapason closing full in man.

What passion cannot Music raise and quell?
When Jubal struck the chorded shell,
His listening brethren stood around,
And, wondering, on their faces fell,
To worship that celestial sound.
Less than a God they thought there could not dwell
Within the hollow of that shell,
That spoke so sweetly and so well.
What passion cannot Music raise and quell?

The trumpet's loud clangor
Excites us to arms,
With shrill notes of anger,
And mortal alarms.
The double double double beat
Of the thundering drum
Cries, Hark! the foes come;
Charge, charge, 't is too late to retreat!

The soft complaining flute
In dying notes discovers
The woes of hopeless lovers,
Whose dirge is whispered by the warbling lute.

Sharp violins proclaim
Their jealous pangs, and desperation,
Fury, frantic indignation,
Depth of pains, and height of passion
For the fair, disdainful dame.

But O, what art can teach,
What human voice can reach,
The sacred organ's praise?
Notes inspiring holy love,
Notes that wing their heavenly ways
To mend the choirs above.

Orpheus could lead the savage race;
And trees uprooted left their place,
Sequacious of the lyre;
But bright Cecilia raised the wonder higher;
When to her organ vocal breath was given,
An angel heard, and straight appeared
Mistaking earth for heaven.

GRAND CHORUS.

As from the power of sacred lays
The spheres began to move,
And sung the great Creator's praise
To all the blessed above;
So, when the last and dreadful hour
This crumbling pageant shall devour,
The trumpet shall be heard on high,
The dead shall live, the living die,
And Music shall untune the sky.

Alexander's Feast; or, the Power of Music

'T WAS at the royal feast, for Persia won
By Philip's warlike son:
Aloft in awful state
The god-like hero sate
On his imperial throne:
His valiant peers were placed around,
Their brows with roses and with myrtles bound;
(So should desert in arms be crown'd.)

The lovely Thais, by his side,
Sate like a blooming Eastern bride
In flower of youth and beauty's pride.
Happy, happy, happy pair!
None but the brave,
None but the brave,
None but the brave deserves the fair.

Chorus: Happy, happy, happy pair!
None but the brave,
None but the brave,
None but the brave deserves the fair.

Timotheus, placed on high
Amid the tuneful choir,
With flying fingers touch'd the lyre:
The trembling notes ascend the sky,
And heavenly joys inspire.
The song began from Jove,
Who left his blissful seats above,
(Such is the power of mighty love.)
A dragon's fiery form belied the god:
Sublime on radiant spires he rode,
When he to fair Olympia press'd:
And while he sought her snowy breast:
Then round her slender waist he curl'd,
And stamp'd an image of himself, a sovereign of the world.
—The listening crowd admire the lofty sound;
"A present deity!" they shout around:
"A present deity!" the vaulted roofs rebound:

With ravished ears
The monarch hears,
Assumes the god;
Affects to nod
And seems to shake the spheres.

Chorus: With ravished ears
The monarch hears,
Assumes the god:
Affects to nod
And seems to shake the spheres.

The praise of Bacchus then the sweet musician sung,
Of Bacchus ever fair and ever young:
The jolly god in triumph comes;
Sound the trumpets, beat the drums!
Flush'd with a purple grace
He shows his honest face:
Now give the hautboys breath; he comes, he comes!
Bacchus, ever fair and young,
Drinking joys did first ordain;
Bacchus' blessings are a treasure,
Drinking is the soldier's pleasure:
Rich the treasure,
Sweet the pleasure,
Sweet is pleasure after pain.

Chorus: Bacchus' blessings are a treasure,
Drinking is the soldier's pleasure:
Rich the treasure,
Sweet the pleasure,
Sweet is pleasure after pain.

Soothed with the sound, the king grew vain;
Fought all his battles o'er again,
And thrice he routed all his foes, and thrice he slew the slain!
The master saw the madness rise;
His glowing cheeks, his ardent eyes;
And, while he heaven and earth defied,
Changed his hand, and check'd his pride.
He chose a mournful muse
Soft pity to infuse:
He sung Darius, great and good;
By too severe a fate,
Fallen, fallen, fallen, fallen,
Fallen from his high estate,
And welt'ring in his blood;
Deserted, at his utmost need,
By those his former bounty fed;
On the bare earth exposed he lies,
With not a friend to close his eyes.
With downcast looks the joyless victor sate,

Revolving in his alter'd soul
  The various turns of chance below;
And, now and then, a sigh he stole;
  And tears began to flow.

Chorus: Revolving in his alter'd soul
  The various turns of chance below;
And, now and then, a sigh he stole;
  And tears began to flow.

The mighty master smiled, to see
That love was in the next degree;
'Twas but a kindred-sound to move,
For pity melts the mind to love.
  Softly sweet, in Lydian measures,
  Soon he soothed his soul to pleasures.
War, he sung, is toil and trouble;
Honour, but an empty bubble;
  Never ending, still beginning,
Fighting still, and still destroying:
  If the world be worth thy winning,
Think, oh! think it worth enjoying:
  Lovely Thais sits beside thee,
  Take the good the gods provide thee.
The many rend the skies with loud applause;
So Love was crown'd, but Music won the cause.

The prince, unable to conceal his pain,
  Gazed on the fair
  Who caused his care,
And sigh'd and look'd, sigh'd and look'd,
Sigh'd and look'd, and sigh'd again:
At length, with love and wine at once opprest,
The vanquish'd victor sunk upon her breast.

Chorus: The prince, unable to conceal his pain,
  Gazed on the fair
  Who caused his care,
And sigh'd and look'd, sigh'd and look'd,
Sigh'd and look'd, and sigh'd again:
At length, with love and wine at once opprest,
The vanquish'd victor sunk upon her breast.

Now strike the golden lyre again:
A louder yet, and yet a louder strain!
Break his bands of sleep asunder,
And rouse him, like a rattling peal of thunder.
Hark, hark! the horrid sound
Has raised up his head:
As awaked from the dead,
And amazed, he stares around.
"Revenge, revenge!" Timotheus cries,
"See the Furies arise!
See the snakes that they rear
How they hiss in their hair,
And the sparkles that flash from their eyes!
Behold a ghastly band,
Each a torch in his hand!
Those are Grecian ghosts, that in battle were slain
And unburied remain
Inglorious on the plain:
Give the vengeance due
To the valiant crew!
Behold how they toss their torches on high,
How they point to the Persian abodes,
And glittering temples of their hostile gods."
The princes applaud with a furious joy:
And the King seized a flambeau with zeal to destroy;
Thais led the way
To light him to his prey,
And like another Helen, fired another Troy!

Chorus: And the King seized a flambeau with zeal to destroy;
Thais led the way
To light him to his prey,
And, like another Helen, fired another Troy!

—Thus, long ago,
Ere heaving bellows learned to blow,
While organs yet were mute,
Timotheus, to his breathing flute
And sounding lyre
Could swell the soul to rage, or kindle soft desire.

At last divine Cecilia came,
Inventress of the vocal frame;
The sweet enthusiast from her sacred store
Enlarged the former narrow bounds,
And added length to solemn sounds,
With nature's mother-wit, and arts unknown before.
Let old Timotheus yield the prize,
Or both divide the crown;
He raised a mortal to the skies,
She drew an angel down.

Grand Chorus: *At last divine Cecilia came,*
Inventress of the vocal frame;
The sweet enthusiast from her sacred store
Enlarged the former narrow bounds,
And added length to solemn sounds,
With nature's mother-wit, and arts unknown before.
Let old Timotheus yield the prize,
Or both divide the crown;
He raised a mortal to the skies,
She drew an angel down.

Ah, How Sweet

Ah, how sweet it is to love!
Ah, how gay is young desire!
And what pleasing pains we prove
When we first approach love's fire!
Pains of love be sweeter far
Than all other pleasures are.

Sighs which are from lovers blown
Do but gently heave the heart:
E'en the tears they shed alone
Cure, like trickling balm, their smart.
Lovers, when they lose their breath,
Bleed away in easy death.

Love and Time with reverence use,
  Treat them like a parting friend;
Nor the golden gifts refuse
  Which in youth sincere they send:
For each year their price is more,
And they less simple than before.

Love, like spring-tides full and high,
  Swells in every youthful vein;
But each tide does less supply,
  Till they quite shrink in again.
If a flow in age appear,
'T is but rain, and runs not clear.

SIR GEORGE ETHEREGE

(1635–1691)

To a Lady Asking Him How Long He Would Love Her

It is not, Celia, in our power
  To say how long our love will last;
It may be we within this hour
  May lose those joys we now do taste:
The Blessèd, that immortal be,
From change in love are only free.

Then since we mortal lovers are,
  Ask not how long our love will last;
But while it does, let us take care
  Each minute be with pleasure passed:
Were it not madness to deny
To live because we're sure to die?

CHARLES SACKVILLE, EARL OF DORSET

(1638–1706)

The Advice

PHYLLIS, for shame, let us improve
A thousand several ways,
These few short minutes stolen by love
From many tedious days.

Whilst you want courage to despise
The censure of the grave,
For all the tyrants in your eyes,
Your heart is but a slave.

My love is full of noble pride,
And never will submit
To let that fop, Discretion, ride
In triumph over wit.

False friends I have, as well as you,
That daily counsel me
Vain frivolous trifles to pursue,
And leave off loving thee.

When I the least belief bestow
On what such fools advise,
May I be dull enough to grow
Most miserably wise.

The Fire of Love

THE fire of love in youthful blood,
Like what is kindled in brushwood,
But for a moment burns;
Yet in that moment makes a mighty noise;
It crackles, and to vapor turns,
And soon itself destroys.

But when crept into aged veins
It slowly burns, and then long remains,
And with a silent heat,
Like fire in logs, it glows and warms 'em long;
And though the flame be not so great,
Yet is the heat as strong.

SIR CHARLES SEDLEY
(1639–1701)

Child and Maiden

AH, CHLORIS! could I now but sit
As unconcern'd as when
Your infant beauty could beget
No pleasure, nor no pain!
When I the dawn used to admire,
And praised the coming day,
I little thought the rising fire
Would take my rest away.

Your charms in harmless childhood lay
Like metals in a mine;
Age from no face takes more away
Than youth conceal'd in thine.
But as your charms insensibly
To their perfection prest,
So love as unperceived did fly,
And in my bosom rest.

My passion with your beauty grew,
While Cupid at my heart,
Still as his mother favour'd you,
Threw a new flaming dart:
Each gloried in their wanton part;
To make a lover, he
Employ'd the utmost of his art—
To make a beauty, she.

To Celia

Not, Celia, that I juster am
  Or better than the rest!
For I would change each hour, like them,
  Were not my heart at rest.

But I am tied to very thee
  By every thought I have;
Thy face I only care to see,
  Thy heart I only crave.

All that in woman is adored
  In thy dear self I find—
For the whole sex can but afford
  The handsome and the kind.

Why then should I seek further store,
  And still make love anew?
When change itself can give no more,
  'Tis easy to be true!

THOMAS OTWAY

(1652–1685)

The Enchantment

I did but look and love awhile,
  'Twas but for one half-hour;
Then to resist I had no will,
  And now I have no power.

To sigh and wish is all my ease;
  Sighs which do heat impart
Enough to melt the coldest ice,
  Yet cannot warm your heart.

O would your pity give my heart
  One corner of your breast,
'Twould learn of yours the winning art,
  And quickly steal the rest.

WILLIAM WALSH

(1663–1708)

Against Marriage

To His Mistress

YES, all the world must sure agree,
He who's secured of having thee,
  Will be entirely blessed;
But t'were in me too great a wrong,
To make one who has been so long
  My queen, my slave at last.

Nor ought those things to be confined,
That were for public good designed:
  Could we, in foolish pride,
Make the sun always with us stay,
'Twould burn our corn and grass away,
  To starve the world beside.

Let not the thoughts of parting fright
Two souls which passion does unite;
  For while our love does last,
Neither will strive to go away;
And why the devil should we stay,
  When once that love is past?

MATTHEW PRIOR

(1664–1721)

To a Child of Quality

Five Years Old, 1704, the Author Then Forty.

LORDS, knights, and squires, the numerous band
  That wear the fair Miss Mary's fetters,
Were summoned by her high command
  To show their passion by their letters.

My pen amongst the rest I took,
  Lest those bright eyes, that cannot read,
Should dart their kindling fires, and look
  The power they have to be obey'd.

Nor quality, nor reputation,
  Forbid me yet my flame to tell;
Dear Five-years-old befriends my passion.
  And I may write till she can spell.

For, while she makes her silkworms beds
  With all the tender things I swear;
Whilst all the house my passion reads,
  In papers round her baby's hair;

She may receive and own my flame;
  For, though the strictest prudes should know it,
She'll pass for a most virtuous dame,
  And I for an unhappy poet.

Then too, alas! when she shall tear
  The rhymes some younger rival sends,
She'll give me leave to write, I fear,
  And we shall still continue friends.

For, as our different ages move,
  'Tis so ordained (would Fate but mend it!)
That I shall be past making love
  When she begins to comprehend it.

Song

THE merchant to secure his treasure,
  Conveys it in a borrowed name:
Euphelia serves to grace my measure;
  But Chloe is my real flame.

My softest verse, my darling lyre,
  Upon Euphelia's toilet lay;
When Chloe noted her desire
  That I should sing, that I should play.

My lyre I tune, my voice I raise;
  But with my numbers mix my sighs:
And while I sing Euphelia's praise,
  I fix my soul on Chloe's eyes.

Fair Chloe blushed: Euphelia frowned:
  I sung, and gazed: I played and trembled:
And Venus to the Loves around
  Remarked, how ill we all dissembled.

To a Lady: She Refusing to Continue a Dispute with Me and Leaving Me in the Argument

SPARE, generous Victor, spare the slave
  Who did unequal war pursue,
That more than triumph he might have
  In being overcome by you.

In the dispute whate'er I said,
  My heart was by my tongue belied;
And in my looks you might have read
  How much I argued on your side.

You, far from danger as from fear,
  Might have sustained an open fight;
For seldom your opinions err,
  Your eyes are always in the right.

Why, fair one, would you not rely
  On reason's force with beauty's joined?
Could I their prevalence deny,
  I must at once be deaf and blind.

Alas! not hoping to subdue,
  I only to the fight aspired:
To keep the beauteous foe in view
  Was all the glory I desired.

But she, howe'er of victory sure,
  Contemns the wreath too long delayed;
And, armed with more immediate power,
  Calls cruel silence to her aid.

Deeper to wound, she shuns the fight:
  She drops her arms, to gain the field:
Secures her conquest by her flight,
  And triumphs when she seems to yield.

So when the Parthian turned his steed,
  And from the hostile camp withdrew,
With cruel skill the backward reed
  He sent; and as he fled, he slew.

The Lady Who Offers Her Looking-Glass to Venus

VENUS, take my votive glass;
Since I am not what I was,
What from this day I shall be,
Venus, let me never see.

WILLIAM CONGREVE
(1670–1729)

Pious Selinda

PIOUS Selinda goes to prayers,
  If I but ask her favor;
And yet the silly fool's in tears
  If she believes I'll leave her;
Would I were free from this restraint,
  Or else had hopes to win her:
Would she could make of me a saint,
  Or I of her a sinner.

AMBROSE PHILIPS
(1671–1749)

To Charlotte Pulteney

TIMELY blossom, Infant fair,
Fondling of a happy pair,
Every morn and every night
Their solicitous delight,
Sleeping, waking, still at ease
Pleasing, without skill to please;
Little gossip, blithe and hale,
Tattling many a broken tale,
Singing many a tuneless song,
Lavish of a heedless tongue;
Simple maiden, void of art,
Babbling out the very heart,
Yet abandon'd to thy will,
Yet imagining no ill,
Yet too innocent to blush;
Like the linnet in the bush
To the mother-linnet's note
Moduling her slender throat;

Chirping forth thy petty joys,
Wanton in the change of toys,
Like the linnet green, in May
Flitting to each bloomy spray;
Wearied then and glad of rest,
Like the linnet in the nest:—
This thy present happy lot
This, in time will be forgot:
Other pleasures, other cares,
Ever-busy Time prepares;
And thou shalt in thy daughter see,
This picture, once, resembled thee.

JOSEPH ADDISON

(1672–1719)

The Spacious Firmament on High

THE spacious firmament on high,
With all the blue ethereal sky,
And spangled heavens, a shining frame,
Their great Original proclaim.
The unwearied sun from day to day
Does his Creator's power display,
And publishes to every land
The work of an Almighty hand.

Soon as the evening shades prevail,
The moon takes up the wondrous tale,
And nightly to the listening earth
Repeats the story of her birth;
Whilst all the stars that round her burn,
And all the planets in their turn,
Confirm the tidings as they roll,
And spread the truth from pole to pole.

What though in solemn silence, all
Move round this dark terrestrial ball?

What though nor real voice nor sound
Amidst their radiant orbs be found?
In Reason's ear they all rejoice,
And utter forth a glorious voice,
Forever singing as they shine:
"The hand that made us is divine!"

GEORGE BERKELEY

(1685–1753)

On the Prospect of Planting Arts and Learning in America

THE Muse, disgusted at an age and clime
Barren of every glorious theme,
In distant lands now waits a better time,
Producing subjects worthy fame:

In happy climes, where from the genial sun
And virgin earth such scenes ensue,
The force of Art by Nature seems outdone,
And fancied beauties by the true:

In happy climes, the seat of Innocence,
Where Nature guides and Virtue rules,
Where men shall not impose, for truth and sense,
The pedantry of courts and schools:

There shall be sung another golden age,
The rise of empire and of arts,
The good and great inspiring epic rage,
The wisest heads and noblest hearts.

Not such as Europe breeds in her decay:
Such as she bred when fresh and young,
When heavenly flame did animate her clay,
By future poets shall be sung.

Westward the course of empire takes its way;
The first four acts already past,
A fifth shall close the drama with the day;
Time's noblest offspring is the last.

JOHN GAY

(1685–1732)

Black-Eyed Susan

All in the Downs the fleet was moored,
The streamers waving in the wind,
When black-eyed Susan came aboard;
"O, where shall I my true-love find?
Tell me, ye jovial sailors, tell me true
If my sweet William sails among the crew."

William, who high upon the yard
Rocked with the billow to and fro,
Soon as her well-known voice he heard
He sighed, and cast his eyes below:
The cord slides swiftly through his glowing hands,
And quick as lightning on the deck he stands.

So the sweet lark, high poised in air,
Shuts close his pinions to his breast
If chance his mate's shrill call he hear,
And drops at once into her nest:—
The noblest captain in the British fleet
Might envy William's lip those kisses sweet.

"O Susan, Susan, lovely dear,
My vows shall ever true remain;
Let me kiss off that falling tear;
We only part to meet again.
Change as ye list, ye winds; my heart shall be
The faithful compass that still points to thee.

"Believe not what the landmen say
  Who tempt with doubts thy constant mind:
They'll tell thee, sailors, when away,
  In every port a mistress find:
Yes, yes, believe them when they tell thee so,
For Thou art present wheresoe'er I go.

"If to fair India's coast we sail,
  Thy eyes are seen in diamonds bright,
Thy breath is Africa's spicy gale,
  Thy skin is ivory so white.
Thus every beauteous object that I view
Wakes in my soul some charm of lovely Sue.

"Though battle call me from thy arms,
  Let not my pretty Susan mourn;
Though cannons roar, yet safe from harms
  William shall to his dear return.
Love turns aside the balls that round me fly,
Lest precious tears should drop from Susan's eye."

The boatswain gave the dreadful word,
  The sails their swelling bosom spread;
No longer must she stay aboard:
  They kissed, she sighed, he hung his head.
Her lessening boat unwilling rows to land;
"Adieu!" she cried; and waved her lily hand.

ALLAN RAMSAY

(1686–1758)

Lochaber No More

Farewell to Lochaber! and farewell, my Jean,
Where heartsome with thee I hae mony day been;
For Lochaber no more, Lochaber no more,
We'll maybe return to Lochaber no more!

These tears that I shed they are a' for my dear,
And no for the dangers attending on wear,
Though borne on rough seas to a far bloody shore,
Maybe to return to Lochaber no more.

Though hurricanes rise, and rise every wind,
They'll ne'er make a tempest like that in my mind;
Though loudest of thunder on louder waves roar,
That's naething like leaving my love on the shore,
To leave thee behind me my heart is sair pained;
By ease that's inglorious no fame can be gained;
And beauty and love's the reward of the brave,
And I must deserve it before I can crave.

Then glory, my Jeany, maun plead my excuse;
Since honor commands me, how can I refuse?
Without it I ne'er can have merit for thee,
And without thy favor I'd better not be.
I gae then, my lass, to win honor and fame,
And if I should luck to come gloriously hame,
I'll bring a heart to thee with love running o'er,
And then I'll leave thee and Lochaber no more.

ALEXANDER POPE

(1688–1744)

Ode to Solitude

HAPPY the man, whose wish and care
A few paternal acres bound,
Content to breathe his native air
In his own ground.

Whose herds with milk, whose fields with bread,
Whose flocks supply him with attire;
Whose trees in summer yield him shade,
In winter, fire.

Blest who can unconcern'dly find
Hours, days, and years slide soft away
In health of body, peace of mind,
Quiet by day,

Sound sleep by night; study and ease
Together mixed; sweet recreation,
And innocence, which most does please
With meditation.

Thus let me live, unseen, unknown;
Thus unlamented let me die;
Steal from the world, and not a stone
Tell where I lie.

The Dying Christian to His Soul

VITAL spark of heavenly flame!
Quit, O quit this mortal frame!
Trembling, hoping, lingering, flying,
O, the pain, the bliss of dying!
Cease, fond nature, cease thy strife,
And let me languish into life!

Hark! they whisper; angels say,
Sister spirit, come away!
What is this absorbs me quite?
Steals my senses, shuts my sight,
Drowns my spirits, draws my breath?
Tell me, my soul, can this be death?

The world recedes; it disappears!
Heaven opens on my eyes! my ears
With sounds seraphic ring:
Lend, lend your wings! I mount! I fly!
O Grave! where is thy victory?
O Death! where is thy sting?

The Universal Prayer

FATHER of all! in every age,
  In every clime adored,
By saint, by savage, and by sage,
  Jehovah, Jove, or Lord!

Thou great First Cause, least understood,
  Who all my sense confined
To know but this, that thou art good,
  And that myself am blind;

Yet gave me, in this dark estate,
  To see the good from ill;
And, binding nature fast in fate,
  Left free the human will:

What conscience dictates to be done,
  Or warns me not to do,
This, teach me more than hell to shun,
  That, more than heaven pursue.

What blessings thy free bounty gives
  Let me not cast away;
For God is paid when man receives,
  To enjoy is to obey.

Yet not to earth's contracted span
  Thy goodness let me bound,
Or think thee Lord alone of man,
  When thousand worlds are round:

Let not this weak, unknowing hand
  Presume thy bolts to throw,
And deal damnation round the land
  On each I judge thy foe.

If I am right, thy grace impart
  Still in the right to stay;
If I am wrong, O, teach my heart
  To find that better way!

Save me alike from foolish pride
And impious discontent
At aught thy wisdom has denied,
Or aught thy goodness lent.

Teach me to feel another's woe,
To hide the fault I see;
That mercy I to others show,
That mercy show to me.

Mean though I am, not wholly so,
Since quickened by thy breath;
O, lead me wheresoe'er I go,
Through this day's life or death!

This day be bread and peace my lot;
All else beneath the sun,
Thou know'st if best bestowed or not,
And let thy will be done.

To thee, whose temple is all space,
Whose altar, earth, sea, skies,
One chorus let all Being raise,
All Nature's incense rise!

HENRY CAREY

(c. 1693–1745)

Sally in Our Alley

OF ALL the girls that are so smart
There's none like pretty Sally;
She is the darling of my heart,
And she lives in our alley.
There is no lady in the land
Is half so sweet as Sally;
She is the darling of my heart,
And she lives in our alley.

Her father he makes cabbage-nets,
And through the streets does cry 'em;
Her mother she sells laces long
To such as please to buy 'em;
But sure such folks could ne'er beget
So sweet a girl as Sally!
She is the darling of my heart,
And she lives in our alley.

When she is by I leave my work,
I love her so sincerely;
My master comes like any Turk,
And bangs me most severely.
But let him bang his bellyful,
I'll bear it all for Sally;
For she's the darling of my heart,
And she lives in our alley.

Of all the days that's in the week
I dearly love but one day,
And that's the day that comes betwixt
The Saturday and Monday;
For then I'm drest all in my best
To walk abroad with Sally;
She is the darling of my heart,
And she lives in our alley.

My master carries me to church,
And often am I blamèd
Because I leave him in the lurch
As soon as text is namèd:
I leave the church in sermon-time,
And slink away to Sally;
She is the darling of my heart,
And she lives in our alley.

When Christmas comes about again,
O, then I shall have money!
I'll hoard it up, and box it all,
And give it to my honey:

I would it were ten thousand pound!
  I'd give it all to Sally;
She is the darling of my heart,
  And she lives in our alley.

My master and the neighbors all
  Make game of me and Sally,
And, but for her, I'd better be
  A slave, and row a galley;
But when my seven long years are out,
  O, then I'll marry Sally!
O, then we'll wed, and then we'll bed,—
  But not in our alley!

DAVID MALET

(1700–1765)

The Birks of Invermay

THE smiling morn, the breathing spring,
Invite the tuneful birds to sing;
And whiie they warble from each spray,
Love melts the universal lay.
Let us, Amanda, timely wise,
Like them improve the hour that flies,
And in soft raptures waste the day
Among the birks of Invermay.

For soon the winter of the year,
And age, life's winter, will appear;
At this, thy living bloom will fade,
As that will strip the verdant shade:
Our taste of pleasure then is o'er;
The feather'd songsters love no more;
And when they droop, and we decay,
Adieu the birks of Invermay.

GEORGE LYTTELTON, LORD LYTTELTON
(1709–1773)

Tell Me, My Heart, if This Be Love

When Delia on the plain appears,
Awed by a thousand tender fears,
I would approach, but dare not move;—
Tell me, my heart, if this be love.

Whene'er she speaks, my ravished ear
No other voice than hers can hear;
No other wit but hers approve;—
Tell me, my heart, if this be love.

If she some other swain commend,
Though I was once his fondest friend,
His instant enemy I prove;—
Tell me, my heart, if this be love.

When she is absent, I no more
Delight in all that pleased before,
The clearest spring, the shadiest grove;—
Tell me, my heart, if this be love.

When fond of power, of beauty vain,
Her nets she spread for every swain,
I strove to hate, but vainly strove;—
Tell me, my heart, if this be love.

WILLIAM SHENSTONE
(1714–c.1763)

Written at an Inn at Henley

To thee, fair freedom! I retire
  From flattery, cards, and dice, and din;
Nor art thou found in mansions higher
  Than the low cot, or humble inn.

'Tis here with boundless power I reign;
  And every health which I begin,
Converts dull port to bright champagne;
  Such freedom crowns it, at an inn.

I fly from pomp, I fly from plate!
  I fly from falsehood's specious grin!
Freedom I love, and form I hate,
  And choose my lodgings at an inn.

Here, waiter! take my sordid ore,
  Which lackeys else might hope to win;
It buys, what courts have not in store;
  It buys me freedom at an inn.

Whoe'er has traveled life's dull round,
  Where'er his stages may have been,
May sigh to think he still has found
  The warmest welcome, at an inn.

THOMAS GRAY
(1716–1771)

Elegy Written in a Country Churchyard

THE curfew tolls the knell of parting day,
  The lowing herd wind slowly o'er the lea,
The ploughman homeward plods his weary way,
  And leaves the world to darkness and to me.

Now fades the glimmering landscape on the sight,
  And all the air a solemn stillness holds,
Save where the beetle wheels his droning flight,
  And drowsy tinklings lull the distant folds:

Save that, from yonder ivy-mantled tower,
  The moping owl does to the moon complain
Of such as, wandering near her secret bower,
  Molest her ancient solitary reign.

Beneath those rugged elms, that yew-tree's shade,
  Where heaves the turf in many a mouldering heap,
Each in his narrow cell forever laid,
  The rude forefathers of the hamlet sleep.

The breezy call of incense-breathing morn,
  The swallow twittering from the straw-built shed,
The cock's shrill clarion, or the echoing horn,
  No more shall rouse them from their lowly bed.

For them no more the blazing hearth shall burn,
  Or busy housewife ply her evening care;
No children run to lisp their sire's return,
  Or climb his knees the envied kiss to share.

Oft did the harvest to their sickle yield,
  Their furrow oft the stubborn glebe has broke;
How jocund did they drive their team afield!
  How bowed the woods beneath their sturdy stroke!

Let not ambition mock their useful toil,
  Their homely joys, and destiny obscure;
Nor grandeur hear with a disdainful smile
  The short and simple annals of the poor.

The boast of heraldry, the pomp of power,
  And all that beauty, all that wealth e'er gave,
Awaits alike the inevitable hour.
  The paths of glory lead but to the grave.

Nor you, ye proud, impute to these the fault,
  If Memory o'er their tomb no trophies raise,
Where, through the long-drawn aisle and fretted vault,
  The pealing anthem swells the note of praise.

Can storied urn or animated bust
  Back to its mansion call the fleeting breath?
Can honor's voice provoke the silent dust,
  Or flattery soothe the dull, cold ear of death?

Perhaps in this neglected spot is laid
  Some heart once pregnant with celestial fire;
Hands, that the rod of empire might have swayed,
  Or waked to ecstasy the living lyre:

But knowledge to their eyes her ample page,
  Rich with the spoils of time, did ne'er unroll;
Chill penury repressed their noble rage,
  And froze the genial current of the soul.

Full many a gem of purest ray serene
  The dark, unfathomed caves of ocean bear;
Full many a flower is born to blush unseen,
  And waste its sweetness on the desert air.

Some village Hampden, that, with dauntless breast,
  The little tyrant of his fields withstood,
Some mute, inglorious Milton here may rest,
  Some Cromwell, guiltless of his country's blood.

Th' applause of listening senates to command,
  The threats of pain and ruin to despise,
To scatter plenty o'er a smiling land,
  And read their history in a nation's eyes,

Their lot forbade: nor circumscribed alone
  Their growing virtues, but their crimes confined;
Forbade to wade through slaughter to a throne,
  And shut the gates of mercy on mankind,

The struggling pangs of conscious truth to hide,
  To quench the blushes of ingenuous shame,
Or heap the shrine of luxury and pride
  With incense kindled at the muse's flame.

Far from the madding crowd's ignoble strife,
  Their sober wishes never learned to stray;
Along the cool sequestered vale of life
  They kept the noiseless tenor of their way.

Yet even these bones from insult to protect,
  Some frail memorial still erected nigh,
With uncouth rhymes and shapeless sculpture decked,
  Implores the passing tribute of a sigh.

Their name, their years, spelt by th' unlettered muse,
  The place of fame and elegy supply;
And many a holy text around she strews,
  That teach the rustic moralist to die.

For who, to dumb forgetfulness a prey,
  This pleasing anxious being e'er resigned,
Left the warm precincts of the cheerful day,
  Nor cast one longing lingering look behind?

On some fond breast the parting soul relies,
  Some pious drops the closing eye requires;
E'en from the tomb the voice of Nature cries,
  E'en in our ashes live their wonted fires.

For thee, who, mindful of th' unhonored dead,
  Dost in these lines their artless tale relate,
If chance, by lonely contemplation led,
  Some kindred spirit shall inquire thy fate,

Haply some hoary-headed swain may say,
  "Oft have we seen him at the peep of dawn
Brushing with hasty steps the dews away,
  To meet the sun upon the upland lawn.

"There at the foot of yonder nodding beech,
  That wreathes its old, fantastic roots so high,
His listless length at noontide would he stretch,
  And pore upon the brook that babbles by.

"Hard by yon wood, now smiling as in scorn,
  Muttering his wayward fancies he would rove;
Now drooping, woeful-wan, like one forlorn,
  Or crazed with care, or crossed in hopeless love.

"One morn I missed him on the customed hill,
  Along the heath, and near his favorite tree;
Another came; nor yet beside the rill,
  Nor up the lawn, nor at the wood was he;

"The next, with dirges due in sad array,
  Slow through the church-way path we saw him borne.
Approach and read (for thou canst read) the lay
  Graved on the stone beneath yon aged thorn."

THE EPITAPH

Here rests his head upon the lap of Earth
  A youth to Fortune and to Fame unknown;
Fair Science frowned not on his humble birth,
  And Melancholy marked him for her own.

Large was his bounty, and his soul sincere,
  Heaven did a recompense as largely send;
He gave to Misery all he had, a tear,
  He gained from Heaven ('t was all he wished) a friend.

No farther seek his merits to disclose,
  Or draw his frailties from their dread abode,
(There they alike in trembling hope repose)
  The bosom of his Father and his God.

WILLIAM COLLINS

(1721–1759)

Ode to Simplicity

O THOU, by Nature taught
To breathe her genuine thought
In numbers warmly pure, and sweetly strong:
Who first, on mountains wild,
In Fancy, loveliest child,
Thy babe, or Pleasure's, nursed the powers of song!

Thou, who with hermit heart,
Disdain'st the wealth of art,
And gauds, and pageant weeds, and trailing pall:
But com'st, a decent maid,
In Attic robe array'd,
O chaste, unboastful Nymph, to thee I call!

By all the honey'd store
On Hybla's thymy shore,
By all her blooms and mingled murmurs dear;
By her whose love-lorn woe
In evening musings slow,
Soothed sweetly sad Electra's poet's ear:

By old Cephisus deep,
Who spread his wavy sweep
In warbled wanderings round thy green retreat;
On whose enamell'd side,
When holy Freedom died,
No equal haunt allured thy future feet:—

O sister meek of Truth,
To my admiring youth
Thy sober aid and native charms infuse!
The flowers that sweetest breathe,
Though Beauty cull'd the wreath,
Still ask thy hand to range their order'd hues.

While Rome could none esteem,
But Virtue's patriot theme,
You loved her hills, and led her laureat band;
But stay'd to sing alone
To one distinguish'd throne;
And turn'd thy face, and fled her alter'd land.

No more, in hall or bower,
The Passions own thy power;
Love, only Love, her forceless numbers mean;
For thou hast left her shrine,
Nor olive more, nor vine,
Shall gain thy feet to bless the servile scene.

Though taste, though genius bless
To some divine excess,
Faint's the cold work till thou inspire the whole;
What each, what all supply
May court, may charm our eye;
Thou, only thou, canst raise the meeting soul!

Of these let others ask,
To aid some mighty task,
I only seek to find thy temperate vale;
Where oft my reed might sound
To maids and shepherds round,
And all thy sons, O Nature, learn my tale.

How Sleep the Brave!

(Written in 1746)

How sleep the Brave who sink to rest
By all their country's wishes blest!
When Spring, with dewy fingers cold,
Returns to deck their hallowed mould,
She there shall dress a sweeter sod
Than Fancy's feet have ever trod.

By fairy hands their knell is rung;
By forms unseen their dirge is sung;
There Honor comes, a pilgrim gray,
To bless the turf that wraps their clay;
And Freedom shall awhile repair,
To dwell a weeping hermit there!

Ode to Evening

If aught of oaten stop or pastoral song
May hope, chaste Eve, to soothe thy modest ear
Like thy own solemn springs,
Thy springs, and dying gales;

O Nymph reserved,—while now the bright-hair'd sun
Sits in yon western tent, whose cloudy skirts
With brede ethereal wove,
O'erhang his wavy bed,

Now air is hush'd, save where the weak-eyed bat
With short shrill shriek flits by on leathern wing,
Or where the beetle winds
His small but sullen horn,

As oft he rises midst the twilight path,
Against the pilgrim borne in heedless hum,—
Now teach me, maid composed,
To breathe some soften'd strain

Whose numbers, stealing through thy dark'ning vale,
May not unseemly with its stillness suit;
As musing slow I hail
Thy genial loved return.

For when thy folding star arising shows
His paly circlet, at his warning lamp
The fragrant Hours, and Elves
Who slept in flowers the day.

And many a Nymph who wreathes her brows with sedge,
And sheds the freshening dew, and, lovelier still,
The pensive Pleasures sweet,
Prepare thy shadowy car.

Then let me rove some wild and heathy scene;
Or find some ruin, 'midst its dreary dells,
Whose walls more awful nod
By thy religious gleams.

Or, if chill blustering winds, or driving rain,
Prevent my willing feet, be mine the hut
That, from the mountain's side,
Views wilds, and swelling floods,

And hamlets brown, and dim-discovered spires;
And hears their simple bell; and marks o'er all
Thy dewy fingers draw
The gradual dusky veil,

While Spring shall pour his showers, as oft he wont,
And bathe thy breathing tresses, meekest Eve!
While Summer loves to sport
Beneath thy lingering light;

While sallow Autumn fills thy lap with leaves;
Or Winter, yelling through the troublous air,
Affrights thy shrinking train,
And rudely rends thy robes;

So long, sure-found beneath the sylvan shed,
Shall Fancy, Friendship, Science, smiling Peace,
Thy gentlest influence own,
And love thy favorite name!

The Passions

An Ode for Music

When Music, heavenly maid, was young,
While yet in early Greece she sung,
The Passions oft, to hear her shell,
Thronged around her magic cell,—
Exulting, trembling, raging, fainting,—
Possessed beyond the muse's painting;
By turns they felt the glowing mind
Disturbed, delighted, raised, refined;
Till once, 't is said, when all were fired,
Filled with fury, rapt, inspired,
From the supporting myrtles round
They snatched her instruments of sound;
And, as they oft had heard apart
  Sweet lessons of her forceful art,
Each (for madness ruled the hour)
Would prove his own expressive power.

First Fear his hand, its skill to try,
  Amid the chords bewildered laid,
And back recoiled, he knew not why,
  E'en at the sound himself had made.

Next Anger rushed; his eyes, on fire,
  In lightnings owned his secret stings:
In one rude clash he struck the lyre,
  And swept with hurried hand the strings.

With woful measures wan Despair,
  Low, sullen sounds, his grief beguiled,—
A solemn, strange, and mingled air;
  'T was sad by fits, by starts 't was wild.

But thou, O Hope, with eyes so fair,—
  What was thy delightful measure?
Still it whispered promised pleasure,
  And bade the lovely scenes at distance hail!

Still would her touch the strain prolong;
  And from the rocks, the woods, the vale,
She called on Echo still, through all the song;
  And where her sweetest theme she chose,
  A soft responsive voice was heard at every close;
And Hope, enchanted, smiled, and waved her golden hair.
And longer had she sung—but, with a frown,
    Revenge impatient rose;
He threw his blood-stained sword in thunder down;
    And, with a withering look,
  The war-denouncing trumpet took,
And blew a blast so loud and dread,
Were ne'er prophetic sounds so full of woe!
    And ever and anon he beat
    The doubling drum with furious heat;
And though, sometimes, each dreary pause between,
    Dejected Pity, at his side,
    Her soul-subduing voice applied,
  Yet still he kept his wild, unaltered mien,
While each strained ball of sight seemed bursting from his head.

  Thy numbers, Jealousy, to naught were fixed,—
    Sad proof of thy distressful state;
  Of differing themes the veering song was mixed;
    And now it courted Love,—now, raving, called on Hate.

With eyes upraised, as one inspired,
Pale Melancholy sate retired;
And from her wild sequestered seat,
In notes by distance made more sweet,
  Poured through the mellow horn her pensive soul:
    And, dashing soft from rocks around,
    Bubbling runnels joined the sound;
  Through glades and glooms the mingled measure stole;
  Or o'er some haunted stream, with fond delay,
    Round an holy calm diffusing,
    Love of peace, and lonely musing,
  In hollow murmurs died away.

But O, how altered was its sprightlier tone
When Cheerfulness, a nymph of healthiest hue,
  Her bow across her shoulder flung,
  Her buskins gemmed with morning dew,
Blew an inspiring air, that dale and thicket rung,—
  The hunter's call, to faun and dryad known!
The oak-crowned sisters, and their chaste-eyed queen,
  Satyrs and sylvan boys, were seen
  Peeping from forth their alleys green:
Brown Exercise rejoiced to hear;
  And Sport leapt up, and seized his beechen spear.

Last came Joy's ecstatic trial:
He, with viny crown advancing,
  First to the lively pipe his hand addrest;
But soon he saw the brisk-awakening viol,
  Whose sweet entrancing voice he loved the best;
They would have thought, who heard the strain,
  They saw, in Tempe's vale, her native maids
  Amidst the festal-sounding shades,
To some unwearied minstrel dancing,
While, as his flying fingers kissed the strings,
Love framed with Mirth a gay fantastic round:
Loose were her tresses seen, her zone unbound;
  And he, amidst his frolic play,
  As if he would the charming air repay,
Shook thousand odors from his dewy wings.

O Music! sphere-descended maid,
Friend of pleasure, wisdom's aid!
Why, goddess, why, to us denied,
Lay'st thou thy ancient lyre aside?
As, in that loved Athenian bower,
You learned an all-commanding power,
Thy mimic soul, O nymph endeared,
Can well recall what then it heard.

Where is thy native simple heart,
Devote to virtue, fancy, art?
Arise, as in that elder time,
Warm, energetic, chaste, sublime!

Thy wonders, in that godlike age,
Fill thy recording sister's page;
'T is said—and I believe the tale—
Thy humblest reed could more prevail,
Had more of strength, diviner rage,
Than all which charms this laggard age,—
E'en all at once together found,—
Cecilia's mingled world of sound.
O, bid our vain endeavors cease;
Revive the just designs of Greece!
Return in all thy simple state,—
Confirm the tales her sons relate!

JEAN ELLIOT

(1727–1805)

A Lament for Flodden

I'VE heard the lilting at our ewe-milking,
Lasses a-lilting before the dawn of day;
But now they are moaning on ilka green loaning—
The Flowers of the Forest are a' wede away.

At bughts, in the morning, nae blithe lads are scorning,
Lasses are lonely and dowie and wae;
Nae daffing, nae gabbing, but sighing and sabbing,
Ilk ane lifts her leglin and hies her away.

In hairst, at the shearing, nae youths now are jeering,
Bandsters are lyart, and runkled, and gray:
At fair or at preaching, nae wooing, nae fleeching—
The Flowers of the Forest are a' wede away.

At e'en, at the gloaming, nae swankies are roaming,
'Bout stacks wi' the lasses at bogle to play;
But ilk ane sits drearie, lamenting her dearie—
The Flowers of the Forest are a' wede away.

Dool and wae for the order sent our lads to the Border!
  The English, for ance, by guile wan the day;
The Flowers of the Forest, that fought aye the foremost,
  The prime o' our land, are cauld in the clay.

We hear nae mair lilting at our ewe-milking;
  Women and bairns are heartless and wae;
Sighing and moaning on ilka green loaning—
  The Flowers of the Forest are a' wede away.

OLIVER GOLDSMITH

(1728–1774)

When Lovely Woman Stoops to Folly

WHEN lovely woman stoops to folly,
  And finds too late that men betray,
What charm can soothe her melancholy?
  What art can wash her guilt away?

The only art her guilt to cover,
  To hide her shame from every eye,
To give repentance to her lover,
  And wring his bosom, is—to die.

Memory

O MEMORY, thou fond deceiver,
  Still importunate and vain,
To former joys recurring ever,
  And turning all the past to pain:

Thou, like the world, th' oppress'd oppressing,
  Thy smiles increase the wretch's woe:
And he who wants each other blessing
  In thee must ever find a foe.

WILLIAM COWPER
(1731–1880)

Loss of the Royal George

TOLL for the brave—
The brave that are no more!
All sunk beneath the wave
Fast by their native shore!

Eight hundred of the brave,
Whose courage well was tried,
Had made the vessel heel
And laid her on her side.

A land-breeze shook the shrouds
And she was overset;
Down went the Royal George,
With all her crew complete.

Toll for the brave!
Brave Kempenfelt is gone;
His last sea-fight is fought,
His work of glory done.

It was not in the battle;
No tempest gave the shock;
She sprang no fatal leak,
She ran upon no rock.

His sword was in its sheath,
His fingers held the pen,
When Kempenfelt went down
With twice four hundred men.

—Weigh the vessel up
Once dreaded by our foes!
And mingle with our cup
The tears that England owes.

Her timbers yet are sound,
And she may float again
Full charged with England's thunder,
And plow the distant main;

But Kempenfelt is gone,
His victories are o'er;
And he and his eight hundred
Shall plow the wave no more.

To Mary Unwin

MARY! I want a lyre with other strings,
Such aid from Heaven as some have feign'd they drew
And eloquence scarce given to mortals, new
And undebased by praise of meaner things;

That ere through age or woe I shed my wings,
I may record thy worth with honor due,
In verse as musical as thou art true,
And that immortalizes whom it sings:

But thou hast little need. There is a Book
By seraphs writ with beams of heavenly light,
On which the eyes of God not rarely look,
A chronicle of actions just and bright—

There all thy deeds, my faithful Mary, shine;
And since thou own'st that praise, I spare thee mine.

To the Same

THE twentieth year is well-nigh past
Since first our sky was overcast;
Ah would that this might be the last!
My Mary!

Thy spirits have a fainter flow,
I see thee daily weaker grow—
'Twas my distress that brought thee low,
My Mary!

Thy needles, once a shining store,
For my sake restless heretofore,
Now rust disused, and shine no more;
My Mary!

For though thou gladly wouldst fulfil
The same kind office for me still,
Thy sight now seconds not thy will,
My Mary!

But well thou play'st the housewife's part,
And all thy threads with magic art
Have wound themselves about this heart,
My Mary!

Thy indistinct expressions seem
Like language utter'd in a dream;
Yet me they charm, whate'er the theme,
My Mary!

Thy silver locks, once auburn bright,
Are still more lovely in my sight
Than golden beams of orient light,
My Mary!

For could I view nor them nor thee,
What sight worth seeing could I see?
The sun would rise in vain for me,
My Mary!

Partakers of thy sad decline
Thy hands their little force resign;
Yet, gently prest, press gently mine,
My Mary!

Such feebleness of limbs thou prov'st
That now at every step thou mov'st
Upheld by two; yet still thou lov'st,
My Mary!

And still to love, though prest with ill,
In wintry age to feel no chill,
With me is to be lovely still,
My Mary!

But ah! by constant heed I know
How oft the sadness that I show
Transforms thy smiles to looks of woe,
My Mary!

And should my future lot be cast
With much resemblance of the past,
Thy worn-out heart will break at last—
My Mary!

I Was a Stricken Deer

I WAS a stricken deer, that left the herd
Long since; with many an arrow deep infixed
My panting side was charged, when I withdrew,
To seek a tranquil death in distant shades.
There was I found by one who had himself
Been hurt by the archers. In his side he bore,
And in his hands and feet, the cruel scars.
With gentle force soliciting the darts,
He drew them forth, and healed, and bade me live.
Since then, with few associates, in remote
And silent woods I wander, far from those
My former partners of the peopled scene;
With few associates, and not wishing more.
Here much I ruminate, as much I may,
With other views of men and manners now
Than once, and others of a life to come.

I see that all are wanderers, gone astray
Each in his own delusions; they are lost
In chase of fancied happiness, still wooed
And never won. Dream after dream ensues;
And still they dream, that they shall still succeed;
And still are disappointed. Rings the world
With the vain stir. I sum up half mankind,
And add two-thirds of the remaining half,
And find the total of their hopes and fears
Dreams, empty dreams.

WILLIAM MICKLE
(1735–1788)

The Sailor's Wife

AND are ye sure the news is true?
  And are ye sure he's weel?
Is this a time to think o' wark?
  Ye jades, lay by your wheel;
Is this the time to spin a thread,
  When Colin's at the door?
Reach down my cloak, I'll to the quay,
  And see him come ashore.
For there's nae luck about the house,
  There's nae luck at a';
There's little pleasure in the house
  When our gudeman's awa.

And gie to me my bigonet,
  My bishop's satin gown;
For I maun tell the baillie's wife
  That Colin's in the town.
My Turkey slippers maun gae on,
  My stockins pearly blue;
It's a' to pleasure our gudeman,
  For he's baith leal and true.

Rise, lass, and mak a clean fireside,
   Put on the muckle pot;
Gie little Kate her button gown
   And Jock his Sunday coat;
And mak their shoon as black as slaes,
   Their hose as white as snaw;
It's a' to please my ain gudeman,
   For he's been long awa.

There's twa fat hens upo' the coop
   Been fed this month and mair;
Mak haste and thraw their necks about,
   That Colin weel may fare;
And spread the table neat and clean,
   Gar ilka thing look braw,
For wha can tell how Colin fared
   When he was far awa?

Sae true his heart, sae smooth his speech,
   His breath like caller air;
His very foot has music in't
   As he comes up the stair.
And will I see his face again?
   And will I hear him speak?
I'm downright dizzy wi' the thought,
   In troth I'm like to greet!

If Colin's weel, and weel content,
   I hae nae mair to crave;
And gin I live to keep him sae,
   I'm blest aboon the lave:
And will I see his face again?
   And will I hear him speak?
I'm downright dizzy wi' the thought,
   In troth I'm like to greet.

For there's nae luck about the house,
   There's nae luck at a';
There's little pleasure in the house
   When our gudeman's awa.

ROBERT CUNNINGHAME-GRAHAM OF GARTMORE

(1735–1797)

If Doughty Deeds My Lady Please

IF DOUGHTY deeds my lady please,
  Right soon I'll mount my steed;
And strong his arm and fast his seat
  That bears frae me the meed.
I'll wear thy colors in my cap,
  Thy picture at my heart,
And he that bends not to thine eye
  Shall rue it to his smart!
    Then tell me how to woo thee, Love;
      O, tell me how to woo thee!
    For thy dear sake nae care I'll take,
      Though ne'er another trow me.

If gay attire delight thine eye,
  I'll dight me in array;
I'll tend thy chamber door all night,
  And squire thee all the day.
If sweetest sounds can win thine ear,
  These sounds I'll strive to catch;
Thy voice I'll steal to woo thysell,
  That voice that nane can match.

But if fond love thy heart can gain,
  I never broke a vow;
Nae maiden lays her skaith to me;
  I never loved but you.
For you alone I ride the ring,
  For you I wear the blue;
For you alone I strive to sing,
  O, tell me how to woo!
    Then tell me how to woo thee, Love;
      O, tell me how to woo thee!
    For thy dear sake nae care I'll take,
      Though ne'er another trow me.

ANNA LETITIA BARBAULD

(1743–1825)

Life

"Animula, vagula, blandula"

  Life! I know not what thou art,
But know that thou and I must part;
And when, or how, or where we met
I own to me 's a secret yet.
But this I know, when thou art fled,
Where'er they lay these limbs, this head,
No clod so valueless shall be,
As all that then remains of me.
O, whither, whither dost thou fly,
Where bend unseen thy trackless course,
  And in this strange divorce,
Ah, tell where I must seek this compound I?

To the vast ocean of empyreal flame,
  From whence thy essence came,
  Dost thou thy flight pursue, when freed
  From matter's base encumbering weed?
    Or dost thou, hid from sight,
    Wait, like some spell-bound knight,
Through blank, oblivious years the appointed hour
To break thy trance and reassume thy power?
Yet canst thou, without thought or feeling be?
O, say what art thou, when no more thou 'rt thee?

Life! we've been long together
Through pleasant and through cloudy weather;
  'T is hard to part when friends are dear,—
  Perhaps 't will cost a sigh, a tear;
  Then steal away, give little warning,
    Choose thine own time;
Say not Good Night,—but in some brighter clime
    Bid me Good Morning.

LADY ANNE LINDSAY
(1750–1825)

Auld Robin Gray

WHEN the sheep are in the fauld, and the kye at hame,
And a' the world to rest are gane,
The waes o' my heart fa' in showers frae my e'e,
While my gudeman lies sound by me.

Young Jamie lo'ed me weel, and sought me for his bride;
But saving a croun he had naething else beside:
To make the croun a pund, young Jamie gaed to sea;
And the croun and the pund were baith for me.

He hadna been awa' a week but only twa,
When my father brak his arm, and the cow was stown awa;
My mother she fell sick, and my Jamie at the sea—
And auld Robin Gray came a-courtin' me.

My father couldna work, and my mother couldna spin;
I toil'd day and night, but their bread I couldna win;
Auld Rob maintain'd them baith, and wi' tears in his e'e
Said, Jennie, for their sakes, O, marry me!

My heart it said nay; I look'd for Jamie back;
But the wind it blew high, and the ship it was a wrack;
His ship it was a wrack—why didna Jamie dee?
Or why do I live to cry, Wae's me?

My father urgit sair: my mother didna speak;
But she look'd in my face till my heart was like to break:
They gi'ed him my hand, but my heart was at the sea;
Sae auld Robin Gray he was gudeman to me.

I hadna been a wife a week but only four,
When mournfu' as I sat on the stane at the door,
I saw my Jamie's wraith, for I couldna think it he
Till he said, I'm come hame to marry thee.

O sair, sair did we greet, and muckle did we say;
We took but ae kiss, and I bad him gang away;
I wish that I were dead, but I'm no like to dee;
And why was I born to say, Wae's me!

I gang like a ghaist, and I carena to spin;
I daurna think on Jamie, for that wad be a sin;
But I'll do my best a gude wife aye to be,
For auld Robin Gray he is kind unto me.

RICHARD BRINSLEY SHERIDAN

(1751–1816)

Let the Toast Pass

HERE'S to the maiden of bashful fifteen;
  Here's to the widow of fifty;
Here's to the flaunting extravagant quean,
  And here's to the housewife that's thrifty.
      Let the toast pass,
      Drink to the lass,
I'll warrant she'll prove an excuse for the glass.

Here's to the charmer whose dimples we prize,
  Now to the maid who has none, sir;
Here's to the girl with a pair of blue eyes,
  And here's to the nymph with but one, sir.
      Let the toast pass, etc.

Here's to the maid with a bosom of snow;
  Now to her that's as brown as a berry;
Here's to the wife with a face full of woe,
  And now to the damsel that's merry.
      Let the toast pass, etc.

For let 'em be clumsy, or let 'em be slim,
  Young or ancient, I care not a feather;
So fill a pint bumper quite up to the brim,
So fill up your glasses, nay, fill to the brim,
  And let us e'en toast them together.
      Let the toast pass, etc.

THOMAS CHATTERTON

(1752–1770)

Minstrel's Song

O, SING unto my roundelay!
  O, drop the briny tear with me!
Dance no more at holiday;
  Like a running river be.
    My love is dead,
    Gone to his death-bed,
    All under the willow-tree.

Black his hair as the winter night,
  White his neck as the summer snow,
Ruddy his face as the morning light;
  Cold he lies in the grave below.
    My love is dead, etc.

Sweet his tongue as the throstle's note;
  Quick in dance as thought can be;
Deft his tabor, cudgel stout;
  O, he lies by the willow-tree!
    My love is dead, etc.

Hark! the raven flaps his wing
  In the briered dell below;
Hark! the death-owl loud doth sing
  To the nightmares as they go.
    My love is dead, etc.

See! the white moon shines on high;
  Whiter is my true-love's shroud,
Whiter than the morning sky,
  Whiter than the evening cloud.
      My love is dead, etc.

Here, upon my true-love's grave
  Shall the barren flowers be laid,
Nor one holy saint to save
  All the coldness of a maid.
      My love is dead, etc.

With my hands I'll bind the briers
  Round his holy corse to gre;
Ouphant fairy, light your fires;
  Here my body still shall be.
      My love is dead, etc.

Come, with acorn-cup and thorn,
  Drain my heart's blood away;
Life and all its good I scorn,
  Dance by night, or feast by day.
      My love is dead, etc.

Water-witches, crowned with reytes,
  Bear me to your lethal tide.
I die! I come! my true-love waits.
  Thus the damsel spake, and died.

WILLIAM BLAKE

(1757–1827)

To the Muses

WHETHER on Ida's shady brow,
  Or in the chambers of the East,
The chambers of the sun that now
  From ancient melody have ceased;

Whether in Heaven ye wander fair,
  Or the green corners of the earth,
Or the blue regions of the air,
  Where the melodious winds have birth;

Whether on crystal rocks ye rove
  Beneath the bosom of the sea,
Wandering in many a coral grove,—
  Fair Nine, forsaking Poetry;

How have you left the ancient love
  That bards of old enjoy'd in you!
The languid strings do scarcely move,
  The sound is forced, the notes are few.

To Spring

O THOU with dewy locks, who lookest down
Through the clear windows of the morning, turn
Thine angel eyes upon our western isle,
Which in full choir hails thy approach, O Spring!

The hills tell one another, and the listening
Valleys hear; all our longing eyes are turn'd
Up to thy bright pavilions: issue forth
And let thy holy feet visit our clime!

Come o'er the eastern hills, and let our winds
Kiss thy perfumèd garments; let us taste
Thy morn and evening breath; scatter thy pearls
Upon our lovesick land that mourns for thee.

O deck her forth with thy fair fingers; pour
Thy soft kisses on her bosom; and put
The golden crown upon her languish'd head,
Whose modest tresses are bound up for thee.

The Piper

PIPING down the valleys wild,
Piping songs of pleasant glee,
On a cloud I saw a child,
And he laughing said to me:—

"Pipe a song about a lamb:"
So I piped with merry cheer.
"Piper, pipe that song again:"
So I piped; he wept to hear.

"Drop thy pipe, thy happy pipe,
Sing thy songs of happy cheer:"
So I sung the same again,
While he wept with joy to hear.

"Piper, sit thee down and write
In a book that all may read—"
So he vanished from my sight;
And I plucked a hollow reed,

And I made a rural pen,
And I stained the water clear,
And I wrote my happy songs
Every child may joy to hear.

The Tiger

TIGER! Tiger! burning bright,
In the forests of the night;
What immortal hand or eye
Could frame thy fearful symmetry?

In what distant deeps or skies
Burned the fire of thine eyes?
On what wings dare he aspire?
What the hand dare seize the fire?

And what shoulder, and what art,
Could twist the sinews of thine heart?
And when thy heart began to beat,
What dread hand? and what dread feet?

What the hammer, what the chain?
In what furnace was thy brain?
What the anvil? what dread grasp
Dare its deadly terrors clasp?

When the stars threw down their spears,
And watered heaven with their tears,
Did he smile his work to see?
Did He, who made the Lamb, make thee!

Tiger! Tiger! burning bright,
In the forests of the night,
What immortal hand or eye
Dare frame thy fearful symmetry?

A Cradle Song

Sleep, sleep, beauty bright,
Dreaming in the joys of night;
Sleep, sleep; in thy sleep
Little sorrows sit and weep.

Sweet babe, in thy face
Soft desires I can trace,
Secret joys and secret smiles,
Little pretty infant wiles.

As thy softest limbs I feel,
Smiles as of the morning steal
O'er thy cheek, and o'er thy breast
Where thy little heart doth rest.

Oh the cunning wiles that creep
In thy little heart asleep!
When thy little heart doth wake,
Then the dreadful light shall break.

Love's Secret

NEVER seek to tell thy love,
  Love that never told can be;
For the gentle wind doth move
  Silently, invisibly.

I told my love, I told my love,
  I told her all my heart,
Trembling, cold, in ghastly fears.
  Ah! she did depart!

Soon after she was gone from me,
  A traveller came by,
Silently, invisibly:
  He took her with a sigh.

ROBERT BURNS

(1759–1796)

The Cotter's Saturday Night

INSCRIBED TO R. AIKEN, ESQ.

"Let not ambition mock their useful toil,
Their homely joys and destiny obscure;
Nor grandeur hear, with a disdainful smile,
The short but simple annals of the poor."

—GRAY.

MY LOVED, my honored, much-respected friend,
  No mercenary bard his homage pays:
With honest pride I scorn each selfish end;
  My dearest meed, a friend's esteem and praise.
To you I sing, in simple Scottish lays,
  The lowly train in life's sequestered scene;
The native feelings strong, the guileless ways;
  What Aiken in a cottage would have been;
Ah! though his worth unknown, far happier there, I ween.

November chill blaws loud wi' angry sugh;
The shortening winter-day is near a close;
The miry beasts retreating frae the pleugh,
The blackening trains o' craws to their repose;
The toilworn cotter frae his labor goes,—
This night his weekly moil is at an end,—
Collects his spades, his mattocks, and his hoes,
Hoping the morn in ease and rest to spend,
And weary, o'er the moor, his course does hameward bend.

At length his lonely cot appears in view,
Beneath the shelter of an aged tree;
Th' expectant wee things, toddlin', stacher through
To meet their dad, wi' flichterin' noise an' glee.
His wee bit ingle, blinking bonnily,
His clean hearthstane, his thriftie wifie's smile,
The lisping infant prattling on his knee,
Does a' his weary carking cares beguile,
And makes him quite forget his labor and his toil.

Belyve[1] the elder bairns come drapping in,
At service out amang the farmers roun;
Some ca' the pleugh, some herd, some tentie[2] rin
A cannie errand to a neibor town;
Their eldest hope, their Jenny, woman grown,
In youthfu' bloom, love sparkling in her e'e,
Comes hame, perhaps, to shew a bra' new gown,
Or deposit her sair-won penny-fee,
To help her parents dear, if they in hardship be.

Wi' joy unfeigned brothers and sisters meet,
An' each for other's weelfare kindly spiers:
The social hours, swift-winged, unnoticed fleet;
Each tells the uncos that he sees or hears;
The parents, partial, eye their hopeful years;
Anticipation forward points the view:
The mother, wi' her needle an' her shears,
Gars auld claes look amaist as weel's the new;
The father mixes a' wi' admonition due.

[1]By and by. [2]Cautious.

Their master's an' their mistress's command,
  The younkers a' are warnèd to obey;
And mind their labors wi' an eydent[1] hand,
  And ne'er, though out o' sight, to jauk or play;
"An' O, be sure to fear the Lord alway!
  An' mind your duty, duly, morn an' night!
Lest in temptation's path ye gang astray,
  Implore his counsel and assisting might;
They never sought in vain that sought the Lord aright!"

But, hark! a rap comes gently to the door.
  Jenny, wha kens the meaning o' the same,
Tells how a neibor lad cam o'er the moor,
  To do some errands and convoy her hame.
The wily mother sees the conscious flame
  Sparkle in Jenny's e'e, and flush her cheek;
Wi' heart-struck anxious care inquires his name,
  While Jenny hafflins[2] is afraid to speak;
Weel pleased the mother hears it's nae wild, worthless rake.

Wi' kindly welcome, Jenny brings him ben;
  A strappin' youth; he taks the mother's e'e;
Blithe Jenny sees the visit 's no ill ta'en;
  The father cracks of horses, pleughs, and kye.
The youngster's artless heart o'erflows wi' joy,
  But blate and lathefu', scarce can weel behave;
The mother, wi' a woman's wiles, can spy
  What makes the youth sae bashfu' an' sae grave;
Weel pleased to think her bairn 's respected like the lave.

O happy love! where love like this is found!
  O heartfelt raptures! bliss beyond compare!
I've pacèd much this weary mortal round,
  And sage experience bids me this declare:—
If Heaven a draught of heavenly pleasure spare,
  One cordial in this melancholy vale,
'T is when a youthful, loving, modest pair
  In other's arms breathe out the tender tale,
Beneath the milk-white thorn that scents the evening gale.

[1]Diligent. [2]Half.

Is there, in human form, that bears a heart,
  A wretch, a villain, lost to love and truth,
That can, with studied, sly, ensnaring art,
  Betray sweet Jenny's unsuspecting youth?
Curse on his perjured arts! dissembling smooth!
  Are honor, virtue, conscience, all exiled?
Is there no pity, no relenting ruth,
  Points to the parents fondling o'er their child,
Then paints the ruined maid, and their distraction wild?

But now the supper crowns their simple board,
  The halesome parritch, chief o' Scotia's food;
The soupe their only hawkie[1] does afford,
  That 'yont the hallan[2] snugly chows her cood;
The dame brings forth, in complimental mood,
  To grace the lad, her weel-hained kebbuck[3] fell,
An' aft he's prest, an' aft he ca's it guid;
  The frugal wifie, garrulous, will tell,
How 't was a towmond[4] auld, sin' lint was i' the bell.

The cheerfu' supper done, wi' serious face,
  They, round the ingle, form a circle wide;
The sire turns o'er, wi' patriarchal grace,
  The big ha'-Bible, ance his father's pride:
His bonnet reverently is laid aside,
  His lyart haffets[5] wearing thin an' bare:
Those strains that once did sweet in Zion glide,
  He wales a portion with judicious care;
And "Let us worship God!" he says with solemn air.

They chant their artless notes in simple guise;
  They tune their hearts, by far the noblest aim:
Perhaps "Dundee's" wild-warbling measures rise,
  Or plaintive "Martyrs," worthy of the name;
Or noble "Elgin" beets the heavenward flame,
  The sweetest far of Scotia's holy lays:
Compared with these, Italian trills are tame;
  The tickled ears no heartfelt raptures raise;
Nae unison hae they with our Creator's praise.

[1]Cow. [2]Partition. [3]Cheese. [4]Twelvemonth. [5]Gray locks.

The priest-like father reads the sacred page,—
How Abram was the friend of God on high;
Or Moses bade eternal warfare wage
With Amalek's ungracious progeny;
Or how the royal bard did groaning lie
Beneath the stroke of Heaven's avenging ire;
Or Job's pathetic plaint, and wailing cry;
Or rapt Isaiah's wild, seraphic fire;
Or other holy seers that tune the sacred lyre.

Perhaps the Christian volume is the theme,—
How guiltless blood for guilty man was shed;
How He, who bore in heaven the second name,
Had not on earth whereon to lay his head:
How his first followers and servants sped;
The precepts sage they wrote to many a land;
How he, who lone in Patmos banishèd,
Saw in the sun a mighty angel stand,
And heard great Bab'lon's doom pronounced by Heaven's command.

Then, kneeling down, to heaven's eternal King,
The saint, the father, and the husband prays:
Hope "springs exulting on triumphant wing,"
That thus they all shall meet in future days;
There ever bask in uncreated rays,
No more to sigh, or shed the bitter tear,
Together hymning their Creator's praise,
In such society, yet still more dear;
While circling Time moves round in an eternal sphere.

Compared with this, how poor Religion's pride,
In all the pomp of method and of art,
When men display to congregations wide,
Devotion's every grace, except the heart!
The Power, incensed, the pageant will desert,
The pompous strain, the sacerdotal stole;
But, haply, in some cottage far apart,
May hear, well pleased, the language of the soul;
And in his Book of Life the inmates poor enroll.

Then homeward all take off their several way;
The youngling cottagers retire to rest:
The parent-pair their secret homage pay,
And proffer up to Heaven the warm request,
That He who stills the raven's clamorous nest,
And decks the lily fair in flowery pride,
Would, in the way his wisdom sees the best,
For them and for their little ones provide;
But, chiefly, in their hearts with grace divine preside.

From scenes like these old Scotia's grandeur springs,
That makes her loved at home, revered abroad;
Princes and lords are but the breath of kings,
"An honest man 's the noblest work of God!"
And certes, in fair Virtue's heavenly road,
The cottage leaves the palace far behind:
What is a lordling's pomp?—a cumbrous load,
Disguising oft the wretch of humankind,
Studied in arts of hell, in wickedness refined!

O Scotia! my dear, my native soil!
For whom my warmest wish to Heaven is sent,
Long may thy hardy sons of rustic toil
Be blest with health, and peace, and sweet content!
And, O, may Heaven their simple lives prevent
From luxury's contagion, weak and vile!
Then, howe'er crowns and coronets be rent,
A virtuous populace may rise the while,
And stand a wall of fire around their much-loved isle.

O Thou! who poured the patriotic tide,
That streamed through Wallace's undaunted heart;
Who dared to nobly stem tyrannic pride,
Or nobly die, the second glorious part,
(The patriot's God peculiarly thou art,
His friend, inspirer, guardian, and reward!)
O, never, never Scotia's realm desert;
But still the patriot and the patriot bard
In bright succession raise, her ornament and guard!

To a Mouse;

On Turning Her up in Her Nest with the Plough, November, 1785.

WEE, sleekit, cowerin', timorous beastie,
O, what a panic 's in thy breastie!
Thou needna start awa sae hasty,
Wi' bickering brattle!
I wad be laith to rin an' chase thee,
Wi' murdering pattle!

I'm truly sorry man's dominion
Has broken nature's social union,
An' justifies that ill opinion
Which makes thee startle
At me, thy poor earth-born companion,
An' fellow-mortal!

I doubtna, whyles, but thou may thieve;
What then? poor beastie, thou maun live!
A daimen-icker[1] in a thrave[2]
'S a sma' request;
I'll get a blessin' wi' the lave,
And never miss 't!

Thy wee bit housie, too, in ruin!
Its silly wa's the win's are strewin'!
An' naething now to big a new ane
O' foggage green!
An' bleak December's winds ensuin',
Baith snell and keen!

Thou saw the fields laid bare an' waste,
An' weary winter comin' fast,
An' cozie here, beneath the blast,
Thou thought to dwell,
Till, crash! the cruel coulter past
Out through thy cell.

[1]Ear of corn. [2]Twenty-four sheaves.

That wee bit heap o' leaves an' stibble
Has cost thee mony a weary nibble!
Now thou's turned out, for a' thy trouble,
But house or hald,
To thole the winter's sleety dribble,
An' cranreuch cauld!

But, Mousie, thou art no thy lane,
In proving foresight may be vain:
The best-laid schemes o' mice an' men
Gang aft a-gley,
An' lea'e us naught but grief and pain,
For promised joy.

Still thou art blest, compared wi' me!
The present only toucheth thee:
But, och! I backward cast my e'e
On prospects drear;
An' forward, though I canna see,
I guess an' fear.

To a Louse

On Seeing One on a Lady's Bonnet at Church

HA! WHARE ye gaun, ye crawlin' ferlie?
Your impudence protects you sairly:
I canna say but ye strunt rarely
Owre gauze an' lace;
Though, faith! I fear ye dine but sparely
On sic a place.

Ye ugly, creepin', blastit wonner,
Detested, shunned by saunt an' sinner,
How dare you set your fit upon her,
Sae fine a lady?
Gae somewhere else, and seek your dinner
On some poor body

Swith, in some beggar's haffet squattle;
There ye may creep and sprawl and sprattle
Wi' ither kindred, jumping cattle,
In shoals and nations:
Whare horn nor bane ne'er daur unsettle
Your thick plantations.

Now haud you there, ye 're out o' sight,
Below the fatt'rels, snug an' tight;
Na, faith ye yet! ye 'll no be right
Till ye 've got on it,
The very tapmost tow'ring height
O' Miss's bonnet.

My sooth; right bauld ye set your nose out,
As plump and gray as ony grozet;
O for some rank, mercurial rozet,
Or fell, red smeddum!
I'd gie you sic a hearty dose o't,
Wad dress your droddum!

I wad na been surprised to spy
You on an auld wife's flannen toy;
Or aiblins some bit duddie boy,
On 's wyliecoat;
But Miss's fine Lunardi, fie!
How daur ye do 't?

O Jenny, dinna toss your head,
An' set your beauties a' abread!
Ye little ken what cursèd speed
The blastie 's makin'!
Thae winks and finger-ends, I dread,
Are notice takin'!

O wad some power the giftie gie us
To see oursel's as ithers see us!
It wad frae monie a blunder free us,
And foolish notion:
What airs in dress an' gait wad lea'e us,
And ev'n devotion!

To a Mountain Daisy

On Turning One Down with the Plough, in April, 1786.

WEE, modest, crimson-tippèd flower,
Thou 's met me in an evil hour,
For I maun crush amang the stoure
Thy slender stem;
To spare thee now is past my power,
Thou bonny gem.

Alas! it's no thy neebor sweet,
The bonnie lark, companion meet,
Bending thee 'mang the dewy weet,
Wi' spreckled breast,
When upward springing, blithe to greet
The purpling east.

Cauld blew the bitter-biting north
Upon thy early, humble birth;
Yet cheerfully thou glinted forth
Amid the storm,
Scarce reared above the parent earth
Thy tender form.

The flaunting flowers our gardens yield
High sheltering woods and wa's maun shield:
But thou beneath the random bield
O' clod or stane,
Adorns the histie stibble-field,
Unseen, alane.

There, in thy scanty mantle clad,
Thy snawie bosom sunward spread,
Thou lifts thy unassuming head
In humble guise;
But now the share uptears thy bed,
And low thou lies!

Such is the fate of artless maid,
Sweet floweret of the rural shade!
By love's simplicity betrayed,
And guileless trust,
Till she, like thee, all soiled, is laid
Low i' the dust.

Such is the fate of simple bard,
On life's rough ocean luckless starred!
Unskilful he to note the card
Of prudent lore,
Till billows rage, and gales blow hard,
And whelm him o'er!

Such fate to suffering worth is given,
Who long with wants and woes has striven,
By human pride or cunning driven
To misery's brink,
Till, wrenched of every stay but Heaven,
He, ruined, sink!

Even thou who mourn'st the daisy's fate,
That fate is thine,—no distant date:
Stern Ruin's ploughshare drives, elate,
Full on thy bloom,
Till crushed beneath the furrow's weight
Shall be thy doom!

Tam o' Shanter

A Tale

Of Brownyis and of Bogillis full is this Buke.
—Gawin Douglas.

When chapman billies[1] leave the street,
And drouthy[2] neibors neibors meet;
As market days are wearing late,
And folk begin to tak the gate,

[1]Shopkeepers. [2]Thirsty.

While we sit bousing at the nappy,[1]
An' getting fou and unco[2] happy,
We think na on the lang Scots miles,
The mosses, waters, slaps[3] and stiles,
That lie between us and our hame,
Where sits our sulky, sullen dame,
Gathering her brows like gathering storm,
Nursing her wrath to keep it warm.

This truth fand honest TAM O' SHANTER,
As he frae Ayr ae night did canter:
(Auld Ayr, wham ne'er a town surpasses,
For honest men and bonie lasses).

O Tam! had'st thou but been sae wise,
As taen thy ain wife Kate's advice!
She tauld thee weel thou was a skellum,[4]
A blethering, blustering, drunken blellum;[5]
That frae November till October,
Ae market-day thou was na sober;
That ilka[6] melder[7] wi' the Miller,
Thou sat as lang as thou had siller;
That ev'ry naig we ca'd[8] a shoe on
The Smith and thee gat roarin fou on;
That at the Lord's house, ev'n on Sunday,
Thou drank wi' Kirkton Jean till Monday;
She prophesied that late or soon,
Thou wad be found, deep drown'd in Doon,
Or catch'd wi' warlocks[9] in the mirk,[10]
By Alloway's auld, haunted kirk.

Ah, gentle dames! it gars[11] me greet,[12]
To think how mony counsels sweet,
How mony lengthen'd, sage advices,
The husband frae the wife despises!

But to our tale:—Ae market night,
Tam had got planted unco right,

[1]Ale. [2]Uncommonly. [3]Gaps. [4]Wretch. [5]Babbler. [6]Every. [7]Grinding.
[8]Driven. [9]Wizards. [10]Darkness. [11]Makes. [12]Weep.

Fast by an ingle,[1] bleezing finely,
Wi' reaming swats[2] that drank divinely;
And at his elbow, Souter Johnie,
His ancient, trusty, drouthy crony:
Tam lo'ed him like a very brither;
They had been fou for weeks thegither.
The night drave on wi' sangs an' clatter;
And aye the ale was growing better:
The Landlady and Tam grew gracious,
Wi' favours secret, sweet and precious:
The Souter tauld his queerest stories;
The Landlord's laugh was ready chorus:
The storm without might rair and rustle,
Tam did na mind the storm a whistle.

Care, mad to see a man sae happy,
E'en drown'd himsel amang the nappy.
As bees flee hame wi' lades o' treasure,
The minutes wing'd their way wi' pleasure;
Kings may be blest, but Tam was glorious,
O'er a' the ills o' life victorious!

But pleasures are like poppies spread,
You seize the flow'r, its bloom is shed;
Or like the snow falls in the river,
A moment white—then melts for ever;
Or like the Borealis race,
That flit ere you can point their place;

Or like the rainbow's lovely form
Evanishing amid the storm.—
Nae man can tether time or tide;
The hour approaches Tam maun ride;
That hour, o' night's black arch the key-stane,
That dreary hour he mounts his beast in;
And sic a night he taks the road in,
As ne'er poor sinner was abroad in.
The wind blew as 't wad blawn its last;
The rattling show'rs rose on the blast;

[1] Fireside. [2] New ale.

The speedy gleams the darkness swallow'd;
Loud, deep, and lang, the thunder bellow'd:
That night, a child might understand,
The Deil had business on his hand.
  Weel mounted on his gray mare, Meg,
A better never lifted leg,
Tam skelpit[1] on thro' dub[2] and mire,
Despising wind, and rain, and fire;
Whiles holding fast his guid blue bonnet;
Whiles crooning o'er some auld Scots sonnet;
Whiles glow'ring round wi' prudent cares,
Lest bogles[3] catch him unawares;
Kirk-Alloway was drawing nigh,
Whare ghaists and houlets[4] nightly cry.—
  By this time he was cross the ford,
Whare in the snaw, the chapman smoor'd;[5]
And past the birks[6] and meikle[7] stane,
Whare drunken Charlie brak's neck-bane;
And thro' the whins,[8] and by the cairn,
Whare hunters fand the murder'd bairn;
And near the thorn, aboon the well,
Whare Mungo's mither hang'd hersel.—
Before him Doon pours all his floods;
The doubling storm roars thro' the woods;
The lightnings flash from pole to pole;
Near and more near the thunders roll:
When, glimmering thro' the groaning trees,
Kirk-Alloway seem'd in a bleeze;
Thro' ilka bore the beams were glancing;
And loud resounded mirth and dancing.—
  Inspiring bold John Barleycorn!
What dangers thou canst make us scorn!
Wi' tippenny we fear nae evil;
Wi' usquebae,[9] we'll face the devil!
The swats sae ream'd[10] in Tammie's noddle,
Fair play, he cared na deils a boddle.[11]
But Maggie stood, right sair astonish'd,
Till, by the heel and hand admonish'd,

[1]Clattered. [2]Puddle. [3]Goblins. [4]Owls. [5]Smothered. [6]Birches. [7]Big. [8]Gorse. [9]Whiskey. [10]Foamed. [11]Copper piece.

She ventured forward on the light;
And vow! Tam saw an unco sight!
Warlocks and witches in a dance;
Nae cotillion brent-new[1] frae France,
But hornpipes, jigs, strathspeys, and reels,
Put life and mettle in their heels.
A winnock-bunker[2] in the east,
There sat auld Nick, in shape o' beast;
A tousie tyke,[3] black, grim, and large,
To gie them music was his charge:
He screw'd the pipes and gart[4] them skirl,[5]
Till roof and rafters a' did dirl.—
Coffins stood round, like open presses,
That shaw'd the Dead in their last dresses;
And (by some devilish cantraip[6] sleight)
Each in its cauld hand held a light.
By which heroic Tam was able
To note upon the haly table,
A murderer's banes, in gibbet-airns;[7]
Twa span-lang, wee, unchristened bairns;
A thief, new-cutted frae a rape,[8]
Wi' his last gasp his gab[9] did gape;
Five tomahawks, wi' blude red-rusted;
Five scimitars, wi' murder crusted;
A garter which a babe had strangled;
A knife, a father's throat had mangled,
Whom his ain son of life bereft,
The grey hairs yet stack to the heft;
Wi' mair of horrible and awfu',
Which even to name wad be unlawfu'.
As Tammie glowr'd, amaz'd and curious,
The mirth and fun grew fast and furious;
The Piper loud and louder blew,
The dancers quick and quicker flew,
They reel'd, they set, they cross'd, they cleekit,[10]
Till ilka carlin swat[11] and reekit,[12]
And coost her duddies[13] to the wark,[14]
And linkit at it in her sark![15]

[1]Brand-new. [2]Window-seat. [3]Shaggy dog. [4]Made. [5]Scream. [6]Magic.
[7]Gibbet-irons. [8]Rope. [9]Mouth. [10]Clutched. [11]Sweated.
[12]Reeked, steamed. [13]Cast her clothes off. [14]Work. [15]Chemise.

Now Tam, O Tam! had they been queans,[1]
A' plump and strapping in their teens!
Their sarks, instead o' creeshie[2] flainen,
Been snaw-white seventeen-hunder linen!—
Thir[3] breeks[4] o' mine, my only pair,
That aince were plush, o' guid blue hair,
I wad hae gi'en them off my hurdies,[5]
For ae blink o' the bonnie burdies;[6]
But wither'd beldams,[7] auld and droll,
Rigwoodie hags wad spean a foal,[8]
Louping[9] an' flinging on a crummock,[10]
I wonder didna turn thy stomach.
But Tam kenn'd what was what fu' brawlie,[11]
There was ae winsome wench and waulie,[12]
That night enlisted in the core,[13]
(Lang after keen'd on Carrick shore;
For mony a beast to dead she shot,
And perish'd mony a bonny boat,
And shook baith meikle corn and bear,
And kept the country-side in fear).
Her cutty-sark,[14] o' Paisley harn,[15]
That while a lassie she had worn,
In longitude tho' sorely scanty,
It was her best, and she was vauntie.[16]—
Ah! little keen'd thy reverend grannie,
That sark she coft[17] for her wee Nannie,
Wi' twa pund Scots ('t was a' her riches),
Wad ever graced a dance o' witches!
But here my muse her wing maun cour;
Sic flights are far beyond her pow'r;
To sing how Nannie lap and flang
(A souple jade she was, and strang),
And how Tam stood, like ane bewitch'd,
And thought his very een enrich'd;
Even Satan glowr'd, and fidged[18] fu' fain,
And hotch'd[19] and blew wi' might and main:

Girls. [2]Greasy. [3]These. [4]Breeches. [5]Hips. [6]Girls. [7]Old Women.
Ancient hags that would wean (by disgust) a foal. [9]Leaping. [10]Staff.
[1]Well. [12]Goodly. [13]Corps, company. [14]Short shirt. [15]Linen.
[6]Proud. [17]Bought. [18]Fidgeted. [19]Squirmed.

Till first ae caper, syne[1] anither,
Tam tint[2] his reason a' thegither,
And roars out, "Weel done, Cutty-sark!"
And in an instant all was dark:
And scarcely had he Maggie rallied,
When out the hellish legion sallied.
As bees bizz out wi' angry fyke,[3]
When plundering herds assail their byke,[4]
As open pussie's[5] mortal foes,
When, pop! she starts before their nose;
As eager runs the market crowd,
When "Catch the thief!" resounds aloud;
So Maggie runs, the witches follow,
Wi' mony an eldritch[6] skreech and hollow.
Ah, Tam! Ah, Tam! thou'll get thy fairin![7]
In hell they'll roast thee like a herrin!
In vain thy Kate awaits thy comin!
Kate soon will be a woefu' woman!
Now, do thy speedy utmost, Meg,
And win the key-stane o' the brig;[8]
There, at them thou thy tail may toss,
A running stream they dare na cross,
But ere the key-stane she could make,
The fient[9] a tail she had to shake!
For Nannie, far before the rest,
Hard upon noble Maggie prest,
And flew at Tam wi' furious ettle;[10]
But little wist she Maggie's mettle!
Ae spring brought off her master hale,
But left behind her ain grey tail:
The carlin claught her by the rump,
And left poor Maggie scarce a stump.
Now, wha this tale o' truth shall read,
Ilk man, and mother's son, take heed:
Whene'er to Drink you are inclin'd,
Or Cutty-sarks rin in your mind,
Think, ye may buy the joys o'er dear;
Remember Tam o' Shanter's mare.

1Then. 2Lost. 3Activity. 4Hive. 5The hare's. 6Unearthly.
7Reward. 8Bridge. 9Devil. 10Aim.

To Mary in Heaven

THOU lingering star, with lessening ray,
  That lov'st to greet the early morn,
Again thou usher'st in the day
  My Mary from my soul was torn.
O Mary! dear departed shade!
  Where is thy place of blissful rest?
See'st thou thy lover lowly laid?
  Hear'st thou the groans that rend his breast?

That sacred hour can I forget,—
  Can I forget the hallowed grove,
Where by the winding Ayr we met
  To live one day of parting love?
Eternity will not efface
  Those records dear of transports past;
Thy image at our last embrace;
  Ah! little thought we 't was our last!

Ayr, gurgling, kissed his pebbled shore,
  O'erhung with wild woods, thickening green;
The fragrant birch, and hawthorn hoar,
  Twined amorous round the raptured scene;
The flowers sprang wanton to be prest,
  The birds sang love on every spray,—
Till soon, too soon, the glowing west
  Proclaimed the speed of wingèd day.

Still o'er these scenes my memory wakes,
  And fondly broods with miser care!
Time but the impression stronger makes,
  As streams their channels deeper wear.
My Mary! dear departed shade!
  Where is thy place of blissful rest?
See'st thou thy lover lowly laid?
  Hear'st thou the groans that rend his breast?

A Farewell

Go FETCH to me a pint o' wine,
An' fill it in a silver tassie,
That I may drink before I go,
A service to my bonnie lassie:
The boat rocks at the pier o' Leith,
Fu' loud the wind blaws frae the ferry,
The ship rides by the Berwick-law,
And I maun leave my bonnie Mary.

The trumpets sound, the banners fly,
The glittering spears are rankèd ready;
The shouts o' war are heard afar,
The battle closes thick and bloody;
But it's not the roar o' sea or shore
Wad make me langer wish to tarry;
Nor shout o' war that's heard afar—
It's leaving thee, my bonnie Mary.

Jean

OF A' the airts[1] the wind can blaw,
I dearly like the west;
For there the bonnie lassie lives,
The lassie I lo'e best.
There wild woods grow, and rivers row,
And monie a hill 's between;
But day and night my fancy's flight
Is ever wi' my Jean.

I see her in the dewy flowers,
I see her sweet and fair;
I hear her in the tunefu' birds,
I hear her charm the air;

[1]The points of the compass.

There's not a bonnie flower that springs
By fountain, shaw, or green;
There's not a bonnie bird that sings,
But minds me of my Jean.

John Anderson My Jo

JOHN ANDERSON my jo, John,
When we were first acquent,
Your locks were like the raven,
Your bonie brow was brent;
But now your brow is beld, John,
Your locks are like the snaw;
But blessings on your frosty pow,
John Anderson my jo.

John Anderson my jo, John,
We clamb the hill thegither;
And monie a canty day, John,
We've had wi' ane anither:
Now we maun totter down, John,
And hand in hand we'll go,
And sleep thegither at the foot,
John Anderson my jo.

O, Saw Ye Bonnie Lesley?

O, SAW ye bonnie Lesley
As she gaed o'er the border?
She's gane, like Alexander,
To spread her conquests farther.

To see her is to love her,
And love but her forever,
For nature made her what she is,
And ne'er made sic anither!

Thou art a queen, fair Lesley,
Thy subjects we, before thee;
Thou art divine, fair Lesley,
The hearts o' men adore thee.

The deil he could na scaith thee,
Or aught that wad belang thee;
He'd look into thy bonnie face,
And say, "I canna wrang thee!"

The Powers aboon will tent thee;
Misfortune sha' na steer thee;
Thou 'rt like themselves sae lovely
That ill they 'll ne'er let near thee.

Return again, fair Lesley,
Return to Caledonie!
That we may brag we hae a lass
There 's nane again sae bonnie.

The Banks o' Doon

YE BANKS and braes o' bonnie Doon
How can ye blume sae fair!
How can ye chant, ye little birds,
And I sae fu' o' care!

Thou'lt break my heart, thou bonnie bird
That sings upon the bough;
Thou minds me o' the happy days
When my fause luve was true.

Thou'lt break my heart, thou bonnie bird
That sings beside thy mate;
For sae I sat, and sae I sang,
And wist na' o' my fate.

Aft hae I roved by bonnie Doon
  To see the woodbine twine,
And ilka bird sang o' its luve;
  And sae did I o' mine.

Wi' lightsome heart I pu'd a rose,
  Frae aff its thorny tree;
And my fause luver staw the rose,
  But left the thorn wi' me.

O My Luve Is Like a Red, Red Rose

O MY luve is like a red, red rose,
  That's newly sprung in June:
O my luve is like the melodie,
  That's sweetly play'd in tune.

As fair art thou, my bonnie lass,
  So deep in luve am I;
And I will luve thee still, my dear,
  Till a' the seas gang dry.

Till a' the seas gang dry, my dear,
  And the rocks melt wi' the sun;
And I will luve thee still, my dear,
  While the sands o' life shall run.

And fare-thee-weel, my only luve!
  And fare-thee-weel a while!
And I will come again, my luve,
  Tho' it were ten thousand mile.

Lament for Culloden

THE lovely lass o' Inverness,
Nae joy nor pleasure can she see;
For e'en and morn she cries, "Alas!"
And aye the saut tear blins her e'e:

"Drumossie moor, Drumossie day,
A waefu' day it was to me!
For there I lost my father dear,
My father dear, and brethren three.

"Their winding-sheet the bluidy clay,
Their graves are growing green to see;
And by them lies the dearest lad
That ever blest a woman's e'e!
Now wae to thee, thou cruel lord,
A bluidy man I trow thou be;
For mony a heart thou hast made sair,
That ne'er did wrang to thine or thee."

Highland Mary

Ye banks and braes and streams around
  The castle o' Montgomery,
Green be your woods, and fair your flowers,
  Your waters never drumlie!
There simmer first unfauld her robes,
  And there the langest tarry;
For there I took the last fareweel
  O' my sweet Highland Mary.

How sweetly bloom'd the gay green birk,
  How rich the hawthorn's blossom,
As underneath their fragrant shade
  I clasp'd her to my bosom!
The golden hours on angel wings
  Flew o'er me and my dearie;
For dear to me as light and life
  Was my sweet Highland Mary.

Wi' monie a vow and lock'd embrace
  Our parting was fu' tender;
And, pledging aft to meet again,
  We tore oursels asunder;

But oh! fell Death's untimely frost,
  That nipt my flower sae early!
Now green's the sod, and cauld's the clay
  That wraps my Highland Mary!

O pale, pale now, those rosy lips
  I aft hae kiss'd sae fondly!
And closed for aye the sparkling glance
  That dwelt on me sae kindly;
And mouldering now in silent dust
  That heart that lo'ed me dearly!
But still within my bosom's core
  Shall live my Highland Mary.

Mary Morison

O MARY, at thy window be!
It is the wish'd, the trysted hour.
Those smiles and glances let me see,
That make the miser's treasure poor.
How blithely wad I bide the stoure,[1]
A weary slave frae sun to sun,
Could I the rich reward secure,
The lovely Mary Morison!

Yestreen when to the trembling string
The dance gaed thro' the lighted ha',
To thee my fancy took its wing,—
I sat, but neither heard nor saw:
Tho' this was fair, and that was braw,
And yon the toast of a' the town,
I sigh'd, and said amang them a',
"Ye are na Mary Morison."

O Mary, canst thou wreck his peace
Wha for thy sake wad gladly dee?
Or canst thou break that heart of his,
Whase only faut is loving thee?

[1]Strife.

If love for love thou wilt na gie,
At least be pity to me shown;
A thought ungentle canna be
The thought o' Mary Morison.

Is There for Honest Poverty?

Is THERE for honest poverty
Wha hangs his head, and a' that?
The coward slave, we pass him by;
We dare be poor for a' that.
For a' that, and a' that,
Our toil 's obscure, and a' that;
The rank is but the guinea's stamp,—
The man 's the gowd for a' that.

What though on hamely fare we dine,
Wear hoddin gray, and a' that?
Gie fools their silks, and knaves their wine,—
A man 's a man for a' that.
For a' that, and a' that,
Their tinsel show, and a' that;
The honest man, though e'er sae poor,
Is king o' men for a' that.

Ye see yon birkie ca'd a lord,
Wha struts, and stares, and a' that,—
Though hundreds worship at his word,
He 's but a coof for a' that;
For a' that, and a' that,
His riband, star, and a' that;
The man of independent mind,
He looks and laughs at a' that.

A prince can mak a belted knight,
A marquis, duke, and a' that;
But an honest man 's aboon his might,—
Guid faith, he maunna fa' that!

For a' that, and a' that;
  Their dignities, and a' that,
The pith o' sense, and pride o' worth,
  Are higher ranks than a' that.

Then let us pray that come it may,—
  As come it will for a' that,—
That sense and worth, o'er a' the earth,
  May bear the gree, and a' that.
For a' that, and a' that,
  It 's coming yet, for a' that,—
When man to man, the warld o'er,
  Shall brothers be for a' that!

Bannockburn

Scots, wha hae wi' Wallace bled,
Scots, wham Bruce has aften led,
Welcome to your gory bed,
          Or to victorie!

Now's the day, and now's the hour;
See the front o' battle lour;
See approach proud Edward's power—
          Chains and slaverie!

Wha will be a traitor knave?
Wha can fill a coward's grave?
Wha sae base as be a slave?
          Let him turn and flee!

Wha, for Scotland's King and Law,
Freedom's sword will strongly draw,
Free-man stand, or Free-man fa',
          Let him follow me!

By Oppression's woes and pains!
By your sons in servile chains!
We will drain our dearest veins,
But they shall be free!

Lay the proud Usurpers low!
Tyrants fall in every foe!
Liberty's in every blow!—
Let us do or die!

SAMUEL ROGERS

(1762–1855)

A Wish

MINE be a cot beside the hill;
A beehive's hum shall soothe my ear;
A willowy brook that turns a mill,
With many a fall shall linger near.

The swallow, oft, beneath my thatch
Shall twitter from her clay-built nest;
Oft shall the pilgrim lift the latch,
And share my meal, a welcome guest.

Around my ivied porch shall spring
Each fragrant flower that drinks the dew,
And Lucy, at her wheel, shall sing
In russet gown and apron blue.

The village-church among the trees,
Where first our marriage-vows were given,
With merry peals shall swell the breeze
And point with taper spire to heaven.

MARY LAMB

(1764–1847)

In Memoriam

A CHILD'S a plaything for an hour;
  Its pretty tricks we try
For that or for a longer space,—
  Then tire, and lay it by.

But I knew one that to itself
  All seasons could control;
That would have mock'd the sense of pain
  Out of a grievèd soul.

Thou straggler into loving arms,
  Young climber-up of knees,
When I forget thy thousand ways
  Then life and all shall cease!

CAROLINA, LADY NAIRNE

(1766–1845)

The Land o' the Leal

I'M WEARING awa', Jean,
Like snaw when it 's thaw, Jean;
I'm wearing awa'
  To the land o' the leal.
There's nae sorrow there, Jean,
There's neither cauld nor care, Jean,
The day is aye fair
  In the land o' the leal.

Ye were aye leal and true, Jean;
Your task 's ended noo, Jean,
And I 'll welcome you
  To the land o' the leal.
Our bonnie bairn 's there, Jean,
She was baith guid and fair, Jean:
O, we grudged her right sair
  To the land o' the leal!

Then dry that tearfu' e'e, Jean,
My soul langs to be free, Jean,
And angels wait on me
  To the land o' the leal!
Now fare ye weel, my ain Jean,
This warld's care is vain, Jean;
We 'll meet and aye be fain
  In the land o' the leal.

JAMES HOGG

(1770–1835)

Kilmeny

BONNY Kilmeny gaed up the glen;
But it wasna to meet Duneira's men,
Nor the rosy monk of the isle to see,
For Kilmeny was pure as pure could be.
It was only to hear the yorlin sing,
And pu' the cress-flower round the spring,—
The scarlet hypp, and the hindberrye,
And the nut that hung frae the hazel-tree;
For Kilmeny was pure as pure could be.
But lang may her minny look o'er the wa',
And lang may she seek i' the green-wood shaw;
Lang the laird of Duneira blame,
And lang, lang greet or Kilmeny come hame.

When many a day had come and fled,
When grief grew calm, and hope was dead,
When mass for Kilmeny's soul had been sung,
When the bedesman had prayed, and the dead-bell rung;
Late, late in a gloamin, when all was still,
When the fringe was red on the westlin hill,
The wood was sear, the moon i' the wane,
The reek o' the cot hung over the plain,—
Like a little wee cloud in the world its lane;
When the ingle lowed with an eiry leme,
Late, late in the gloamin Kilmeny came hame!

"Kilmeny, Kilmeny, where have you been?
Lang hae we sought baith holt and den,—
By linn, by ford, and green-wood tree;
Yet you are halesome and fair to see.
Where got you that joup o' the lily sheen?
That bonny snood of the birk sae green?
And these roses, the fairest that ever was seen?
Kilmeny, Kilmeny, where have you been?"

Kilmeny looked up with a lovely grace,
But nae smile was seen on Kilmeny's face;
As still was her look, and as still was her ee,
As the stillness that lay on the emerant lea,
Or the mist that sleeps on a waveless sea.
For Kilmeny had been she knew not where,
And Kilmeny had seen what she could not declare.
Kilmeny had been where the cock never crew,
Where the rain never fell, and the wind never blew;
But it seemed as the harp of the sky had rung,
And the airs of heaven played round her tongue,
When she spake of the lovely forms she had seen,
And a land where sin had never been,—
A land of love, and a land of light,
Withouten sun or moon or night;
Where the river swa'd a living stream,
And the light a pure celestial beam:
The land of vision it would seem,
A still, an everlasting dream.

In yon green-wood there is a waik,
And in that waik there is a wene,
And in that wene there is a maike,
That neither has flesh, blood, nor bane;
And down in yon green-wood he walks his lane.
In that green wene Kilmeny lay,
Her bosom happed wi' the flowerets gay;
But the air was soft, and the silence deep,
And bonny Kilmeny fell sound asleep;
She kend nae mair, nor opened her ee,
Till waked by the hymns of a far countrye.

She awaked on a couch of the silk sae slim,
All striped wi' the bars of the rainbow's rim;
And lovely beings around were rife,
Who erst had travelled mortal life;
And aye they smiled, and 'gan to speer:
"What spirit has brought this mortal here?"

"Lang have I journeyed the world wide,"
A meek and reverend fere replied;
"Baith night and day I have watched the fair
Eident a thousand years and mair.
Yes, I have watched o'er ilk degree,
Wherever blooms femenitye;
But sinless virgin, free of stain,
In mind and body, fand I nane.
Never, since the banquet of time,
Found I a virgin in her prime,
Till late this bonny maiden I saw,
As spotless as the morning snaw.
Full twenty years she has lived as free
As the spirits that sojourn in this countrye.
I have brought her away frae the snares of men,
That sin or death she may never ken."

They clasped her waist and her hands sae fair;
They kissed her cheek, and they kemed her hair;
And round came many a blooming fere,
Saying, "Bonny Kilmeny, ye 're welcome here;

Women are freed of the littand scorn;
O, blest be the day Kilmeny was born!
Now shall the land of the spirits see,
Now shall it ken, what a woman may be!
Many a lang year in sorrow and pain,
Many a lang year through the world we 've gane,
Commissioned to watch fair womankind,
For it 's they who nurice the immortal mind.
We have watched their steps as the dawning shone,
And deep in the greenwood walks alone;
By lily bower and silken bed
The viewless tears have o'er them shed;
Have soothed their ardent minds to sleep,
Or left the couch of love to weep.
We have seen! we have seen! but the time must come,
And the angels will weep at the day of doom!

"O, would the fairest of mortal kind
Aye keep the holy truths in mind,
That kindred spirits their motions see,
Who watch their ways with anxious e'e,
And grieve for the guilt of humanitye!
O, sweet to Heaven the maiden's prayer,
And the sigh that heaves a bosom sae fair!
And dear to Heaven the words of truth
And the praise of virtue frae beauty's mouth!
And dear to the viewless forms of air
The minds that kythe as the body fair!

"O bonny Kilmeny! free frae stain,
If ever you seek the world again,—
That world of sin, of sorrow and fear,—
O, tell of the joys that are waiting here;
And tell of the signs you shall shortly see;
Of the times that are now, and the times that shall be."

They lifted Kilmeny, they led her away,
And she walked in the light of a sunless day;
The sky was a dome of crystal bright,
The fountain of vision, and fountain of light;

The emerald fields were of dazzling glow,
And the flowers of everlasting blow.
Then deep in the stream her body they laid,
That her youth and beauty never might fade;
And they smiled on heaven, when they saw her lie
   In the stream of life that wandered by.

And she heard a song,—she heard it sung,
She kend not where; but sae sweetly it rung,
It fell on her ear like a dream of the morn,—
"O, blest be the day Kilmeny was born!
Now shall the land of the spirits see,
Now shall it ken, what a woman may be!
The sun that shines on the world sae bright,
A borrowed gleid frae the fountain of light;
And the moon that sleeks the sky sae dun,
Like a gouden bow, or a beamless sun,
Shall wear away, and be seen nae mair;
And the angels shall miss them, travelling the air.
But lang, lang after baith night and day,
When the sun and the world have edyed away,
When the sinner has gane to his waesome doom,
Kilmeny shall smile in eternal bloom!"

   They bore her away, she wist not how,
For she felt not arm nor rest below;
But so swift they wained her through the light,
'T was like the motion of sound or sight;
They seemed to split the gales of air,
And yet nor gale nor breeze was there.
Unnumbered groves below them grew;
They came, they past, and backward flew,
Like floods of blossoms gliding on,
In moment seen, in moment gone.
O, never vales to mortal view
Appeared like those o'er which they flew,
That land to human spirits given,
The lowermost vales of the storied heaven;
From whence they can view the world below,
And heaven's blue gates with sapphires glow,—
More glory yet unmeet to know.

They bore her far to a mountain green,
To see what mortal never had seen;
And they seated her high on a purple sward,
And bade her heed what she saw and heard,
And note the changes the spirits wrought;
For now she lived in the land of thought.—
She looked, and she saw nor sun nor skies,
But a crystal dome of a thousand dyes;
She looked, and she saw nae land aright,
But an endless whirl of glory and light;
And radiant beings went and came,
Far swifter than wind or the linkèd flame;
She hid her een frae the dazzling view;
She looked again, and the scene was new.

She saw a sun on a summer sky,
And clouds of amber sailing by;
A lovely land beneath her lay,
And that land had glens and mountains gray;
And that land had valleys and hoary piles,
And marlèd seas, and a thousand isles;
Its fields were speckled, its forests green,
And its lakes were all of the dazzling sheen,
Like magic mirrors, where slumbering lay
The sun and the sky and the cloudlet gray,
Which heaved and trembled, and gently swung;
On every shore they seemed to be hung;
For there they were seen on their downward plain
A thousand times and a thousand again;
In winding lake and placid firth,—
Little peaceful heavens in the bosom of earth.

Kilmeny sighed and seemed to grieve,
For she found her heart to that land did cleave;
She saw the corn wave on the vale;
She saw the deer run down the dale;
She saw the plaid and the broad claymore,
And the brows that the badge of freedom bore;
And she thought she had seen the land before.

She saw a lady sit on a throne,
The fairest that ever the sun shone on:
A lion licked her hand of milk,
And she held him in a leish of silk;
And a leifu' maiden stood at her knee,
With a silver wand and melting ee;
Her sovereign shield till love stole in,
And poisoned all the fount within.

Then a gruff untoward bedesman came,
And hundit the lion on his dame;
And the guardian maid wi' the dauntless ee,
She dropped a tear, and left her knee;
And she saw till the queen frae the lion fled,
Till the bonniest flower of the world lay dead;
A coffin was set on a distant plain,
And she saw the red blood fall like rain:
Then bonny Kilmeny's heart grew sair,
And she turned away, and could look nae mair.

Then the gruff grim carle girnèd amain,
And they trampled him down, but he rose again;
And he baited the lion to deeds of weir,
Till he lapped the blood to the kingdom dear;
And weening his head was danger-preef,
When crowned with the rose and clover leaf,
He gowled at the carle, and chased him away
To feed wi' the deer on the mountain gray.
He gowled at the carle, and he gecked at Heaven;
But his mark was set, and his arles given.
Kilmeny a while her een withdrew;
She looked again, and the scene was new.

She saw below her fair unfurled
One half of all the glowing world,
Where oceans rolled, and rivers ran,
To bound the aims of sinful man.
She saw a people, fierce and fell,
Burst frae their bounds like fiends of hell;
There lilies grew, and the eagle flew,
And she herked on her ravening crew,

Till the cities and towers were wrapt in a blaze,
And the thunder it roared o'er the lands and the seas.
The widows they wailed, and the red blood ran,
And she threatened an end to the race of man:
She never lened, nor stood in awe,
Till caught by the lion's deadly paw.
Oh! then the eagle swinked for life,
And brainzelled up a mortal strife;
But flew she north, or flew she south,
She met wi' the gowl of the lion's mouth.

With a mooted wing and waefu' maen,
The eagle sought her eiry again;
But lang may she cower in her bloody nest,
And lang, lang sleek her wounded breast,
Before she sey another flight,
To play wi' the norland lion's might.

But to sing the sights Kilmeny saw,
So far surpassing nature's law,
The singer's voice wad sink away,
And the string of his harp wad cease to play.
But she saw till the sorrows of man were by,
And all was love and harmony;—
Till the stars of heaven fell calmly away,
Like the flakes of snaw on a winter's day.

Then Kilmeny begged again to see
The friends she had left in her own countrye,
To tell the place where she had been,
And the glories that lay in the land unseen;
To warn the living maidens fair,
The loved of heaven, the spirits' care,
That all whose minds unmeled remain
Shall bloom in beauty when time is gane.

With distant music, soft and deep,
They lulled Kilmeny sound asleep;
And when she awakened, she lay her lane,
All happed with flowers in the green-wood wene.

When seven long years had come and fled;
When grief was calm, and hope was dead;
When scarce was remembered Kilmeny's name,
Late, late in a gloamin, Kilmeny came hame!
And O, her beauty was fair to see,
But still and steadfast was her ee!
Such beauty bard may never declare,
For there was no pride nor passion there;
And the soft desire of maidens' een
In that mild face could never be seen.
Her seymar was the lily flower,
And her cheek the moss-rose in the shower;
And her voice like the distant melodye
That floats along the twilight sea.
But she loved to raike the lanely glen,
And keeped afar frae the haunts of men;
Her holy hymns unheard to sing,
To suck the flowers and drink the spring.
But wherever her peaceful form appeared,
The wild beasts of the hills were cheered;
The wolf played blythely round the field;
The lordly byson lowed and kneeled;
The dun deer wooed with manner bland,
And cowered aneath her lily hand.
And when at even the woodlands rung,
When hymns of other worlds she sung
In ecstasy of sweet devotion,
O, then the glen was all in motion!
The wild beasts of the forest came,
Broke from their bughts and faulds the tame,
And goved around, charmed and amazed;
Even the dull cattle crooned, and gazed,
And murmured, and looked with anxious pain
For something the mystery to explain.
The buzzard came with the throstle-cock,
The corby left her houf in the rock;
The blackbird alang wi' the eagle flew;
The hind came tripping o'er the dew;
The wolf and the kid their raike began;
And the tod, and the lamb, and the leveret ran;
The hawk and the hern attour them hung,

And the merl and the mavis forhooyed their young;
And all in a peaceful ring were hurled:
It was like an eve in a sinless world!

When a month and day had come and gane,
Kilmeny sought the green-wood wene;
There laid her down on the leaves sae green,
And Kilmeny on earth was never mair seen.
But O the words that fell from her mouth
Were words of wonder, and words of truth!
But all the land were in fear and dread,
For they kend na whether she was living or dead.
It wasna her hame, and she couldna remain;
She left this world of sorrow and pain,
And returned to the land of thought again.

The Skylark

Bird of the wilderness,
Blithesome and cumberless,
Sweet be thy matin o'er moorland and lea!
Emblem of happiness,
Blest is thy dwelling-place,—
O, to abide in the desert with thee!
Wild is thy lay and loud
Far in the downy cloud,
Love gives it energy, love gave it birth.
Where, on thy dewy wing,
Where art thou journeying?
Thy lay is in heaven, thy love is on earth.
O'er fell and fountain sheen,
O'er moor and mountain green,
O'er the red streamer that heralds the day,
Over the cloudlet dim,
Over the rainbow's rim,
Musical cherub, soar, singing, away!
Then, when the gloaming comes,
Low in the heather blooms

Sweet will thy welcome and bed of love be!
Emblem of happiness,
Blest is thy dwelling-place,—
O, to abide in the desert with thee!

WILLIAM WORDSWORTH

(1770–1850)

Tintern Abbey

FIVE years have past; five summers, with the length
Of five long winters! and again I hear
These waters,[1] rolling from their mountain-springs
With a soft inland murmur.—Once again
Do I behold these steep and lofty cliffs,
That on a wild, secluded scene impress
Thoughts of more deep seclusion, and connect
The landscape with the quiet of the sky.
The day is come when I again repose
Here, under this dark sycamore, and view
These plots of cottage-ground, these orchard-tufts,
Which at this season, with their unripe fruits,
Are clad in one green hue, and lose themselves
Mid groves and copses. Once again I see
These hedge-rows, hardly hedge-rows, little lines
Of sportive wood run wild: these pastoral farms,
Green to the very door; and wreaths of smoke
Sent up, in silence, from among the trees!
With some uncertain notice, as might seem
Of vagrant dwellers in the houseless woods,
Or of some hermit's cave, where by his fire
The hermit sits alone.
These beauteous forms,
Through a long absence, have not been to me

[1]The River Wye.

As is a landscape to a blind man's eye;
But oft, in lonely rooms, and mid the din
Of towns and cities, I have owed to them,
In hours of weariness, sensations sweet,
Felt in the blood, and felt along the heart;
And passing even into my purer mind,
With tranquil restoration:—feelings too
Of unremembered pleasure: such, perhaps,
As have no slight or trivial influence
On that best portion of a good man's life,
His little, nameless, unremembered acts
Of kindness and of love. Nor less, I trust,
To them I may have owed another gift,
Of aspect more sublime; that blessèd mood,
In which the burden of the mystery,
In which the heavy and the weary weight
Of all this unintelligible world,
Is lightened,—that serene and blessèd mood,
In which the affections gently lead us on,
Until, the breath of this corporeal frame
And even the motion of our human blood
Almost suspended, we are laid asleep
In body, and become a living soul:
While with an eye made quiet by the power
Of harmony, and the deep power of joy,
We see into the life of things.
If this
Be but a vain belief, yet, O, how oft—
In darkness and amid the many shapes
Of joyless daylight; when the fretful stir
Unprofitable, and the fever of the world,
Have hung upon the beatings of my heart—
How oft, in spirit, have I turned to thee,
O sylvan Wye! thou wanderer through the woods,
How often has my spirit turned to thee!

And now, with gleams of half-extinguished thought,
With many recognitions dim and faint,
And somewhat of a sad perplexity,
The picture of the mind revives again:
While here I stand, not only with the sense

Of present pleasure, but with pleasing thoughts
That in this moment there is life and food
For future years. And so I dare to hope,
Though changed, no doubt, from what I was when first
I came among these hills; when like a roe
I bounded o'er the mountains, by the sides
Of the deep rivers, and the lonely streams,
Wherever nature led: more like a man
Flying from something that he dreads, than one
Who sought the thing he loved. For nature then
(The coarser pleasures of my boyish days
And their glad animal movements all gone by)
To me was all in all.—I cannot paint
What then I was. The sounding cataract
Haunted me like a passion: the tall rock,
The mountain, and the deep and gloomy wood,
Their colors and their forms, were then to me
An appetite; a feeling and a love,
That had no need of a remoter charm
By thoughts supplied, nor any interest
Unborrowed from the eye.—That time is past,
And all its aching joys are now no more,
And all its dizzy raptures. Not for this
Faint I, nor mourn nor murmur; other gifts
Have followed; for such loss, I would believe,
Abundant recompense. For I have learned
To look on nature, not as in the hour
Of thoughtless youth; but hearing oftentimes
The still, sad music of humanity,
Nor harsh nor grating, though of ample power
To chasten and subdue. And I have felt
A presence that disturbs me with the joy
Of elevated thoughts; a sense sublime
Of something far more deeply interfused,
Whose dwelling is the light of setting suns,
And the round ocean, and the living air,
And the blue sky, and in the mind of man:
A motion and a spirit, that impels
All thinking things, all objects of all thought,
And rolls through all things. Therefore am I still
A lover of the meadows and the woods,

And mountains; and of all that we behold
From this green earth; of all the mighty world
Of eye, and ear,—both what they half create,
And what perceive; well pleased to recognize
In nature and the language of the sense,
The anchor of my purest thoughts, the nurse,
The guide, the guardian of my heart, and soul
Of all my moral being.
Nor perchance,
If I were not thus taught, should I the more
Suffer my genial spirits to decay:
For thou art with me here upon the banks
Of this fair river; thou my dearest friend,
My dear, dear friend; and in thy voice I catch
The language of my former heart, and read
My former pleasures in the shooting lights
Of thy wild eyes. O, yet a little while
May I behold in thee what I was once,
My dear, dear sister! and this prayer I make,
Knowing that Nature never did betray
The heart that loved her; 't is her privilege,
Through all the years of this our life, to lead
From joy to joy: for she can so inform
The mind that is within us, so impress
With quietness and beauty, and so feed
With lofty thoughts, that neither evil tongues,
Rash judgments, nor the sneers of selfish men,
Nor greetings where no kindness is, nor all
The dreary intercourse of daily life,
Shall e'er prevail against us, or disturb
Our cheerful faith, that all which we behold
Is full of blessings. Therefore let the moon
Shine on thee in thy solitary walk;
And let the misty mountain-winds be free
To blow against thee: and, in after years,
When these wild ecstasies shall be matured
Into a sober pleasure; when thy mind
Shall be a mansion for all lovely forms,
Thy memory be as a dwelling-place
For all sweet sounds and harmonies; O, then,
If solitude or fear or pain or grief

Should be thy portion, with what healing thoughts
Of tender joy wilt thou remember me,
And these my exhortations! Nor, perchance,—
If I should be where I no more can hear
Thy voice, nor catch from thy wild eyes these gleams
Of past existence,—wilt thou then forget
That on the banks of this delightful stream
We stood together; and that I, so long
A worshipper of Nature, hither came
Unwearied in that service: rather say
With warmer love,—O, with far deeper zeal
Of holier love. Nor wilt thou then forget
That after many wanderings, many years
Of absence, these steep woods and lofty cliffs,
And this green pastoral landscape, were to me
More dear, both for themselves and for thy sake!

She Dwelt Among the Untrodden Ways

SHE dwelt among the untrodden ways
Beside the springs of Dove,
A maid whom there were none to praise
And very few to love:

A violet by a mossy stone
Half hidden from the eye!
—Fair as a star, when only one
Is shining in the sky.

She lived unknown, and few could know
When Lucy ceased to be;
But she is in her grave, and, oh,
The difference to me!

Three Years She Grew

THREE years she grew in sun and shower;
Then Nature said, "A lovelier flower

On earth was never sown:
This child I to myself will take;
She shall be mine, and I will make
A lady of my own.

"Myself will to my darling be
Both law and impulse; and with me
The girl, in rock and plain,
In earth and heaven, in glade and bower,
Shall feel an overseeing power
To kindle or restrain.

"She shall be sportive as the fawn
That wild with glee across the lawn
Or up the mountain springs;
And hers shall be the breathing balm,
And hers the silence and the calm,
Of mute insensate things.

"The floating clouds their state shall lend
To her; for her the willow bend;
Nor shall she fail to see
E'en in the motions of the storm
Grace that shall mould the maiden's form
By silent sympathy.

"The stars of midnight shall be dear
To her; and she shall lean her ear
In many a secret place
Where rivulets dance their wayward round,
And beauty born of murmuring sound
Shall pass into her face.

"And vital feelings of delight
Shall rear her form to stately height,
Her virgin bosom swell;
Such thoughts to Lucy I will give
While she and I together live
Here in this happy dell."

'Thus Nature spake. The work was done,
How soon my Lucy's race was run!
She died, and left to me
This heath, this calm and quiet scene;
The memory of what has been,
And nevermore will be.

My Heart Leaps Up

My heart leaps up when I behold
A rainbow in the sky;
So was it when my life began,
So is it now I am a man,
So be it when I shall grow old,
Or let me die!
The Child is father of the Man;
And I could wish my days to be
Bound each to each by natural piety.

The Solitary Reaper

Behold her, single in the field,
Yon solitary Highland Lass!
Reaping and singing by herself;
Stop here, or gently pass!
Alone she cuts and binds the grain,
And sings a melancholy strain;
O listen! for the vale profound
Is overflowing with the sound.

No nightingale did ever chaunt
More welcome notes to weary bands
Of travelers in some shady haunt,
Among Arabian sands;

A voice so thrilling ne'er was heard,
In springtime from the cuckoo bird,
Breaking the silence of the seas
Among the farthest Hebrides.

Will no one tell me what she sings?—
Perhaps the plaintive numbers flow
For old, unhappy, far-off things,
And battles long ago:
Or is it some more humble lay,
Familiar matter of to-day?
Some natural sorrow, loss or pain,
That has been, and may be again?

Whate'er the theme, the maiden sang
As if her song could have no ending;
I saw her singing at her work,
And o'er the sickle bending;—
I listened, motionless and still;
And, as I mounted up the hill,
The music in my heart I bore,
Long after it was heard no more.

She Was a Phantom of Delight

SHE was a phantom of delight
When first she gleamed upon my sight;
A lovely apparition, sent
To be a moment's ornament;
Her eyes as stars of twilight fair;
Like Twilight's, too, her dusky hair;
But all things else about her drawn
From May-time and the cheerful dawn;
A dancing shape, an image gay,
To haunt, to startle, and waylay.

I saw her upon nearer view,
A spirit, yet a woman too!
Her household motions light and free,
And steps of virgin-liberty;
A countenance in which did meet
Sweet records, promises as sweet;
A creature not too bright or good
For human nature's daily food,
For transient sorrows, simple wiles,
Praise, blame, love, kisses, tears, and smiles.

And now I see with eye serene
The very pulse of the machine;
A being breathing thoughtful breath,
A traveller between life and death:
The reason firm, the temperate will,
Endurance, foresight, strength, and skill;
A perfect woman, nobly planned
To warn, to comfort, and command;
And yet a spirit still, and bright
With something of an angel-light.

Daffodils

I WANDERED lonely as a cloud
   That floats on high o'er vales and hills,
When all at once I saw a crowd,—
   A host of golden daffodils
Beside the lake, beneath the trees,
Fluttering and dancing in the breeze.

Continuous as the stars that shine
   And twinkle on the Milky Way,
They stretched in never-ending line
   Along the margin of a bay:
Ten thousand saw I, at a glance,
Tossing their heads in sprightly dance.

The waves beside them danced, but they
  Outdid the sparkling waves in glee;
A poet could not but be gay
  In such a jocund company;
I gazed—and gazed—but little thought
What wealth the show to me had brought.

For oft, when on my couch I lie,
  In vacant or in pensive mood,
They flash upon that inward eye
  Which is the bliss of solitude;
And then my heart with pleasure fills,
And dances with the daffodils.

Ode to Duty

Stern Daughter of the Voice of God!
O Duty! if that name thou love
Who art a light to guide, a rod
To check the erring, and reprove;
Thou, who art victory and law
When empty terrors overawe,
From vain temptations dost set free,
And calm'st the weary strife of frail humanity!

There are who ask not if thine eye
Be on them; who, in love and truth
Where no misgiving is, rely
Upon the genial sense of youth:
Glad hearts! without reproach or blot,
Who do thy work, and know it not:
Oh! if through confidence misplaced
They fail, thy saving arms, dread Power! around them cast.

Serene will be our days and bright
And happy will our nature be,
When love is an unerring light,
And joy its own security.

And they a blissful course may hold
Ev'n now, who, not unwisely bold,
Live in the spirit of this creed;
Yet seek thy firm support, according to their need.

I, loving freedom, and untried,
No sport of every random gust,
Yet being to myself a guide,
Too blindly have reposed my trust:
And oft, when in my heart was heard
Thy timely mandate, I deferr'd
The task, in smoother walks to stray;
But thee I now would serve more strictly, if I may.

Through no disturbance of my soul
Or strong compunction in me wrought,
I supplicate for thy control,
But in the quietness of thought:
Me this uncharter'd freedom tires;
I feel the weight of chance desires:
My hopes no more must change their name;
I long for a repose that ever is the same.

Stern Lawgiver! yet thou dost wear
The Godhead's most benignant grace;
Nor know we anything so fair
As is the smile upon thy face:
Flowers laugh before thee on their beds,
And fragrance in thy footing treads;
Thou dost preserve the stars from wrong;
And the most ancient heavens, through thee, are fresh and strong.

To humbler functions, awful Power!
I call thee: I myself commend
Unto thy guidance from this hour;
Oh let my weakness have an end!
Give unto me, made lowly wise,
The spirit of self-sacrifice;
The confidence of reason give;
And in the light of truth thy bondman let me live.

Ode on Intimations of Immortality

FROM RECOLLECTIONS OF EARLY CHILDHOOD

THERE was a time when meadow, grove, and stream,
The earth, and every common sight,
To me did seem
Appareled in celestial light,
The glory and the freshness of a dream.
It is not now as it hath been of yore;—
Turn wheresoe'er I may,
By night or day,
The things which I have seen I now can see no more.

The Rainbow comes and goes,
And lovely is the Rose,
The Moon doth with delight
Look round her when the heavens are bare,
Waters on a starry night
Are beautiful and fair;
The sunshine is a glorious birth;
But yet I know, where'er I go,
That there hath passed away a glory from the earth.

Now, while the birds thus sing a joyous song,
And while the young lambs bound
As to the tabor's sound,
To me alone there came a thought of grief:
A timely utterance gave that thought relief,
And I again am strong:
The cataracts blow their trumpets from the steep;
No more shall grief of mine the season wrong;
I hear the Echoes through the mountains throng,
The Winds come to me from the fields of sleep,
And all the earth is gay;
Land and sea
Give themselves up to jollity,

And with the heart of May
Doth every Beast keep holiday;—
Thou Child of Joy,
Shout round me, let me hear thy shouts, thou happy Shepherd-boy!

Ye blessèd Creatures, I have heard the call
Ye to each other make; I see
The heavens laugh with you in your jubilee;
My heart is at your festival,
My head hath its coronal,
The fullness of your bliss, I feel—I feel it all.
Oh evil day! if I were sullen
While Earth herself is adorning,
This sweet May-morning,
And the Children are culling
On every side,
In a thousand valleys far and wide,
Fresh flowers; while the sun shines warm,
And the Babe leaps up on his Mother's arm:—
I hear, I hear, with joy I hear!
—But there's a Tree, of many, one,
A single Field which I have looked upon,
Both of them speak of something that is gone:
The Pansy at my feet
Doth the same tale repeat:
Whither is fled the visionary gleam?
Where is it now, the glory and the dream?

Our birth is but a sleep and a forgetting:
The Soul that rises with us, our life's Star,
Hath had elsewhere its setting,
And cometh from afar:
Not in entire forgetfulness,
And not in utter nakedness,
But trailing clouds of glory do we come
From God, who is our home:
Heaven lies about us in our infancy!
Shades of the prison-house begin to close
Upon the growing Boy,
But He beholds the light, and whence it flows,
He sees it in his joy;

The Youth, who daily farther from the east
   Must travel, still is Nature's Priest,
   And by the vision splendid
   Is on his way attended;
At length the Man perceives it die away,
And fade into the light of common day.

Earth fills her lap with pleasures of her own;
Yearnings she hath in her own natural kind,
And, even with something of a Mother's mind,
   And no unworthy aim,
   The homely Nurse doth all she can
To make her Foster-child, her Inmate Man,
   Forget the glories he hath known,
And that imperial palace whence he came.

Behold the Child among his new-born blisses,
A six years' Darling of a pigmy size!
See, where 'mid work of his own hand he lies,
Fretted by sallies of his mother's kisses,
With light upon him from his father's eyes!
See, at his feet, some little plan or chart,
Some fragment from his dream of human life,
Shaped by himself with newly-learnéd art;
   A wedding or a festival,
   A mourning or a funeral;
         And this hath now his heart,
   And unto this he frames his song:
         Then will he fit his tongue
To dialogues of business, love, or strife;
   But it will not be long
   Ere this be thrown aside,
   And with new joy and pride
The little Actor cons another part;
Filling from time to time his "humorous stage"
With all the Persons, down to palsied Age,
That Life brings with her in her equipage;
   As if his whole vocation
   Were endless imitation.

Thou, whose exterior semblance doth belie
  Thy Soul's immensity;
Thou best Philosopher, who yet dost keep
Thy heritage, thou Eye among the blind,
That, deaf and silent, read'st the eternal deep,
Haunted for ever by the eternal mind,—
  Mighty Prophet! Seer bless'd!
  On whom those truths do rest,
Which we are toiling all our lives to find,
In darkness lost, the darkness of the grave;
Thou, over whom thy Immortality
Broods like the Day, a Master o'er a Slave,
A Presence which is not to be put by;
Thou little Child, yet glorious in the might
Of heaven-born freedom on thy being's height,
Why with such earnest pains dost thou provoke
The years to bring the inevitable yoke,
Thus blindly with thy blessedness at strife?
Full soon thy Soul shall have her earthly freight,
And custom lie upon thee with a weight,
Heavy as frost, and deep almost as life!

  O joy! that in our embers
  Is something that doth live,
  That nature yet remembers
  What was so fugitive!
The thought of our past years in me doth breed
Perpetual benediction: not indeed
For that which is most worthy to be bless'd—
Delight and liberty, the simple creed
Of Childhood, whether busy or at rest,
With new-fledged hope still fluttering in his breast:—
    Not for these I raise
    The song of thanks and praise;
  But for those obstinate questionings
  Of sense and outward things,
  Fallings from us, vanishings;
  Blank misgivings of a Creature
Moving about in worlds not realized,
High instincts before which our mortal Nature
Did tremble like a guilty Thing surprised:

But for those first affections,
Those shadowy recollections,
Which, be they what they may,
Are yet the fountain light of all our day,
Are yet a master light of all our seeing;
Uphold us, cherish, and have power to make
Our noisy years seem moments in the being
Of the eternal Silence: truths that wake,
To perish never;
Which neither listlessness, nor mad endeavor,
Nor Man nor Boy,
Nor all that is at enmity with joy,
Can utterly abolish or destroy!
Hence in a season of calm weather
Though inland far we be,
Our Souls have sight of that immortal sea
Which brought us hither,
Can in a moment travel thither,
And see the Children sport upon the shore,
And hear the mighty waters rolling evermore.

Then sing, ye Birds, sing, sing a joyous song!
And let the young Lambs bound
As to the tabor's sound!
We in thought will join your throng,
Ye that pipe and ye that play,
Ye that through your hearts to-day
Feel the gladness of the May!
What though the radiance which was once so bright
Be now for ever taken from my sight,
Though nothing can bring back the hour
Of splendor in the grass, of glory in the flower;
We will grieve not, rather find
Strength in what remains behind;
In the primal sympathy
Which having been must ever be;
In the soothing thoughts that spring
Out of human suffering;
In the faith that looks through death,
In years that bring the philosophic mind.

And O, ye Fountains, Meadows, Hills, and Groves,
Forebode not any severing of our loves!
Yet in my heart of hearts I feel your might;
I only have relinquished one delight
To live beneath your more habitual sway.
I love the Brooks which down their channels fret,
Even more than when I tripped lightly as they;
The innocent brightness of a new-born Day
        Is lovely yet;
The Clouds that gather round the setting sun
Do take a sober coloring from an eye
That hath kept watch o'er man's mortality;
Another race hath been, and other palms are won.
Thanks to the human heart by which we live,
Thanks to its tenderness, its joys, and fears,
To me the meanest flower that blows can give
Thoughts that do often lie too deep for tears.

Composed Upon Westminster Bridge

September 3, 1802

EARTH has not anything to show more fair:
Dull would he be of soul who could pass by
A sight so touching in its majesty:
This City now doth, like a garment, wear
The beauty of the morning; silent, bare,
Ships, towers, domes, theatres, and temples lie
Open unto the fields, and to the sky;
All bright and glittering in the smokeless air.
Never did sun more beautifully steep
In his first splendor valley, rock, or hill;
Ne'er saw I, never felt, a calm so deep!
The river glideth at his own sweet will:
Dear God! the very houses seem asleep;
And all that mighty heart is lying still!

It Is a Beauteous Evening

It is a beauteous evening, calm and free;
The holy time is quiet as a Nun
Breathless with adoration; the broad sun
Is sinking down in its tranquillity;
The gentleness of heaven is on the sea:
Listen! the mighty Being is awake,
And doth with his eternal motion make
A sound like thunder—everlastingly.
Dear Child! dear Girl! that walkest with me here,
If thou appear'st untouched by solemn thought,
Thy nature is not therefore less divine:
Thou liest in Abraham's bosom all the year;
And worshipp'st at the Temple's inner shrine,
God being with thee when we know it not.

On the Extinction of the Venetian Republic

Once did She hold the gorgeous East in fee
And was the safeguard of the West; the worth
Of Venice did not fall below her birth,
Venice, the eldest child of Liberty.
She was a maiden city, bright and free:
No guile seduced, no force could violate;
And when she took unto herself a mate,
She must espouse the everlasting Sea.
And what if she had seen those glories fade,
Those titles vanish, and that strength decay,—
Yet shall some tribute of regret be paid
When her long life hath reach'd its final day:
Men are we, and must grieve when even the shade
Of that which once was great is pass'd away.

Milton! Thou Shouldst Be Living at This Hour

MILTON! thou shouldst be living at this hour:
England hath need of thee: she is a fen
Of stagnant waters: altar, sword, and pen,
Fireside, the heroic wealth of hall and bower,
Have forfeited their ancient English dower
Of inward happiness. We are selfish men;
Oh! raise us up, return to us again;
And give us manners, virtue, freedom, power.
Thy soul was like a Star, and dwelt apart:
Thou hadst a voice whose sound was like the sea:
Pure as the naked heavens, majestic, free,
So didst thou travel on life's common way,
In cheerful godliness; and yet thy heart
The lowliest duties on herself did lay.

The World Is too Much with Us

THE World is too much with us; late and soon,
Getting and spending, we lay waste our powers;
Little we see in nature that is ours;
We have given our hearts away, a sordid boon!
This sea that bares her bosom to the moon;
The winds that will be howling at all hours,
And are up-gathered now like sleeping flowers;
For this, for everything, we are out of tune;
It moves us not.—Great God! I'd rather be
A Pagan suckled in a creed outworn,
So might I, standing on this pleasant lea,
Have glimpses that would make me less forlorn;
Have sight of Proteus rising from the sea,
Or hear old Triton blow his wreathèd horn.

SIR WALTER SCOTT

(1771–1832)

Waken, Lords and Ladies Gay

WAKEN, lords and ladies gay,
On the mountain dawns the day;
  All the jolly chase is here,
  With hawk and horse and hunting-spear!
Hounds are in their couples yelling,
Hawks are whistling, horns are knelling,
  Merrily, merrily mingle they,
  "Waken, lords and ladies gay."

Waken, lords and ladies gay,
The mist has left the mountain gray,
  Springlets in the dawn are steaming,
  Diamonds on the brake are gleaming,
And foresters have busy been
To track the buck in thicket green:
  Now we come to chant our lay,
  "Waken, lords and ladies gay."

Waken, lords and ladies gay,
To the greenwood haste away;
  We can show you where he lies,
  Fleet of foot and tall of size;
We can show the marks he made
When 'gainst the oak his antlers frayed;
  You shall see him brought to bay;
  Waken, lords and ladies gay.

Louder, louder chant the lay,
Waken, lords and ladies gay!
  Tell them, youth and mirth and glee
  Run a course as well as we;
Time, stern huntsman, who can balk,
Stanch as hound and fleet as hawk?
  Think of this, and rise with day,
  Gentle lords and ladies gay!

Lochinvar

OH, YOUNG Lochinvar is come out of the west:
Through all the wide border his steed was the best;
And save his good broadsword he weapons had none;
He rode all unarmed and he rode all alone.
So faithful in love, and so dauntless in war,
There never was knight like the young Lochinvar!

He stayed not for brake, and he stopped not for stone;
He swam the Esk River where ford there was none:
But ere he alighted at Netherby gate,
The bride had consented, the gallant came late;
For a laggard in love, and a dastard in war,
Was to wed the fair Ellen of brave Lochinvar.

So boldly he entered the Netherby Hall,
Among bride'smen, and kinsmen, and brothers, and all:
Then spoke the bride's father, his hand on his sword
(For the poor craven bridegroom said never a word),
"O come ye in peace here, or come ye in war,
Or to dance at our bridal, young Lord Lochinvar?"—

"I long wooed your daughter, my suit you denied;—
Love swells like the Solway, but ebbs like its tide!
And now am I come, with this lost love of mine,
To lead but one measure, drink one cup of wine:
There are maidens in Scotland more lovely by far,
That would gladly be bride to the young Lochinvar."

The bride kissed the goblet: the knight took it up,
He quaffed off the wine, and he threw down the cup.
She looked down to blush, and she looked up to sigh,
With a smile on her lips, and a tear in her eye.
He took her soft hand, ere her mother could bar,—
"Now tread we a measure!" said young Lochinvar.

So stately his form, and so lovely her face,
That never a hall such a galliard did grace:

While her mother did fret, and her father did fume,
And the bridegroom stood dangling his bonnet and plume;
And the bride-maidens whispered, " 'T were better by far
To have matched our fair cousin with young Lochinvar."

One touch to her hand, and one word in her ear,
When they reached the hall door, and the charger stood near;
So light to the croupe the fair lady he swung,
So light to the saddle before her he sprung!
"She is won! we are gone, over bank, bush, and scaur:
They'll have fleet steeds that follow," quoth young Lochinvar.

There was mounting 'mong Graemes of the Netherby clan:
Forsters, Fenwicks, and Musgraves, they rode and they ran;
There was racing and chasing on Canobie Lee,
But the lost bride of Netherby ne'er did they see.
So daring in love, and so dauntless in war,
Have ye e'er heard of gallant like young Lochinvar?

Coronach

He is gone on the mountain,
  He is lost to the forest,
Like a summer-dried fountain
  When our need was the sorest.
The font, reappearing,
  From the rain-drops shall borrow,
But to us comes no cheering,
  To Duncan no morrow!

The hand of the reaper
  Takes the ears that are hoary;
But the voice of the weeper
  Wails manhood in glory.
The autumn winds rushing
  Waft the leaves that are searest,
But our flower was in flushing
  When blighting was nearest.

Fleet foot on the correi,
  Sage counsel in cumber,
Red hand in the foray,
  How sound is thy slumber!
Like the dew on the mountain,
  Like the foam on the river,
Like the bubble on the fountain,
  Thou art gone, and forever!

Soldier, Rest

SOLDIER, rest! thy warfare o'er,
  Sleep the sleep that knows not breaking;
Dream of battled fields no more,
  Days of danger, nights of waking.
In our isle's enchanted hall,
  Hands unseen thy couch are strewing,
Fairy strains of music fall,
  Every sense in slumber dewing.
Soldier, rest! thy warfare o'er,
Dream of fighting fields no more;
Sleep the sleep that knows not breaking,
Morn of toil, nor night of waking.

No rude sound shall reach thine ear,
  Armor's clang, or war-steed champing,
Trump nor pibroch summon here
  Mustering clan, or squadron tramping.
Yet the lark's shrill fife may come
  At the daybreak from the fallow,
And the bittern sound his drum,
  Booming from the sedgy shallow.
Ruder sounds shall none be near,
Guards nor warders challenge here;
Here's no war-steed's neigh and champing,
Shouting clans or squadrons stamping.

Huntsman, rest! thy chase is done,
  While our slumberous spells assail ye,
Dream not, with the rising sun,
  Bugles here shall sound reveille.
Sleep! the deer is in his den;
  Sleep! thy hounds are by thee lying;
Sleep! nor dream in yonder glen
  How thy gallant steed lay dying.
Huntsman, rest! thy chase is done;
Think not of the rising sun,
For, at dawning to assail ye,
Here no bugles sound reveille.

Proud Maisie

Proud Maisie is in the wood,
  Walking so early;
Sweet Robin sits on the bush,
  Singing so rarely.

"Tell me, thou bonny bird,
  When shall I marry me?"
—"When six braw gentlemen
  Kirkward shall carry ye."

"Who makes the bridal bed,
  Birdie say truly?"
—"The gray-headed sexton
  That delves the grave duly.

"The glowworm o'er grave and stone
  Shall light thee steady;
The owl from the steeple sing
  Welcome, proud lady."

SAMUEL TAYLOR COLERIDGE

(1772–1834)

Kubla Khan

IN XANADU did Kubla Khan
A stately pleasure-dome decree:
Where Alph, the sacred river, ran
Through caverns measureless to man
  Down to a sunless sea.
So twice five miles of fertile ground
With walls and towers were girdled round:
And there were gardens bright with sinuous rills
Where blossom'd many an incense-bearing tree:
And here were forests ancient as the hills,
Enfolding sunny spots of greenery.

  But O! that deep romantic chasm which slanted
Down the green hill athwart a cedarn cover!
A savage place! as holy and enchanted
As e'er beneath a waning moon was haunted
By woman wailing for her demon-lover!
And from this chasm, with ceaseless turmoil seething
As if this earth in fast thick pants were breathing,
A mighty fountain momently was forced;
Amid whose swift half-intermitted burst
Huge fragments vaulted like rebounding hail,
Or chaffy grain beneath the thresher's flail:
And mid these dancing rocks at once and ever
It flung up momently the sacred river.
Five miles meandering with a mazy motion
Through wood and dale the sacred river ran,
Then reach'd the caverns measureless to man,
And sank in tumult to a lifeless ocean:
And 'mid this tumult Kubla heard from far
Ancestral voices prophesying war!

    The shadow of the dome of pleasure
  Floated midway on the waves;

Where was heard the mingled measure
From the fountain and the caves.
It was a miracle of rare device,
A sunny pleasure-dome with caves of ice!

A damsel with a dulcimer
In a vision once I saw:
It was an Abyssinian maid,
And on her dulcimer she play'd,
Singing of Mount Abora.
Could I revive within me
Her symphony and song,
To such a deep delight 'twould win me,
That with music loud and long,
I would build that dome in air,
That sunny dome! those caves of ice!
And all who heard should see them there,
And all should cry, Beware! Beware!
His flashing eyes, his floating hair!
Weave a circle round him thrice,
And close your eyes with holy dread,
For he on honey-dew hath fed,
And drunk the milk of Paradise.

The Rime of the Ancient Mariner

PART THE FIRST

An ancient Mariner meeteth three Gallants bidden to a wedding-feast, and detaineth one.

IT IS an ancient Mariner,
And he stoppeth one of three.
"By thy long grey beard and glittering eye,
Now wherefore stopp'st thou me?

The Bridegroom's doors are opened wide,
And I am next of kin;
The guests are met, the feast is set:
May'st hear the merry din."

He holds him with his skinny hand,
"There was a ship," quoth he.
"Hold off! unhand me, grey-beard loon!"
Eftsoons his hand dropt he.

The Wedding-Guest is spell-bound by the eye of the old seafaring man, and constrained to hear his tale.

He holds him with his glittering eye—
The Wedding-Guest stood still,
And listens like a three years' child:
The Mariner hath his will.

The Wedding-Guest sat on a stone:
He cannot choose but hear;
And thus spake on that ancient man,
The bright-eyed Mariner.

The Mariner tells how the ship sailed southward with a good wind and fair weather, till it reached the Line.

"The ship was cheered, the harbour cleared,
Merrily did we drop
Below the kirk, below the hill,
Below the lighthouse top.

"The Sun came up upon the left,
Out of the sea came he!
And he shone bright, and on the right
Went down into the sea.

"Higher and higher every day,
Till over the mast at noon—"
The Wedding-Guest here beat his breast,
For he heard the loud bassoon.

The Wedding-Guest heareth the bridal music; but the mariner continueth his tale.

The bride hath paced into the hall,
Red as a rose is she;
Nodding their heads before her goes
The merry minstrelsy.

The Wedding-Guest he beat his breast,
Yet he cannot choose but hear;
And thus spake on that ancient man,
The bright-eyed Mariner.

The ship drawn y a storm toward the south ole.

"And now the Storm-blast came, and he
Was tyrannous and strong:
He struck with his o'ertaking wings,
And chased us south along.

"With sloping masts and dipping prow,
As who pursued with yell and blow
Still treads the shadow of his foe
And forward bends his head,
The ship drove fast, loud roared the blast,
And southward ay we fled.

The land of ice, nd of fearful ounds, where no ving thing was o be seen.

"And now there came both mist and snow
And it grew wondrous cold:
And ice, mast-high, came floating by,
As green as emerald.

"And through the drifts the snowy clifts
Did send a dismal sheen:
Nor shapes of men nor beasts we ken—
The ice was all between.

"The ice was here, the ice was there,
The ice was all around:
It cracked and growled, and roared and howled,
Like noises in a swound!

ill a great seaird, called the lbatross, came hrough the now-fog, and as received ith great joy nd hospitality.

"At length did cross an Albatross:
Thorough the fog it came;
As if it had been a Christian soul,
We hailed it in God's name.

"It ate the food it ne'er had eat,
And round and round it flew.
The ice did split with a thunder-fit;
The helmsman steered us through!

And lo! the Albatross proveth a bird of good omen, and followeth the ship as it returned northward through fog and floating ice.

"And a good south wind sprung up behind;
The Albatross did follow,
And every day, for food or play,
Came to the mariner's hollo!

"In mist or cloud, on mast or shroud,
It perched for vespers nine;
Whiles all the night, through fog-smoke white,
Glimmered the white moonshine."

The ancient Mariner inhospitably killeth the pious bird of good omen.

"God save thee, ancient Mariner!
From the fiends, that plague thee thus!—
Why look'st thou so?"—"With my cross-bow
I shot the Albatross."

PART THE SECOND

"The Sun now rose upon the right:
Out of the sea came he,
Still hid in mist, and on the left
Went down into the sea.

"And the good south wind still blew behind,
But no sweet bird did follow,
Nor any day for food or play
Came to the mariner's hollo!

His shipmates cry out against the ancient Mariner for killing the bird of good luck.

"And I had done a hellish thing,
And it would work 'em woe:
For all averred, I had killed the bird
That made the breeze to blow.
Ah wretch! said they, the bird to slay,
That made the breeze to blow!

But when the fog cleared off, they justify the same and thus make themselves accomplices in the crime.

"Nor dim nor red, like God's own head,
The glorious Sun uprist:
Then all averred, I had killed the bird
That brought the fog and mist.
'Twas right, said they, such birds to slay,
That bring the fog and mist.

The fair breeze continues; the ship enters the Pacific Ocean, and sails northward, even till it reaches the Line.

"The fair breeze blew, the white foam flew,
The furrow followed free;
We were the first that ever burst
Into that silent sea.

The ship hath been suddenly becalmed.

"Down dropt the breeze, the sails dropt down,
'Twas sad as sad could be;
And we did speak only to break
The silence of the sea!

"All in a hot and copper sky,
The bloody Sun, at noon,
Right up above the mast did stand,
No bigger than the Moon.

"Day after day, day after day,
We stuck, nor breath nor motion;
As idle as a painted ship
Upon a painted ocean.

And the Albatross begins to be avenged.

"Water, water, every where,
And all the boards did shrink;
Water, water, every where,
Nor any drop to drink.

"The very deep did rot: O Christ!
That ever this should be!
Yea, slimy things did crawl with legs
Upon the slimy sea.

"About, about, in reel and rout
The death-fires danced at night;
The water, like a witch's oils,
Burnt green, and blue and white.

A Spirit had followed them; one of the invisible inhabitants of this planet neither departed souls nor angels; concerning whom the learned Jew, Josephus and the Platonic Constantinopolitan, Michael Psellus, may be consulted. They are very numerous, and there is no climate or element without one or more.

"And some in dreams assuréd were
Of the Spirit that plagued us so;
Nine fathom deep he had followed us
From the land of mist and snow.

"And every tongue, through utter drought,
Was withered at the root;
We could not speak, no more than if
We had been choked with soot.

The shipmates, in their sore distress, would fain throw the whole guilt on the ancient Mariner: in sign whereof they hang the dead sea-bird round his neck.

"Ah! well a-day! what evil looks
Had I from old and young!
Instead of the cross, the Albatross
About my neck was hung.

PART THE THIRD

"There passed a weary time. Each throat
Was parched, and glazed each eye.
A weary time! a weary time!
How glazed each weary eye,
When looking westward, I beheld
A something in the sky.

The ancient Mariner beholdeth a sign in the element afar off.

"At first it seemed a little speck,
And then it seemed a mist;
It moved and moved, and took at last
A certain shape, I wist.

"A speck, a mist, a shape, I wist!
And still it neared and neared:
As if it dodged a water-sprite,
It plunged and tacked and veered.

At its nearest approach, it seemeth him to be a ship; and at a dear ransom he freeth his speech from the bonds of thirst.

"With throats unslaked, with black lips baked,
We could nor laugh nor wail;
Through utter drought all dumb we stood!
I bit my arm, I sucked the blood,
And cried, 'A sail! a sail!'

"With throats unslaked, with black lips baked,
Agape they heard me call:
Gramercy! they for joy did grin,
And all at once their breath drew in,
As they were drinking all.

lash of joy;

" 'See! see!' (I cried) 'she tacks no more!
'Hither to work us weal;
Without a breeze, without a tide,
She steadies with upright keel!'

d horror ows. For can e a ship that ies onward hout wind or e?

"The western wave was all a-flame.
The day was well nigh done!
Almost upon the western wave
Rested the broad bright Sun;
When that strange shape drove suddenly
Betwixt us and the Sun.

"And straight the Sun was flecked with bars,
(Heaven's Mother send us grace!)
As if through a dungeon-grate he peered
With broad and burning face.

seemeth him the skeleton ship.

"Alas! (thought I, and my heart beat loud)
How fast she nears and nears!
Are those her sails that glance in the Sun,
Like restless gossameres?

d its ribs are n as bars on face of the ing Sun.

"Are those her ribs through which the Sun
Did peer, as through a grate?
And is that Woman all her crew?
Is that a DEATH? and are there two?
Is DEATH that woman's mate?

e Spectre-man and her ath-mate, and other on rd the leton ship.

"Her lips were red, her looks were free,
Her locks were yellow as gold:
Her skin was as white as leprosy,
The Nightmare Life-in-Death was she,
Who thicks man's blood with cold.

Death and Life-in-Death have diced for the ship's crew, and she (the latter) winneth the ancient Mariner.

"The naked hulk alongside came,
And the twain was casting dice;
'The game is done! I've won, I've won!'
Quoth she, and whistles thrice.

No twilight within the courts of the sun.

"The Sun's rim dips; the stars rush out:
At one stride comes the dark;
With far-heard whisper, o'er the sea,
Off shot the spectre-bark.

"We listened and looked sideways up!
Fear at my heart, as at a cup,
My life-blood seemed to sip!

At the rising of the Moon,

The stars were dim, and thick the night,
The steersman's face by his lamp gleamed white;
From the sails the dew did drip—
Till clomb above the eastern bar
The hornèd Moon, with one bright star
Within the nether tip.

One after another,

"One after one, by the star-dogged Moon,
Too quick for groan or sigh,
Each turned his face with a ghastly pang,
And cursed me with his eye.

His ship-mates drop down dead;

"Four times fifty living men,
(And I heard nor sigh nor groan)
With heavy thump, a lifeless lump,
They dropped down one by one.

But Life-in-Death begins her work on the ancient Mariner.

"The souls did from their bodies fly,—
They fled to bliss or woe!
And every soul, it passed me by,
Like the whizz of my cross-bow!"

PART THE FOURTH

The Wedding-Guest feareth that a Spirit is talking to him;

"I fear thee, ancient Mariner!
I fear thy skinny hand!
And thou art long, and lank, and brown,
As is the ribbed sea-sand.

"I fear thee and thy glittering eye,
And thy skinny hand, so brown."—
"Fear not, fear not, thou Wedding-Guest!
This body dropt not down.

t the ancient ariner assureth n of his bodily ., and pro- ːdeth to relate horrible nance.

"Alone, alone, all, all alone,
Alone on a wide wide sea!
And never a saint took pity on
My soul in agony.

despiseth the atures of the m.

"The many men, so beautiful!
And they all dead did lie:
And a thousand thousand slimy things
Lived on; and so did I.

d envieth that y should live, d so many lie ad.

"I looked upon the rotting sea,
And drew my eyes away;
I looked upon the rotting deck,
And there the dead men lay.

"I looked to heaven, and tried to pray;
But or ever a prayer had gusht,
A wicked whisper came, and made
My heart as dry as dust.

"I closed my lids, and kept them close,
And the balls like pulses beat;
For the sky and the sea, and the sea and the sky
Lay like a load on my weary eye,
And the dead were at my feet.

t the curse eth for him in eye of the ad men.

"The cold sweat melted from their limbs,
Nor rot nor reek did they:
The look with which they looked on me
Had never passed away.

"An orphan's curse would drag to hell
A spirit from on high;
But oh! more horrible than that
Is the curse in a dead man's eye!
Seven days, seven nights, I saw that curse,
And yet I could not die

In his loneliness and fixedness he yearneth towards the journeying Moon and the stars that still sojourn, yet still move onward; and everywhere the blue sky belongs to them, and is their appointed rest, and their native country and their own natural homes, which they enter unannounced, as lords that are certainly expected and yet there is a silent joy at their arrival.

"The moving Moon went up the sky,
And nowhere did abide:
Softly she was going up,
And a star or two beside—

"Her beams bemocked the sultry main,
Like April hoar-frost spread;
But where the ship's huge shadow lay,
The charmèd water burnt alway
A still and awful red.

"Beyond the shadow of the ship,
I watched the water-snakes:
They moved in tracks of shining white,
And when they reared, the elfish light
Fell off in hoary flakes.

By the light of the Moon he beholdeth God's creatures of the great calm.

"Within the shadow of the ship
I watched their rich attire:
Blue, glossy green, and velvet black,
They coiled and swam; and every track
Was a flash of golden fire.

Their beauty and their happiness.

"O happy living things! no tongue
Their beauty might declare:
A spring of love gushed from my heart,
And I blessed them unaware:
Sure my kind saint took pity on me,
And I blessed them unaware.

He blesseth them in his heart.

"The selfsame moment I could pray;
And from my neck so free
The Albatross fell off, and sank
Like lead into the sea."

The spell begins to break.

PART THE FIFTH

"Oh sleep! it is a gentle thing,
Beloved from pole to pole!
To Mary Queen the praise be given!
She sent the gentle sleep from Heaven,
That slid into my soul.

By grace of the holy Mother, the ancient Mariner is refreshed with rain.

"The silly buckets on the deck,
That had so long remained,
I dreamt that they were filled with dew;
And when I awoke, it rained.

"My lips were wet, my throat was cold,
My garments all were dank;
Sure I had drunken in my dreams,
And still my body drank.

"I moved, and could not feel my limbs:
I was so light—almost
I thought that I had died in sleep,
And was a blessed ghost.

He heareth sounds and seeth strange sights and commotions in the sky and the element.

"And soon I heard a roaring wind:
It did not come anear;
But with its sound it shook the sails,
That were so thin and sere.

"The upper air burst into life!
And a hundred fire-flags sheen,
To and fro they were hurried about!
And to and fro, and in and out,
The wan stars danced between.

"And the coming wind did roar more loud,
And the sails did sigh like sedge;
And the rain poured down from one black cloud;
The Moon was at its edge.

"The thick black cloud was cleft, and still
The Moon was at its side:
Like waters shot from some high crag,
The lightning fell with never a jag,
A river steep and wide.

The bodies of the ship's crew are inspired, and the ship moves on;

"The loud wind never reached the ship,
Yet now the ship moved on!
Beneath the lightning and the Moon
The dead men gave a groan.

"They groaned, they stirred, they all uprose,
Nor spake, nor moved their eyes;
It had been strange, even in a dream,
To have seen those dead men rise.

"The helmsman steered, the ship moved on;
Yet never a breeze up blew;
The mariners all 'gan work the ropes,
Where they were wont to do;
They raised their limbs like lifeless tools—
We were a ghastly crew.

but not by the souls of the men, nor by daemons of earth or middle air, but by a blessed troop of angelic spirits, sent down by the invocation of the guardian saint.

"The body of my brother's son
Stood by me, knee to knee:
The body and I pulled at one rope,
But he said nought to me."

"I fear thee, ancient Mariner!"
"Be calm, thou Wedding-Guest!
'Twas not those souls that fled in pain,
Which to their corses came again,
But a troop of spirits blest:

"For when it dawned—they dropt their arms,
And clustered round the mast;
Sweet sounds rose slowly through their mouths,
And from their bodies passed.

"Around, around, flew each sweet sound,
Then darted to the Sun;
Slowly the sounds came back again,
Now mixed, now one by one.

"Sometimes a-dropping from the sky
I heard the sky-lark sing;
Sometimes all little birds that are,
How they seemed to fill the sea and air
With their sweet jargoning!

"And now 'twas like all instruments,
Now like a lonely flute;
And now it is an angel's song,
That makes the heavens be mute.

"It ceased; yet still the sails made on
A pleasant noise till noon,
A noise like of a hidden brook
In the leafy month of June,
That to the sleeping woods all night
Singeth a quiet tune.

"Till noon we quietly sailed on,
Yet never a breeze did breathe:
Slowly and smoothly went the ship,
Moved onward from beneath.

he lonesome pirit from the uth-pole rries on the ip as far as e Line, in edience to the gelic troop, ut still requir- h vengeance.

"Under the keel nine fathom deep,
From the land of mist and snow,
The spirit slid: and it was he
That made the ship to go.
The sails at noon left off their tune,
And the ship stood still also.

"The Sun, right up above the mast,
Had fixed her to the ocean:
But in a minute she 'gan stir,
With a short uneasy motion—
Backwards and forwards half her length
With a short uneasy motion.

"Then, like a pawing horse let go,
She made a sudden bound:
It flung the blood into my head,
And I fell down in a swound.

he Polar Spirit's llow daemons, e invisible habitants of e element, ke part in his rong; and two; f them relate,

"How long in that same fit I lay,
I have not to declare;
But ere my living life returned,
I heard and in my soul discerned
Two voices in the air.

one to the other, that penance long and heavy for the ancient Mariner hath been accorded to the Polar Spirit, who returneth southward.

" 'Is it he?' quoth one, 'Is this the man?
By him who died on cross,
With his cruel bow he laid full low
The harmless Albatross.

" 'The spirit who bideth by himself
In the land of mist and snow,
He loved the bird that loved the man
Who shot him with his bow.'

"The other was a softer voice,
As soft as honeydew:
Quoth he, 'The man hath penance done,
And penance more will do.'

PART THE SIXTH

First Voice

" 'But tell me, tell me! speak again,
Thy soft response renewing—
What makes that ship drive on so fast?
What is the ocean doing?'

Second Voice

" 'Still as a slave before his lord,
The ocean hath no blast;
His great bright eye most silently
Up to the Moon is cast—

" 'If he may know which way to go;
For she guides him smooth or grim.
See, brother, see! how graciously
She looketh down on him.'

First Voice

The Mariner hath been cast into a trance; for the angelic power causeth the vessel to drive northward faster than human life could endure.

" 'But why drives on that ship so fast,
Without or wave or wind?'

Second Voice

" 'The air is cut away before,
And closes from behind.

"'Fly, brother, fly! more high, more high!
Or we shall be belated:
For slow and slow that ship will go,
When the Mariner's trance is abated.'

The super-natural motion is retarded; the Mariner awakes, and his penance begins anew.

"I woke, and we were sailing on
As in a gentle weather:
'Twas night, calm night, the moon was high;
The dead men stood together.

"All stood together on the deck,
For a charnel-dungeon fitter:
All fixed on me their stony eyes,
That in the Moon did glitter.

"The pang, the curse, with which they died,
Had never passed away:
I could not draw my eyes from theirs,
Nor turn them up to pray.

The curse is finally expiated.

"And now this spell was snapt: once more
I viewed the ocean green,
And looked far forth, yet little saw
Of what had else been seen—

"Like one, that on a lonesome road
Doth walk in fear and dread,
And having once turned round walks on,
And turns no more his head;
Because he knows, a frightful fiend
Doth close behind him tread.

"But soon there breathed a wind on me,
Nor sound nor motion made:
Its path was not upon the sea,
In ripple or in shade.

"It raised my hair, it fanned my cheek
Like a meadow-gale of spring—
It mingled strangely with my fears,
Yet it felt like a welcoming.

"Swiftly, swiftly flew the ship
Yet she sailed softly too:
Sweetly, sweetly blew the breeze—
On me alone it blew.

And the ancient Mariner beholdeth his native country.

"Oh! dream of joy! is this indeed
The light-house top I see?
Is this the hill? is this the kirk?
Is this mine own countree?

"We drifted o'er the harbour-bar,
And I with sobs did pray—
O let me be awake, my God!
Or let me sleep alway.

"The harbour-bay was clear as glass,
So smoothly it was strewn!
And on the bay the moonlight lay,
And the shadow of the Moon.

"The rock shone bright, the kirk no less,
That stands above the rock:
The moonlight steeped in silentness
The steady weathercock.

"And the bay was white with silent light
Till rising from the same,
Full many shapes, that shadows were,
In crimson colours came.

The Angelic spirits leave the dead bodies,

"A little distance from the prow
Those crimson shadows were:
I turned my eyes upon the deck—
Oh, Christ! what saw I there!

And appear in their own forms of light.

"Each corse lay flat, lifeless and flat,
And, by the holy rood!
A man all light, a seraph-man,
On every corse there stood.

"This seraph-band, each waved his hand:
It was a heavenly sight!
They stood as signals to the land,
Each one a lovely light:

"This seraph-band, each waved his hand,
No voice did they impart—
No voice; but oh! the silence sank
Like music on my heart.

"But soon I heard the dash of oars,
I heard the Pilot's cheer;
My head was turned perforce away,
And I saw a boat appear.

"The Pilot and the Pilot's boy,
I heard them coming fast:
Dear Lord in Heaven! it was a joy
The dead men could not blast.

"I saw a third—I heard his voice:
It is the Hermit good!
He singeth loud his godly hymns
That he makes in the wood.
He'll shrive my soul, he'll wash away
The Albatross's blood.

PART THE SEVENTH

The Hermit of the Wood,

"This Hermit good lives in that wood
Which slopes down to the sea.
How loudly his sweet voice he rears!
He loves to talk with marineres
That come from a far countree.

"He kneels at morn, and noon, and eve—
He hath a cushion plump:
It is the moss that wholly hides
The rotted old oak-stump.

"The skiff-boat neared: I heard them talk,
'Why, this is strange, I trow!
Where are those lights so many and fair,
That signal made but now?'

Approacheth the ship with wonder.

" 'Strange, by my faith!' the Hermit said—
'And they answered not our cheer!
The planks look warped! and see those sails,
How thin they are and sere!
I never saw aught like to them,
Unless perchance it were

" 'Brown skeletons of leaves that lag
My forest-brook along;
When the ivy-tod is heavy with snow,
And the owlet whoops to the wolf below,
That eats the she-wolf's young.'

" 'Dear Lord! it hath a fiendish look'—
(The Pilot made reply)
'I am a-feared'—'Push on, push on!'
Said the Hermit cheerily.

"The boat came closer to the ship,
But I nor spake nor stirred;
The boat came close beneath the ship,
And straight a sound was heard.

The ship suddenly sinketh.

"Under the water it rumbled on,
Still louder and more dread:
It reached the ship, it split the bay;
The ship went down like lead.

The ancient Mariner is saved in the Pilot's boat.

"Stunned by that loud and dreadful sound,
Which sky and ocean smote,
Like one that hath been seven days drowned
My body lay afloat;
But swift as dreams, myself I found
Within the Pilot's boat.

"Upon the whirl, where sank the ship,
The boat spun round and round;
And all was still, save that the hill
Was telling of the sound.

"I moved my lips—the Pilot shrieked
And fell down in a fit;
The holy Hermit raised his eyes,
And prayed where he did sit.

"I took the oars: the Pilot's boy,
Who now doth crazy go,
Laughed loud and long, and all the while
His eyes went to and fro.
'Ha! ha!' quoth he, 'full plain I see,
The Devil knows how to row.'

"And now, all in my own countree,
I stood on the firm land!
The Hermit stepped forth from the boat,
And scarcely he could stand.

e ancient ariner nestly reateth the rmit to shrive n; and the ance of life ls on him.

" 'O shrive me, shrive me, holy man!'
The Hermit crossed his brow.
'Say quick,' quoth he, 'I bid thee say—
What manner of man art thou?'

"Forthwith this frame of mine was wrenched
With a woeful agony,
Which forced me to begin my tale;
And then it left me free.

d ever and n throughout future life an ny constrain- him to travel m land to land,

"Since then, at an uncertain hour,
That agony returns:
And till my ghastly tale is told,
This heart within me burns.

"I pass, like night, from land to land;
I have strange power of speech;
That moment that his face I see,
I know the man that must hear me:
To him my tale I teach.

"What loud uproar bursts from that door!
The wedding-guests are there:
But in the garden-bower the bride
And bride-maids singing are:
And hark the little vesper bell,
Which biddeth me to prayer!

"O Wedding-Guest! this soul hath been
Alone on a wide wide sea:
So lonely 'twas, that God Himself
Scarce seemèd there to be.

"O sweeter than the marriage-feast,
'Tis sweeter far to me,
To walk together to the kirk
With a goodly company!—

"To walk together to the kirk,
And all together pray,
While each to his great Father bends,
Old men, and babes, and loving friends,
And youths and maidens gay!

and to teach, by his own example, love and reverence to all things that God made and loveth.

"Farewell, farewell! but this I tell
To thee, thou Wedding-Guest!
He prayeth well, who loveth well
Both man and bird and beast.

"He prayeth best, who loveth best
All things both great and small;
For the dear God who loveth us,
He made and loveth all."

The Mariner, whose eye is bright,
Whose beard with age is hoar,
Is gone: and now the Wedding-Guest
Turned from the bridegroom's door.

He went like one that hath been stunned,
And is of sense forlorn:
A sadder and a wiser man,
He rose the morrow morn.

Christabel

PART THE FIRST

'Tis the middle of night by the castle clock,
And the owls have awakened the crowing cock,
Tu—whit!——Tu—whoo!
And hark, again! the crowing cock,
How drowsily it crew.

Sir Leoline, the Baron rich,
Hath a toothless mastiff bitch;
From her kennel beneath the rock
She maketh answer to the clock,
Four for the quarters, and twelve for the hour;
Ever and aye, by shine and shower,
Sixteen short howls, not over loud;
Some say, she sees my lady's shroud.

Is the night chilly and dark?
The night is chilly, but not dark.
The thin gray cloud is spread on high,
It covers but not hides the sky.
The moon is behind, and at the full;
And yet she looks both small and dull
The night is chill, the cloud is gray:
'Tis a month before the month of May,
And the Spring comes slowly up this way.

The lovely lady, Christabel,
Whom her father loves so well,
What makes her in the wood so late,
A furlong from the castle gate?
She had dreams all yesternight
Of her own betrothéd knight;
And she in the midnight wood will pray
For the weal of her lover that's far away

She stole along, she nothing spoke,
The sighs she heaved were soft and low,
And naught was green upon the oak
But moss and rarest mistletoe:
She kneels beneath the huge oak tree,
And in silence prayeth she.

The lady sprang up suddenly,
The lovely lady, Christabel!
It moaned as near, as near can be,
But what it is she cannot tell.—
On the other side it seems to be,
Of the huge, broad-breasted, old oak tree.

The night is chill; the forest bare;
Is it the wind that moaneth bleak?
There is not wind enough in the air
To move away the ringlet curl
From the lovely lady's cheek—
There is not wind enough to twirl
The one red leaf, the last of its clan,
That dances as often as dance it can,
Hanging so light, and hanging so high,
On the topmost twig that looks up at the sky.

Hush, beating heart of Christabel!
Jesu, Maria, shield her well!
She folded her arms beneath her cloak,
And stole to the other side of the oak.
What sees she there?

There she sees a damsel bright,
Dressed in a silken robe of white,
That shadowy in the moonlight shone:
The neck that made that white robe wan,
Her stately neck, and arms were bare;
Her blue-veined feet unsandaled were;
And wildly glittered here and there
The gems entangled in her hair.

I guess, 'twas frightful there to see
A lady so richly clad as she—
Beautiful exceedingly!

"Mary mother, save me now!"
Said Christabel; "and who art thou?"

The lady strange made answer meet,
And her voice was faint and sweet:—
"Have pity on my sore distress,
I scarce can speak for weariness:
Stretch forth thy hand, and have no fear!"
Said Christabel, "How camest thou here?"
And the lady, whose voice was faint and sweet,
Did thus pursue her answer meet:—

"My sire is of a noble line,
And my name is Geraldine:
Five warriors seized me yestermorn,
Me, even me, a maid forlorn:
They choked my cries with force and fright,
And tied me on a palfrey white.
The palfrey was as fleet as wind,
And they rode furiously behind.
They spurred amain, their steeds were white:
And once we crossed the shade of night.
As sure as Heaven shall rescue me,
I have no thought what men they be;
Nor do I know how long it is
(For I have lain entranced, I wis)
Since one, the tallest of the five,
Took me from the palfrey's back,
A weary woman, scarce alive.
Some muttered words his comrades spoke:
He placed me underneath this oak;
He swore they would return with haste;
Whither they went I cannot tell—
I thought I heard, some minutes past,
Sounds as of a castle bell.
Stretch forth thy hand," thus ended she,
"And help a wretched maid to flee."

Then Christabel stretched forth her hand,
And comforted fair Geraldine:
"O well, bright dame! may you command
The service of Sir Leoline;
And gladly our stout chivalry
Will he send forth, and friends withal,
To guide and guard you safe and free
Home to your noble father's hall."

She rose: and forth with steps they passed
That strove to be, and were not, fast.
Her gracious stars the lady bless'd,
And thus spake on sweet Christabel:
"All our household are at rest,
The hall as silent as the cell;
Sir Leoline is weak in health,
And may not well awakened be,
But we will move as if in stealth;
And I beseech your courtesy,
This night, to share your couch with me."

They crossed the moat, and Christabel
Took the key that fitted well;
A little door she opened straight,
All in the middle of the gate;
The gate that was ironed within and without,
Where an army in battle array had marched out.
The lady sank, belike through pain,
And Christabel with might and main
Lifted her up, a weary weight,
Over the threshold of the gate:
Then the lady rose again,
And moved, as she were not in pain.

So free from danger, free from fear,
They crossed the court: right glad they were.
And Christabel devoutly cried
To the lady by her side,
"Praise we the Virgin all divine,

Who hath rescued thee from thy distress!"
"Alas, alas!" said Geraldine,
"I cannot speak for weariness."
So free from danger, free from fear,
They crossed the court: right glad they were.

Outside her kennel, the mastiff old
Lay fast asleep, in moonshine cold.
The mastiff old did not awake,
Yet she an angry moan did make!
And what can ail the mastiff bitch?
Never till now she uttered yell
Beneath the eye of Christabel.
Perhaps it is the owlet's scritch:
For what can ail the mastiff bitch?

They passed the hall, that echoes still,
Pass as lightly as you will!
The brands were flat, the brands were dying,
Amid their own white ashes lying;
But when the lady passed, there came
A tongue of light, a fit of flame;
And Christabel saw the lady's eye,
And nothing else saw she thereby,
Save the boss of the shield of Sir Leoline tall,
Which hung in a murky old niche in the wall.
"O softly tread," said Christabel,
"My father seldom sleepeth well."

Sweet Christabel her feet doth bare,
And jealous of the listening air
They steal their way from stair to stair,
Now in glimmer, and now in gloom,
And now they pass the Baron's room,
As still as death, with stifled breath!
And now have reached her chamber door;
And now doth Geraldine press down
The rushes of the chamber floor.

The moon shines dim in the open air,
And not a moonbeam enters here.
But they without its light can see
The chamber carved so curiously,
Carved with figures strange and sweet,
All made out of the carver's brain,
For a lady's chamber meet:
The lamp with twofold silver chain
Is fastened to an angel's feet.

The silver lamp burns dead and dim;
But Christabel the lamp will trim.
She trimmed the lamp, and made it bright,
And left it swinging to and fro,
While Geraldine, in wretched plight,
Sank down upon the floor below.

"O weary lady, Geraldine,
I pray you, drink this cordial wine!
It is a wine of virtuous powers;
My mother made it of wild flowers."

"And will your mother pity me,
Who am a maiden most forlorn?"
Christabel answered—"Woe is me!
She died the hour that I was born.
I have heard the gray-haired friar tell
How on her death-bed she did say,
That she should hear the castle-bell
Strike twelve upon my wedding-day.
O mother dear! that thou wert here!"
"I would," said Geraldine, "she were!"
But soon with altered voice, said she—
"Off, wandering mother! Peak and pine!
I have power to bid thee flee."
Alas! what ails poor Geraldine?
Why stares she with unsettled eye?
Can she the bodiless dead espy?
And why with hollow voice cries she,
"Off, woman, off! this hour is mine—

Though thou her guardian spirit be,
Off, woman, off! 'tis given to me."

Then Christabel knelt by the lady's side,
And raised to heaven her eyes so blue—
"Alas!" said she, "this ghastly ride—
Dear lady! it hath wildered you!"
The lady wiped her moist cold brow,
And faintly said, " 'Tis over now!"

Again the wild-flower wine she drank:
Her fair large eyes 'gan glitter bright,
And from the floor whereon she sank,
The lofty lady stood upright:
She was most beautiful to see,
Like a lady of a far countree.
And thus the lofty lady spake—
"All they who live in the upper sky,
Do love you, holy Christabel!
And you love them, and for their sake
And for the good which me befell,
Even I in my degree will try,
Fair maiden, to requite you well.
But now unrobe yourself; for I
Must pray, ere yet in bed I lie."

Quoth Christabel, "So let it be!"
And as the lady bade, did she.
Her gentle limbs did she undress,
And lay down in her loveliness.

But through her brain of weal and woe
So many thoughts moved to and fro,
That vain it were her lids to close;
So half-way from the bed she rose,
And on her elbow did recline
To look at the lady Geraldine.

Beneath the lamp the lady bowed,
And slowly rolled her eyes around;

Then drawing in her breath aloud,
Like one that shuddered, she unbound
The cincture from beneath her breast:
Her silken robe, and inner vest,
Dropped to her feet, and full in view,
Behold! her bosom and half her side—
A sight to dream of, not to tell!
O shield her! shield sweet Christabel!

Yet Geraldine nor speaks nor stirs;
Ah! what a stricken look was hers!
Deep from within she seems half-way
To lift some weight with sick assay;
And eyes the maid and seeks delay;
Then suddenly, as one defied,
Collects herself in scorn and pride,
And lay down by the Maiden's side!—
And in her arms the maid she took,
        Ah well-a-day!
And with low voice and doleful look
These words did say:

"In the touch of this bosom there worketh a spell,
Which is lord of thy utterance, Christabel!
Thou knowest to-night, and wilt know to-morrow,
This mark of my shame, this seal of my sorrow;
        But vainly thou warrest,
          For this is alone in
        Thy power to declare,
          That in the dim forest
        Thou heard'st a low moaning,
And found'st a bright lady, surpassingly fair;
And didst bring her home with thee in love and in charity,
To shield her and shelter her from the damp air."

THE CONCLUSION TO PART THE FIRST

It was a lovely sight to see
The Lady Christabel, when she
Was praying at the old oak tree.

Amid the jaggéd shadows
Of mossy leafless boughs,
Kneeling in the moonlight,
To make her gentle vows;
Her slender palms together pressed,
Heaving sometimes on her breast;
Her face resigned to bliss or bale—
Her face, oh call it fair not pale,
And both blue eyes more bright than clear,
Each about to have a tear.

With open eyes (ah woe is me!)
Asleep, and dreaming fearfully,
Fearfully dreaming, yet, I wis,
Dreaming that alone, which is—
O sorrow and shame! Can this be she,
The lady, who knelt at the old oak tree?
And lo! the worker of these harms,
That holds the maiden in her arms,
Seems to slumber still and mild,
As a mother with her child.

A star hath set, a star hath risen,
O Geraldine! since arms of thine
Have been the lovely lady's prison.
O Geraldine! one hour was thine—
Thou'st had thy will! By tairn and rill,
The night-birds all that hour were still.
But now they are jubilant anew.
From cliff and tower, tu—whoo! tu—whoo!
Tu—whoo! tu—whoo! from wood and fell!

And see! the lady Christabel
Gathers herself from out her trance;
Her limbs relax, her countenance
Grows sad and soft; the smooth thin lids
Close o'er her eyes; and tears she sheds—
Large tears that leave the lashes bright!
And oft the while she seems to smile
As infants at a sudden light!

Yea, she doth smile, and she doth weep,
Like a youthful hermitess,
Beauteous in a wilderness,
Who, praying always, prays in sleep.
And, if she move unquietly,
Perchance, 'tis but the blood so free
Comes back and tingles in her feet.
No doubt, she hath a vision sweet.
What if her guardian spirit 'twere,
What if she knew her mother near?
But this she knows, in joys and woes,
That saints will aid if men will call:
For the blue sky bends over all.

PART THE SECOND

Each matin bell, the Baron saith,
Knells us back to a world of death.
These words Sir Leoline first said,
When he rose and found his lady dead:
These words Sir Leoline will say
Many a morn to his dying day!

And hence the custom and law began
That still at dawn the sacristan,
Who duly pulls the heavy bell,
Five and forty beads must tell
Between each stroke—a warning knell,
Which not a soul can choose but hear
From Bratha Head to Wyndermere.

Saith Bracy the bard, "So let it knell!
And let the drowsy sacristan
Still count as slowly as he can!
There is no lack of such, I ween,
As well fill up the space between.
In Langdale Pike and Witch's Lair,
And Dungeon-ghyll so foully rent,
With ropes of rock and bells of air
Three sinful sextons' ghosts are pent,

Who all give back, one after t'other,
The death-note to their living brother;
And oft too, by the knell offended,
Just as their one! two! three! is ended,
The devil mocks the doleful tale
With a merry peal from Borrowdale."
The air is still! through mist and cloud
That merry peal comes ringing loud;
And Geraldine shakes off her dread,
And rises lightly from the bed,
Puts on her silken vestments white,
And tricks her hair in lovely plight,
And nothing doubting of her spell
Awakens the lady Christabel.
"Sleep you, sweet lady Christabel?
I trust that you have rested well."

And Christabel awoke and spied
The same who lay down by her side—
O rather say, the same whom she
Raised up beneath the old oak tree!
Nay, fairer yet! and yet more fair!
For she belike hath drunken deep
Of all the blessedness of sleep!
And while she spake, her looks, her air,
Such gentle thankfulness declare,
That (so it seemed) her girded vests
Grew tight beneath her heaving breasts.
"Sure I have sinned!" said Christabel,
"Now heaven be praised if all be well!"
And in low faltering tones, yet sweet,
Did she the lofty lady greet
With such perplexity of mind
As dreams too lively leave behind.

So quickly she rose, and quickly arrayed
Her maiden limbs, and having prayed
That He, who on the cross did groan,
Might wash away her sins unknown,
She forthwith led fair Geraldine
To meet her sire, Sir Leoline.

The lovely maid and the lady tall
Are pacing both into the hall,
And pacing on through page and groom,
Enter the Baron's presence-room.

The Baron rose, and while he pressed
His gentle daughter to his breast,
With cheerful wonder in his eyes
The lady Geraldine espies,
And gave such welcome to the same,
As might beseem so bright a dame!

But when he heard the lady's tale,
And when she told her father's name,
Why waxed Sir Leoline so pale,
Murmuring o'er the name again,
Lord Roland de Vaux of Tryermaine?
Alas! they had been friends in youth;
But whispering tongues can poison truth;
And constancy lives in realms above;
And life is thorny; and youth is vain;
And to be wroth with one we love
Doth work like madness in the brain.
And thus it chanced, as I divine,
With Roland and Sir Leoline.
Each spake words of high disdain
And insult to his heart's best brother:
They parted—ne'er to meet again!
But never either found another
To free the hollow heart from paining—
They stood aloof, the scars remaining,
Like cliffs which had been rent asunder;
A dreary sea now flows between:
But neither heat, nor frost, nor thunder,
Shall wholly do away, I ween,
The marks of that which once hath been.

Sir Leoline, a moment's space,
Stood gazing on the damsel's face:
And the youthful Lord of Tryermaine
Came back upon his heart again.

O then the Baron forgot his age,
His noble heart swelled high with rage;
He swore by the wounds in Jesu's side
He would proclaim it far and wide,
With trump and solemn heraldry,
That they, who thus had wronged the dame
Were base as spotted infamy!
"And if they dare deny the same,
My herald shall appoint a week,
And let the recreant traitors seek
My tourney court—that there and then
I may dislodge their reptile souls
From the bodies and forms of men!"
He spake: his eye in lightning rolls!
For the lady was ruthlessly seized; and he kenned
In the beautiful lady the child of his friend!

And now the tears were on his face,
And fondly in his arms he took
Fair Geraldine, who met the embrace,
Prolonging it with joyous look.
Which when she viewed, a vision fell
Upon the soul of Christabel,
The vision of fear, the touch and pain!
She shrunk and shuddered, and saw again—
(Ah, woe is me! Was it for thee,
Thou gentle maid! such sights to see?)
Again she saw that bosom old,
Again she felt that bosom cold,
And drew in her breath with a hissing sound:
Whereat the Knight turned wildly round,
And nothing saw, but his own sweet maid
With eyes upraised, as one that prayed.

The touch, the sight, had passed away,
And in its stead that vision bless'd,
Which comforted her after-rest,
While in the lady's arms she lay,
Had put a rapture in her breast,
And on her lips and o'er her eyes
Spread smiles like light!

With new surprise,
"What ails then my belovéd child?"
The Baron said.—His daughter mild
Made answer, "All will yet be well!"
I ween, she had no power to tell
Aught else: so mighty was the spell.

Yet he who saw this Geraldine
Had deemed her sure a thing divine.
Such sorrow with such grace she blended,
As if she feared she had offended
Sweet Christabel, that gentle maid!
And with such lowly tones she prayed
She might be sent without delay
Home to her father's mansion.
"Nay!
Nay, by my soul!" said Leoline.
"Ho! Bracy the bard, the charge be thine!
Go thou, with music sweet and loud,
And take two steeds with trappings proud,
And take the youth whom thou lov'st best
To bear thy harp, and learn thy song,
And clothe you both in solemn vest,
And over the mountains haste along,
Lest wandering folk, that are abroad,
Detain you on the valley road.

"And when he has crossed the Irthing flood,
My merry bard! he hastes, he hastes
Up Knorren Moor, through Halegarth Wood,
And reaches soon that castle good
Which stands and threatens Scotland's wastes.

"Bard Bracy! bard Bracy! your horses are fleet,
Ye must ride up the hall, your music so sweet,
More loud than your horses' echoing feet!
And loud and loud to Lord Roland call,
Thy daughter is safe in Langdale hall!
Thy beautiful daughter is safe and free—
Sir Leoline greets thee thus through me.

He bids thee come without delay
With all thy numerous array;
And take thy lovely daughter home:
And he will meet thee on the way
With all his numerous array
White with their panting palfreys' foam:
And, by mine honor! I will say,
That I repent me of the day
When I spake words of fierce disdain
To Roland de Vaux of Tryermaine!—
—For since that evil hour hath flown,
Many a summer's sun hath shone;
Yet ne'er found I a friend again
Like Roland de Vaux of Tryermaine."

The lady fell, and clasped his knees,
Her face upraised, her eyes o'erflowing;
And Bracy replied, with faltering voice,
His gracious hail on all bestowing:
"Thy words, thou sire of Christabel.
Are sweeter than my harp can tell;
Yet might I gain a boon of thee,
This day my journey should not be;
So strange a dream hath come to me,
That I had vowed with music loud
To clear yon wood from thing unbless'd,
Warned by a vision in my rest!
For in my sleep I saw that dove,
That gentle bird, whom thou dost love,
And call'st by thy own daughter's name—
Sir Leoline! I saw the same,
Fluttering, and uttering fearful moan,
Among the green herbs in the forest alone.
Which when I saw and when I heard,
I wondered what might ail the bird;
For nothing near it could I see,
Save the grass and green herbs underneath the old tree.

"And in my dream, methought, I went
To search out what might there be found;

And what the sweet bird's trouble meant,
That thus lay fluttering on the ground.
I went and peered, and could descry
No cause for her distressful cry;
But yet for her dear lady's sake
I stooped, methought, the dove to take,
When lo! I saw a bright green snake
Coiled around its wings and neck,
Green as the herbs on which it couched,
Close by the dove's its head it crouched;
And with the dove it heaves and stirs,
Swelling its neck as she swelled hers!
I woke; it was the midnight hour,
The clock was echoing in the tower;
But though my slumber was gone by,
This dream it would not pass away—
It seems to live upon my eye!
And thence I vowed this self-same day
With music strong and saintly song
To wander through the forest bare,
Lest aught unholy loiter there."

Thus Bracy said: the Baron, the while,
Half-listening heard him with a smile;
Then turned to Lady Geraldine,
His eyes made up of wonder and love;
And said in courtly accents fine,
"Sweet maid, Lord Roland's beauteous dove,
With arms more strong than harp or song,
Thy sire and I will crush the snake!"
He kissed her forehead as he spake,
And Geraldine in maiden wise
Casting down her large bright eyes,
With blushing cheek and courtesy fine
She turned her from Sir Leoline;
Softly gathering up her train,
That o'er her right arm fell again;
And folded her arms across her chest,
And couched her head upon her breast,
And looked askance at Christabel——
Jesu, Maria, shield her well!

A snake's small eye blinks dull and shy,
And the lady's eyes they shrunk in her head,
Each shrunk up to a serpent's eye,
And with somewhat of malice, and more of dread,
At Christabel she looked askance!—
One moment—and the sight was fled!
But Christabel in dizzy trance
Stumbling on the unsteady ground
Shuddered aloud, with a hissing sound;
And Geraldine again turned round,
And like a thing that sought relief,
Full of wonder and full of grief,
She rolled her large bright eyes divine
Wildly on Sir Leoline.

The maid, alas! her thoughts are gone,
She nothing sees—no sight but one!
The maid, devoid of guile and sin,
I know not how, in fearful wise,
So deeply had she drunken in
That look, those shrunken serpent eyes,
That all her features were resigned
To this sole image in her mind:
And passively did imitate
That look of dull and treacherous hate!
And thus she stood, in dizzy trance,
Still picturing that look askance
With forced unconscious sympathy
Full before her father's view——
As far as such a look could be
In eyes so innocent and blue!

And, when the trance was o'er, the maid
Paused awhile, and inly prayed:
Then falling at the Baron's feet,
"By my mother's soul do I entreat
That thou this woman send away!"
She said: and more she could not say:
For what she knew she could not tell,
O'er-mastered by the mighty spell.

Why is thy cheek so wan and wild,
Sir Leoline? Thy only child
Lies at thy feet, thy joy, thy pride,
So fair, so innocent, so mild;
The same, for whom thy lady died!
O, by the pangs of her dear mother
Think thou no evil of thy child!
For her, and thee, and for no other,
She prayed the moment ere she died:
Prayed that the babe for whom she died,
Might prove her dear lord's joy and pride!
  That prayer her deadly pangs beguiled, Sir Leoline!
  And wouldst thou wrong thy only child,
    Her child and thine?

Within the Baron's heart and brain
If thoughts, like these, had any share,
They only swelled his rage and pain,
And did but work confusion there.
His heart was cleft with pain and rage,
His cheeks they quivered, his eyes were wild,
Dishonored thus in his old age;
Dishonored by his only child,
And all his hospitality
To the insulted daughter of his friend
By more than woman's jealousy
Brought thus to a disgraceful end—
He rolled his eye with stern regard
Upon the gentle minstrel bard,
And said in tones abrupt, austere—
"Why, Bracy! dost thou loiter here?
I bade thee hence!" The bard obeyed;
And turning from his own sweet maid,
The agéd knight, Sir Leoline,
Led forth the lady Geraldine!

THE CONCLUSION TO PART THE SECOND

A little child, a limber elf,
Singing, dancing to itself,

A fairy thing with red round cheeks,
That always finds, and never seeks,
Makes such a vision to the sight
As fills a father's eyes with light;
And pleasures flow in so thick and fast
Upon his heart, that he at last
Must needs express his love's excess
With words of unmeant bitterness.
Perhaps 'tis pretty to force together
Thoughts so all unlike each other;
To mutter and mock a broken charm,
To dally with wrong that does no harm.
Perhaps 'tis tender too and pretty
At each wild word to feel within
A sweet recoil of love and pity.
And what, if in a world of sin
(O sorrow and shame should this be true!)
Such giddiness of heart and brain
Comes seldom save from rage and pain,
So talks as it's most used to do.

ROBERT SOUTHEY

(1774–1843)

The Battle of Blenheim

IT WAS a summer evening,—
Old Kaspar's work was done,
And he before his cottage door
Was sitting in the sun;
And by him sported on the green
His little grandchild Wilhelmine.

She saw her brother Peterkin
Roll something large and round,
Which he beside the rivulet,
In playing there, had found;
He came to ask what he had found
That was so large and smooth and round.

Old Kaspar took it from the boy,
 Who stood expectant by;
And then the old man shook his head,
 And, with a natural sigh,—
" 'T is some poor fellow's skull," said he,
"Who fell in the great victory.

"I find them in the garden,
 For there's many hereabout;
And often, when I go to plough,
 The ploughshare turns them out;
For many thousand men," said he,
"Were slain in the great victory."

"Now tell us what 't was all about,"
 Young Peterkin he cries;
And little Wilhelmine looks up
 With wonder-waiting eyes,—
"Now tell us all about the war,
And what they fought each other for."

"It was the English," Kaspar cried,
 "Who put the French to rout;
But what they fought each other for
 I could not well make out;
But everybody said," quoth he,
"That 't was a famous victory.

"My father lived at Blenheim then,
 Yon little stream hard by;
They burnt his dwelling to the ground,
 And he was forced to fly;
So with his wife and child he fled,
Nor had he where to rest his head.

"With fire and sword the country round
 Was wasted far and wide;
And many a childing mother there,
 And new-born baby died;
But things like that, you know, must be
At every famous victory.

"They say it was a shocking sight
After the field was won,—
For many thousand bodies here
Lay rotting in the sun;
But things like that, you know, must be
After a famous victory.

"Great praise the Duke of Marlborough won,
And our good Prince Eugene."
"Why, 't was a very wicked thing!"
Said little Wilhelmine.
"Nay, nay, my little girl!" quoth he,
"It was a famous victory.

"And everybody praised the duke
Who this great fight did win."
"But what good came of it at last?"
Quoth little Peterkin.
"Why, that I cannot tell," said he;
"But 't was a famous victory."

WALTER SAVAGE LANDOR
(1775–1864)

Rose Aylmer

AH, WHAT avails the sceptred race!
Ah, what the form divine!
What every virtue, every grace!
Rose Aylmer, all were thine.

Rose Aylmer, whom these wakeful eyes
May weep, but never see,
A night of memories and sighs
I consecrate to thee.

Proud Word You Never Spoke

PROUD word you never spoke, but you will speak
  Four not exempt from pride some future day.
Resting on one white hand a warm wet cheek
  Over my open volume you will say,
  "This man loved *me!*" then rise and trip away.

An Ancient Rhyme

THE burden of an ancient rhyme
Is, "by the forelock seize on Time."
Time in some corner heard it said;
Pricking his ears, away he fled;
And, seeing me upon the road,
A hearty curse on me bestowed.
"What if I do the same by thee?
How wouldst thou like it?" thundered he,
And, without answer thereupon,
Seizing *my* forelock . . . it was gone.

To Robert Browning

THERE is delight in singing, tho' none hear
Beside the singer: and there is delight
In praising, tho' the praiser sit alone
And see the praised far off him, far above.
Shakespeare is not our poet, but the world's,
Therefore on him no speech! and brief for thee,
Browning! Since Chaucer was alive and hale,
No man hath walked along our roads with step

So active, so inquiring eye, or tongue
So varied in discourse. But warmer climes
Give brighter plumage, stronger wing: the breeze
Of Alpine heights thou playest with, borne on
Beyond Sorrento and Amalfi, where
The Siren waits thee, singing sing for song.

On His Seventy-Fifth Birthday

I STROVE with none; for none was worth my strife,
  Nature I loved, and next to Nature, Art;
I warmed both hands before the fire of life,
  It sinks, and I am ready to depart.

CHARLES LAMB
(1775–1834)

The Old Familiar Faces

I HAVE had playmates, I have had companions,
In my days of childhood, in my joyful schooldays;
All, all are gone, the old familiar faces.

I have been laughing, I have been carousing,
Drinking late, sitting late, with my bosom cronies;
All, all are gone, the old familiar faces.

I loved a Love once, fairest among women:
Closed are her doors on me, I must not see her,—
All, all are gone, the old familiar faces.

I have a friend, a kinder friend has no man
Like an ingrate, I left my friend abruptly;
Left him, to muse on the old familiar faces.

Ghost-like I paced round the haunts of my childhood,
Earth seemed a desert I was bound to traverse,
Seeking to find the old familiar faces.

Friend of my bosom, thou more than a brother,
Why wert not thou born in my father's dwelling?
So might we talk of the old familiar faces.

How some they have died, and some they have left me,
And some are taken from me; all are departed;
All, all are gone, the old familiar faces.

Hester

When maidens such as Hester die,
Their place ye may not well supply,
Though ye among a thousand try,
With vain endeavor.

A month or more hath she been dead,
Yet cannot I by force be led
To think upon the wormy bed
And her together.

A springy motion in her gait,
A rising step, did indicate
Of pride and joy no common rate,
That flushed her spirit;

I know not by what name beside
I shall it call;—if 't was not pride,
It was a joy to that allied,
She did inherit.

Her parents held the Quaker rule,
Which doth the human feeling cool;
But she was trained in nature's school,
Nature had blessed her.

A waking eye, a prying mind,
A heart that stirs, is hard to bind;
A hawk's keen sight ye cannot blind,—
Ye could not Hester.

My sprightly neighbor, gone before
To that unknown and silent shore!
Shall we not meet as heretofore
Some summer morning,

When from thy cheerful eyes a ray
Hath struck a bliss upon the day,—
A bliss that would not go away,—
A sweet forewarning?

THOMAS CAMPBELL
(1777–1844)

Lord Ullin's Daughter

A CHIEFTAIN, to the Highlands bound,
Cries, "Boatman, do not tarry!
And I'll give thee a silver pound,
To row us o'er the ferry."

"Now who be ye, would cross Lochgyle,
This dark and stormy water?"
"O, I'm the chief of Ulva's isle,
And this Lord Ullin's daughter.

"And fast before her father's men
Three days we 've fled together,
For should he find us in the glen,
My blood would stain the heather.

"His horsemen hard behind us ride;
  Should they our steps discover,
Then who will cheer my bonny bride
  When they have slain her lover?"

Out spoke the hardy Highland wight,
  "I'll go, my chief,—I'm ready:—
It is not for your silver bright;
  But for your winsome lady:

"And by my word! the bonny bird
  In danger shall not tarry:
So, though the waves are raging white,
  I'll row you o'er the ferry."

By this the storm grew loud apace,
  The water-wraith was shrieking;
And in the scowl of heaven each face
  Grew dark as they were speaking.

But still as wilder blew the wind,
  And as the night grew drearer,
Adown the glen rode armèd men,
  Their trampling sounded nearer.

"O, haste thee, haste!" the lady cries,
  "Though tempests round us gather;
I'll meet the raging of the skies,
  But not an angry father."

The boat has left a stormy land,
  A stormy sea before her,—
When, O, too strong for human hand,
  The tempest gathered o'er her.

And still they rowed amidst the roar
  Of waters fast prevailing:
Lord Ullin reached that fatal shore,
  His wrath was changed to wailing.

For sore dismayed, through storm and shade,
His child he did discover:
One lovely hand she stretched for aid,
And one was round her lover.

"Come back! come back!" he cried in grief,
"Across this stormy water:
And I'll forgive your Highland chief,
My daughter!—O my daughter!"

'T was vain;—the loud waves lashed the shore,
Return or aid preventing;
The waters wild went o'er his child,
And he was left lamenting.

Ye Mariners of England

Ye mariners of England!
That guard our native seas;
Whose flag has braved a thousand years
The battle and the breeze!
Your glorious standard launch again
To match another foe!
And sweep through the deep,
While the stormy winds do blow;
While the battle rages loud and long,
And the stormy winds do blow.

The spirits of your fathers
Shall start from every wave!
For the deck it was their field of fame,
And Ocean was their grave:
Where Blake and mighty Nelson fell
Your manly hearts shall glow,
As ye sweep through the deep,
While the stormy winds do blow;
While the battle rages loud and long,
And the stormy winds do blow.

Britannia needs no bulwarks,
No towers along the steep;
Her march is o'er the mountain-waves,
Her home is on the deep.
With thunders from her native oak
She quells the floods below,
As they roar on the shore,
When the stormy winds do blow;
When the battle rages loud and long,
And the stormy winds do blow.

The meteor flag of England
Shall yet terrific burn;
Till danger's troubled night depart,
And the star of peace return.
Then, then, ye ocean warriors!
Our song and feast shall flow
To the fame of your name,
When the storm has ceased to blow;
When the fiery fight is heard no more,
And the storm has ceased to blow.

Song to the Evening Star

STAR that bringest home the bee,
And sett'st the weary laborer free!
If any star shed peace, 'tis thou
  That send'st it from above,
Appearing when Heaven's breath and brow
  Are sweet as hers we love.

Come to the luxuriant skies,
Whilst the landscape's odors rise,
Whilst far-off lowing herds are heard
  And songs when toil is done,
From cottages whose smoke unstirr'd
  Curls yellow in the sun.

Star of love's soft interviews,
Parted lovers on thee muse;
Their remembrancer in Heaven
  Of thrilling vows thou art,
Too delicious to be riven
  By absence from the heart.

The First Kiss

How delicious is the winning
Of a kiss at love's beginning,
When two mutual hearts are sighing
For the knot there's no untying.

Yet remember, midst your wooing,
Love has bliss, but love has ruing;
Other smiles may make you fickle,
Tears for other charms may trickle.

Love he comes, and Love he tarries,
Just as fate or fancy carries,—
Longest stays when sorest chidden,
Laughs and flies when pressed and bidden

Bind the sea to slumber stilly,
Bind its odor to the lily,
Bind the aspen ne'er to quiver,—
Then bind Love to last forever!

Love's a fire that needs renewal
Of fresh beauty for its fuel;
Love's wing moults when caged and captured,—
Only free he soars enraptured.

Can you keep the bee from ranging,
Or the ring-dove's neck from changing?
No! nor fettered Love from dying
In the knot there's no untying.

The Soldier's Dream

Our bugles sang truce,—for the night-cloud had lowered,
And the sentinel stars set their watch in the sky;
And thousands had sunk on the ground over-powered,
The weary to sleep, and the wounded to die.

When reposing that night on my pallet of straw,
By the wolf-scaring fagot that guarded the slain;
At the dead of the night a sweet vision I saw,
And thrice ere the morning I dreamt it again.

Methought from the battle-field's dreadful array,
Far, far I had roamed on a desolate track:
'T was autumn,—and sunshine arose on the way
To the home of my fathers, that welcomed me back.

I flew to the pleasant fields traversed so oft
In life's morning march, when my bosom was young;
I heard my own mountain-goats bleating aloft,
And knew the sweet strain that the corn-reapers sung.

Then pledged we the wine-cup, and fondly I swore,
From my home and my weeping friends never to part;
My little ones kissed me a thousand times o'er,
And my wife sobbed aloud in her fulness of heart.

"Stay, stay with us,—rest, thou art weary and worn;"
And fain was their war-broken soldier to stay;—
But sorrow returned with the dawning of morn,
And the voice in my dreaming ear melted away.

THOMAS MOORE

(1779–1852)

The Harp That Once Through Tara's Halls

THE harp that once through Tara's halls
  The soul of music shed,
Now hangs as mute on Tara's walls
  As if that soul were fled.
So sleeps the pride of former days,
  So glory's thrill is o'er,
And hearts that once beat high for praise
  Now feel that pulse no more!

No more to chiefs and ladies bright
  The harp of Tara swells;
The chord alone that breaks at night
  Its tale of ruin tells.
Thus Freedom now so seldom wakes,
  The only throb she gives
Is when some heart indignant breaks,
  To show that still she lives.

The Minstrel-Boy

THE Minstrel-boy to the war is gone,
  In the ranks of death you'll find him;
His father's sword he has girded on,
  And his wild harp slung behind him.—
"Land of song!" said the warrior-bard,
  "Though all the world betrays thee,
One sword, at least, thy rights shall guard,
  One faithful harp shall praise thee!"

The Minstrel fell!—but the foeman's chain
Could not bring his proud soul under;
The harp he loved ne'er spoke again,
For he tore its chords asunder;
And said, "No chains shall sully thee,
Thou soul of love and bravery!
Thy songs were made for the pure and free,
They shall never sound in slavery!"

Oft, in the Stilly Night

Oft, in the stilly night,
Ere Slumber's chain has bound me,
Fond Memory brings the light
Of other days around me:
The smiles, the tears,
Of boyhood's years,
The words of love then spoken;
The eyes that shone,
Now dimmed and gone,
The cheerful hearts now broken!
Thus, in the stilly night,
Ere Slumber's chain has bound me,
Sad Memory brings the light
Of other days around me.

When I remember all
The friends so linked together
I've seen around me fall,
Like leaves in wintry weather,
I feel like one
Who treads alone
Some banquet-hall deserted,
Whose lights are fled,
Whose garlands dead,
And all but him departed!

Thus, in the stilly night,
   Ere Slumber's chain has bound me,
Sad Memory brings the light
   Of other days around me.

At the Mid Hour of Night

At the mid hour of night, when stars are weeping, I fly
To the lone vale we loved, when life shone warm in thine eye;
And I think oft, if spirits can steal from the regions of air
To revisit past scenes of delight, thou wilt come to me there,
And tell me our love is remember'd, even in the sky!

Then I sing the wild song it once was rapture to hear,
When our voices commingling breathed like one on the ear;
And as Echo far off through the vale my sad orison rolls,
I think, oh my Love! 'tis thy voice, from the Kingdom of Souls
Faintly answering still the notes that once were so dear.

LEIGH HUNT

(1784–1859)

Jenny Kissed Me

Jenny kissed me when we met,
   Jumping from the chair she sat in.
Time, you thief! who love to get
   Sweets into your list, put that in.
Say I'm weary, say I'm sad;
   Say that health and wealth have missed me;
Say I'm growing old, but add—
                  Jenny kissed me!

Abou Ben Adhem

ABOU BEN ADHEM (may his tribe increase!)
Awoke one night from a deep dream of peace,
And saw within the moonlight in his room,
Making it rich and like a lily in bloom,
An angel writing in a book of gold:
Exceeding peace had made Ben Adhem bold,
And to the presence in the room he said,
"What writest thou?" The vision raised its head,
And, with a look made of all sweet accord,
Answered, "The names of those who love the Lord."
"And is mine one?" said Abou. "Nay, not so,"
Replied the angel. Abou spoke more low,
But cheerly still; and said, "I pray thee, then,
Write me as one that loves his fellow-men."

The angel wrote, and vanished. The next night
It came again, with a great wakening light,
And showed the names whom love of God had blessed,—
And, lo! Ben Adhem's name led all the rest!

ALLAN CUNNINGHAM

(1784–1842)

A Wet Sheet and a Flowing Sea

A WET sheet and a flowing sea,
  A wind that follows fast
And fills the white and rustling sail
  And bends the gallant mast;
And bends the gallant mast, my boys,
  While like the eagle free
Away the good ship flies, and leaves
  Old England on the lee.

O for a soft and gentle wind!
  I heard a fair one cry;
But give to me the snoring breeze
  And white waves heaving high;
And white waves heaving high, my lads,
  The good ship tight and free—
The world of waters is our home,
  And merry men are we.

There's tempest in yon hornèd moon,
  And lightning in yon cloud;
But hark the music, mariners!
  The wind is piping loud;
The wind is piping loud, my boys,
  The lightning flashes free—
While the hollow oak our palace is,
  Our heritage the sea.

BRYAN WALLER PROCTER

(Barry Cornwall)

(1787–1874)

The Sea

THE sea! the sea! the open sea!
The blue, the fresh, the ever free!
Without a mark, without a bound,
It runneth the earth's wide regions round;
It plays with the clouds; it mocks the skies;
Or like a cradled creature lies.

I'm on the sea! I'm on the sea!
I am where I would ever be;
With the blue above, and the blue below,
And silence wheresoe'er I go;
If a storm should come and awake the deep,
What matter? *I* shall ride and sleep.

I love, O, how I love to ride
On the fierce, foaming, bursting tide,
When every mad wave drowns the moon,
Or whistles aloft his tempest tune,
And tells how goeth the world below,
And why the sou'west blasts do blow.

I never was on the dull, tame shore,
But I loved the great sea more and more,
And backwards flew to her billowy breast,
Like a bird that seeketh its mother's nest;
And a mother she was, and is, to me;
For I was born on the open sea!

The waves were white, and red the morn,
In the noisy hour when I was born;
And the whale it whistled, the porpoise rolled,
And the dolphins bared their backs of gold;
And never was heard such an outcry wild
As welcomed to life the ocean-child!

I've lived since then, in calm and strife,
Full fifty summers, a sailor's life,
With wealth to spend and a power to range,
But never have sought nor sighed for change;
And Death, whenever he comes to me,
Shall come on the wild, unbounded sea!

GEORGE GORDON BYRON, LORD BYRON

(1788–1824)

She Walks in Beauty

SHE walks in beauty, like the night
  Of cloudless climes and starry skies,
And all that's best of dark and bright
  Meet in her aspect and her eyes,
Thus mellowed to that tender light
  Which heaven to gaudy day denies.

One shade the more, one ray the less,
  Had half impaired the nameless grace
Which waves in every raven tress
  Or softly lightens o'er her face,
Where thoughts serenely sweet express
  How pure, how dear their dwelling-place.

And on that cheek and o'er that brow
  So soft, so calm, yet eloquent,
The smiles that win, the tints that glow,
  But tell of days in goodness spent,—
A mind at peace with all below,
  A heart whose love is innocent.

There Be None of Beauty's Daughters

THERE be none of Beauty's daughters
  With a magic like thee;
And like music on the waters
  Is thy sweet voice to me:
When, as if its sound were causing
The charmèd ocean's pausing,
The waves lie still and gleaming,
And the lull'd winds seem dreaming:

And the midnight moon is weaving
  Her bright chain o'er the deep,
Whose breast is gently heaving
  As an infant's asleep:
So the spirit bows before thee,
To listen and adore thee;
With a full but soft emotion
Like the swell of Summer's ocean.

So We'll Go No More A-Roving

So WE'LL go no more a-roving
  So late into the night,
Though the heart be still as loving,
  And the moon be still as bright.

For the sword outwears its sheath,
  And the soul wears out the breast,
And the heart must pause to breathe,
  And love itself have rest.

Though the night was made for loving,
  And the day returns too soon,
Yet we'll go no more a-roving
  By the light of the moon.

When We Two Parted

WHEN we two parted
  In silence and tears,
Half broken-hearted
  To sever for years,
Pale grew thy cheek and cold,
  Colder thy kiss;
Truly that hour foretold
  Sorrow to this.

The dew of the morning
  Sunk chill on my brow—
It felt like the warning
  Of what I feel now.
Thy vows are all broken,
  And light is thy fame;
I hear thy name spoken,
  And share in its shame.

They name thee before me,
  A knell to mine ear;
A shudder comes o'er me—
  Why wert thou so dear?
They know not I knew thee,
  Who knew thee too well:—
Long, long shall I rue thee,
  Too deeply to tell.

In secret we met—
  In silence I grieve,
That thy heart could forget,
  Thy spirit deceive.
If I should meet thee
  After long years,
How should I greet thee?—
  With silence and tears.

The Destruction of Sennacherib

The Assyrian came down like the wolf on the fold,
And his cohorts were gleaming in purple and gold;
And the sheen of their spears was like stars on the sea,
When the blue wave rolls nightly on deep Galilee.

Like the leaves of the forest when summer is green,
That host with their banners at sunset were seen:
Like the leaves of the forest when autumn hath blown,
That host on the morrow lay withered and strown.

For the Angel of Death spread his wings on the blast,
And breathed in the face of the foe as he passed;
And the eyes of the sleepers waxed deadly and chill,
And their hearts but once heaved, and forever grew still!

And there lay the steed with his nostril all wide,
But through it there rolled not the breath of his pride:
And the foam of his gasping lay white on the turf,
And cold as the spray of the rock-beating surf.

And there lay the rider distorted and pale,
With the dew on his brow, and the rust on his mail;
And the tents were all silent, the banners alone,
The lances unlifted, the trumpet unblown.

And the widows of Ashur are loud in their wail,
And the idols are broke in the temple of Baal;
And the might of the Gentile, unsmote by the sword,
Hath melted like snow in the glance of the Lord!

The Prisoner of Chillon

ETERNAL spirit of the chainless mind!
Brightest in dungeons, Liberty! thou art,
For there thy habitation is the heart,—
The heart which love of thee alone can bind;
And when thy sons to fetters are consigned,—
To fetters, and the damp vault's dayless gloom,—
Their country conquers with their martyrdom,
And Freedom's fame finds wings on every wind.
Chillon! thy prison is a holy place,
And thy sad floor an altar,—for 't was trod,
Until his very steps have left a trace
Worn, as if thy cold pavement were a sod,
By Bonnivard!—May none those marks efface!
For they appeal from tyranny to God.

My hair is gray, but not with years,
Nor grew it white
In a single night,
As men's have grown from sudden fears:
My limbs are bowed, though not with toil,
But rusted with a vile repose,
For they have been a dungeon's spoil,
And mine has been the fate of those

To whom the goodly earth and air
Are banned, and barred,—forbidden fare;
But this was for my father's faith
I suffered chains and courted death;
That father perished at the stake
For tenets he would not forsake;
And for the same his lineal race
In darkness found a dwelling-place;
We were seven,—who now are one,
  Six in youth, and one in age,
Finished as they had begun,
  Proud of Persecution's rage;
One in fire, and two in field,
Their belief with blood have sealed!
Dying as their father died,
For the God their foes denied;
Three were in a dungeon cast,
Of whom this wreck is left the last.

There are seven pillars of Gothic mould
In Chillon's dungeons deep and old,
There are seven columns, massy and gray,
Dim with a dull imprisoned ray,—
A sunbeam which hath lost its way,
And through the crevice and the cleft
Of the thick wall is fallen and left,
Creeping o'er the floor so damp,
Like a marsh's meteor lamp,—
And in each pillar there is a ring,
  And in each ring there is a chain;
That iron is a cankering thing,
  For in these limbs its teeth remain
With marks that will not wear away,
Till I have done with this new day,
Which now is painful to these eyes,
Which have not seen the sun to rise
For years,--I cannot count them o'er,
I lost their long and heavy score
When my last brother drooped and died,
And I lay living by his side.

They chained us each to a column stone,
And we were three, yet each alone;
We could not move a single pace,
We could not see each other's face,
But with that pale and livid light
That made us strangers in our sight;
And thus together, yet apart,
Fettered in hand, but pined in heart;
'T was still some solace, in the dearth
Of the pure elements of earth,
To hearken to each other's speech,
And each turn comforter to each
With some new hope, or legend old,
Or song heroically bold;
But even these at length grew cold.
Our voices took a dreary tone,
An echo of the dungeon-stone,
  A grating sound,—not full and free
  As they of yore were wont to be;
  It might be fancy,—but to me
They never sounded like our own.

I was the eldest of the three,
  And to uphold and cheer the rest
  I ought to do—and did—my best,
And each did well in his degree.
  The youngest, whom my father loved,
Because our mother's brow was given
To him, with eyes as blue as heaven,—
  For him my soul was sorely moved;
And truly might it be distrest
To see such bird in such a nest;
For he was beautiful as day
  (When day was beautiful to me
  As to young eagles, being free),—
  A polar day, which will not see
A sunset till its summer's gone,
  Its sleepless summer of long light,
The snow-clad offspring of the sun;
  And thus he was as pure and bright,
And in his natural spirit gay,

With tears for naught but others' ills,
And then they flowed like mountain rills,
Unless he could assuage the woe
Which he abhorred to view below.

The other was as pure of mind,
But formed to combat with his kind;
Strong in his frame, and of a mood
Which 'gainst the world in war had stood,
And perished in the foremost rank
  With joy;—but not in chains to pine;
His spirit withered with their clank,
  I saw it silently decline,—
And so perchance in sooth did mine;
But yet I forced it on to cheer
Those relics of a home so dear.
He was a hunter of the hills,
  Had followed there the deer and wolf;
  To him this dungeon was a gulf
And fettered feet the worst of ills.
  Lake Leman lies by Chillon's walls:
A thousand feet in depth below
Its massy waters meet and flow;
Thus much the fathom-line was sent
From Chillon's snow-white battlement,
  Which round about the wave inthralls;
A double dungeon wall and wave
Have made,—and like a living grave.
Below the surface of the lake
The dark vault lies wherein we lay,
We heard it ripple night and day;
  Sounding o'er our heads it knocked;
And I have felt the winter's spray
Wash through the bars when winds were high
And wanton in the happy sky;
  And then the very rock hath rocked,
  And I have felt it shake, unshocked,
Because I could have smiled to see
The death that would have set me free.

I said my nearer brother pined,
I said his mighty heart declined,
He loathed and put away his food;
It was not that 't was coarse and rude,
For we were used to hunter's fare,
And for the like had little care;
The milk drawn from the mountain goat
Was changed for water from the moat.
Our bread was such as captives' tears
Have moistened many a thousand years,
Since man first pent his fellow-men
Like brutes within an iron den;
But what were these to us or him?
These wasted not his heart or limb;
My brother's soul was of that mould
Which in a palace had grown cold,
Had his free breathing been denied
The range of the steep mountain's side;
But why delay the truth?—he died.
I saw, and could not hold his head,
Nor reach his dying hand,—nor dead,—
Though hard I strove, but strove in vain,
To rend and gnash my bonds in twain.
He died,—and they unlocked his chain,
And scooped for him a shallow grave
Even from the cold earth of our cave.
I begged them, as a boon, to lay
His corse in dust whereon the day
Might shine,—it was a foolish thought,
But then within my brain it wrought,
That even in death his free-born breast
In such a dungeon could not rest.
I might have spared my idle prayer,—
They coldly laughed, and laid him there.
The flat and turfless earth above
The being we so much did love;
His empty chain above it leant,
Such murder's fitting monument!

But he, the favorite and the flower,
Most cherished since his natal hour,

His mother's image in fair face,
The infant love of all his race,
His martyred father's dearest thought,
My latest care, for whom I sought
To hoard my life, that his might be
Less wretched now, and one day free;
He, too, who yet had held untired
A spirit natural or inspired,—
He, too, was struck, and day by day
Was withered on the stalk away.
O God! it is a fearful thing
To see the human soul take wing
In any shape, in any mood:—
I've seen it rushing forth in blood,
I've seen it on the breaking ocean
Strive with a swoln convulsive motion,
I've seen the sick and ghastly bed
Of Sin delirious with its dread:
But these were horrors,—this was woe
Unmixed with such,—but sure and slow:
He faded, and so calm and meek,
So softly worn, so sweetly weak,
So tearless, yet so tender,—kind,
And grieved for those he left behind;
With all the while a cheek whose bloom
Was as a mockery of the tomb,
Whose tints as gently sunk away
As a departing rainbow's ray,—
An eye of most transparent light,
That almost made the dungeon bright,
And not a word of murmur,—not
A groan o'er his untimely lot,—
A little talk of better days,
A little hope my own to raise,
For I was sunk in silence,—lost
In this last loss, of all the most;
And then the sighs he would suppress
Of fainting nature's feebleness,
More slowly drawn, grew less and less:
I listened, but I could not hear,—
I called, for I was wild with fear;

I knew 't was hopeless, but my dread
Would not be thus admonishèd;
I called, and thought I heard a sound,—
I burst my chain with one strong bound,
And rushed to him:—I found him not,
I only stirred in this black spot,
I only lived,—*I* only drew
The accursèd breath of dungeon-dew;
The last—the sole—the dearest link
Between me and the eternal brink,
Which bound me to my failing race,
Was broken in this fatal place.
One on the earth, and one beneath,—
My brothers—both had ceased to breathe.
I took that hand which lay so still,
Alas! my own was full as chill;
I had not strength to stir or strive,
But felt that I was still alive,—
A frantic feeling when we know
That what we love shall ne'er be so.
    I know not why
    I could not die,
I had no earthly hope—but faith,
And that forbade a selfish death.

What next befell me then and there
  I know not well—I never knew.
First came the loss of light and air,
  And then of darkness too;
I had no thought, no feeling—none:
Among the stones I stood a stone,
And was, scarce conscious what I wist,
As shrubless crags within the mist;
For all was blank and bleak and gray;
It was not night,—it was not day;
It was not even the dungeon-light,
So hateful to my heavy sight;
But vacancy absorbing space,
And fixedness, without a place:
There were no stars—no earth—no time—
No check—no change—no good—no crime:

But silence, and a stirless breath
Which neither was of life nor death:—
A sea of stagnant idleness,
Blind, boundless, mute, and motionless.

A light broke in upon my brain,—
  It was the carol of a bird;
It ceased, and then it came again,—
  The sweetest song ear ever heard,
And mine was thankful till my eyes
Ran over with the glad surprise,
And they that moment could not see
I was the mate of misery;
But then by dull degrees came back
My senses to their wonted track,
I saw the dungeon walls and floor
Close slowly round me as before,
I saw the glimmer of the sun
Creeping as it before had done,
But through the crevice where it came
That bird was perched, as fond and tame,
  And tamer than upon the tree;
A lovely bird, with azure wings,
And song that said a thousand things,
  And seemed to say them all for me.
I never saw its like before,
I ne'er shall see its likeness more.
It seemed, like me, to want a mate,
But was not half so desolate,
And it was come to love me when
None lived to love me so again,
And cheering from my dungeon's brink,
Had brought me back to feel and think.
I know not if it late were free,
  Or broke its cage to perch on mine,
But knowing well captivity,
  Sweet bird! I could not wish for thine!
Or if it were, in wingèd guise,
A visitant from Paradise:
For—Heaven forgive that thought! the while
Which made me both to weep and smile—

I sometimes deemed that it might be
My brother's soul come down to me;
But then at last away it flew,
And then 't was mortal,—well I knew,
For he would never thus have flown,
And left me twice so doubly lone,—
Lone—as the corse within its shroud,
Lone—as a solitary cloud,
  A single cloud on a sunny day,
While all the rest of heaven is clear,
A frown upon the atmosphere,
That hath no business to appear
  When skies are blue and earth is gay.

A kind of change came in my fate,
My keepers grew compassionate;
I know not what had made them so,
They were inured to sights of woe,
But so it was:—my broken chain
With links unfastened did remain,
And it was liberty to stride
Along my cell from side to side,
And up and down, and then athwart,
And tread it over every part;
And round the pillars one by one,
Returning where my walk begun,
Avoiding only, as I trod,
My brothers' graves without a sod;
For if I thought with heedless tread
My step profaned their lowly bed,
My breath came gaspingly and thick,
And my crushed heart fell blind and sick.

I made a footing in the wall,
  It was not therefrom to escape,
For I had buried one and all
  Who loved me in a human shape:
And the whole earth would henceforth be
A wider prison unto me:
No child,—no sire,—no kin had I,
No partner in my misery;

I thought of this and I was glad,
For thought of them had made me mad;
But I was curious to ascend
To my barred windows, and to bend
Once more, upon the mountains high,
The quiet of a loving eye.

I saw them,—and they were the same,
They were not changed like me in frame;
I saw their thousand years of snow
On high,—their wide long lake below,
And the blue Rhone in fullest flow;
I heard the torrents leap and gush
O'er channelled rock and broken bush;
I saw the white-walled distant town,
And whiter sails go skimming down;
And then there was a little isle,
Which in my very face did smile,
  The only one in view;
A small green isle, it seemed no more,
Scarce broader than my dungeon floor,
But in it there were three tall trees,
And o'er it blew the mountain breeze,
And by it there were waters flowing,
And on it there were young flowers growing,
  Of gentle breath and hue.
The fish swam by the castle wall,
And they seemed joyous each and all;
The eagle rode the rising blast,
Methought he never flew so fast
As then to me he seemed to fly,
And then new tears came in my eye,
And I felt troubled,—and would fain
I had not left my recent chain;
And when I did descend again,
The darkness of my dim abode
Fell on me as a heavy load;
It was as in a new-dug grave
Closing o'er one we sought to save,
And yet my glance, too much oppressed,
Had almost need of such a rest.

It might be months, or years, or days,
  I kept no count,—I took no note,
I had no hope my eyes to raise,
  And clear them of their dreary mote;
At last men came to set me free,
  I asked not why and recked not where,
It was at length the same to me,
Fettered or fetterless to be,
I learned to love despair.
And thus when they appeared at last,
And all my bonds aside were cast,
These heavy walls to me had grown
A hermitage, and all my own!
And half I felt as they were come
To tear me from a second home;
With spiders I had friendship made,
And watched them in their sullen trade,
Had seen the mice by moonlight play,
And why should I feel less than they?
We were all inmates of one place,
And I, the monarch of each race,
Had power to kill,—yet, strange to tell!
In quiet we had learned to dwell,—
My very chains and I grew friends,
So much a long communion tends
To make us what we are:—even I
Regained my freedom with a sigh.

The Night Before Waterloo

THERE was a sound of revelry by night,
And Belgium's capital had gather'd then
Her Beauty and her Chivalry, and bright
The lamps shone o'er fair women and brave men;
A thousand hearts beat happily; and when
Music arose with its voluptuous swell,
Soft eyes look'd love to eyes which spake again,
And all went merry as a marriage bell;
But hush! hark! a deep sound strikes like a rising knell!

Did ye not hear it?—No; 'twas but the wind,
Or the car rattling o'er the stony street;
On with the dance! let joy be unconfined;
No sleep till morn, when Youth and Pleasure meet
To chase the glowing Hours with flying feet.
But hark! that heavy sound breaks in once more,
As if the clouds its echo would repeat;
And nearer, clearer, deadlier than before!
Arm! arm! it is—it is—the cannon's opening roar!

Ah! then and there was hurrying to and fro,
And gathering tears, and tremblings of distress,
And cheeks all pale, which but an hour ago
Blush'd at the praise of their own loveliness;
And there were sudden partings, such as press
The life from out young hearts, and choking sighs
Which ne'er might be repeated: who could guess
If ever more should meet those mutual eyes,
Since upon night so sweet such awful morn could rise!

And there was mounting in hot haste: the steed,
The mustering squadron, and the clattering car,
Went pouring forward with impetuous speed,
And swiftly forming in the ranks of war;
And the deep thunder peal on peal afar;
And near, the beat of the alarming drum
Roused up the soldier ere the morning star;
While throng'd the citizens with terror dumb,
Or whispering with white lips—"The foe!
They come! they come!"

Last noon beheld them full of lusty life,
Last eve in Beauty's circle proudly gay,
The midnight brought the signal-sound of strife,
The morn the marshalling in arms—the day
Battle's magnificently stern array!
The thunder-clouds close o'er it, which when rent
The earth is cover'd thick with other clay,
Which her own clay shall cover, heap'd and pent,
Rider and horse—friend, foe,—in one red burial blent!

The Isles of Greece

THE isles of Greece, the isles of Greece!
  Where burning Sappho loved and sung,
Where grew the arts of war and peace,—
  Where Delos rose, and Phœbus sprung!
Eternal summer gilds them yet,
But all, except their sun, is set.

The Scian and the Teian muse,
  The hero's harp, the lover's lute,
Have found the fame your shores refuse;
  Their place of birth alone is mute
To sounds which echo further west
Than your sires' "Islands of the Blest."

The mountains look on Marathon—
  And Marathon looks on the sea;
And musing there an hour alone,
  I dreamed that Greece might still be free;
For standing on the Persians' grave,
I could not deem myself a slave.

A king sate on the rocky brow
  Which looks o'er sea-born Salamis;
And ships, by thousands, lay below,
  And men in nations;—all were his!
He counted them at break of day—
And when the sun set where were they?

And where are they? and where art thou,
  My country? On thy voiceless shore
The heroic lay is tuneless now—
  The heroic bosom beats no more!

And must thy lyre, so long divine,
Degenerate into hands like mine?

'Tis something, in the dearth of fame,
  Though linked among a fettered race,
To feel at least a patriot's shame,
  Even as I sing, suffuse my face;
For what is left the poet here?
For Greeks a blush—for Greece a tear.

Must *we* but weep o'er days more blest?
  Must *we* but blush?—Our fathers bled.
Earth! render back from out thy breast
  A remnant of our Spartan dead!
Of the three hundred grant but three,
To make a new Thermopylæ!

What, silent still? and silent all?
  Ah! no;—the voices of the dead
Sound like a distant torrent's fall,
  And answer, "Let one living head,
But one arise,—we come, we come!"
'Tis but the living who are dumb.

In vain—in vain: strike other chords;
  Fill high the cup with Samian wine!
Leave battles to the Turkish hordes,
  And shed the blood of Scio's vine!
Hark! rising to the ignoble call—
How answers each bold Bacchanal!

You have the Pyrrhic dance as yet,
  Where is the Pyrrhic phalanx gone?
Of two such lessons, why forget
  The nobler and the manlier one?
You have the letters Cadmus gave—
Think ye he meant them for a slave?

Fill high the bowl with Samian wine!
  We will not think of themes like these!
It made Anacreon's song divine:
  He served—but served Polycrates—
A tyrant; but our masters then
Were still, at least, our countrymen.

The tyrant of the Chersonese
  Was freedom's best and bravest friend;
That tyrant was Miltiades!
  Oh! that the present hour would lend
Another despot of the kind!
Such chains as his were sure to bind.

Fill high the bowl with Samian wine!
  On Suli's rock, and Parga's shore,
Exists the remnant of a line
  Such as the Doric mothers bore;
And there, perhaps, some seed is sown,
The Heracleidan blood might own.

Trust not for freedom to the Franks—
  They have a king who buys and sells:
In native swords, and native ranks,
  The only hope of courage dwells;
But Turkish force, and Latin fraud,
Would break your shield, however broad.

Fill high the bowl with Samian wine!
  Our virgins dance beneath the shade—
I see their glorious black eyes shine;
  But gazing on each glowing maid,
My own the burning tear-drop laves,
To think such breasts must suckle slaves.

Place me on Sunium's marbled steep,
  Where nothing, save the waves and I,
May hear our mutual murmurs sweep;
  There, swan-like, let me sing and die:
A land of slaves shall ne'er be mine—
Dash down yon cup of Samian wine!

The Sea

THERE is a pleasure in the pathless woods,
There is a rapture on the lonely shore,
There is society where none intrudes
By the deep sea, and music in its roar:
I love not man the less, but nature more,
From these our interviews, in which I steal
From all I may be, or have been before,
To mingle with the universe, and feel
What I can ne'er express, yet cannot all conceal.

Roll on, thou deep and dark blue Ocean,—roll!
Ten thousand fleets sweep over thee in vain;
Man marks the earth with ruin,—his control
Stops with the shore;—upon the watery plain
The wrecks are all thy deed, nor doth remain
A shadow of man's ravage, save his own,
When, for a moment, like a drop of rain,
He sinks into thy depths with bubbling groan,
Without a grave, unknelled, uncoffined, and unknown.

His steps are not upon thy paths,—thy fields
Are not a spoil for him,—thou dost arise
And shake him from thee; the vile strength he wields
For earth's destruction thou dost all despise,
Spurning him from thy bosom to the skies,
And send'st him, shivering in thy playful spray
And howling, to his gods, where haply lies
His petty hope in some near port or bay,
And dashest him again to earth:—there let him lay.

The armaments which thunderstrike the walls
Of rock-built cities, bidding nations quake
And monarchs tremble in their capitals,
The oak leviathans, whose huge ribs make
Their clay creator the vain title take
Of lord of thee and arbiter of war,—
These are thy toys, and, as the snowy flake,
They melt into thy yeast of waves, which mar
Alike the Armada's pride or spoils of Trafalgar.

Thy shores are empires, changed in all save thee;
Assyria, Greece, Rome, Carthage, what are they?
Thy waters wasted them while they were free,
And many a tyrant since; their shores obey
The stranger, slave, or savage; their decay
Has dried up realms to deserts: not so thou;
Unchangeable save to thy wild waves' play,
Time writes no wrinkles on thine azure brow;
Such as creation's dawn beheld, thou rollest now.

Thou glorious mirror, where the Almighty's form
Glasses itself in tempests; in all time,
Calm or convulsed,—in breeze, or gale, or storm,
Icing the pole, or in the torrid clime
Dark-heaving; boundless, endless, and sublime,
The image of Eternity,—the throne
Of the Invisible! even from out thy slime
The monsters of the deep are made; each zone
Obeys thee; thou goest forth, dread, fathomless, alone.

And I have loved thee, Ocean! and my joy
Of youthful sports was on thy breast to be
Borne, like thy bubbles, onward; from a boy
I wantoned with thy breakers,—they to me
Were a delight; and if the freshening sea
Made them a terror, 't was a pleasing fear;
For I was as it were a child of thee,
And trusted to thy billows far and near,
And laid my hand upon thy mane,—as I do here.

FITZ-GREENE HALLECK
(1790–1867)

Joseph Rodman Drake

GREEN be the turf above thee,
  Friend of my better days!
None knew thee but to love thee,
  Nor named thee but to praise.

Tears fell, when thou wert dying,
  From eyes unused to weep,
And long, where thou art lying,
  Will tears the cold turf steep.

When hearts, whose truth was proven,
  Like thine, are laid in earth,
There should a wreath be woven
  To tell the world their worth;

And I, who woke each morrow
  To clasp thy hand in mine,
Who shared thy joy and sorrow,
  Whose weal and woe were thine,

It should be mine to braid it
  Around thy faded brow,
But I've in vain essayed it,
  And feel I cannot now.

While memory bids me weep thee,
  Nor thoughts nor words are free,
The grief is fixed too deeply
  That mourns a man like thee.

CHARLES WOLFE

(1791–1823)

The Burial of Sir John Moore

Not a drum was heard, not a funeral note,
As his corse to the rampart we hurried;
Not a soldier discharged his farewell shot
O'er the grave where our hero we buried.

We buried him darkly, at dead of night,
The sods with our bayonets turning;
By the struggling moonbeam's misty light,
And the lantern dimly burning.

No useless coffin enclosed his breast,
Not in sheet or in shroud we wound him,
But he lay like a warrior taking his rest,
With his martial cloak around him.

Few and short were the prayers we said,
And we spoke not a word of sorrow;
But we steadfastly gazed on the face that was dead,
And we bitterly thought of the morrow.

We thought, as we hollowed his narrow bed
And smoothed down his lonely pillow,
That the foe and the stranger would tread o'er his head,
And we far away on the billow!

Lightly they'll talk of the spirit that's gone,
And o'er his cold ashes upbraid him;
But little he'll reck, if they let him sleep on
In the grave where a Briton has laid him.

But half of our weary task was done
When the clock struck the note for retiring;
And we heard the distant and random gun
Of the enemy sullenly firing.

Slowly and sadly we laid him down,
  From the field of his fame fresh and gory:
We carved not a line, and we raised not a stone,
  But we left him alone with his glory.

PERCY BYSSHE SHELLEY
(1792–1822)

Ozymandias

I MET a traveler from an antique land
Who said: Two vast and trunkless legs of stone
Stand in the desert. Near them on the sand,
Half sunk, a shatter'd visage lies, whose frown
And wrinkled lip and sneer of cold command
Tell that its sculptor well those passions read
Which yet survive, stamp'd on these lifeless things,
The hand that mock'd them and the heart that fed;
And on the pedestal these words appear:
"My name is Ozymandias, king of kings:
Look on my works, ye Mighty, and despair!"
Nothing beside remains. Round the decay
Of that colossal wreck, boundless and bare,
The lone and level sands stretch far away.

Ode to the West Wind

O WILD West Wind, thou breath of Autumn's being,
Thou, from whose unseen presence the leaves dead
Are driven, like ghosts from an enchanter fleeing,

Yellow, and black, and pale, and hectic red,
Pestilence-stricken multitudes: O thou,
Who chariotest to their dark wintry bed

The wingèd seeds, where they lie cold and low,
Each like a corpse within its grave, until
Thine azure sister of the Spring shall blow

Her clarion o'er the dreaming earth, and fill
(Driving sweet buds like flocks to feed in air)
With living hues and odours plain and hill:

Wild Spirit, which art moving everywhere;
Destroyer and preserver; hear, oh, hear!

II

Thou on whose stream, mid the steep sky's commotion,
Loose clouds like earth's decaying leaves are shed,
Shook from the tangled boughs of Heaven and Ocean,

Angels of rain and lightning: there are spread
On the blue surface of thine airy surge,
Like the bright hair uplifted from the head

Of some fierce Maenad, even from the dim verge
Of the horizon to the zenith's height,
The locks of the approaching storm. Thou dirge

Of the dying year, to which this closing night
Will be the dome of a vast sepulchre,
Vaulted with all thy congregated might

Of vapours, from whose solid atmosphere
Black rain, and fire, and hail will burst: oh, hear!

III

Thou who didst waken from his summer dreams
The blue Mediterranean, where he lay,
Lulled by the coil of his crystàlline streams,

Beside a pumice isle in Baiae's bay,
And saw in sleep old palaces and towers
Quivering within the wave's intenser day,

All overgrown with azure moss and flowers
So sweet, the sense faints picturing them! Thou
For whose path the Atlantic's level powers

Cleave themselves into chasms, while far below
The sea-blooms and the oozy woods which wear
The sapless foliage of the ocean, know

Thy voice, and suddenly grow gray with fear,
And tremble and despoil themselves: oh, hear!

IV

If I were a dead leaf thou mightest bear;
If I were a swift cloud to fly with thee;
A wave to pant beneath thy power, and share

The impulse of thy strength, only less free
Than thou, O uncontrollable! If even
I were as in my boyhood, and could be

The comrade of thy wanderings over heaven,
As then, when to outstrip thy skyey speed
Scarce seemed a vision; I would ne'er have striven

As thus with thee in prayer in my sore need.
Oh, lift me as a wave, a leaf, a cloud!
I fall upon the thorns of life! I bleed!

A heavy weight of hours has chained and bowed
One too like thee: tameless, and swift, and proud.

V

Make me thy lyre, even as the forest is:
What if my leaves are falling like its own!
The tumult of thy mighty harmonies

Will take from both a deep, autumnal tone,
Sweet though in sadness. Be thou, Spirit fierce,
My spirit! Be thou me, impetuous one!

Drive my dead thoughts over the universe
Like withered leaves to quicken a new birth!
And, by the incantation of this verse,

Scatter, as from an unextinguished hearth
Ashes and sparks, my words among mankind!
Be through my lips to unawakened earth

The trumpet of a prophecy! O Wind,
If Winter comes, can Spring be far behind?

Indian Serenade

I ARISE from dreams of thee
  In the first sweet sleep of night,
When the winds are breathing low,
  And the stars are shining bright.
I arise from dreams of thee,
  And a spirit in my feet
Has led me—who knows how?—
  To thy chamber-window, sweet!

The wandering airs they faint
  On the dark, the silent stream,—
The champak odors fail
  Like sweet thoughts in a dream;
The nightingale's complaint,
  It dies upon her heart,
As I must die on thine,
  O, belovèd as thou art!

O, lift me from the grass!
  I die, I faint, I fail!
Let thy love in kisses rain
  On my lips and eyelids pale.
My cheek is cold and white, alas!
  My heart beats loud and fast:
O, press it close to thine again,
  Where it will break at last!

Love's Philosophy

THE fountains mingle with the river,
  And the rivers with the ocean;
The winds of heaven mix forever,
  With a sweet emotion;
Nothing in the world is single;
  All things by a law divine
In one another's being mingle:—
  Why not I with thine?

See! the mountains kiss high heaven,
  And the waves clasp one another;
No sister flower would be forgiven
  If it disdained its brother;
And the sunlight clasps the earth,
  And the moonbeams kiss the sea:—
What are all these kissings worth,
  If thou kiss not me?

The Cloud

I BRING fresh showers for the thirsting flowers,
    From the seas and the streams;
I bear light shade for the leaves when laid
    In their noonday dreams.
From my wings are shaken the dews that waken
    The sweet buds every one,
When rocked to rest on their mother's breast,
    As she dances about the sun.
I wield the flail of the lashing hail,
    And whiten the green plains under;
And then again I dissolve it in rain,
    And laugh as I pass in thunder.

I sift the snow on the mountains below,
 And their great pines groan aghast;
And all the night 'tis my pillow white,
 While I sleep in the arms of the blast.
Sublime on the towers of my skyey bowers,
 Lightning my pilot sits;
In a cavern under is fettered the thunder,
 It struggles and howls at fits;

Over earth and ocean, with gentle motion,
 This pilot is guiding me,
Lured by the love of the genii that move
 In the depths of the purple sea;
Over the rills, and the crags, and the hills,
 Over the lakes and the plains,
Wherever he dream, under mountain or stream,
 The Spirit he loves remains;
And I all the while bask in heaven's blue smile,
 Whilst he is dissolving in rains.

The sanguine sunrise, with his meteor eyes,
 And his burning plumes outspread,
Leaps on the back of my sailing rack
 When the morning-star shines dead,
As on the jag of a mountain crag,
 Which an earthquake rocks and swings,
An eagle alit one moment may sit
 In the light of its golden wings.
And when Sunset may breathe, from the lit sea beneath
 Its ardors of rest and of love,
And the crimson pall of eve may fall
 From the depth of heaven above,
With wings folded I rest, on mine airy nest,
 As still as a brooding dove.

That orbèd maiden with white fire laden,
 Whom mortals call the moon,
Glides glimmering o'er my fleece-like floor,
 By the midnight breezes strewn;

And wherever the beat of her unseen feet,
Which only the angels hear,
May have broken the woof of my tent's thin roof,
The stars peep behind her and peer;
And I laugh to see them whirl and flee,
Like a swarm of golden bees,
When I widen the rent in my wind-built tent,
Till the calm rivers, lakes, and seas,
Like strips of the sky fallen through me on high,
Are each paved with the moon and these.

I bind the sun's throne with a burning zone,
And the moon's with a girdle of pearl;
The volcanoes are dim, and the stars reel and swim
When the whirlwinds my banner unfurl.
From cape to cape, with a bridge-like shape,
Over a torrent sea,
Sunbeam-proof, I hang like a roof,
The mountains its columns be.
The triumphal arch through which I march
With hurricane, fire, and snow,
When the powers of the air are chained to my chair,
Is the million-colored bow;
The sphere-fire above its soft colors wove,
While the moist earth was laughing below.

I am the daughter of earth and water,
And the nursling of the sky:
I pass through the pores of the ocean and shores;
I change, but I cannot die.
For after the rain when with never a stain,
The pavilion of heaven is bare,
And the winds and sunbeams with their convex gleams,
Build up the blue dome of air,
I silently laugh at my own cenotaph,
And out of the caverns of rain,
Like a child from the womb, like a ghost from the tomb,
I arise and unbuild it again.

To a Skylark

HAIL to thee, blithe spirit!
Bird thou never wert,
That from heaven, or near it,
Pourest thy full heart
In profuse strains of unpremeditated art.

Higher still and higher
From the earth thou springest,
Like a cloud of fire;
The blue deep thou wingest,
And singing still dost soar, and soaring ever singest.

In the golden lightning
Of the setting sun,
O'er which clouds are brightening,
Thou dost float and run;
Like an unbodied joy whose race is just begun.

The pale purple even
Melts around thy flight;
Like a star of heaven,
In the broad daylight
Thou art unseen, but yet I hear thy shrill delight.

Keen as are the arrows
Of that silver sphere,
Whose intense lamp narrows
In the white dawn clear,
Until we hardly see, we feel that it is there.

All the earth and air
With thy voice is loud,
As, when night is bare,
From one lonely cloud
The moon rains out her beams, and heaven is overflowed.

What thou art we know not;
  What is most like thee?
From rainbow clouds there flow not
  Drops so bright to see,
As from thy presence showers a rain of melody.

Like a poet hidden
  In the light of thought,
Singing hymns unbidden,
  Till the world is wrought
To sympathy with hopes and fears it heeded not;

Like a high-born maiden
  In a palace tower,
Soothing her love-laden
  Soul in secret hour
With music sweet as love, which overflows her bower;

Like a glow-worm golden,
  In a dell of dew,
Scattering unbeholden
  Its aerial hue
Among the flowers and grass which screen it from the view;

Like a rose embowered
  In its own green leaves,
By warm winds deflowered,
  Till the scent it gives
Makes faint with too much sweet these heavy-wingèd thieves.

Sound of vernal showers
  On the twinkling grass,
Rain-awakened flowers,
  All that ever was
Joyous and fresh and clear thy music doth surpass.

Teach us, sprite or bird,
  What sweet thoughts are thine;
I have never heard
  Praise of love or wine
That panted forth a flood of rapture so divine.

Chorus hymeneal,
  Or triumphant chant,
Matched with thine, would be all
  But an empty vaunt,—
A thing wherein we feel there is some hidden want.

What objects are the fountains
  Of thy happy strain?
What fields, or waves, or mountains?
  What shapes of sky or plain?
What love of thine own kind? What ignorance of pain?

With thy clear, keen joyance
  Languor cannot be:
Shadow of annoyance
  Never come near thee:
Thou lovest; but ne'er knew love's sad satiety.

Waking or asleep,
  Thou of death must deem
Things more true and deep
  Than we mortals dream,
Or how could thy notes flow in such a crystal stream?

We look before and after,
  And pine for what is not;
Our sincerest laughter
  With some pain is fraught;
Our sweetest songs are those that tell of saddest thought.

Yet if we could scorn
  Hate and pride and fear,
If we were things born
  Not to shed a tear,
I know not how thy joy we ever should come near.

Better than all measures
  Of delightful sound,
Better than all treasures
  That in books are found,
Thy skill to poet were, thou scorner of the ground!

Teach me half the gladness
  That thy brain must know,
Such harmonious madness
  From my lips would flow,
The world should listen then, as I am listening now.

I Fear Thy Kisses, Gentle Maiden

I FEAR thy kisses, gentle maiden;
  Thou needest not fear mine;
My spirit is too deeply laden
  Ever to burden thine.

I fear thy mien, thy tones, thy motion;
  Thou needest not fear mine;
Innocent is the heart's devotion
  With which I worship thine.

To Night

SWIFTLY walk o'er the western wave,
    Spirit of Night!
Out of the misty eastern cave,
Where all the long and lone daylight,
Thou wovest dreams of joy and fear,
Which make thee terrible and dear,—
    Swift be thy flight!

Wrap thy form in a mantle gray,
    Star-inwrought!
Blind with thine hair the eyes of Day;
Kiss her until she be wearied out,
Then wander o'er city, and sea, and land,
Touching all with thine opiate wand—
    Come, long-sought!

When I arose and saw the dawn,
        I sighed for thee;
When light rode high, and the dew was gone,
And noon lay heavy on flower and tree,
And the weary Day turned to his rest,
Lingering like an unloved guest,
        I sighed for thee.

Thy brother Death came, and cried,
        Wouldst thou me?
Thy sweet child Sleep, the filmy-eyed,
Murmured like a noontide bee,
Shall I nestle near thy side?
Wouldst thou me?—And I replied,
        No, not thee!

Death will come when thou art dead,
        Soon, too soon—
Sleep will come when thou art fled;
Of neither would I ask the boon
I ask of thee, beloved Night—
Swift be thine approaching flight,
        Come soon, soon!

Music, When Soft Voices Die

Music, when soft voices die,
Vibrates in the memory—
Odors when sweet violets sicken,
Live within the sense they quicken.

Rose leaves, when the rose is dead,
Are heap'd for the beloved's bed;
And so thy thoughts, when thou art gone,
Love itself shall slumber on.

To ——

One word is too often profaned
  For me to profane it,
One feeling too falsely disdained
  For thee to disdain it;
One hope is too like despair
  For prudence to smother,
And pity from thee more dear
  Than that from another.

I can give not what men call love;
  But wilt thou accept not
The worship the heart lifts above
  And the Heavens reject not:
The desire of the moth for the star,
  Of the night for the morrow,
The devotion to something afar
  From the sphere of our sorrow?

O World! O Life! O Time

O World! O Life! O Time
On whose last steps I climb,
  Trembling at that where I had stood before;
When will return the glory of your prime?
  No more—O never more!

Out of the day and night
A joy has taken flight:
  Fresh spring, and summer, and winter hoar
Move my faint heart with grief, but with delight
  No more—O never more!

When the Lamp Is Shattered

When the lamp is shattered
The light in the dust lies dead;
When the cloud is scattered,
The rainbow's glory is shed.
When the lute is broken,
Sweet tones are remembered not;
When the lips have spoken,
Loved accents are soon forgot.

As music and splendor
Survive not the lamp and the lute,
The heart's echoes render
No song when the spirit is mute,—
No song but sad dirges,
Like the wind through a ruined cell,
Or the mournful surges
That ring the dead seaman's knell.

When hearts have once mingled,
Love first leaves the well-built nest;
The weak one is singled
To endure what it once possessed.
O Love! who bewailest
The frailty of all things here,
Why choose you the frailest
For your cradle, your home, and your bier?

Its passions will rock thee
As the storms rock the ravens on high;
Bright reason will mock thee
Like the sun from a wintry sky.
From thy nest every rafter
Will rot, and thine eagle home
Leave thee naked to laughter,
When leaves fall and cold winds come.

JOHN CLARE
(1793–1864)

Written In Northampton County Asylum

I AM! yet what I am who cares, or knows?
  My friends forsake me like a memory lost.
I am the self-consumer of my woes;
  They rise and vanish, an oblivious host,
Shadows of life, whose very soul is lost.
And yet I am—I live—though I am toss'd

Into the nothingness of scorn and noise,
  Into the living sea of waking dream,
Where there is neither sense of life, nor joys,
  But the huge shipwreck of my own esteem
And all that's dear. Even those I loved the best
Are strange—nay, they are stranger than the rest.

I long for scenes where man has never trod—
  For scenes where woman never smiled or wept—
There to abide with my Creator, God,
  And sleep as I in childhood sweetly slept,
Full of high thoughts, unborn. So let me lie,—
The grass below; above, the vaulted sky.

HENRY FRANCIS LYTE
(1793–1847)

A Lost Love

I MEET thy pensive, moonlight face;
  Thy thrilling voice I hear;
And former hours and scenes retrace,
  Too fleeting, and too dear!

Then sighs and tears flow fast and free,
  Though none is nigh to share;
And life has nought beside for me
  So sweet as this despair.

There are crush'd hearts that will not break;
  And mine, methinks, is one;
Or thus I should not weep and wake,
  And thou to slumber gone.

I little thought it thus could be
  In days more sad and fair—
That earth could have a place for me,
  And thou no longer there.

Yet death cannot our hearts divide,
  Or make thee less my own:
'Twere sweeter sleeping at thy side
  Than watching here alone.

Yet never, never can we part,
  While Memory holds her reign:
Thine, thine is still this wither'd heart,
  Till we shall meet again.

WILLIAM CULLEN BRYANT

(1794–1878)

Thanatopsis

To HIM who, in the love of Nature, holds
Communion with her visible forms, she speaks
A various language: for his gayer hours
She has a voice of gladness, and a smile
And eloquence of beauty; and she glides
Into his darker musings with a mild
And healing sympathy, that steals away
Their sharpness, ere he is aware. When thoughts

Of the last bitter hour come like a blight
Over thy spirit, and sad images
Of the stern agony, and shroud, and pall,
And breathless darkness, and the narrow house,
Make thee to shudder, and grow sick at heart,
Go forth under the open sky, and list
To Nature's teachings, while from all around—
Earth and her waters, and the depths of air—
Comes a still voice:—Yet a few days, and thee
The all-beholding sun shall see no more
In all his course; nor yet in the cold ground,
Where thy pale form was laid, with many tears,
Nor in the embrace of ocean, shall exist
Thy image. Earth, that nourished thee, shall claim
Thy growth, to be resolved to earth again;
And, lost each human trace, surrendering up
Thine individual being, shalt thou go
To mix forever with the elements;
To be a brother to the insensible rock,
And to the sluggish clod, which the rude swain
Turns with his share, and treads upon. The oak
Shall send his roots abroad, and pierce thy mould.
  Yet not to thine eternal resting-place
Shalt thou retire alone,—nor couldst thou wish
Couch more magnificent. Thou shalt lie down
With patriarchs of the infant world,—with kings,
The powerful of the earth,—the wise, the good,
Fair forms, and hoary seers of ages past,
All in one mighty sepulchre. The hills,
Rock-ribbed, and ancient as the sun; the vales
Stretching in pensive quietness between;
The venerable woods; rivers that move
In majesty, and the complaining brooks,
That make the meadows green; and, poured round all,
Old ocean's gray and melancholy waste,—
Are but the solemn decorations all
Of the great tomb of man! The golden sun,
The planets, all the infinite host of heaven,
Are shining on the sad abodes of death,
Through the still lapse of ages. All that tread
The globe are but a handful to the tribes

That slumber in its bosom. Take the wings
Of morning, pierce the Barcan wilderness,
Or lose thyself in the continuous woods
Where rolls the Oregon, and hears no sound
Save his own dashings,—yet the dead are there!
And millions in those solitudes, since first
The flight of years began, have laid them down
In their last sleep,—the dead reign there alone!
So shalt thou rest; and what if thou withdraw
In silence from the living, and no friend
Take note of thy departure? All that breathe
Will share thy destiny. The gay will laugh
When thou art gone, the solemn brood of care
Plod on, and each one, as before, will chase
His favorite phantom; yet all these shall leave
Their mirth and their employments, and shall come
And make their bed with thee. As the long train
Of ages glide away, the sons of men—
The youth in life's green spring, and he who goes
In the full strength of years, matron and maid,
And the sweet babe, and the gray-headed man—
Shall, one by one, be gathered to thy side
By those who in their turn shall follow them.

So live, that when thy summons comes to join
The innumerable caravan that moves
To the pale realms of shade, where each shall take
His chamber in the silent halls of death,
Thou go not, like the quarry-slave at night,
Scourged to his dungeon, but, sustained and soothed
By an unfaltering trust, approach thy grave
Like one who wraps the drapery of his couch
About him, and lies down to pleasant dreams.

To a Waterfowl

Whither, midst falling dew,
While glow the heavens with the last steps of day,
Far, through their rosy depths, dost thou pursue
Thy solitary way?

Vainly the fowler's eye
Might mark thy distant flight to do thee wrong,
As, darkly painted on the crimson sky,
Thy figure floats along.

Seek'st thou the plashy brink
Of weedy lake, or marge of river wide,
Or where the rocking billows rise and sink
On the chafed ocean-side?

There is a Power whose care
Teaches thy way along that pathless coast,—
The desert and illimitable air,—
Lone wandering, but not lost.

All day thy wings have fanned,
At that far height, the cold, thin atmosphere,
Yet stoop not, weary, to the welcome land,
Though the dark night is near.

And soon that toil shall end;
Soon shalt thou find a summer home, and rest,
And scream among thy fellows; reeds shall bend,
Soon, o'er thy sheltered nest.

Thou 'rt gone, the abyss of heaven
Hath swallowed up thy form; yet, on my heart
Deeply hath sunk the lesson thou hast given,
And shall not soon depart:

He who, from zone to zone,
Guides through the boundless sky thy certain flight,
In the long way that I must tread alone,
Will lead my steps aright.

A Forest Hymn

The groves were God's first temples. Ere man learned
To hew the shaft, and lay the architrave,
And spread the roof above them,—ere he framed
The lofty vault, to gather and roll back
The sound of anthems; in the darkling wood,
Amidst the cool and silence, he knelt down,
And offered to the Mightiest solemn thanks
And supplication. For his simple heart
Might not resist the sacred influences
Which, from the stilly twilight of the place,
And from the gray old trunks that high in heaven
Mingled their mossy boughs, and from the sound
Of the invisible breath that swayed at once
All their green tops, stole over him, and bowed
His spirit with the thought of boundless power
And inaccessible majesty. Ah, why
Should we, in the world's riper years, neglect
God's ancient sanctuaries, and adore
Only among the crowd, and under roofs
That our frail hands have raised? Let me, at least,
Here, in the shadow of this aged wood,
Offer one hymn,—thrice happy if it find
Acceptance in his ear.

Father, thy hand
Hath reared these venerable columns, thou
Didst weave this verdant roof. Thou didst look down
Upon the naked earth, and forthwith rose
All these fair ranks of trees. They in thy sun
Budded, and shook their green leaves in thy breeze,
And shot towards heaven. The century-living crow,
Whose birth was in their tops, grew old and died
Among their branches, till at last they stood,
As now they stand, massy and tall and dark,
Fit shrine for humble worshipper to hold
Communion with his Maker. These dim vaults,
These winding aisles, of human pomp or pride

Report not. No fantastic carvings show
The boast of our vain race to change the form
Of thy fair works. But thou art here,—thou fill'st
The solitude. Thou art in the soft winds
That run along the summit of these trees
In music; thou art in the cooler breath
That from the inmost darkness of the place
Comes, scarcely felt; the barky trunks, the ground,
The fresh moist ground, are all instinct with thee.
Here is continual worship;—nature, here,
In the tranquillity that thou dost love,
Enjoys thy presence. Noiselessly around,
From perch to perch, the solitary bird
Passes; and yon clear spring, that, midst its herbs,
Wells softly forth and wandering steeps the roots
Of half the mighty forest, tells no tale
Of all the good it does. Thou hast not left
Thyself without a witness, in these shades,
Of thy perfections. Grandeur, strength, and grace
Are here to speak of thee. This mighty oak,—
By whose immovable stem I stand and seem
Almost annihilated,—not a prince,
In all that proud old world beyond the deep,
E'er wore his crown as loftily as he
Wears the green coronal of leaves with which
Thy hand has graced him. Nestled at his root
Is beauty, such as blooms not in the glare
Of the broad sun. That delicate forest flower
With scented breath, and look so like a smile,
Seems, as it issues from the shapeless mould,
An emanation of the indwelling Life,
A visible token of the upholding Love,
That are the soul of this wide universe.

My heart is awed within me when I think
Of the great miracle that still goes on,
In silence, round me,—the perpetual work
Of thy creation, finished, yet renewed
Forever. Written on thy works I read
The lesson of thy own eternity.
Lo! all grow old and die; but see again,

How on the faltering footsteps of decay
Youth presses,—ever gay and beautiful youth
In all its beautiful forms. These lofty trees
Wave not less proudly that their ancestors
Moulder beneath them. O, there is not lost
One of Earth's charms! upon her bosom yet,
After the flight of untold centuries,
The freshness of her far beginning lies,
And yet shall lie. Life mocks the idle hate
Of his arch-enemy Death,—yea, seats himself
Upon the tyrant's throne, the sepulchre,
And of the triumphs of his ghastly foe
Makes his own nourishment. For he came forth
From thine own bosom, and shall have no end.

There have been holy men who hid themselves
Deep in the woody wilderness, and gave
Their lives to thought and prayer, till they outlive
The generation born with them, nor seemed
Less aged than the hoary trees and rocks
Around them;—and there have been holy men
Who deemed it were not well to pass life thus.
But let me often to these solitudes
Retire, and in thy presence reassure
My feeble virtue. Here its enemies,
The passions, at thy plainer footsteps shrink
And tremble, and are still. O God! when thou
Dost scare the world with tempests, set on fire
The heavens with falling thunderbolts, or fill,
With all the waters of the firmament,
The swift dark whirlwind that uproots the woods
And drowns the villages; when, at thy call,
Uprises the great deep, and throws himself
Upon the continent, and overwhelms
Its cities,—who forgets not, at the sight
Of these tremendous tokens of thy power,
His pride, and lays his strifes and follies by?
O, from these sterner aspects of thy face
Spare me and mine, nor let us need the wrath
Of the mad unchainèd elements to teach
Who rules them. Be it ours to meditate,

In these calm shades, thy milder majesty,
And to the beautiful order of thy works
Learn to conform the order of our lives.

America

O MOTHER of a mighty race,
Yet lovely in thy youthful grace!
The elder dames, thy haughty peers,
Admire and hate thy blooming years;
With words of shame
And taunts of scorn they join thy name.

For on thy cheeks the glow is spread
That tints thy morning hills with red;
Thy step,—the wild deer's rustling feet
Within thy woods are not more fleet;
Thy hopeful eye
Is bright as thine own sunny sky.

Ay, let them rail, those haughty ones,
While safe thou dwellest with thy sons.
They do not know how loved thou art,
How many a fond and fearless heart
Would rise to throw
Its life between thee and the foe.

They know not, in their hate and pride,
What virtues with thy children bide,—
How true, how good, thy graceful maids
Make bright, like flowers, the valley shades;
What generous men
Spring, like thine oaks, by hill and glen;

What cordial welcomes greet the guest
By thy lone rivers of the west;
How faith is kept, and truth revered,
And man is loved, and God is feared,
In woodland homes,
And where the ocean border foams.

There's freedom at thy gates, and rest
For earth's down-trodden and opprest,
A shelter for the hunted head,
For the starved laborer toil and bread.
Power, at thy bounds,
Stops, and calls back his baffled hounds.

O fair young mother! on thy brow
Shall sit a nobler grace than now.
Deep in the brightness of thy skies,
The thronging years in glory rise,
And, as they fleet,
Drop strength and riches at thy feet.

Thine eye, with every coming hour,
Shall brighten, and thy form shall tower;
And when thy sisters, elder born,
Would brand thy name with words of scorn,
Before thine eye
Upon their lips the taunt shall die.

JOSEPH RODMAN DRAKE

(1795–1820)

The American Flag

When Freedom, from her mountain height,
Unfurled her standard to the air,
She tore the azure robe of night,
And set the stars of glory there!
She mingled with its gorgeous dyes
The milky baldric of the skies,
And striped its pure, celestial white
With streakings of the morning light;
Then, from his mansion in the sun,
She called her eagle-bearer down,
And gave into his mighty hand
The symbol of her chosen land!

Majestic monarch of the cloud!
  Who rear'st aloft thy regal form,
To hear the tempest trumping loud,
And see the lightning lances driven,
  When strive the warriors of the storm,
And rolls the thunder-drum of heaven,—
Child of the Sun! to thee 't is given
  To guard the banner of the free,
To hover in the sulphur smoke,
To ward away the battle-stroke,
And bid its blendings shine afar,
Like rainbows on the cloud of war,
  The harbingers of victory!

Flag of the brave! thy folds shall fly,
The sign of hope and triumph high!
When speaks the signal-trumpet tone,
And the long line comes gleaming on,
Ere yet the life-blood, warm and wet,
Has dimmed the glistening bayonet,
Each soldier's eye shall brightly turn
To where thy sky-born glories burn,
And, as his springing steps advance,
Catch war and vengeance from the glance.

And when the cannon-mouthings loud
Heave in wild wreaths the battle shroud,
And gory sabres rise and fall
Like shoots of flame on midnight's pall,
Then shall thy meteor glances glow,
  And cowering foes shall shrink beneath
Each gallant arm that strikes below
  That lovely messenger of death.

Flag of the seas! on ocean wave
Thy stars shall glitter o'er the brave;
When death, careering on the gale,
Sweeps darkly round the bellied sail,
And frighted waves rush wildly back
Before the broadside's reeling rack,

Each dying wanderer of the sea
Shall look at once to heaven and thee,
And smile to see thy splendors fly
In triumph o'er his closing eye.

Flag of the free heart's hope and home,
By angel hands to valor given!
Thy stars have lit the welkin dome,
And all thy hues were born in heaven.
Forever float that standard sheet!
Where breathes the foe but falls before us,
With Freedom's soil beneath our feet,
And Freedom's banner streaming o'er us!

THOMAS CARLYLE

(1795–1881)

To-Day

So HERE hath been dawning
Another blue day:
Think, wilt thou let it
Slip useless away.

Out of Eternity
This new day was born;
Into Eternity,
At night, will return.

Behold it aforetime
No eye ever did;
So soon it for ever
From all eyes is hid.

Here hath been dawning
Another blue day:
Think, wilt thou let it
Slip useless away.

JOHN KEATS
(1795–1821)

Ode on a Grecian Urn

THOU still unravish'd bride of quietness,
  Thou foster-child of silence and slow time,
Sylvan historian, who canst thus express
  A flowery tale more sweetly than our rhyme:
What leaf-fring'd legend haunts about thy shape
  Of deities or mortals, or of both,
    In Tempe or the dales of Arcady?
  What men or gods are these? What maidens loth?
What mad pursuit? What struggle to escape?
    What pipes and timbrels? What wild ecstasy?

Heard melodies are sweet, but those unheard
  Are sweeter; therefore, ye soft pipes, play on;
Not to the sensual ear, but, more endear'd,
  Pipe to the spirit ditties of no tone:
Fair youth, beneath the trees, thou canst not leave
  Thy song, nor ever can those trees be bare;
    Bold Lover, never, never canst thou kiss,
Though winning near the goal—yet, do not grieve;
  She cannot fade, though thou hast not thy bliss,
  For ever wilt thou love, and she be fair!

Ah, happy, happy boughs! that cannot shed
  Your leaves, nor ever bid the Spring adieu;
And, happy melodist, unwearied,
  For ever piping songs for ever new;
More happy love! more happy, happy love!
  For ever warm and still to be enjoy'd,
    For ever panting, and for ever young;
All breathing human passion far above,
  That leaves a heart high-sorrowful and cloy'd,
    A burning forehead, and a parching tongue

Who are these coming to the sacrifice?
To what green altar, O mysterious priest,
Lead'st thou that heifer lowing at the skies,
And all her silken flanks with garlands drest?
What little town by river or sea shore,
Or mountain-built with peaceful citadel,
Is emptied of this folk, this pious morn?
And, little town, thy streets for evermore
Will silent be; and not a soul to tell
Why thou art desolate, can e'er return.

O Attic shape! Fair attitude! with brede
Of marble men and maidens overwrought,
With forest branches and the trodden weed;
Thou, silent form, dost tease us out of thought
As doth eternity: Cold Pastoral!
When old age shall this generation waste,
Thou shalt remain, in midst of other woe
Than ours, a friend to man, to whom thou say'st,
"Beauty is truth, truth beauty,"—that is all
Ye know on earth, and all ye need to know.

Ode to the Nightingale

My heart aches, and a drowsy numbness pains
My sense, as though of hemlock I had drunk,
Or emptied some dull opiate to the drains
One minute past, and Lethe-wards had sunk:
'Tis not through envy of thy happy lot,
But being too happy in thine happiness,—
That thou, light-wingèd Dryad of the trees,
In some melodious plot
Of beechen green, and shadows numberless,
Singest of summer in full-throated ease.

O, for a draught of vintage! that hath been
Cool'd a long age in the deep-delved earth,
Tasting of Flora and the country green,
Dance, and Provencal song, and sunburnt mirth!

O for a beaker full of the warm South,
Full of the true, the blushful Hippocrene,
With beaded bubbles winking at the brim,
And purple-stained mouth;
That I might drink, and leave the world unseen,
And with thee fade away into the forest dim:

Fade far away, dissolve, and quite forget
What thou among the leaves has never known,
The weariness, the fever, and the fret
Here, where men sit and hear each other groan;
Where palsy shakes a few, sad, last gray hairs,
Where youth grows pale, and spectre-thin, and dies;
Where but to think is to be full of sorrow
And leaden-eyed despairs,
Where Beauty cannot keep her lustrous eyes,
Or new Love pine at them beyond to-morrow.

Away! away! for I will fly to thee,
Not charioted by Bacchus and his pards,
But on the viewless wings of Poesy,
Though the dull brain perplexes and retards:
Already with thee! tender is the night,
And haply the Queen-Moon is on her throne,
Cluster'd around by all her starry Fays;
But here there is no light,
Save what from heaven is with the breezes blown
Through verdurous glooms and winding mossy ways.

I cannot see what flowers are at my feet,
Nor what soft incense hangs upon the boughs,
But, in embalmed darkness, guess each sweet
Wherewith the seasonable month endows
The grass, the thicket, and the fruit-tree wild;
White hawthorn, and the pastoral eglantine;
Fast fading violets cover'd up in leaves;
And mid-May's eldest child,
The coming musk-rose, full of dewy wine,
The murmurous haunt of flies on summer eves.

Darkling I listen; and, for many a time
  I have been half in love with easeful Death,
Call'd him soft names in many a musèd rhyme,
  To take into the air my quiet breath;
Now more than ever seems it rich to die,
  To cease upon the midnight with no pain,
    While thou art pouring forth thy soul abroad
      In such an ecstasy!
  Still wouldst thou sing, and I have ears in vain—
    To thy high requiem become a sod.

Thou wast not born for death, immortal Bird!
  No hungry generations tread thee down;
The voice I hear this passing night was heard
  In ancient days by emperor and clown:
Perhaps the self-same song that found a path
  Through the sad heart of Ruth, when, sick for home,
    She stood in tears amid the alien corn;
      The same that oft-times hath
  Charm'd magic casements, opening on the foam
    Of perilous seas, in faery lands forlorn.

Forlorn! the very word is like a bell
  To toll me back from thee to my sole self!
Adieu! the fancy cannot cheat so well
  As she is fam'd to do, deceiving elf.
Adieu! adieu! thy plaintive anthem fades
  Past the near meadows, over the still stream,
    Up the hill-side; and now 'tis buried deep
      In the next valley-glades:
  Was it a vision, or a waking dream?
    Fled is that music:—Do I wake or sleep?

To Autumn

Season of mists and mellow fruitfulness,
  Close bosom-friend of the maturing sun;
Conspiring with him how to load and bless
  With fruit the vines that round the thatch-eves run;

To bend with apples the moss'd cottage-trees,
  And fill all fruit with ripeness to the core;
    To swell the gourd, and plump the hazel shells
With a sweet kernel; to set budding more,
  And still more, later flowers for the bees,
  Until they think warm days will never cease,
    For Summer has o'er-brimmed their clammy cells.

Who hath not seen thee oft amid thy store?
  Sometimes whoever seeks abroad may find
Thee sitting careless on a granary floor,
  Thy hair soft-lifted by the winnowing wind;
Or on a half-reap'd furrow sound asleep,
  Drows'd with the fume of poppies, while thy hook
    Spares the next swath and all its twined flowers:
And sometimes like a gleaner thou dost keep
  Steady thy laden head across a brook;
  Or by a cyder-press, with patient look,
    Thou watchest the last oozings hours by hours.

Where are the songs of Spring? Ay, where are they?
  Think not of them, thou hast thy music too,—
While barred clouds bloom the soft-dying day,
  And touch the stubble-plains with rosy hue;
  Then in a wailful choir the small gnats mourn
    Among the river sallows, borne aloft
      Or sinking as the light wind lives or dies;
  And full-grown lambs loud bleat from hilly bourn;
    Hedge-crickets sing; and now with treble soft
    The red-breast whistles from a garden-croft;
      And gathering swallows twitter in the skies.

Fancy

EVER let the Fancy roam,
Pleasure never is at home:
At a touch sweet Pleasure melteth,
Like to bubbles when rain pelteth;

Then let wingèd Fancy wander
Through the thought still spread beyond her:
Open wide the mind's cage-door,
She 'll dart forth, and cloudward soar.

O sweet Fancy! let her loose;
Summer's joys are spoilt by use,
And the enjoying of the Spring
Fades as does its blossoming:
Autumn's red-lipped fruitage too,
Blushing through the mist and dew,
Cloys with tasting. What do then?
Sit thee by the ingle, when
The sear fagot blazes bright,
Spirit of a winter's night;
When the soundless earth is muffled,
And the cakèd snow is shuffled
From the ploughboy's heavy shoon;
When the Night doth meet the Noon
In a dark conspiracy
To banish Even from her sky.
—Sit thee there, and send abroad
With a mind self-overawed
Fancy, high-commissioned:—send her!
She has vassals to attend her;
She will bring, in spite of frost,
Beauties that the earth hath lost;
She will bring thee, all together,
All delights of summer weather;
All the buds and bells of May
From dewy sward or thorny spray;
All the heapèd Autumn's wealth,
With a still, mysterious stealth;
She will mix these pleasures up
Like three fit wines in a cup,
And thou shalt quaff it:—thou shalt hear
Distant harvest-carols clear;
Rustle of the reapèd corn;
Sweet birds antheming the morn;
And in the same moment—hark!
'T is the early April lark,

Or the rooks, with busy caw,
Foraging for sticks and straw.
Thou shalt, at one glance, behold
The daisy and the marigold;
White-plumed lilies, and the first
Hedge-grown primrose that hath burst;
Shaded hyacinth, alway
Sapphire queen of the mid-May;
And every leaf, and every flower
Pearlèd with the self-same shower.
Thou shalt see the field-mouse peep
Meagre from its cellèd sleep;
And the snake all winter-thin
Cast on sunny bank its skin;
Freckled nest-eggs thou shalt see
Hatching in the hawthorn tree,
When the hen-bird's wing doth rest
Quiet on her mossy nest;
Then the hurry and alarm
When the bee-hive casts its swarm;
Acorns ripe down-pattering
While the autumn breezes sing.

O sweet Fancy! let her loose;
Everything is spoilt by use:
Where 's the cheek that doth not fade,
Too much gazed at? Where 's the maid
Whose lip mature is ever new?
Where 's the eye, however blue,
Doth not weary? Where 's the face
One would meet in every place?
Where's the voice, however soft,
One would hear so very oft?
At a touch sweet Pleasure melteth
Like to bubbles when rain pelteth.
Let then wingèd Fancy find
Thee a mistress to thy mind:
Dulcet-eyed as Ceres' daughter,
Ere the god of torment taught her
How to frown and how to chide;
With a waist and with a side

White as Hebe's, when her zone
Slipt its golden clasp, and down
Fell her kirtle to her feet
While she held the goblet sweet,
And Jove grew languid.—Break the mesh
Of the Fancy's silken leash:
Quickly break her prison-string,
And such joys as these she 'll bring:
—Let the wingèd Fancy roam,
Pleasure never is at home.

The Mermaid Tavern

SOULS of Poets dead and gone,
What Elysium have ye known,
Happy field or mossy cavern,
Choicer than the Mermaid Tavern,
Have ye tippled drink more fine
Than mine host's Canary wine?
Or are fruits of Paradise
Sweeter than those dainty pies
Of venison? O generous food!
Dressed as though bold Robin Hood
Would, with his maid Marian,
Sup and bowse from horn and can.

I have heard that on a day
Mine host's sign-board flew away,
Nobody knew whither, till
An astrologer's old quill
To a sheepskin gave the story,
Said he saw you in your glory,
Underneath a new old sign
Sipping beverage divine,
And pledging with contented smack
The Mermaid in the Zodiac!

Souls of Poets dead and gone,
What Elysium have ye known,
Happy field or mossy cavern,
Choicer than the Mermaid Tavern?

La Belle Dame Sans Merci

"O WHAT can ail thee, knight-at-arms,
Alone and palely loitering?
The sedge is wither'd from the lake,
And no birds sing.

"O what can ail thee, knight-at-arms,
So haggard and so woe-begone?
The squirrel's granary is full,
And the harvest's done.

"I see a lily on thy brow
With anguish moist and fever dew;
And on thy cheek a fading rose
Fast withereth too."

"I met a lady in the meads,
Full beautiful—a faery's child,
Her hair was long, her foot was light,
And her eyes were wild.

"I made a garland for her head,
And bracelets too, and fragrant zone;
She look'd at me as she did love,
And made sweet moan.

"I set her on my pacing steed
And nothing else saw all day long,
For sideways would she lean, and sing
A faery's song.

"She found me roots of relish sweet,
  And honey wild and manna dew,
And sure in language strange she said,
    'I love thee true!'

"She took me to her elfin grot,
  And there she wept and sigh'd full sore,
And there I shut her wild, wild eyes
    With kisses four.

"And there she lullèd me asleep,
  And there I dream'd—Ah! woe betide!
The latest dream I ever dream'd
    On the cold hill's side.

"I saw pale kings and princes too,
  Pale warriors, death-pale were they all;
Who cried—'La belle Dame sans Merci
    Hath thee in thrall!'

"I saw their starved lips in the gloam
  With horrid warning gapèd wide,
And I awoke and found me here
    On the cold hill's side.

"And this is why I sojourn here
  Alone and palely loitering,
Though the sedge is wither'd from the lake,
    And no birds sing."

On First Looking into Chapman's Homer

Much have I travelled in the realms of gold,
  And many goodly states and kingdoms seen;
  Round many western islands have I been
Which bards in fealty to Apollo hold.

Oft of one wide expanse had I been told
  That deep-browed Homer ruled as his demesne:
  Yet did I never breathe its pure serene
Till I heard Chapman speak out loud and bold;
Then felt I like some watcher of the skies
  When a new planet swims into his ken;
Or like stout Cortez, when with eagle eyes
  He stared at the Pacific—and all his men
Looked at each other with a wild surmise—
  Silent, upon a peak in Darien.

To One Who Has Been Long in City Pent

To ONE who has been long in city pent,
'Tis very sweet to look into the fair
And open face of heaven,—to breathe a prayer
Full in the smile of the blue firmament.
Who is more happy, when, with heart's content,
Fatigued he sinks into some pleasant lair
Of wavy grass, and reads a debonair
And gentle tale of love and languishment?
Returning home at evening, with an ear
Catching the notes of Philomel,—an eye
Watching the sailing cloudlet's bright career,
He mourns that day so soon has glided by:
E'en like the passage of an angel's tear
That falls through the clear ether silently.

The Poetry of Earth Is Never Dead

THE poetry of earth is never dead;
When all the birds are faint with the hot sun
And hide in cooling trees, a voice will run
From hedge to hedge about the new-mown mead.

That is the grasshopper's,—he takes the lead
In summer luxury,—he has never done
With his delights; for, when tired out with fun,
He rests at ease beneath some pleasant weed.
The poetry of earth is ceasing never.
On a lone winter evening, when the frost
Has wrought a silence, from the stove there shrills
The cricket's song, in warmth increasing ever,
And seems, to one in drowsiness half lost,
The grasshopper's among some grassy hills.

On Seeing the Elgin Marbles

My spirit is too weak; mortality
Weighs heavily on me like unwilling sleep,
And each imagined pinnacle and steep
Of godlike hardship tells me I must die
Like a sick eagle looking at the sky.
Yet 'tis a gentle luxury to weep
That I have not the cloudy winds to keep
Fresh for the opening of the morning's eye.
Such dim-conceivèd glories of the brain
Bring round the heart an indescribable feud;
So do these wonders a most dizzy pain,
That mingles Grecian grandeur with the rude
Wasting of old Time—with a billowy main,
A sun, a shadow of a magnitude.

When I Have Fears That I May Cease to Be

When I have fears that I may cease to be
  Before my pen has glean'd my teeming brain,
Before high-piled books, in charactery,
  Hold like rich garners the full ripen'd grain;

When I behold, upon the night's starr'd face,
  Huge cloudy symbols of a high romance,
And think that I may never live to trace
  Their shadows, with the magic hand of chance;
And when I feel, fair creature of an hour,
  That I shall never look upon thee more,
Never have relish in the faery power
  Of unreflecting love;—then on the shore
Of the wide world I stand alone, and think
Till love and fame to nothingness do sink.

Bright Star

BRIGHT star, would I were stedfast as thou art—
  Not in lone splendour hung aloft the night
And watching, with eternal lids apart,
  Like nature's patient, sleepless Eremite,
The moving waters at their priestlike task
  Of pure ablution round earth's human shores,
Or gazing on the new soft-fallen mask
  Of snow upon the mountains and the moors—
No—yet still stedfast, still unchangeable,
  Pillow'd upon my fair love's ripening breast,
To feel for ever its soft fall and swell,
  Awake for ever in a sweet unrest,
Still, still to hear her tender-taken breath,
And so live ever—or else swoon to death.

HARTLEY COLERIDGE

(1796–1849)

She Is Not Fair to Outward View

SHE is not fair to outward view,
  As many maidens be;
Her loveliness I never knew
  Until she smiled on me:

O, then I saw her eye was bright,—
A well of love, a spring of light.

But now her looks are coy and cold;
  To mine they ne'er reply;
And yet I cease not to behold
  The love-light in her eye:
Her very frowns are fairer far
Than smiles of other maidens are!

THOMAS HOOD

(c. 1799–1845)

Silence

THERE is a silence where hath been no sound;
There is a silence where no sound may be;
In the cold grave, under the deep, deep sea,
Or in wide desert, where no life is found,
Which hath been mute, and still must sleep profound.
No voice is hushed, no life treads silently;
But cloud, and cloudy shadows wander free,
That never spoke, over the idle ground.
But in green ruins, in the desolate walls
Of antique palaces, where Man hath been,
Though the dun fox, or wild hyena, calls,
And owls, that flit continually between,
Shriek to the echo, and the low winds moan,
There the true Silence is, self-conscious and alone.

The Death Bed

WE WATCH'D her breathing thro' the night,
  Her breathing soft and low,
As in her breast the wave of life
  Kept heaving to and fro.

So silently we seem'd to speak,
  So slowly moved about,
As we had lent her half our powers
  To eke her living out.

Our very hopes belied our fears,
  Our fears our hopes belied—
We thought her dying when she slept,
  And sleeping when she died.

For when the morn came dim and sad
  And chill with early showers,
Her quiet eyelids closed—she had
  Another morn than ours.

The Song of the Shirt

WITH fingers weary and worn,
  With eyelids heavy and red,
A woman sat, in unwomanly rags,
  Plying her needle and thread,—
    Stitch! stitch! stitch!
In poverty, hunger, and dirt;
  And still with a voice of dolorous pitch
She sang the "Song of the Shirt!"

"Work! work! work
  While the cock is crowing aloof!
And work—work—work
  Till the stars shine through the roof!
It 's, O, to be a slave
  Along with the barbarous Turk,
Where woman has never a soul to save,
  If this is Christian work!

"Work—work—work
  Till the brain begins to swim!
Work—work—work
  Till the eyes are heavy and dim!

Seam, and gusset, and band,
  Band, and gusset, and seam,—
Till over the buttons I fall asleep,
  And sew them on in a dream!

"O men with sisters dear!
  O men with mothers and wives!
It is not linen you 're wearing out,
  But human creatures' lives!
    Stitch—stitch—stitch,
  In poverty, hunger, and dirt,—
Sewing at once, with a double thread,
  A shroud as well as a shirt!

"But why do I talk of death,—
  That phantom of grisly bone?
I hardly fear his terrible shape,
  It seems so like my own,—
It seems so like my own
  Because of the fasts I keep;
O God! that bread should be so dear,
  And flesh and blood so cheap!

"Work—work—work!
  My labor never flags;
And what are its wages? A bed of straw,
  A crust of bread—and rags,
That shattered roof—and this naked floor—
  A table—a broken chair—
And a wall so blank my shadow I thank
  For sometimes falling there!

"Work—work—work
  From weary chime to chime!
Work—work—work
  As prisoners work for crime!
Band, and gusset, and seam,
  Seam, and gusset, and band,—
Till the heart is sick and the brain benumbed,
  As well as the weary hand.

"Work—work—work
  In the dull December light?
And work—work—work
  When the weather is warm and bright!
While underneath the eaves
  The brooding swallows cling,
As if to show me their sunny backs,
  And twit me with the Spring.

"O, but to breathe the breath
  Of the cowslip and primrose sweet,—
With the sky above my head,
  And the grass beneath my feet!
For only one short hour
  To feel as I used to feel,
Before I knew the woes of want
  And the walk that costs a meal!

"O, but for one short hour,—
  A respite, however brief!
No blessèd leisure for love or hope,
  But only time for grief!
A little weeping would ease my heart;
  But in their briny bed
My tears must stop, for every drop
  Hinders needle and thread!"

With fingers weary and worn,
  With eyelids heavy and red,
A woman sat, in unwomanly rags,
  Plying her needle and thread,—
    Stitch! stitch! stitch!
  In poverty, hunger, and dirt;
And still with a voice of dolorous pitch—
Would that its tone could reach the rich!—
  She sang this "Song of the Shirt!"

THOMAS BABINGTON, LORD MACAULAY

(1800–1859)

Horatius at the Bridge

LARS PORSENA of Clusium,
  By the Nine Gods he swore
That the great house of Tarquin
  Should suffer wrong no more.
By the Nine Gods he swore it,
  And named a trysting-day,
And bade his messengers ride forth,
East and west and south and north,
  To summon his array.

East and west and south and north
  The messengers ride fast,
And tower and town and cottage
  Have heard the trumpet's blast.
Shame on the false Etruscan
  Who lingers in his home,
When Porsena of Clusium
  Is on the march for Rome!

The horsemen and the footmen
  Are pouring in amain
From many a stately market-place,
  From many a fruitful plain,
From many a lonely hamlet,
  Which, hid by beech and pine,
Like an eagle's nest hangs on the crest
  Of purple Apennine:

From lordly Volaterræ,
  Where scowls the far-famed hold
Piled by the hands of giants
  For godlike kings of old;

From sea-girt Populonia,
  Whose sentinels descry
Sardinia's snowy mountain-tops
  Fringing the southern sky;

From the proud mart of Pisæ,
  Queen of the western waves,
Where ride Massilia's triremes,
  Heavy with fair-haired slaves;
From where sweet Clanis wanders
  Through corn and vines and flowers,
From where Cortona lifts to heaven
  Her diadem of towers.

Tall are the oaks whose acorns
  Drop in dark Auser's rill;
Fat are the stags that champ the boughs
  Of the Ciminian hill;
Beyond all streams, Clitumnus
  Is to the herdsman dear;
Best of all pools the fowler loves
  The great Volsinian mere.

But now no stroke of woodman
  Is heard by Auser's rill;
No hunter tracks the stag's green path
  Up the Ciminian hill;
Unwatched along Clitumnus
  Grazes the milk-white steer;
Unharmed the water-fowl may dip
  In the Volsinian mere.

The harvests of Arretium,
  This year, old men shall reap;
This year, young boys in Umbro
  Shall plunge the struggling sheep;
And in the vats of Luna,
  This year, the must shall foam
Round the white feet of laughing girls
  Whose sires have marched to Rome.

There be thirty chosen prophets,
  The wisest of the land,
Who always by Lars Porsena
  Both morn and evening stand.
Evening and morn the Thirty
  Have turned the verses o'er,
Traced from the right on linen white
  By mighty seers of yore;

And with one voice the Thirty
  Have their glad answer given:
"Go forth, go forth, Lars Porsena,—
  Go forth, beloved of Heaven!
Go, and return in glory
  To Clusium's royal dome,
And hang round Nurscia's altars
  The golden shields of Rome!"

And now hath every city
  Sent up her tale of men;
The foot are fourscore thousand,
  The horse are thousands ten.
Before the gates of Sutrium
  Is met the great array;
A proud man was Lars Porsena
  Upon the trysting-day.

For all the Etruscan armies
  Were ranged beneath his eye,
And many a banished Roman,
  And many a stout ally;
And with a mighty following,
  To join the muster came
The Tusculan Mamilius,
  Prince of the Latian name.

But by the yellow Tiber
  Was tumult and affright;
From all the spacious champaign
  To Rome men took their flight.

A mile around the city
  The throng stopped up the ways;
A fearful sight it was to see
  Through two long nights and days.

For aged folk on crutches,
  And women great with child,
And mothers, sobbing over babes
  That clung to them and smiled,
And sick men borne in litters
  High on the necks of slaves,
And troops of sunburned husbandmen
  With reaping-hooks and staves,

And droves of mules and asses
  Laden with skins of wine,
And endless flocks of goats and sheep,
  And endless herds of kine,
And endless trains of wagons,
  That creaked beneath the weight
Of corn-sacks and of household goods,
  Choked every roaring gate.

Now, from the rock Tarpeian,
  Could the wan burghers spy
The line of blazing villages
  Red in the midnight sky.
The Fathers of the City,
  They sat all night and day,
For every hour some horseman came
  With tidings of dismay.

To eastward and to westward
  Have spread the Tuscan bands,
Nor house, nor fence, nor dovecote
  In Crustumerium stands.
Verbenna down to Ostia
  Hath wasted all the plain;
Astur hath stormed Janiculum,
  And the stout guards are slain.

I wis, in all the Senate
  There was no heart so bold
But sore it ached, and fast it beat,
  When that ill news was told.
Forthwith up rose the Consul,
  Up rose the Fathers all;
In haste they girded up their gowns,
  And hied them to the wall.

They held a council, standing
  Before the River-gate;
Short time was there, ye well may guess,
  For musing or debate.
Out spake the Consul roundly:
  "The bridge must straight go down;
For, since Janiculum is lost,
  Naught else can save the town."

Just then a scout came flying,
  All wild with haste and fear:
"To arms! to arms! Sir Consul,—
  Lars Porsena is here."
On the low hills to westward
  The Consul fixed his eye,
And saw the swarthy storm of dust
  Rise fast along the sky.

And nearer fast and nearer
  Doth the red whirlwind come;
And louder still, and still more loud,
From underneath that rolling cloud,
Is heard the trumpets' war-note proud,
  The trampling and the hum.
And plainly and more plainly
  Now through the gloom appears,
Far to left and far to right,
In broken gleams of dark-blue light,
The long array of helmets bright,
  The long array of spears.

And plainly and more plainly,
  Above that glimmering line,
Now might ye see the banners
  Of twelve fair cities shine;
But the banner of proud Clusium
  Was highest of them all,—
The terror of the Umbrian,
  The terror of the Gaul.

And plainly and more plainly
  Now might the burghers know,
By port and vest, by horse and crest,
  Each warlike Lucumo:
There Cilnius of Arretium
  On his fleet roan was seen;
And Astur of the fourfold shield,
Girt with the brand none else may wield;
Tolumnius with the belt of gold,
And dark Verbenna from the hold
  By reedy Thrasymene.

Fast by the royal standard,
  O'erlooking all the war,
Lars Porsena of Clusium
  Sat in his ivory car.
By the right wheel rode Mamilius,
  Prince of the Latian name;
And by the left false Sextus,
  That wrought the deed of shame.

But when the face of Sextus
  Was seen among the foes,
A yell that rent the firmament
  From all the town arose.
On the house-tops was no woman
  But spat towards him and hissed,
No child but screamed out curses,
  And shook its little fist.

But the Consul's brow was sad,
  And the Consul's speech was low,
And darkly looked he at the wall,
  And darkly at the foe:
"Their van will be upon us
  Before the bridge goes down;
And if they once may win the bridge,
  What hope to save the town?"

Then out spake brave Horatius,
  The Captain of the gate:
"To every man upon this earth
  Death cometh soon or late.
And how can man die better
  Than facing fearful odds
For the ashes of his fathers
  And the temples of his gods,

"And for the tender mother
  Who dandled him to rest,
And for the wife who nurses
  His baby at her breast,
And for the holy maidens
  Who feed the eternal flame,—
To save them from false Sextus
  That wrought the deed of shame?

"Hew down the bridge, Sir Consul,
  With all the speed ye may;
I, with two more to help me,
  Will hold the foe in play.
In you strait path a thousand
  May well be stopped by three:
Now who will stand on either hand,
  And keep the bridge with me?"

Then out spake Spurius Lartius,—
  A Ramnian proud was he:
"Lo, I will stand at thy right hand,
  And keep the bridge with thee."

And out spake strong Herminius,—
  Of Titian blood was he:
"I will abide on thy left side,
  And keep the bridge with thee."

"Horatius," quoth the Consul,
  "As thou sayest so let it be."
And straight against that great array
  Went forth the dauntless three.
For Romans in Rome's quarrel
  Spared neither land nor gold,
Nor son nor wife, nor limb nor life,
  In the brave days of old.

Then none was for a party—
  Then all were for the state;
Then the great man helped the poor,
  And the poor man loved the great;
Then lands were fairly portioned!
  Then spoils were fairly sold:
The Romans were like brothers
  In the brave days of old.

Now Roman is to Roman
  More hateful than a foe,
And the tribunes beard the high,
  And the fathers grind the low.
As we wax hot in faction,
  In battle we wax cold;
Wherefore men fight not as they fought
  In the brave days of old.

Now while the three were tightening
  Their harness on their backs,
The Consul was the foremost man
  To take in hand an axe;
And fathers, mixed with commons,
  Seized hatchet, bar, and crow,
And smote upon the planks above,
  And loosed the props below.

Meanwhile the Tuscan army,
  Right glorious to behold,
Came flashing back the noonday light,
Rank behind rank, like surges bright
  Of a broad sea of gold.
Four hundred trumpets sounded
  A peal of warlike glee,
As that great host with measured tread,
And spears advanced, and ensigns spread,
Rolled slowly towards the bridge's head,
  Where stood the dauntless three.

The three stool calm and silent,
  And looked upon the foes,
And a great shout of laughter
  From all the vanguard rose;
And forth three chiefs came spurring
  Before that deep array;
To earth they sprang, their swords they drew,
And lifted high their shields, and flew
  To win the narrow way.

Aunus, from green Tifernum,
  Lord of the Hill of Vines;
And Seius, whose eight hundred slaves
  Sicken in Ilva's mines;
And Picus, long to Clusium
  Vassal in peace and war,
Who led to fight his Umbrian powers
From that gray crag where, girt with towers,
The fortress of Nequinum lowers
  O'er the pale waves of Nar.

Stout Lartius hurled down Aunus
  Into the stream beneath;
Herminius struck at Seius,
  And clove him to the teeth;
At Picus brave Horatius
  Darted one fiery thrust,
And the proud Umbrian's gilded arms
  Clashed in the bloody dust.

Then Ocnus of Falerii
  Rushed on the Roman three;
And Lausulus of Urgo,
  The rover of the sea;
And Aruns of Volsinium,
  Who slew the great wild boar,—
The great wild boar that had his den
Amidst the reeds of Cosa's fen,
And wasted fields, and slaughtered men,
  Along Albinia's shore.

Herminius smote down Aruns;
  Lartius laid Ocnus low;
Right to the heart of Lausulus
  Horatius sent a blow:
"Lie there," he cried, "fell pirate!
  No more, aghast and pale,
From Ostia's walls the crowd shall mark
The track of thy destroying bark;
No more Campania's hinds shall fly
To woods and caverns, when they spy
  Thy thrice-accursèd sail!"

But now no sound of laughter
  Was heard among the foes;
A wild and wrathful clamor
  From all the vanguard rose.
Six spears' length from the entrance,
  Halted that mighty mass,
And for a space no man came forth
  To win the narrow pass.

But, hark! the cry is Astur:
  And lo! the ranks divide;
And the great lord of Luna
  Comes with his stately stride.
Upon his ample shoulders
  Clangs loud the fourfold shield,
And in his hand he shakes the brand
  Which none but he can wield.

He smiled on those bold Romans,
  A smile serene and high;
He eyed the flinching Tuscans,
  And scorn was in his eye.
Quoth he, "The she-wolf's litter
  Stand savagely at bay;
But will ye dare to follow,
  If Astur clears the way?"

Then, whirling up his broadsword
  With both hands to the height,
He rushed against Horatius,
  And smote with all his might.
With shield and blade Horatius
  Right deftly turned the blow.
The blow, though turned, came yet too nigh;
It missed his helm, but gashed his thigh.
The Tuscans raised a joyful cry
  To see the red blood flow.

He reeled, and on Herminius
  He leaned one breathing-space,
Then, like a wild-cat mad with wounds,
  Sprang right at Astur's face.
Through teeth and skull and helmet
  So fierce a thrust he sped,
The good sword stood a handbreadth out
  Behind the Tuscan's head.

And the great lord of Luna
  Fell at that deadly stroke,
As falls on Mount Avernus
  A thunder-smitten oak.
Far o'er the crashing forest
  The giant arms lie spread;
And the pale augurs, muttering low
  Gaze on the blasted head.

On Astur's throat Horatius
  Right firmly pressed his heel,
And thrice and four times tugged amain,
  Ere he wrenched out the steel.
And "See," he cried, "the welcome,
  Fair guests, that waits you here!
What noble Lucumo comes next
  To taste our Roman cheer?"

But at his haughty challenge
  A sullen murmur ran,
Mingled with wrath and shame and dread,
  Along that glittering van.
There lacked not men of prowess,
  Nor men of lordly race,
For all Etruria's noblest
  Were round the fatal place.

But all Etruria's noblest
  Felt their hearts sink to see
On the earth the bloody corpses,
  In the path the dauntless three;
And from the ghastly entrance,
  Where those bold Romans stood,
All shrank,—like boys who, unaware,
Ranging the woods to start a hare,
Come to the mouth of the dark lair
Where, growling low, a fierce old bear
  Lies amidst bones and blood.

Was none who would be foremost
  To lead such dire attack;
But those behind cried "Forward!"
  And those before cried "Back!"
And backward now and forward
  Wavers the deep array;
And on the tossing sea of steel
To and fro the standards reel,
And the victorious trumpet-peal
  Dies fitfully away.

Yet one man for one moment
  Strode out before the crowd;
Well known was he to all the three,
  And they gave him greeting loud:
"Now welcome, welcome, Sextus!
  Now welcome to thy home!
Why dost thou stay, and turn away?
  Here lies the road to Rome."

Thrice looked he at the city;
  Thrice looked he at the dead;
And thrice came on in fury,
  And thrice turned back in dread;
And, white with fear and hatred,
  Scowled at the narrow way
Where, wallowing in a pool of blood,
  The bravest Tuscans lay.

But meanwhile axe and lever
  Have manfully been plied;
And now the bridge hangs tottering
  Above the boiling tide.
"Come back, come back, Horatius!"
  Loud cried the Fathers all,—
"Back, Lartius! back, Herminius!
  Back, ere the ruin fall!"

Back darted Spurius Lartius,—
  Herminius darted back;
And, as they passed, beneath their feet
  They felt the timbers crack.
But when they turned their faces,
  And on the farther shore
Saw brave Horatius stand alone,
  They would have crossed once more;

But with a crash like thunder
  Fell every loosened beam,
And, like a dam, the mighty wreck
  Lay right athwart the stream;

And a long shout of triumph
  Rose from the walls of Rome,
As to the highest turret-tops
  Was splashed the yellow foam.

And like a horse unbroken,
  When first he feels the rein,
The furious river struggled hard,
  And tossed his tawny mane,
And burst the curb, and bounded,
  Rejoicing to be free;
And whirling down, in fierce career,
Battlement and plank and pier,
  Rushed headlong to the sea.

Alone stood brave Horatius,
  But constant still in mind,—
Thrice thirty thousand foes before,
  And the broad flood behind.
"Down with him!" cried false Sextus,
  With a smile on his pale face;
"Now yield thee," cried Lars Porsena,
  "Now yield thee to our grace!"

Round turned he, as not deigning
  Those craven ranks to see;
Naught spake he to Lars Porsena,
  To Sextus naught spake he;
But he saw on Palatinus
  The white porch of his home;
And he spake to the noble river
  That rolls by the towers of Rome:

"O Tiber! Father Tiber!
  To whom the Romans pray,
A Roman's life, a Roman's arms,
  Take thou in charge this day!"
So he spake, and, speaking, sheathed
  The good sword by his side,
And, with his harness on his back,
  Plunged headlong in the tide.

No sound of joy or sorrow
  Was heard from either bank,
But friends and foes in dumb surprise,
With parted lips and straining eyes,
  Stood gazing where he sank;
And when above the surges
  They saw his crest appear,
All Rome sent forth a rapturous cry,
And even the ranks of Tuscany
  Could scarce forbear to cheer.

But fiercely ran the current,
  Swollen high by months of rain;
And fast his blood was flowing,
  And he was sore in pain,
And heavy with his armor,
  And spent with changing blows;
And oft they thought him sinking,
  But still again he rose.

Never, I ween, did swimmer,
  In such an evil case,
Struggle through such a raging flood
  Safe to the landing-place;
But his limbs were borne up bravely
  By the brave heart within,
And our good Father Tiber
  Bare bravely up his chin.

"Curse on him!" quoth false Sextus,—
  "Will not the villain drown?
But for this stay, ere close of day
  We should have sacked the town!"
"Heaven help him!" quoth Lars Porsena,
  "And bring him safe to shore;
For such a gallant feat of arms
  Was never seen before."

And now he feels the bottom;
Now on dry earth he stands;
Now round him throng the Fathers
To press his gory hands;
And now, with shouts and clapping,
And noise of weeping loud,
He enters through the River-gate,
Borne by the joyous crowd.

They gave him of the corn-land,
That was of public right,
As much as two strong oxen
Could plough from morn till night;
And they made a molten image,
And set it up on high,—
And there it stands unto this day
To witness if I lie.

It stands in the Comitium,
Plain for all folk to see,—
Horatius in his harness,
Halting upon one knee;
And underneath is written,
In letters all of gold,
How valiantly he kept the bridge
In the brave days of old.

And still his name sounds stirring
Unto the men of Rome,
As the trumpet-blast that cries to them
To charge the Volscian home;
And wives still pray to Juno
For boys with hearts as bold
As his who kept the bridge so well
In the brave days of old.

And in the nights of winter,
When the cold north-winds blow,
And the long howling of the wolves
Is heard amidst the snow;

When round the lonely cottage
  Roars loud the tempest's din,
And the good logs of Algidus
  Roar louder yet within;

When the oldest cask is opened,
  And the largest lamp is lit;
When the chestnuts glow in the embers,
  And the kid turns on the spit;
When young and old in circle
  Around the firebrands close;
When the girls are weaving baskets,
  And the lads are shaping bows;

When the goodman mends his armor,
  And trims his helmet's plume;
When the goodwife's shuttle merrily
  Goes flashing through the loom;
With weeping and with laughter
  Still is the story told,
How well Horatius kept the bridge
  In the brave days of old.

THOMAS LOVELL BEDDOES

(1803–1849)

Dream-Pedlary

IF THERE were dreams to sell,
  What would you buy?
Some cost a passing bell;
  Some a light sigh
That shakes from Life's fresh crown
Only a rose leaf down.
If there were dreams to sell,
Merry and sad to tell,
And the crier rang the bell,
  What would you buy?

A cottage lone and still,
  With bowers nigh,
Shadowy, my woes to still
  Until I die.
Each pearl from Life's fresh crown
Fain would I shake me down;
Were dreams to have at will,
This would best heal my ill,
  This would I buy.

But there were dreams to sell,
  Ill didst thou buy;
Life is a dream, they tell,
  Waking, to die.
Dreaming a dream to prize
Is wishing ghosts to rise;
And, if I had the spell
To call the buried well,
  Which one would I?

If there are ghosts to raise,
  What shall I call,
Out of hell's murky haze,
  Heaven's blue pall?
Raise my loved, long-lost boy
To lead me to his joy—
There are no ghosts to raise;
Out of death lead no ways;
  Vain is the call.

Know'st thou not ghosts to sue,
  No love thou hast.
Else lie, as I will do,
  And breathe thy last.
So out of Life's fresh crown
Fall like a rose leaf down.
Thus are the ghosts to woo;
Thus are all dreams made true,
  Ever to last!

RALPH WALDO EMERSON

(1803–1882)

Concord Hymn

SUNG AT THE COMPLETION OF THE CONCORD MONUMENT, APRIL 19, 1836.

By the rude bridge that arched the flood,
Their flag to April's breeze unfurled,
Here once the embattled farmers stood,
And fired the shot heard round the world.

The foe long since in silence slept;
Alike the conqueror silent sleeps;
And Time the ruined bridge has swept
Down the dark stream which seaward creeps.

On this green bank, by this soft stream,
We set to-day a votive stone;
That memory may their deed redeem,
When, like our sires, our sons are gone.

Spirit, that made those heroes dare
To die, or leave their children free,
Bid Time and Nature gently spare
The shaft we raise to them and thee.

The Rhodora

Lines on Being Asked, Whence Is the Flower?

In May, when sea-winds pierced our solitudes,
I found the fresh rhodora in the woods,
Spreading its leafless blooms in a damp nook,
To please the desert and the sluggish brook:

The purple petals fallen in the pool
  Made the black waters with their beauty gay,—
Here might the red-bird come his plumes to cool,
  And court the flower that cheapens his array.
Rhodora! if the sages ask thee why
This charm is wasted on the marsh and sky.
Tell them, dear, that if eyes were made for seeing,
Then beauty is its own excuse for being.
  Why thou wert there, O rival of the rose!
I never thought to ask; I never knew,
  But in my simple ignorance suppose
The self-same Power that brought me there brought you.

Brahma

If the red slayer think he slays,
  Or if the slain think he is slain,
They know not well the subtle ways
  I keep, and pass, and turn again.

Far or forgot to me is near;
  Shadow and sunlight are the same;
The vanished gods to me appear;
  And one to me are shame and fame.

They reckon ill who leave me out;
  When me they fly, I am the wings;
I am the doubter and the doubt,
  And I the hymn the Brahmin sings.

The strong gods pine for my abode,
  And pine in vain the sacred Seven;
But thou, meek lover of the good!
  Find me, and turn thy back on heaven.

Days

DAUGHTERS of Time, the hypocritic Days,
Muffled and dumb like barefoot dervishes,
And marching single in an endless file,
Bring diadems and fagots in their hands.
To each they offer gifts after his will,
Bread, kingdoms, stars, and sky that holds them all.
I, in my pleachèd garden, watched the pomp,
Forgot my morning wishes, hastily
Took a few herbs and apples, and the Day
Turned and departed silent. I, too late,
Under her solemn fillet saw the scorn.

JAMES CLARENCE MANGAN

(1803–1849)

Dark Rosaleen

O MY Dark Rosaleen,
  Do not sigh, do not weep!
The priests are on the ocean green,
  They march along the deep.
There's wine from the royal Pope,
  Upon the ocean green;
And Spanish ale shall give you hope,
  My Dark Rosaleen!
  My own Rosaleen!
Shall glad your heart, shall give you hope,
Shall give you health, and help, and hope,
  My Dark Rosaleen!

Over hills, and thro' dales,
  Have I roam'd for your sake;
All yesterday I sail'd with sails
  On river and on lake.
The Erne, at its highest flood,
  I dash'd across unseen.
For there was lightning in my blood,
  My Dark Rosaleen!
  My own Rosaleen!
O, there was lightning in my blood,
Red lightning lighten'd thro' my blood,
  My Dark Rosaleen!

All day long, in unrest,
  To and fro do I move.
The very soul within my breast
  Is wasted for you, love!
The heart in my bosom faints
  To think of you, my Queen,
My life of life, my saint of saints,
  My Dark Rosaleen!
  My own Rosaleen!
To hear your sweet and sad complaints,
My life, my love, my saint of saints,
  My Dark Rosaleen!

Woe and pain, pain and woe,
  Are my lot, night and noon,
To see your bright face clouded so,
  Like to the mournful moon.
But yet will I rear your throne
  Again in golden sheen;
'Tis you shall reign, shall reign alone,
  My Dark Rosaleen!
  My own Rosaleen!
'Tis you shall have the golden throne,
'Tis you shall reign, and reign alone,
  My Dark Rosaleen!

Over dews, over sands,
  Will I fly, for your weal:
Your holy delicate white hands
  Shall girdle me with steel.
At home, in your emerald bowers,
  From morning's dawn till e'en,
You'll pray for me, my flower of flowers,
  My Dark Rosaleen!
  My fond Rosaleen!
You'll think of me through daylight hours,
My virgin flower, my flower of flowers,
  My Dark Rosaleen!

I could scale the blue air,
  I could plough the high hills,
O, I could kneel all night in prayer,
  To heal your many ills!
And one beamy smile from you
  Would float like light between
My toils and me, my own, my true,
  My Dark Rosaleen!
  My fond Rosaleen!
Would give me life and soul anew,
A second life, a soul anew,
  My Dark Rosaleen!

O, the Erne shall run red,
  With redundance of blood,
The earth shall rock beneath our tread,
  And flames wrap hill and wood,
And gun-peal and slogan-cry
  Wake many a glen serene,
Ere you shall fade, ere you shall die,
  My Dark Rosaleen!
  My own Rosaleen!
The Judgment Hour must first be nigh,
Ere you can fade, ere you can die,
  My Dark Rosaleen!

ELIZABETH BARRETT BROWNING
(1806–1861)

A Musical Instrument

WHAT was he doing, the great god Pan,
  Down in the reeds by the river?
Spreading ruin and scattering ban,
Splashing and paddling with hoofs of a goat,
And breaking the golden lilies afloat
  With the dragon-fly on the river.

He tore out a reed, the great god Pan,
  From the deep cool bed of the river:
The limpid water turbidly ran,
And the broken lilies a-dying lay,
And the dragon-fly had fled away,
  Ere he brought it out of the river.

High on the shore sate the great god Pan,
  While turbidly flowed the river;
And hacked and hewed as a great god can,
With his hard bleak steel at the patient reed,
Till there was not a sign of a leaf indeed
  To prove it fresh from the river.

He cut it short, did the great god Pan
  (How tall it stood in the river!)
Then drew the pith, like the heart of a man,
Steadily from the outside ring,
And notched the poor dry empty thing
  In holes, as he sate by the river.

"This is the way," laughed the great god Pan
  (Laughed while he sate by the river),
"The only way, since gods began
To make sweet music, they could succeed."
Then, dropping his mouth to a hole in the reed
  He blew in power by the river.

Sweet, sweet, sweet, O Pan!
  Piercing sweet by the river!
Blinding sweet, O great god Pan!
The sun on the hill forgot to die,
And the lilies revived, and the dragon-fly
  Came back to dream on the river.

Yet half a beast is the great god Pan,
  To laugh as he sits by the river,
Making a poet out of a man:
The true gods sigh for the cost and pain,—
For the reed which grows nevermore again
  As a reed with the reeds in the river.

Grief

I TELL you, hopeless grief is passionless;
  That only men incredulous of despair,
  Half-taught in anguish, through the midnight air
Beat upward to God's throne in loud access
Of shrieking and reproach. Full desertness,
  In souls as countries, lieth silent-bare
  Under the blanching, vertical eye-glare
Of the absolute Heavens. Deep-hearted man, express
Grief for thy Dead in silence like to death—
  Most like a monumental statue set
In everlasting watch and moveless woe
Till itself crumble to the dust beneath.
  Touch it; the marble eyelids are not wet:
If it could weep, it could arise and go.

I Thought How Once Theocritus Had Sung

I THOUGHT how once Theocritus had sung
Of the sweet years, the dear and wish'd-for years,
Who each one in a gracious hand appears
To bear a gift for mortals old or young:

And, as I mused it in his antique tongue,
I saw in gradual vision through my tears
The sweet, sad years, the melancholy years—
Those of my own life, who by turns had flung
A shadow across me. Straightway I was 'ware,
So weeping, how a mystic Shape did move
Behind me, and drew me backward by the hair;
And a voice said in mastery, while I strove,
"Guess now who holds thee?"—"Death," I said. But there
The silver answer rang—"Not Death, but Love."

Unlike Are We

UNLIKE as we, unlike, O princely Heart!
Unlike our uses and our destinies.
Our ministering two angels look surprise
On one another, as they strike athwart
Their wings in passing. Thou, bethink thee, art
A guest for queens to social pageantries,
With gages from a hundred brighter eyes
Than tears even can make mine, to play thy part
Of chief musician. What hast *thou* to do
With looking from the lattice-lights at me,
A poor, tired, wandering singer, singing through
The dark, and leaning up a cypress tree?
The chrism is on thine head,—on mine, the dew,—
And Death must dig the level where these agree.

Go From Me

GO FROM me. Yet I feel that I shall stand
Henceforward in thy shadow. Nevermore
Alone upon the threshold of my door
Of individual life, I shall command

The uses of my soul, nor lift my hand
Serenely in the sunshine as before,
Without the sense of that which I forbore, . . .
Thy touch upon the palm. The widest land
Doom takes to part us, leaves thy heart in mine
With pulses that beat double. What I do
And what I dream include thee, as the wine
Must taste of its own grapes. And when I sue
God for myself, he hears that name of thine,
And sees within my eyes the tears of two.

The Face of all the World Is Changed

THE face of all the world is changed, I think,
Since first I heard the footsteps of thy soul
Move still, oh, still, beside me, as they stole
Betwixt me and the dreadful outer brink
Of obvious death, where I, who thought to sink,
Was caught up into love, and taught the whole
Of life in a new rhythm. The cup of dole
God gave for baptism, I am fain to drink,
And praise its sweetness, Sweet, with thee anear.
The name of country, heaven, are changed away
For where thou art or shalt be, there or here;
And this . . . this lute and song . . . loved yesterday,
(The singing angels know) are only dear
Because thy name moves right in what they say.

What Can I Give Thee Back

WHAT can I give thee back, O liberal
And princely giver, who hast brought the gold
And purple of thine heart, unstained, untold,
And laid them on the outside of the wall

For such as I to take or leave withal,
In unexpected largesse? Am I cold,
Ungrateful, that for these most manifold
High gifts, I render nothing back at all?
Not so; not cold,—but very poor instead.
Ask God who knows. For frequent tears have run
The colors from my life, and left so dead
And pale a stuff, it were not fitly done
To give the same as pillow to thy head.
Go farther! let it serve to trample on.

If Thou Must Love Me

If thou must love me, let it be for naught
Except for love's sake only. Do not say,
"I love her for her smile—her look—her way
Of speaking gently,—for a trick of thought
That falls in well with mine, and certes brought
A sense of pleasant ease on such a day"—
For these things in themselves, Belovèd, may
Be changed, or change for thee,—and love, so wrought,
May be unwrought so. Neither love me for
Thine own dear pity's wiping my cheeks dry,—
A creature might forget to weep, who bore
Thy comfort long, and lose thy love thereby!
But love me for love's sake, that evermore
Thou mayst love on, through love's eternity.

When Our Two Souls Stand Up Erect and Strong

When our two souls stand up erect and strong,
Face to face, silent, drawing nigh and nigher,
Until the lengthening wings break into fire
At either curvèd point,—what bitter wrong

Can the earth do to us, that we should not long
Be here contented? Think. In mounting higher,
The angels would press on us, and aspire
To drop some golden orb of perfect song
Into our deep dear silence. Let us stay
Rather on earth, Belovèd, where the unfit
Contrarious moods of men recoil away
And isolate pure spirits, and permit
A place to stand and love in for a day,
With darkness and the death-hour rounding it.

Say Over Again

SAY over again, and yet once over again,
That thou dost love me. Though the word repeated
Should seem "a cuckoo-song," as thou dost treat it,
Remember, never to the hill or plain,
Valley and wood, without her cuckoo-strain,
Comes the fresh spring in all her green completed.
Beloved, I, amid the darkness greeted
By a doubtful spirit-voice, in that doubt's pain
Cry: "Speak once more—thou lovest!" Who can fear
Too many stars, though each in heaven shall roll,—
Too many flowers, though each shall crown the year?
Say thou dost love me, love me, love me,—toll
The silver iterance!—only minding, dear,
To love me also in silence, with thy soul.

My Letters! All Dead Paper

MY LETTERS! all dead paper, . . . mute and white!—
And yet they seem alive and quivering
Against my tremulous hands which loose the string
And let them drop down on my knee to-night.

This said, . . . he wished to have me in his sight
Once, as a friend: this fixed a day in spring
To come and touch my hand . . . a simple thing,
Yet I wept for it! this, . . . the paper's light . . .
Said, *Dear, I love thee;* and I sank and quailed
As if God's future thundered on my past.
This said, *I am thine,*—and so its ink has paled
With lying at my heart that beat too fast.
And this . . . O Love, thy words have ill availed,
If what this said, I dared repeat at last!

First Time He Kissed Me

FIRST time he kissed me, he but only kissed
The fingers of this hand wherewith I write;
And, ever since, it grew more clean and white,
Slow to world-greetings, quick with its "O list!"
When the angels speak. A ring of amethyst
I could not wear here, plainer to my sight
Than that first kiss. The second passed in height
The first, and sought the forehead, and half missed,
Half falling on the hair. O, beyond meed!
That was the chrism of love, which love's own crown,
With sanctifying sweetness, did precede.
The third upon my lips was folded down
In perfect, purple state; since when, indeed,
I have been proud, and said, "My love, my own!"

How Do I Love Thee?

How do I love thee? Let me count the ways.
I love thee to the depth and breadth and height
My soul can reach, when feeling out of sight
For the ends of Being and ideal Grace.

I love thee to the level of every day's
Most quiet need, by sun and candlelight.
I love thee freely, as men strive for Right;
I love thee purely, as they turn from Praise.
I love thee with the passion put to use
In my old griefs, and with my childhood's faith.
I love thee with a love I seemed to lose
With my lost saints,—I love thee with the breath,
Smiles, tears, of all my life!—and, if God choose,
I shall but love thee better after death.

HENRY WADSWORTH LONGFELLOW

(1807–1882)

Hymn to the Night

'Ασπασίη, τρίλλιστος.

I HEARD the trailing garments of the Night
Sweep through her marble halls!
I saw her sable skirts all fringed with light
From the celestial walls!

I felt her presence, by its spell of might,
Stoop o'er me from above;
The calm, majestic presence of the Night,
As of the one I love.

I heard the sounds of sorrow and delight,
The manifold, soft chimes,
That fill the haunted chambers of the Night,
Like some old poet's rhymes.

From the cool cisterns of the midnight air
  My spirit drank repose;
The fountain of perpetual peace flows there,—
  From those deep cisterns flows.

O holy Night! from thee I learn to bear
  What man has borne before!
Thou layest thy finger on the lips of Care,
  And they complain no more.

Peace! Peace! Orestes-like I breathe this prayer!
  Descend with broad-winged flight,
The welcome, the thrice-prayed for, the most fair,
  The best-belovèd Night!

My Lost Youth

OFTEN I think of the beautiful town
  That is seated by the sea;
Often in thought go up and down
The pleasant streets of that dear old town,
  And my youth comes back to me.
    And a verse of a Lapland song
    Is haunting my memory still:
    "A boy's will is the wind's will,
And the thoughts of youth are long, long thoughts."

I can see the shadowy lines of its trees,
  And catch, in sudden gleams,
The sheen of the far-surrounding seas,
And islands that were the Hesperides
  Of all my boyish dreams.
    And the burden of that old song,
    It murmurs and whispers still:
    "A boy's will is the wind's will,
And the thoughts of youth are long, long thoughts."

I remember the black wharves and the slips,
  And the sea-tides tossing free;
And Spanish sailors with bearded lips,
And the beauty and mystery of the ships,
  And the magic of the sea.
    And the voice of that wayward song
    Is singing and saying still:
    "A boy's will is the wind's will,
And the thoughts of youth are long, long thoughts."

I remember the bulwarks by the shore,
  And the fort upon the hill;
The sunrise gun, with its hollow roar,
The drum-beat repeated o'er and o'er,
  And the bugle wild and shrill.
    And the music of that old song
    Throbs in my memory still:
    "A boy's will is the wind's will,
And the thoughts of youth are long, long thoughts."

I remember the sea-fight far away,
  How it thundered o'er the tide!
And the dead captains, as they lay
In their graves, o'erlooking the tranquil bay
  Where they in battle died.
    And the sound of that mournful song
    Goes through me with a thrill:
    "A boy's will is the wind's will,
And the thoughts of youth are long, long thoughts."

I can see the breezy dome of groves,
  The shadows of Deering's Woods;
And the friendships old and the early loves
Come back with a Sabbath sound, as of doves
  In quiet neighborhoods.
    And the verse of that sweet old song,
    It flutters and murmurs still:
    "A boy's will is the wind's will,
And the thoughts of youth are long, long thoughts."

I remember the gleams and glooms that dart
  Across the school-boy's brain;
The song and the silence in the heart,
That in part are prophecies, and in part
  Are longings wild and vain.
    And the voice of that fitful song
    Sings on, and is never still:
    "A boy's will is the wind's will,
And the thoughts of youth are long, long thoughts."

There are things of which I may not speak;
  There are dreams that cannot die;
There are thoughts that make the strong heart weak,
And bring a pallor into the cheek,
  And a mist before the eye.
    And the words of that fatal song
    Come over me like a chill:
    "A boy's will is the wind's will,
And the thoughts of youth are long, long thoughts."

Strange to me now are the forms I meet
  When I visit the dear old town;
But the native air is pure and sweet,
And the trees that o'ershadow each well-known street,
  As they balance up and down,
    Are singing the beautiful song,
    Are sighing and whispering still:
    "A boy's will is the wind's will,
And the thoughts of youth are long, long thoughts."

And Deering's Woods are fresh and fair,
  And with joy that is almost pain
My heart goes back to wander there,
And among the dreams of the days that were,
  I find my lost youth again.
    And the strange and beautiful song,
    The groves are repeating it still:
    "A boy's will is the wind's will,
And the thoughts of youth are long, long thoughts."

JOHN GREENLEAF WHITTIER

(1807–1892)

Ichabod

So FALLEN! so lost! the light withdrawn
Which once he wore!
The glory from his gray hairs gone
Forevermore!

Revile him not, the Tempter hath
A snare for all;
And pitying tears, not scorn and wrath,
Befit his fall!

Oh, dumb be passion's stormy rage,
When he who might
Have lighted up and led his age,
Falls back in night.

Scorn! would the angels laugh, to mark
A bright soul driven,
Fiend-goaded, down the endless dark,
From hope and heaven!

Let not the land once proud of him
Insult him now,
Nor brand with deeper shame his dim,
Dishonored brow.

But let its humbled sons, instead,
From sea to lake,
A long lament, as for the dead,
In sadness make.

Of all we loved and honored, naught
Save power remains;
A fallen angel's pride of thought,
Still strong in chains.

All else is gone; from those great eyes
The soul has fled;
When faith is lost, when honor dies,
The man is dead!

Then pay the reverence of old days
To his dead fame;
Walk backward, with averted gaze,
And hide the shame!

CAROLINA ELIZABETH SARAH NORTON

(1808–1876)

I Do Not Love Thee

I DO not love thee!—no! I do not love thee!
And yet when thou art absent I am sad;
And envy even the bright blue sky above thee,
Whose quiet stars may see thee and be glad.

I do not love thee!—yet, I know not why,
Whate'er thou dost seems still well done, to me:
And often in my solitude I sigh
That those I do love are not more like thee!

I do not love thee!—yet, I know not why,
I hate the sound (though those who speak be dear)
Which breaks the lingering echo of the tone
Thy voice of music leaves upon my ear.

I do not love thee!—yet thy speaking eyes,
With their deep, bright, and most expressive blue,
Between me and the midnight heaven arise,
Oftener than any eyes I ever knew.

I know I do not love thee! yet, alas!
Others will scarcely trust my candid heart;
And oft I catch them smiling as they pass,
Because they see me gazing where thou art.

EDWARD FITZGERALD

(1809–1883)

The Rubaiyat of Omar Khayyam

I

Wake! For the Sun, who scatter'd into flight
The Stars before him from the Field of Night,
Drives Night along with them from Heav'n, and strikes
The Sultan's Turret with a Shaft of Light.

II

Before the phantom of False morning died,
Methought a Voice within the Tavern cried,
"When all the Temple is prepared within,
"Why nods the drowsy Worshipper outside?"

III

And, as the Cock crew, those who stood before
The Tavern shouted—"Open then the Door!
"You know how little while we have to stay,
"And, once departed, may return no more."

IV

Now the New Year reviving old Desires,
The thoughtful Soul to Solitude retires,
Where the White Hand of Moses on the Bough
Puts out, and Jesus from the Ground suspires.

V

Iram indeed is gone with all his Rose,
And Jamshyd's sev'n-ringed Cup where no one knows;
  But still a Ruby kindles in the Vine,
And many a Garden by the Water blows.

VI

And David's lips are lockt; but in divine
High-piping Pehlevi, with "Wine! Wine! Wine!
  "Red Wine!"—the Nightingale cries to the Rose
That sallow cheek of hers to' incardine.

VII

Come, fill the Cup, and in the fire of Spring
Your Winter-garment of Repentance fling:
  The Bird of Time has but a little way
To flutter—and the Bird is on the Wing.

VIII

Whether at Naishapur or Babylon,
Whether the Cup with sweet or bitter run,
  The wine of Life keeps oozing drop by drop,
The Leaves of Life keep falling one by one.

IX

Each morn a thousand Roses brings, you say;
Yes, but where leaves the Rose of Yesterday?
  And this first Summer month that brings the Rose
Shall take Jamshyd and Kaikobad away.

X

Well, let it take them! What have we to do
With Kaikobad the Great, or Kaikhosru?
  Let Zal and Rustum bluster as they will,
Or Hatim call to Supper—heed not you.

XI

With me along the strip of Herbage strown
That just divides the desert from the sown,
  Where name of Slave and Sultan is forgot—
And Peace to Mahmud on his golden Throne!

XII

A Book of Verses underneath the Bough,
A Jug of Wine, a Loaf of Bread—and Thou
  Beside me singing in the Wilderness—
Oh, Wilderness were Paradise enow!

XIII

Some for the Glories of This World; and some
Sigh for the Prophet's Paradise to come;
  Ah, take the Cash, and let the Credit go,
Nor heed the rumble of a distant Drum!

XIV

Look to the blowing Rose about us—"Lo,
"Laughing," she says, "into the world I blow,
  "At once the silken tassel of my Purse
"Tear, and its Treasure on the Garden throw."

XV

And those who husbanded the Golden grain,
And those who flung it to the winds like Rain,
  Alike to no such aureate Earth are turn'd
As, buried once, Men want dug up again.

XVI

The Worldly Hope men set their Hearts upon
Turns Ashes—or it prospers; and anon,
  Like Snow upon the Desert's dusty Face,
Lighting a little hour or two—is gone.

XVII

Think, in this batter'd Caravanserai
Whose Portals are alternate Night and Day,
  How Sultan after Sultan with his Pomp
Abode his destined Hour, and went his way.

XVIII

They say the Lion and the Lizard keep
The Courts where Jamshyd gloried and drank deep:
  And Bahram, that great Hunter—the Wild Ass
Stamps o'er his Head, but cannot break his Sleep.

XIX

I sometimes think that never blows so red
The Rose as where some buried Cæsar bled;
  That every Hyacinth the Garden wears
Dropt in her Lap from some once lovely Head.

XX

And this reviving Herb whose tender Green
Fledges the River-Lip on which we lean—
  Ah, lean upon it lightly! for who knows
From what once lovely Lip it springs unseen!

XXI

Ah, my Belovèd, fill the Cup that clears
TO-DAY of past Regrets and future Fears:
  To-morrow!—Why, To-morrow I may be
Myself with Yesterday's Sev'n thousand Years.

XXII

For some we loved, the loveliest and the best
That from his Vintage rolling Time hath prest,
  Have drunk their Cup a Round or two before.
And one by one crept silently to rest.

XXIII

And we, that now make merry in the Room
They left, and Summer dresses in new bloom,
  Ourselves must we beneath the Couch of Earth
Descend—ourselves to make a Couch—for whom?

XXIV

Ah, make the most of what we yet may spend,
Before we too into the Dust descend;
  Dust into Dust, and under Dust to lie,
Sans Wine, sans Song, sans Singer, and—sans End!

XXV

Alike for those who for To-day prepare,
And those that after some To-morrow stare,
  A Muezzin from the Tower of Darkness cries,
"Fools! your Reward is neither Here nor There."

XXVI

Why, all the Saints and Sages who discuss'd
Of the Two Worlds so wisely—they are thrust
  Like foolish Prophets forth; their Words to Scorn
Are scatter'd, and their Mouths are stopt with Dust.

XXVII

Myself when young did eagerly frequent
Doctor and Saint, and heard great argument
  About it and about: but evermore
Came out by the same door where in I went.

XXVIII

With them the seed of Wisdom did I sow,
And with mine own hand wrought to make it grow;
  And this was all the Harvest that I reap'd—
"I came like Water, and like Wind I go."

XXIX

Into this Universe, and *Why* not knowing
Nor *Whence,* like Water willy-nilly flowing;
And out of it, as Wind along the Waste,
I know not *Whither,* willy-nilly blowing.

XXX

What, without asking, hither hurried *Whence?*
And, without asking, *whither* hurried hence!
Oh, many a Cup of this forbidden Wine
Must drown the memory of that insolence!

XXXI

Up from Earth's Centre through the Seventh Gate
I rose, and on the Throne of Saturn sate,
And many a Knot unravel'd by the Road;
But not the Master-knot of Human Fate.

XXXII

There was the Door to which I found no Key;
There was the Veil through which I might not see:
Some little talk a while of ME and THEE
There was—and then no more of THEE and ME.

XXXIII

Earth could not answer, nor the Seas that mourn
In flowing Purple, of their Lord forlorn;
Nor rolling Heaven, with all his Signs reveal'd
And hidden by the sleeve of Night and Morn.

XXXIV

Then of the THEE in ME who works behind
The Veil, I lifted up my hands to find
A Lamp amid the Darkness; and I heard,
As from Without—"THE ME WITHIN THEE BLIND!"

XXXV

Then to the Lip of this poor earthen Urn
I lean'd, the Secret of my Life to learn:
  And Lip to Lip it murmur'd—"While you live,
"Drink!—for, once dead, you never shall return."

XXXVI

I think the Vessel, that with fugitive
Articulation answer'd, once did live
  And drink; and Ah! the passive Lip I kiss'd,
How many Kisses might it take—and give!

XXXVII

For I remember stopping by the way
To watch a Potter thumping his wet Clay:
  And with its all-obliterated Tongue
It murmur'd—"Gently, Brother, gently, pray!"

XXXVIII

And has not such a Story from of Old
Down Man's successive generations roll'd
  Of such a clod of saturated Earth
Cast by the Maker into Human mould?

XXXIX

And not a drop that from our Cups we throw
For earth to drink of, but may steal below
  To quench the fire of Anguish in some Eye
There hidden—far beneath, and long ago.

XL

As then the Tulip for her morning sup
Of Heav'nly Vintage from the soil looks up,
  Do you devoutly do the like, till Heav'n
To Earth invert you—like an empty Cup.

XLI

Perplext no more with Human or Divine,
To-morrow's tangle to the winds resign,
  And lose your fingers in the tresses of
The Cypress-slender Minister of Wine.

XLII

And if the Wine you drink, the Lip you press,
End in what All begins and ends in—Yes;
  Think then you are TO-DAY what YESTERDAY
You were—TO-MORROW you shall not be less.

XLIII

So when that Angel of the darker Drink
At last shall find you by the river-brink,
  And, offering his Cup, invite your Soul
Forth to your Lips to quaff—you shall not shrink.

XLIV

Why, if the Soul can fling the Dust aside,
And naked on the Air of Heaven ride,
  Were't not a Shame—were't not a Shame for him
In this clay carcase crippled to abide?

XLV

'Tis but a Tent where takes his one day's rest
A Sultan to the realm of Death addrest;
  The Sultan rises, and the dark Ferrash
Strikes, and prepares it for another Guest.

XLVI

And fear not lest Existence closing your
Account, and mine, should know the like no more;
  The Eternal Saki from that Bowl has pour'd
Millions of Bubbles like us, and will pour.

XLVII

When You and I behind the Veil are past,
Oh, but the long, long while the World shall last,
Which of our Coming and Departure heeds
As the Sea's self should heed a pebble-cast.

XLVIII

A Moment's Halt—a momentary taste
Of BEING from the Well amid the Waste—
And lo!—the phantom Caravan has reach'd
The NOTHING it set out from—Oh, make haste!

XLIX

Would you that spangle of Existence spend
About THE SECRET—quick about it, Friend!
A Hair perhaps divides the False and True—
And upon what, prithee, may life depend?

L

A Hair perhaps divides the False and True;
Yes; and a single Alif were the clue—
Could you but find it—to the Treasure-house,
And peradventure to THE MASTER too;

LI

Whose secret Presence, through Creation's veins
Running Quicksilver-like eludes your pains;
Taking all shapes from Mah to Mahi; and
They change and perish all—but He remains;

LII

A moment guess'd—then back behind the Fold
Immerst of Darkness round the Drama roll'd
Which, for the Pastime of Eternity,
He doth Himself contrive, enact, behold.

LIII

But if in vain, down on the stubborn floor
Of Earth, and up to Heav'n's unopening Door,
  You gaze To-DAY, while You are You—how then
To-MORROW, You when shall be You no more?

LIV

Waste not your Hour, nor in the vain pursuit
Of This and That endeavor and dispute;
  Better be jocund with the fruitful Grape
Than sadden after none, or bitter, Fruit.

LV

You know, my Friends, with what a brave Carouse
I made a Second Marriage in my house;
  Divorced old barren Reason from my Bed,
And took the Daughter of the Vine to Spouse.

LVI

For "Is" and "Is-NOT" though with Rule and Line
And "UP-AND-DOWN" by Logic I define,
  Of all that one should care to fathom, I
Was never deep in anything but—Wine.

LVII

Ah, but my Computations, People say,
Reduced the Year to better reckoning?—Nay,
  'Twas only striking from the Calendar
Unborn To-morrow, and dead Yesterday.

LVIII

And lately, by the Tavern Door agape,
Came shining through the Dusk an Angel Shape
  Bearing a Vessel on his Shoulder; and
He bid me taste of it; and 'twas—the Grape!

LIX

The Grape that can with Logic absolute
The Two-and-Seventy jarring Sects confute:
  The sovereign Alchemist that in a trice
Life's leaden metal into Gold transmute:

LX

The mighty Mahmud, Allah breathing Lord,
That all the misbelieving and black Horde
  Of fears and Sorrows that infest the Soul
Scatters before him with his whirlwind Sword.

LXI

Why, be this Juice the growth of God, who dare
Blaspheme the twisted tendril as a Snare?
  A Blessing, we should use it, should we not?
And if a Curse—why, then, Who set it there?

LXII

I must abjure the Balm of Life, I must,
Scared by some After-reckoning ta'en on trust,
  Or lured with Hope of some Diviner Drink,
To fill the Cup—when crumbled into Dust!

LXIII

O threats of Hell and Hopes of Paradise!
One thing at least is certain—*This* Life flies;
  One thing is certain and the rest is Lies;
The Flower that once has blown for ever dies.

LXIV

Strange, is it not? that of the myriads who
Before us pass'd the door of Darkness through,
  Not one returns to tell us of the Road,
Which to discover we must travel too.

LXV

The Revelations of Devout and Learn'd
Who rose before us, and as Prophets burn'd,
Are all but Stories, which, awoke from Sleep
They told their comrades, and to Sleep return'd.

LXVI

I sent my Soul through the Invisible,
Some letter of that After-life to spell:
And by and by my Soul return'd to me,
And answered "I Myself am Heav'n and Hell:"

LXVII

Heav'n but the Vision of fulfill'd Desire,
And Hell the Shadow from a Soul on fire,
Cast on the Darkness into which Ourselves,
So late emerged from, shall so soon expire.

LXVIII

We are no other than a moving row
Of Magic Shadow-shapes that come and go
Round with the Sun-illumined Lantern held
In Midnight by the Master of the Show;

LXIX

But helpless Pieces of the Game He plays
Upon his Chequer-board of Nights and Days;
Hither and thither moves, and checks, and slays,
And one by one back in the Closet lays.

LXX

The Ball no question makes of Ayes and Noes,
But Here or There as strikes the Player goes;
And He that toss'd you down into the Field,
He knows about it all—HE knows—HE knows!

LXXI

The Moving Finger writes; and, having writ,
Moves on: nor all your Piety nor Wit
  Shall lure it back to cancel half a Line,
Nor all your Tears wash out a Word of it.

LXXII

And that inverted Bowl they call the Sky,
Whereunder crawling coop'd we live and die,
  Lift not your hands to *It* for help—for It
As impotently moves as you or I.

LXXIII

With Earth's first Clay They did the Last Man knead,
And there of the Last Harvest sow'd the Seed:
  And the first Morning of Creation wrote
What the Last Dawn of Reckoning shall read.

LXXIV

YESTERDAY *This* Day's Madness did prepare;
TO-MORROW'S Silence, Triumph, or Despair:
  Drink! for you know not whence you came, nor why:
Drink! for you know not why you go, nor where.

LXXV

I tell you this—When, started from the Goal,
Over the flaming shoulders of the Foal
  Of Heav'n Parwin and Mushtari they flung,
In my predestined Plot of Dust and Soul

LXXVI

The Vine had struck a fiber: which about
If clings my Being—let the Dervish flout;
  Of my Base metal may be filed a Key,
That shall unlock the Door he howls without.

LXXVII

And this I know: whether the one True Light
Kindle to Love, or Wrath consume me quite,
One Flash of It within the Tavern caught
Better than in the Temple lost outright.

LXXVIII

What! out of senseless Nothing to provoke
A conscious Something to resent the yoke
Of unpermitted Pleasure, under pain
Of Everlasting Penalties, if broke!

LXXIX

What! from his helpless Creature be repaid
Pure Gold for what he lent him dross-allay'd--
Sue for a Debt he never did contract,
And cannot answer—Oh the sorry trade!

LXXX

Oh Thou, who didst with pitfall and with gin
Beset the Road I was to wander in,
Thou wilt not with Predestined Evil round
Enmesh, and then impute my Fall to Sin!

LXXXI

Oh Thou, who Man of baser Earth didst make,
And ev'n with Paradise devise the Snake:
For all the Sin wherewith the Face of Man
Is blacken'd—Man's forgiveness give—and take!

LXXXII

As under cover of departing Day
Slunk hunger-stricken Ramazan away,
Once more within the Potter's house alone
I stood, surrounded by the Shapes of Clay.

LXXXIII

Shapes of all Sorts and Sizes, great and small,
That stood along the floor and by the wall;
And some loquacious Vessels were; and some
Listen'd perhaps, but never talk'd at all.

LXXXIV

Said one among them—"Surely not in vain
"My substance of the common Earth was ta'en
"And to this Figure moulded, to be broke,
"Or tramped back to Shapeless Earth again."

LXXXV

Then said a Second—"Ne'er a peevish Boy
"Would break the Bowl from which he drank in joy;
"And He that with his hand the Vessel made
"Will surely not in after Wrath destroy."

LXXXVI

After a momentary silence spake
Some Vessel of a more ungainly Make;
"They sneer at me for leaning all awry:
"What! did the Hand then of the Potter shake?"

LXXXVII

Whereat some one of the loquacious Lot—
I think a Sufi pipkin—waxing hot—
"All this of Pot and Potter—Tell me then,
"Who is the Potter, pray, and who the Pot?"

LXXXVIII

"Why," said another, "Some there are who tell
"Of one who threatens he will toss to Hell
"The luckless Pots he marr'd in baking—Pish!
"He's a Good Fellow, and 'twill all be well."

LXXXIX

"Well," murmur'd one, "Let whoso make or buy,
"My Clay with long Oblivion is gone dry:
"But fill me with the old familiar Juice,
"Methinks I might recover by and by."

XC

So while the Vessels one by one were speaking,
The little Moon look'd in that all were seeking:
And then they jogg'd each other, "Brother! Brother!
"Now for the Porter's shoulder-knot a-creaking!"

XCI

Ah, with the Grape my fading Life provide,
And wash the Body whence the Life has died,
And lay me, shrouded in the living Leaf,
By some not unfrequented Garden-side.

XCII

That ev'n my buried Ashes such as snare
Of Vintage shall fling up into the Air
As not a True-believer passing by
But shall be overtaken unaware.

XCIII

Indeed the Idols I have loved so long
Have done my credit in this World much wrong:
Have drown'd my Glory in a shallow Cup,
And sold my Reputation for a Song.

XCIV

Indeed, indeed, Repentance oft before
I swore—but was I sober when I swore?
And then and then came Spring, and Rose-in-hand
My thread-bare Penitence apieces tore.

XCV

And much as Wine has play'd the Infidel,
And robb'd me of my Robe of Honor—Well,
I wonder often what the Vintners buy
One half so precious as the stuff they sell.

XCVI

Yet Ah, that Spring should vanish with the Rose!
That Youth's sweet-scented manuscript should close!
The Nightingale that in the branches sang,
Ah whence, and whither flown again, who knows?

XCVII

Would but the Desert of the Fountain yield
One glimpse—if dimly, yet indeed, reveal'd,
To which the fainting Traveler might spring,
As springs the trampled herbage of the field!

XCVIII

Would but some winged Angel ere too late
Arrest the yet unfolded Roll of Fate,
And make the stern Recorder otherwise
Enregister, or quite obliterate!

XCIX

Ah Love! could you and I with Him conspire
To grasp this sorry Scheme of Things entire,
Would not we shatter it to bits—and then
Re-mould it nearer to the Heart's Desire!

C

Yon rising Moon that looks for us again—
How oft hereafter will she wax and wane;
How oft hereafter rising look for us
Through this same Garden—and for *one* in vain!

CI

And when like her, oh Saki, you shall pass
Among the Guests Star-scatter'd on the Grass,
   And in your joyous errand reach the spot
Where I made One—turn down an empty Glass!

ALFRED, LORD TENNYSON

(1809–1892)

Mariana

"Mariana in the moated grange."
MEASURE FOR MEASURE.

WITH blackest moss the flower-plots
   Were thickly crusted, one and all:
The rusted nails fell from the knots
   That held the pear to the gable-wall.
The broken sheds look'd sad and strange:
   Unlifted was the clinking latch;
   Weeded and worn the ancient thatch
Upon the lonely moated grange.
      She only said, "My life is dreary,
         He cometh not," she said;
      She said, "I am aweary, aweary,
         I would that I were dead!"

Her tears fell with the dews at even;
   Her tears fell ere the dews were dried;
She could not look on the sweet heaven,
   Either at morn or eventide.
After the flitting of the bats,
   When thickest dark did trance the sky,
   She drew her casement-curtain by,
And glanced athwart the glooming flats.

She only said, "The night is dreary,
He cometh not," she said;
She said, "I am aweary, aweary,
I would that I were dead!"

Upon the middle of the night,
Waking she heard the night-fowl crow:
The cock sung out an hour ere light:
From the dark fen the oxen's low
Came to her: without hope of change,
In sleep she seem'd to walk forlorn,
Till cold winds woke the gray-eyed morn
About the lonely moated grange.
She only said, "The day is dreary,
He cometh not," she said;
She said, "I am aweary, aweary,
I would that I were dead!"

About a stone-cast from the wall
A sluice with blacken'd waters slept,
And o'er it many, round and small,
The cluster'd marish-mosses crept.
Hard by a poplar shook alway,
All silver-green with gnarled bark:
For leagues no other tree did mark
The level waste, the rounding gray.
She only said, "My life is dreary,
He cometh not," she said,
She said, "I am aweary, aweary,
I would that I were dead!"

And ever when the moon was low,
And the shrill winds were up and away,
In the white curtain, to and fro,
She saw the gusty shadow sway.
But when the moon was very low,
And wild winds bound within their cell,
The shadow of the poplar fell
Upon her bed, across her brow.

She only said, "The night is dreary,
He cometh not," she said;
She said, "I am aweary, aweary,
I would that I were dead!"

All day within the dreamy house,
The doors upon their hinges creak'd;
The blue fly sung in the pane; the mouse
Behind the mouldering wainscot shriek'd,
Or from the crevice peer'd about.
Old faces glimmer'd thro' the doors,
Old footsteps trod the upper floors,
Old voices called her from without.
She only said, "My life is dreary,
He cometh not," she said;
She said, "I am aweary, aweary,
I would that I were dead!"

The sparrow's chirrup on the roof,
The slow clock ticking, and the sound
Which to the wooing wind aloof
The poplar made, did all confound
Her sense; but most she loathed the hour
When the thick-moted sunbeam lay
Athwart the chambers, and the day
Was sloping toward his western bower.
Then, said she, "I am very dreary,
He will not come," she said;
She wept, "I am aweary, aweary,
Oh God, that I were dead!"

The Lady of Shalott

PART I

ON EITHER side the river lie
Long fields of barley and of rye,

That clothe the wold and meet the sky;
And through the field the road runs by
        To many-towered Camelot;
And up and down the people go,
Gazing where the lilies blow
Round an island there below,
        The island of Shalott.

Willows whiten, aspens quiver,
Little breezes dusk and shiver
Through the wave that runs for ever
By the island in the river
        Flowing down to Camelot.
Four gray walls, and four gray towers,
Overlook a space of flowers,
And the silent isle imbowers
        The Lady of Shalott.

By the margin, willow-veiled,
Slide the heavy barges trailed
By slow horses; and unhailed
The shallop flitteth silken-sailed
        Skimming down to Camelot:
But who hath seen her wave her hand?
Or at the casement seen her stand?
Or is she known in all the land,
        The Lady of Shalott?

Only reapers, reaping early
In among the bearded barley,
Hear a song that echoes cheerly
From the river winding clearly,
        Down to towered Camelot;
And by the moon the reaper weary,
Piling sheaves in uplands airy,
Listening, whispers " 'Tis the fairy
        Lady of Shalott."

PART II

There she weaves by night and day
A magic web with colors gay.

She has heard a whisper say,
A curse is on her if she stay
        To look down to Camelot.
She knows not what the curse may be,
And so she weaveth steadily,
And little other care hath she,
        The Lady of Shalott.

And moving through a mirror clear
That hangs before her all the year,
Shadows of the world appear.
There she sees the highway near
        Winding down to Camelot;
There the river eddy whirls,
And there the surly village-churls,
And the red cloaks of market girls,
        Pass onward from Shalott.

Sometimes a troop of damsels glad,
An abbot on an ambling pad,
Sometimes a curly shepherd-lad,
Or long-haired page in crimson clad,
        Goes by to towered Camelot;
And sometimes through the mirror blue
The knights come riding two and two:
She hath no loyal knight and true,
        The Lady of Shalott.

But in her web she still delights
To weave the mirror's magic sights,
For often through the silent nights
A funeral, with plumes and lights
        And music, went to Camelot;
Or when the moon was overhead,
Came two young lovers lately wed:
"I am half sick of shadows," said
        The Lady of Shalott.

PART III

A bow-shot from her bower-eaves,
He rode between the barley-sheaves,

The sun came dazzling through the leaves
And flamed upon the brazen greaves
Of bold Sir Lancelot.
A red-cross knight for ever kneeled
To a lady in his shield,
That sparkled on the yellow field,
Beside remote Shalott.

The gemmy bridle glittered free,
Like to some branch of stars we see
Hung in the golden Galaxy.
The bridle bells rang merrily
As he rode down to Camelot;
And from his blazoned baldric slung
A mighty silver bugle hung,
And as he rode his armor rung,
Beside remote Shalott.

All in the blue unclouded weather
Thick-jeweled shone the saddle-leather,
The helmet and the helmet-feather
Burned like one burning flame together,
As he rode down to Camelot;
As often through the purple night,
Below the starry clusters bright,
Some bearded meteor, trailing light,
Moves over still Shalott.

His broad clear brow in sunlight glowed;
On burnished hooves his war-horse trode;
From underneath his helmet flowed
His coal-black curls as on he rode,
As he rode down to Camelot.
From the bank and from the river
He flashed into the crystal mirror,
"Tirra lirra," by the river
Sang Sir Lancelot.

She left the web, she left the loom,
She made three paces through the room,

She saw the water-lily bloom,
She saw the helmet and the plume,
She looked down to Camelot.
Out flew the web and floated wide;
The mirror cracked from side to side;
"The curse is come upon me," cried
The Lady of Shalott.

PART IV

In the stormy east-wind straining,
The pale yellow woods were waning,
The broad stream in his banks complaining,
Heavily the low sky raining
Over towered Camelot;
Down she came and found a boat
Beneath a willow left afloat,
And round about the prow she wrote
The Lady of Shalott.

And down the river's dim expanse
Like some bold seër in a trance,
Seeing all his own mischance—
With a glassy countenance
Did she look to Camelot.
And at the closing of the day
She loosed the chain, and down she lay;
The broad stream bore her far away,
The Lady of Shalott.

Lying, robed in snowy white
That loosely flew to left and right—
The leaves upon her falling light—
Through the noises of the night
She floated down to Camelot;
And as the boat-head wound along
The willowy hills and fields among,
They heard her singing her last song,
The Lady of Shalott.

Heard a carol, mournful, holy,
Chanted loudly, chanted lowly,
Till her blood was frozen slowly,
And her eyes were darkened wholly,
Turned to towered Camelot.
For ere she reached upon the tide
The first house by the water-side,
Singing in her song she died,
The Lady of Shalott.

Under tower and balcony,
By garden-wall and gallery,
A gleaming shape she floated by,
Dead-pale between the houses high,
Silent into Camelot.
Out upon the wharfs they came,
Knight and burgher, lord and dame,
And round the prow they read her name,
The Lady of Shalott.

Who is this? and what is here?
And in the lighted palace near
Died the sound of royal cheer;
And they crossed themselves for fear,
All the knights at Camelot:
But Lancelot mused a little space;
He said, "She has a lovely face;
God in his mercy lend her grace,
The Lady of Shalott."

The Lotos-Eaters

"COURAGE!" he said, and pointed toward the land,
"This mounting wave will roll us shoreward soon."
In the afternoon they came unto a land
In which it seemèd always afternoon.

All round the coast the languid air did swoon,
Breathing like one that hath a weary dream.
Full-faced above the valley stood the moon;
And, like a downward smoke, the slender stream
Along the cliff to fall and pause and fall did seem.

A land of streams! some, like a downward smoke,
Slow-dropping veils of thinnest lawn, did go;
And some through wavering lights and shadows broke,
Rolling a slumbrous sheet of foam below.
They saw the gleaming river seaward flow
From the inner land; far off, three mountain-tops,
Three silent pinnacles of agéd snow,
Stood sunset-flushed; and, dewed with showery drops,
Up-clomb the shadowy pine above the woven copse.

The charméd sunset lingered low adown
In the red West; through mountain clefts the dale
Was seen far inland, and the yellow down
Bordered with palm, and many a winding vale
And meadow, set with slender galingale;
A land where all things always seemed the same!
And round about the keel with faces pale,
Dark faces pale against that rosy flame,
The mild-eyed melancholy Lotos-eaters came.

Branches they bore of that enchanted stem,
Laden with flower and fruit, whereof they gave
To each, but whoso did receive of them
And taste, to him the gushing of the wave
Far far away did seem to mourn and rave
On alien shores; and if his fellow spake,
His voice was thin, as voices from the grave;
And deep-asleep he seemed, yet all awake,
And music in his ears his beating heart did make.

They sat them down upon the yellow sand,
Between the sun and moon upon the shore;
And sweet it was to dream of Fatherland,
Of child, and wife, and slave; but evermore

Most weary seemed the sea, weary the oar,
Weary the wandering fields of barren foam.
Then some one said, "We will return no more";
And all at once they sang, "Our island home
Is far beyond the wave; we will no longer roam."

Choric Song

I

There is sweet music here that softer falls
Than petals from blown roses on the grass,
Or night-dews on still waters between walls
Of shadowy granite, in a gleaming pass;
Music that gentlier on the spirit lies,
Than tired eyelids upon tired eyes;
Music that brings sweet sleep down from the blissful skies.
Here are cool mosses deep,
And through the moss the ivies creep,
And in the stream the long-leaved flowers weep,
And from the craggy ledge the poppy hangs in sleep.

II

Why are we weighed upon with heaviness,
And utterly consumed with sharp distress,
While all things else have rest from weariness?
All things have rest: why should we toil alone,
We only toil, who are the first of things,
And make perpetual moan,
Still from one sorrow to another thrown;
Nor ever fold our wings,
And cease from wanderings,
Nor steep our brows in slumber's holy balm;
Nor harken what the inner spirit sings,
"There is no joy but calm!"—
Why should we only toil, the roof and crown of things?

III

Lo! in the middle of the wood,
The folded leaf is wooed from out the bud
With winds upon the branch, and there
Grows green and broad, and takes no care,
Sun-steeped at noon, and in the moon
Nightly dew-fed; and turning yellow
Falls, and floats adown the air.
Lo! sweetened with the summer light,
The full-juiced apple, waxing over-mellow,
Drops in a silent autumn night.
All its allotted length of days
The flower ripens in its place,
Ripens and fades, and falls, and hath no toil,
Fast-rooted in the fruitful soil.

IV

Hateful is the dark-blue sky,
Vaulted o'er the dark-blue sea.
Death is the end of life; ah, why
Should life all labor be?
Let us alone. Time driveth onward fast,
And in a little while our lips are dumb.
Let us alone. What is it that will last?
All things are taken from us, and become
Portions and parcels of the dreadful past.
Let us alone. What pleasure can we have
To war with evil? Is there any peace
In ever climbing up the climbing wave?
All things have rest, and ripen toward the grave
In silence—ripen, fall, and cease:
Give us long rest or death, dark death, or dreamful ease.

V

How sweet it were, hearing the downward stream,
With half-shut eyes ever to seem
Falling asleep in a half-dream!
To dream and dream, like yonder amber light,
Which will not leave the myrrh-bush on the height;

To hear each other's whispered speech;
Eating the Lotos day by day,
To watch the crisping ripples on the beach,
And tender curving lines of creamy spray;
To lend our hearts and spirits wholly
To the influence of mild-minded melancholy;
To muse and brood and live again in memory,
With those old faces of our infancy
Heaped over with a mound of grass,
Two handfuls of white dust, shut in an urn of brass!

VI

Dear is the memory of our wedded lives,
And dear the last embraces of our wives
And their warm tears; but all hath suffered change;
For surely now our household hearths are cold,
Our sons inherit us, our looks are strange,
And we should come like ghosts to trouble joy.
Or else the island princes over-bold
Have eat our substance, and the minstrel sings
Before them of the ten years' war in Troy,
And our great deeds, as half-forgotten things.
Is there confusion in the little isle?
Let what is broken so remain.
The Gods are hard to reconcile;
'Tis hard to settle order once again.
There *is* confusion worse than death,
Trouble on trouble, pain on pain,
Long labor unto agéd breath,
Sore task to hearts worn out by many wars
And eyes grown dim with gazing on the pilot-stars.

VII

But, propped on beds of amaranth and moly,
How sweet—while warm airs lull us, blowing lowly—
With half-dropped eyelid still,
Beneath a heaven dark and holy,
To watch the long bright river drawing slowly
His waters from the purple hill—

To hear the dewy echoes calling
From cave to cave through the thick-twined vine—
To watch the emerald-colored water falling
Through many a woven acanthus-wreath divine!
Only to hear and see the far-off sparkling brine,
Only to hear were sweet, stretched out beneath the pine.

VIII

The Lotos blooms below the barren peak,
The Lotos blows by every winding creek;
All day the wind breathes low with mellower tone;
Through every hollow cave and alley lone
Round and round the spicy downs the yellow Lotos-dust is blown.
We have had enough of action, and of motion we,
Rolled to starboard, rolled to larboard, when the surge was seething free,
Where the wallowing monster spouted his foam-fountains in the sea.
Let us swear an oath, and keep it with an equal mind,
In the hollow Lotos-land to live and lie reclined
On the hills like Gods together, careless of mankind.
For they lie beside their nectar, and the bolts are hurled
Far below them in the valleys, and the clouds are lightly curled
Round their golden houses, girdled with the gleaming world;
Where they smile in secret, looking over wasted lands,
Blight and famine, plague and earthquake, roaring deeps and fiery sands,
Clanging fights, and flaming towns, and sinking ships, and praying hands.
But they smile, they find a music centered in a doleful song
Steaming up, a lamentation and an ancient tale of wrong,
Like a tale of little meaning though the words are strong;
Chanted from an ill-used race of men that cleave the soil,
Sow the seed, and reap the harvest with enduring toil,
Storing yearly little dues of wheat, and wine and oil;
Till they perish and they suffer—some, 'tis whispered—down in hell
Suffer endless anguish, others in Elysian valleys dwell,
Resting weary limbs at last on beds of asphodel.
Surely, surely, slumber is more sweet than toil, the shore
Than labor in the deep mid-ocean, wind and wave and oar;
O, rest ye, brother mariners, we will not wander more.

Ulysses

IT LITTLE profits that an idle king,
By this still hearth, among these barren crags,
Matched with an aged wife, I mete and dole
Unequal laws unto a savage race,
That hoard, and sleep, and feed, and know not me.
I cannot rest from travel: I will drink
Life to the lees: all times I have enjoyed
Greatly, have suffer'd greatly, both with those
That loved me, and alone; on shore, and when
Through scudding drifts the rainy Hyades
Vext the dim sea: I am become a name;
For always roaming with a hungry heart
Much have I seen and known, cities of men
And manners, climates, councils, governments,
Myself not least, but honor'd of them all;
And drunk delight of battle with my peers,
Far on the ringing plains of windy Troy.
I am a part of all that I have met;
Yet all experience is an arch wherethrough
Gleams that untravelled world, whose margin fades
Forever and forever when I move.
How dull it is to pause, to make an end,
To rust unburnished, not to shine in use!
As though to breathe were life. Life piled on life
Were all too little, and of one to me
Little remains: but every hour is saved
From that eternal silence, something more,
A bringer of new things; and vile it were
For some three suns to store and hoard myself,
And this gray spirit yearning in desire
To follow knowledge, like a sinking star,
Beyond the utmost bound of human thought.
  This is my son, mine own Telemachus,
To whom I leave the scepter and the isle—
Well-loved of me, discerning to fulfil
This labor, by slow prudence to make mild
A rugged people, and through soft degrees
Subdue them to the useful and the good.

Most blameless is he, centred in the sphere
Of common duties, decent not to fail
In offices of tenderness, and pay
Meet adoration to my household gods,
When I am gone. He works his work, I mine.
There lies the port: the vessel puffs her sail:
There gloom the dark broad seas. My mariners,
Souls that have toiled and wrought, and thought with me—
That ever with a frolic welcome took
The thunder and the sunshine, and opposed
Free hearts, free foreheads—you and I are old;
Old age hath yet his honor and his toil;
Death closes all: but something ere the end,
Some work of noble note, may yet be done,
Not unbecoming men that strove with Gods.
The lights begin to twinkle from the rocks:
The long day wanes: the slow moon climbs: the deep
Moans round with many voices. Come, my friends,
'Tis not too late to seek a newer world.
Push off, and sitting well in order smite
The sounding furrows; for my purpose holds
To sail beyond the sunset, and the baths
Of all the western stars, until I die.
It may be that the gulfs will wash us down:
It may be we shall touch the Happy Isles,
And see that great Achilles, whom we knew.
Though much is taken, much abides; and though
We are not now that strength which in old days
Moved earth and heaven; that which we are, we are;
One equal temper of heroic hearts,
Made weak by time and fate, but strong in will
To strive, to seek, to find, and not to yield.

Locksley Hall

COMRADES, leave me here a little, while as yet 't is early morn,—
Leave me here, and when you want me, sound upon the bugle horn.

'T is the place, and all around it, as of old, the curlews call,
Dreary gleams about the moorland, flying over Locksley Hall:

Locksley Hall, that in the distance overlooks the sandy tracts,
And the hollow ocean-ridges roaring into cataracts.

Many a night from yonder ivied casement, ere I went to rest,
Did I look on great Orion sloping slowly to the west.

Many a night I saw the Pleiads, rising through the mellow shade,
Glitter like a swarm of fire-flies tangled in a silver braid.

Here about the beach I wandered, nourishing a youth sublime
With the fairy tales of science, and the long result of time;

When the centuries behind me like a fruitful land reposed;
When I clung to all the present for the promise that it closed;

When I dipt into the future far as human eye could see,—
Saw the vision of the world, and all the wonder that would be.

In the spring a fuller crimson comes upon the robin's breast;
In the spring the wanton lapwing gets himself another crest;

In the spring a livelier iris changes on the burnished dove;
In the spring a young man's fancy lightly turns to thoughts of love.

Then her cheek was pale and thinner than should be for one so young,
And her eyes on all my motions with a mute observance hung.

And I said, "My cousin Amy, speak, and speak the truth to me;
Trust me, cousin, all the current of my being sets to thee."

On her pallid cheek and forehead came a color and a light,
As I have seen the rosy red flushing in the northern night.

And she turned,—her bosom shaken with a sudden storm of sighs;
All the spirit deeply dawning in the dark of hazel eyes,—

Saying, "I have hid my feelings, fearing they should do me wrong;"
Saying, "Dost thou love me, cousin?" weeping, "I have loved thee long."

Love took up the glass of time, and turned it in his glowing hands;
Every moment, lightly shaken, ran itself in golden sands.

Love took up the harp of life, and smote on all the chords with might;
Smote the chord of self, that, trembling, passed in music out of sight.

Many a morning on the moorland did we hear the copses ring,
And her whisper thronged my pulses with the fulness of the spring.

Many an evening by the waters did we watch the stately ships,
And our spirits rushed together at the touching of the lips.

O my cousin, shallow-hearted! O my Amy, mine no more!
O the dreary, dreary moorland! O the barren, barren shore!

Falser than all fancy fathoms, falser than all songs have sung,—
Puppet to a father's threat, and servile to a shrewish tongue!

Is it well to wish thee happy?—having known me; to decline
On a range of lower feelings and a narrower heart than mine!

Yet it shall be: thou shalt lower to his level day by day,
What is fine within thee growing coarse to sympathize with clay.

As the husband is, the wife is; thou art mated with a clown,
And the grossness of his nature will have weight to drag thee down.

He will hold thee, when his passion shall have spent its novel force,
Something better than his dog, a little dearer than his horse.

What is this? his eyes are heavy,—think not they are glazed with wine.
Go to him; it is thy duty,—kiss him; take his hand in thine.

It may be my lord is weary, that his brain is overwrought,—
Soothe him with thy finer fancies, touch him with thy lighter thought.

He will answer to the purpose, easy things to understand,—
Better thou wert dead before me, though I slew thee with my hand.

Better thou and I were lying, hidden from the heart's disgrace,
Rolled in one another's arms, and silent in a last embrace.

Cursed be the social wants that sin against the strength of youth!
Cursed be the social lies that warp us from the living truth!

Cursed be the sickly forms that err from honest nature's rule!
Cursed be the gold that gilds the straitened forehead of the fool!

Well—'t is well that I should bluster!—Hadst thou less unworthy proved,
Would to God—for I had loved thee more than ever wife was loved.

Am I mad, that I should cherish that which bears but bitter fruit?
I will pluck it from my bosom, though my heart be at the root.

Never! though my mortal summers to such length of years should come
As the many-wintered crow that leads the clanging rookery home.

Where is comfort? in division of the records of the mind?
Can I part her from herself, and love her, as I knew her, kind?

I remembered one that perished; sweetly did she speak and move;
Such a one do I remember, whom to look at was to love.

Can I think of her as dead, and love her for the love she bore?
No,—she never loved me truly; love is love forevermore.

Comfort? comfort scorned of devils! this is truth the poet sings,
That a sorrow's crown of sorrow is remembering happier things.

Drug thy memories, lest thou learn it, lest thy heart be put to proof,
In the dead, unhappy night, and when the rain is on the roof.

Like a dog, he hunts in dreams; and thou art staring at the wall,
Where the dying night-lamp flickers, and the shadows rise and fall.

Then a hand shall pass before thee, pointing to his drunken sleep,
To thy widowed marriage-pillows, to the tears that thou wilt weep.

Thou shalt hear the "Never, never," whispered by the phantom years,
And a song from out the distance in the ringing of thine ears;

And an eye shall vex thee, looking ancient kindness on thy pain.
Turn thee, turn thee on thy pillow; get thee to thy rest again.

Nay, but nature brings thee solace; for a tender voice will cry;
'T is a purer life than thine, a lip to drain thy trouble dry.

Baby lips will laugh me down; my latest rival brings thee rest,—
Baby fingers, waxen touches, press me from the mother's breast.

O, the child too clothes the father with a dearness not his due.
Half is thine and half is his: it will be worthy of the two.

O, I see thee old and formal, fitted to thy petty part,
With a little hoard of maxims preaching down a daughter's heart.

"They were dangerous guides, the feelings—she herself was not exempt—
Truly, she herself had suffered"—Perish in thy self-contempt!

Overlive it—lower yet—be happy! wherefore should I care?
I myself must mix with action, lest I wither by despair.

What is that which I should turn to, lighting upon days like these?
Every door is barred with gold, and opens but to golden keys.

Every gate is thronged with suitors, all the markets overflow.
I have but an angry fancy: what is that which I should do?

I had been content to perish, falling on the foeman's ground,
When the ranks are rolled in vapor, and the winds are laid with sound.

But the jingling of the guinea helps the hurt that honor feels,
And the nations do but murmur, snarling at each other's heels.

Can I but relive in sadness? I will turn that earlier page.
Hide me from my deep emotion, O thou wondrous mother-age!

Make me feel the wild pulsation that I felt before the strife,
When I heard my days before me, and the tumult of my life;

Yearning for the large excitement that the coming years would yield,
Eager-hearted as a boy when first he leaves his father's field,

And at night along the dusky highway near and nearer drawn,
Sees in heaven the light of London flaring like a dreary dawn;

And his spirit leaps within him to be gone before him then,
Underneath the light he looks at, in among the throngs of men;

Men, my brothers, men the workers, ever reaping something new:
That which they have done but earnest of the things that they shall do:

For I dipt into the future, far as human eye could see,
Saw the vision of the world, and all the wonder that would be;

Saw the heavens fill with commerce, argosies of magic sails,
Pilots of the purple twilight, dropping down with costly bales;

Heard the heavens fill with shouting, and there rained a ghastly dew
From the nations' airy navies grappling in the central blue;

Far along the world-wide whisper of the southwind rushing warm,
With the standards of the peoples plunging through the thunder-storm;

Till the war-drum throbbed no longer, and the battle-flags were furled
In the parliament of man, the federation of the world.

There the common sense of most shall hold a fretful realm in awe,
And the kindly earth shall slumber, lapt in universal law.

So I triumphed ere my passion sweeping through me left me dry,
Left me with a palsied heart, and left me with the jaundiced eye;

Eye, to which all order festers, all things here are out of joint.
Science moves, but slowly, slowly, creeping on from point to point:

Slowly comes a hungry people, as a lion, creeping nigher,
Glares at one that nods and winks behind a slowly dying fire.

Yet I doubt not through the ages one increasing purpose runs,
And the thoughts of men are widened with the process of the suns.

What is that to him that reaps not harvest of his youthful joys,
Though the deep heart of existence beat forever like a boy's?

Knowledge comes, but wisdom lingers; and I linger on the shore,
And the individual withers, and the world is more and more.

Knowledge comes, but wisdom lingers, and he bears a laden breast,
Full of sad experience moving toward the stillness of his rest.

Hark! my merry comrades call me, sounding on the bugle horn,—
They to whom my foolish passion were a target for their scorn;

Shall it not be scorn to me to harp on such a mouldered string?
I am shamed through all my nature to have loved so slight a thing.

Weakness to be wroth with weakness! woman's pleasure, woman's pain—
Nature made them blinder motions bounded in a shallower brain;

Woman is the lesser man, and all thy passions, matched with mine,
Are as moonlight unto sunlight, and as water unto wine—

Here at least, where nature sickens, nothing. Ah for some retreat
Deep in yonder shining Orient, where my life began to beat!

Where in wild Mahratta-battle fell my father, evil-starred;
I was left a trampled orphan, and a selfish uncle's ward.

Or to burst all links of habit,—there to wander far away,
On from island unto island at the gateways of the day,—

Larger constellations burning, mellow moons and happy skies,
Breadths of tropic shade and palms in cluster, knots of Paradise.

Never comes the trader, never floats an European flag,—
Slides the bird o'er lustrous woodland, swings the trailer from the crag,—

Droops the heavy-blossomed bower, hangs the heavy-fruited tree,—
Summer isles of Eden lying in dark-purple spheres of sea.

There, methinks, would be enjoyment more than in this march of mind—
In the steamship, in the railway, in the thoughts that shake mankind.

There the passions, cramped no longer, shall have scope and breathing-space;
I will take some savage woman, she shall rear my dusky race.

Iron-jointed, supple-sinewed, they shall dive, and they shall run,
Catch the wild goat by the hair, and hurl their lances in the sun,

Whistle back the parrot's call, and leap the rainbows of the brooks,
Not with blinded eyesight poring over miserable books—

Fool, again the dream, the fancy! but I know my words are wild,
But I count the gray barbarian lower than the Christian child.

I, to herd with narrow foreheads, vacant of our glorious gains,
Like a beast with lower pleasures, like a beast with lower pains!

Mated with a squalid savage,—what to me were sun or clime?
I, the heir of all the ages, in the foremost files of time,—

I, that rather held it better men should perish one by one,
Than that earth should stand at gaze like Joshua's moon in Ajalon!

Not in vain the distance beacons. Forward, forward let us range;
Let the great world spin forever down the ringing grooves of change.

Through the shadow of the globe we sweep into the younger day:
Better fifty years of Europe than a cycle of Cathay.

Mother-age, (for mine I knew not,) help me as when life begun,—
Rift the hills, and roll the waters, flash the lightnings, weigh the sun,—

O, I see the crescent promise of my spirit hath not set;
Ancient founts of inspiration well through all my fancy yet.

Howsoever these things be, a long farewell to Locksley Hall!
Now for me the woods may wither, now for me the roof-tree fall.

Comes a vapor from the margin, blackening over heath and holt,
Cramming all the blast before it, in its breast a thunderbolt.

Let it fall on Locksley Hall, with rain or hail, or fire or snow;
For the mighty wind arises, roaring seaward, and I go.

Break, Break, Break

BREAK, break, break,
  On thy cold gray stones, O sea!
And I would that my tongue could utter
  The thoughts that arise in me.

O well for the fisherman's boy
  That he shouts with his sister at play!
O well for the sailor lad
  That he sings in his boat on the bay!

And the stately ships go on,
  To the haven under the hill;
But O for the touch of a vanished hand,
  And the sound of a voice that is still!

Break, break, break,
  At the foot of thy crags, O sea!
But the tender grace of a day that is dead
  Will never come back to me.

The Splendor Falls on Castle Walls

THE splendor falls on castle walls
  And snowy summits old in story:
The long light shakes across the lakes,
  And the wild cataract leaps in glory.
Blow, bugle, blow, set the wild echoes flying,
Blow, bugle; answer, echoes, dying, dying, dying.

O hark, O hear! how thin and clear,
  And thinner, clearer, farther going!
O sweet and far from cliff and scar
  The horns of Elfland faintly blowing!

Blow, let us hear the purple glens replying:
Blow, bugle; answer, echoes, dying, dying, dying.

O love, they die in yon rich sky,
They faint on hill or field or river:
Our echoes roll from soul to soul,
And grow for ever and for ever.
Blow, bugle, blow, set the wild echoes flying,
And answer, echoes, answer, dying, dying, dying.

Tears, Idle Tears

Tears, idle tears, I know not what they mean,
Tears from the depth of some divine despair
Rise in the heart, and gather to the eyes,
In looking on the happy autumn fields,
And thinking of the days that are no more.

Fresh as the first beam glittering on a sail,
That brings our friends up from the under world;
Sad as the last which reddens over one
That sinks with all we love below the verge,—
So sad, so fresh, the days that are no more.

Ah, sad and strange as in dark summer dawns
The earliest pipe of half-awakened birds
To dying ears, when unto dying eyes
The casement slowly grows a glimmering square;
So sad, so strange, the days that are no more.

Dear as remembered kisses after death,
And sweet as those by hopeless fancy feigned
On lips that are for others; deep as love,
Deep as first love, and wild with all regret,—
O Death in Life, the days that are no more.

Strong Son of God, Immortal Love

STRONG Son of God, immortal Love,
  Whom we, that have not seen thy face,
  By faith, and faith alone, embrace,
Believing where we cannot prove;

Thine are these orbs of light and shade;
  Thou madest Life in man and brute;
  Thou madest Death; and lo, thy foot
Is on the skull which thou hast made.

Thou wilt not leave us in the dust:
  Thou madest man, he knows not why;
  He thinks he was not made to die;
And thou hast made him: thou art just.

Thou seemest human and divine,
  The highest, holiest manhood, thou:
  Our wills are ours, we know not how;
Our wills are ours, to make them thine.

Our little systems have their day;
  They have their day and cease to be:
  They are but broken lights of thee,
And thou, O Lord, art more than they.

We have but faith: we cannot know;
  For knowledge is of things we see;
  And yet we trust it comes from thee,
A beam in darkness: let it grow.

Let knowledge grow from more to more,
  But more of reverence in us dwell;
  That mind and soul, according well,
May make one music as before,

But vaster. We are fools and slight;
  We mock thee when we do not fear:
  But help thy foolish ones to bear;
Help thy vain worlds to bear thy light.

Forgive what seemed my sin in me;
  What seemed my worth since I began;
  For merit lives from man to man,
And not from man, O Lord, to thee.

Forgive my grief for one removed,
  Thy creature, whom I found so fair.
  I trust he lives in thee, and there
I find him worthier to be loved.

Forgive these wild and wandering cries,
  Confusions of a wasted youth;
  Forgive them where they fail in truth,
And in thy wisdom make me wise.

Ring Out, Wild Bells

RING out, wild bells, to the wild sky,
    The flying cloud, the frosty light;
    The year is dying in the night;
Ring out, wild bells, and let him die.

Ring out the old, ring in the new,
    Ring, happy bells, across the snow;
    The year is going, let him go;
Ring out the false, ring in the true.

Ring out the grief that saps the mind,
    For those that here we see no more;
    Ring out the feud of rich and poor,
Ring in redress to all mankind.

Ring out a slowly dying cause,
    And ancient forms of party strife;
    Ring in the nobler modes of life,
With sweeter manners, purer laws.

Ring out the want, the care, the sin,
    The faithless coldness of the times;
    Ring out, ring out my mournful rhymes,
But ring the fuller minstrel in.

Ring out false pride in place and blood,
    The civic slander and the spite;
    Ring in the love of truth and right,
Ring in the common love of good.

Ring out old shapes of foul disease;
    Ring out the narrowing lust of gold;
    Ring out the thousand wars of old,
Ring in the thousand years of peace.

Ring in the valiant man and free,
    The larger heart, the kindlier hand;
    Ring out the darkness of the land,
Ring in the Christ that is to be.

Crossing the Bar

SUNSET and evening star,
  And one clear call for me!
And may there be no moaning of the bar,
  When I put out to sea,

But such a tide as moving seems asleep,
  Too full for sound and foam,
When that which drew from out the boundless deep
  Turns again home.

Twilight and evening bell,
 And after that the dark!
And may there be no sadness of farewell,
 When I embark;

For tho' from out our bourne of Time and Place
 The flood may bear me far,
I hope to see my Pilot face to face
 When I have crost the bar.

EDGAR ALLAN POE

(1809–1849)

To Science

SCIENCE! true daughter of Old Time thou art!
 Who alterest all things with thy peering eyes.
Why preyest thou thus upon the poet's heart,
 Vulture, whose wings are dull realities?
How should he love thee? or how deem thee wise,
 Who wouldst not leave him in his wandering
To seek for treasure in the jewelled skies,
 Albeit he soared with an undaunted wing?
Hast thou not dragged Diana from her car,
 And driven the Hamadryad from the wood
To seek some shelter in a happier star?
 Hast thou not torn the Naiad from her flood,
The Elfin from the green grass, and from me
The summer dream beneath the tamarind tree?

To Helen

HELEN, thy beauty is to me
 Like those Nicæan barks of yore
That gently, o'er a perfumed sea,
 The weary, wayworn wanderer bore
 To his own native shore.

On desperate seas long wont to roam,
  Thy hyacinth hair, thy classic face,
Thy Naiad airs, have brought me home
  To the glory that was Greece
And the grandeur that was Rome.

Lo! in yon brilliant window-niche
  How statue-like I see thee stand,
  The agate lamp within thy hand!
Ah, Psyche, from the regions which
  Are Holy Land!

Israfel

And the angel Israfel, whose heart-strings are a lute, and who has the sweetest voice of all God's creatures.—KORAN.

IN HEAVEN a spirit doth dwell
  Whose heart-strings are a lute;
None sing so wildly well
As the angel Israfel,
And the giddy stars (so legends tell),
Ceasing their hymns, attend the spell
  Of his voice, all mute.

Tottering above
  In her highest noon,
  The enamored moon
Blushes with love,
  While, to listen, the red levin
  (With the rapid Pleiads, even,
  Which were seven)
  Pauses in Heaven.

And they say (the starry choir
  And the other listening things)
That Israfeli's fire
Is owing to that lyre
  By which he sits and sings,
The trembling living wire
  Of those unusual strings.

But the skies that angel trod,
  Where deep thoughts are a duty,
Where Love's a grown-up God,
Where the Houri glances are
  Imbued with all the beauty
Which we worship in a star.

Therefore thou art not wrong,
  Israfeli, who despisest
An unimpassioned song;
To thee the laurels belong,
  Best bard, because the wisest:
Merrily live, and long!

The ecstasies above
  With thy burning measures suit:
Thy grief, thy joy, thy hate, thy love,
  With the fervor of thy lute:
  Well may the stars be mute!

Yes, Heaven is thine; but this
  Is a world of sweets and sours;
  Our flowers are merely—flowers,
And the shadow of thy perfect bliss
  Is the sunshine of ours.

If I could dwell
Where Israfel
  Hath dwelt, and he where I,
He might not sing so wildly well
  A mortal melody,
While a bolder note than this might swell
  From my lyre within the sky.

To One in Paradise

THOU wast all that to me, love,
For which my soul did pine:
A green isle in the sea, love,
A fountain and a shrine
All wreathed with fairy fruits and flowers,
And all the flowers were mine.

Ah, dream too bright to last!
Ah, starry Hope, that didst arise
But to be overcast!
A voice from out the Future cries,
"On! on!"—but o'er the Past
(Dim gulf!) my spirit hovering lies
Mute, motionless, aghast.

For, alas! alas! with me
The light of Life is o'er!
No more—no more—no more—
(Such language holds the solemn sea
To the sands upon the shore)
Shall bloom the thunder-blasted tree,
Or the stricken eagle soar.

And all my days are trances,
And all my nightly dreams
Are where thy gray eye glances,
And where thy footstep gleams—
In what ethereal dances,
By what eternal streams.

The Raven

ONCE upon a midnight dreary, while I pondered, weak and weary,
Over many a quaint and curious volume of forgotten lore,
While I nodded, nearly napping, suddenly there came a tapping,
As of some one gently rapping, rapping at my chamber door.
" 'Tis some visitor," I muttered, "tapping at my chamber door—
Only this and nothing more."

Ah, distinctly I remember it was in the bleak December,
And each separate dying ember wrought its ghost upon the floor.
Eagerly I wished the morrow; vainly I had sought to borrow
From my books surcease of sorrow—sorrow for the lost Lenore,
For the rare and radiant maiden whom the angels name Lenore—
Nameless *here* for evermore.

And the silken, sad, uncertain rustling of each purple curtain
Thrilled me—filled me with fantastic terrors never felt before;
So that now, to still the beating of my heart, I stood repeating,
" 'Tis some visitor entreating entrance at my chamber door—
Some late visitor entreating entrance at my chamber door—
This it is and nothing more."

Presently my soul grew stronger: hesitating then no longer,
"Sir," said I, "or Madam, truly your forgiveness I implore;
But the fact is I was napping, and so gently you came rapping,
And so faintly you came tapping, tapping at my chamber door,
That I scarce was sure I heard you"—here I opened wide the door—
Darkness there and nothing more.

Deep into that darkness peering, long I stood there, wondering, fearing,
Doubting, dreaming dreams no mortal ever dared to dream before;
But the silence was unbroken, and the stillness gave no token,
And the only word there spoken was the whispered word "Lenore!"
This I whispered, and an echo murmured back the word "Lenore!"
Merely this and nothing more.

Back into the chamber turning, all my soul within me burning,
Soon again I heard a tapping, somewhat louder than before.

"Surely," said I, "surely that is something at my window lattice;
Let me see, then, what thereat is, and this mystery explore,—
Let my heart be still a moment and this mystery explore—
'Tis the wind and nothing more."

Open here I flung the shutter, when, with many a flirt and flutter,
In there stepped a stately Raven of the saintly days of yore.
Not the least obeisance made he, not a minute stopped or stayed he,
But with mien of lord or lady perched above my chamber door—
Perched upon a bust of Pallas just above my chamber door—
Perched and sat, and nothing more.

Then, this ebony bird beguiling my sad fancy into smiling
By the grave and stern decorum of the countenance it wore,
"Though thy crest be shorn and shaven, thou," I said, "art sure no craven,
Ghastly, grim, and ancient Raven, wandering from the nightly shore:
Tell me what thy lordly name is on the night's Plutonian shore!"
Quoth the Raven, "Nevermore."

Much I marveled this ungainly fowl to hear discourse so plainly,
Though its answer little meaning, little relevancy bore;
For we cannot help agreeing that no living human being
Ever yet was blessed with seeing bird above his chamber door—
Bird or beast upon the sculptured bust above his chamber door—
With such name as "Nevermore."

But the Raven, sitting lonely on the placid bust, spoke only
That one word, as if his soul in that one word he did outpour.
Nothing farther then he uttered, not a feather then he fluttered;
Till I scarcely more than muttered, "Other friends have flown before:
On the morrow *he* will leave me, as my hopes have flown before."
Then the bird said, "Nevermore."

Startled at the stillness broken by reply so aptly spoken,
"Doubtless," said I, "what it utters is its only stock and store,
Caught from some unhappy master whom unmerciful Disaster
Followed fast and followed faster till his songs one burden bore,
Till the dirges of his hope that melancholy burden bore
Of 'Never—nevermore.'"

But the Raven still beguiling my sad fancy into smiling,
Straight I wheeled a cushioned seat in front of bird and bust and door;
Then, upon the velvet sinking, I betook myself to linking
Fancy unto fancy, thinking what this ominous bird of yore,
What this grim, ungainly, ghastly, gaunt, and ominous bird of yore
Meant in croaking "Nevermore."

This I sat engaged in guessing, but no syllable expressing
To the fowl, whose fiery eyes now burned into my "bosom's" core;
This and more I sat divining, with my head at ease reclining
On the cushion's velvet lining that the lamplight gloated o'er,
But whose velvet violet lining with the lamplight gloating o'er,
She shall press, ah, nevermore!

Then, methought, the air grew denser, perfumed from an unseen censer
Swung by seraphim whose foot-falls tinkled on the tufted floor.
"Wretch," I cried, "thy God hath lent thee—by these angels he hath sent thee
Respite—respite and nepenthe from thy memories of Lenore!
Quaff, oh quaff this kind nepenthe, and forget this lost Lenore!"
Quoth the Raven, "Nevermore."

"Prophet!" said I, "thing of evil! prophet still, if bird or devil!
Whether Tempter sent, or whether tempest tossed thee here ashore,
Desolate yet all undaunted, on this desert land enchanted—
On this home by Horror haunted—tell me truly, I implore:
Is there—*is* there balm in Gilead?—tell me—tell me, I implore!"
Quoth the Raven, "Nevermore."

"Prophet!" said I, "thing of evil—prophet still, if bird or devil!
By that Heaven that bends above us, by that God we both adore,
Tell this soul with sorrow laden if, within the distant Aidenn,
It shall clasp a sainted maiden whom the angels name Lenore:
Clasp a rare and radiant maiden whom the angels name Lenore!"
Quoth the Raven, "Nevermore."

"Be that word our sign of parting, bird or fiend!" I shrieked, upstarting:
"Get thee back into the tempest and the Night's Plutonian shore!
Leave no black plume as a token of that lie thy soul hath spoken!
Leave my loneliness unbroken! quit the bust above my door!

Take thy beak from out my heart, and take thy form from off my door!"
Quoth the Raven, "Nevermore."

And the Raven, never flitting, still is sitting, still is sitting
On the pallid bust of Pallas just above my chamber door;
And his eyes have all the seeming of a demon's that is dreaming,
And the lamp-light o'er him streaming throws his shadow on the floor;
And my soul from out that shadow that lies floating on the floor
Shall be lifted—nevermore!

Ulalume

THE skies they were ashen and sober;
The leaves they were crispèd and sere,
The leaves they were withering and sere;
It was night in the lonesome October
Of my most immemorial year;
It was hard by the dim lake of Auber,
In the misty mid region of Weir:
It was down by the dank tarn of Auber,
In the ghoul-haunted woodland of Weir.

Here once, through an alley Titanic
Of cypress, I roamed with my Soul—
Of cypress, with Psyche, my Soul.
These were days when my heart was volcanic
As the scoriac rivers that roll,
As the lavas that restlessly roll
Their sulphurous currents down Yaanek
In the ultimate climes of the pole,
That groan as they roll down Mount Yaanek
In the realms of the boreal pole.

Our talk had been serious and sober,
But our thoughts they were palsied and sere,
Our memories were treacherous and sere,
For we knew not the month was October,

And we marked not the night of the year,
(Ah, night of all nights in the year!)
We noted not the dim lake of Auber
(Though once we had journeyed down here),
Remembered not the dank tarn of Auber
Nor the ghoul-haunted woodland of Weir.

And now, as the night was senescent
And star-dials pointed to morn,
As the star-dials hinted of morn,
At the end of our path a liquescent
And nebulous lustre was born,
Out of which a miraculous crescent
Arose with a duplicate horn,
Astarte's bediamonded crescent
Distinct with its duplicate horn.

And I said—"She is warmer than Dian:
She rolls through an ether of sighs,
She revels in a region of sighs:
She has seen that the tears are not dry on
These cheeks, where the worm never dies,
And has come past the stars of the Lion
To point us the path to the skies,
To the Lethean peace of the skies:
Come up, in despite of the Lion,
To shine on us with her bright eyes:
Come up through the lair of the Lion,
With love in her luminous eyes."

But Psyche, uplifting her finger,
Said—"Sadly this star I mistrust,
Her pallor I strangely mistrust:
Oh, hasten!—oh, let us not linger!
Oh, fly!—let us fly!—for we must."
In terror she spoke, letting sink her
Wings until they trailed in the dust;
In agony sobbed, letting sink her
Plumes till they trailed in the dust,
Till they sorrowfully trailed in the dust.

replied—"This is nothing but dreaming:
Let us on by this tremulous light!
Let us bathe in this crystalline light!
Its sibyllic splendor is beaming
With hope and in beauty to-night:
See, it flickers up the sky through the night!
Ah, we safely may trust to its gleaming,
And be sure it will lead us aright:
We safely may trust to a gleaming
That cannot but guide us aright,
Since it flickers up to Heaven through the night."

Thus I pacified Psyche and kissed her,
And tempted her out of her gloom,
And conquered her scruples and gloom;
And we passed to the end of the vista,
But were stopped by the door of a tomb,
By the door of a legended tomb;
And I said—"What is written, sweet sister,
On the door of this legended tomb?"
She replied—"Ulalume—Ulalume—
'Tis the vault of thy lost Ulalume!"

Then my heart it grew ashen and sober
As the leaves that were crispèd and sere,
As the leaves that were withering and sere,
And I cried—"It was surely October
On this very night of last year
That I journeyed—I journeyed down here,
That I brought a dread burden down here:
On this night of all nights in the year,
Ah, what demon has tempted me here?
Well I know, now, this dim lake of Auber,
This misty mid region of Weir:
Well I know, now, this dank tarn of Auber,
This ghoul-haunted woodland of Weir."

Annabel Lee

It was many and many a year ago,
  In a kingdom by the sea,
That a maiden lived, whom you may know
  By the name of Annabel Lee;
And this maiden she lived with no other thought
  Than to love, and be loved by me.

I was a child and she was a child,
  In this kingdom by the sea;
But we loved with a love that was more than love,
  I and my Annabel Lee,—
With a love that the wingèd seraphs of heaven
  Coveted her and me.

And this was the reason that long ago,
  In this kingdom by the sea,
A wind blew out of a cloud, chilling
  My beautiful Annabel Lee;
So that her high-born kinsmen came,
  And bore her away from me,
To shut her up in a sepulchre,
  In this kingdom by the sea.

The angels, not so happy in heaven,
  Went envying her and me.
Yes! that was the reason (as all men know)
  In this kingdom by the sea,
That the wind came out of the cloud by night,
  Chilling and killing my Annabel Lee.

But our love it was stronger by far than the love
  Of those who were older than we,
  Of many far wiser than we;
And neither the angels in heaven above,
  Nor the demons down under the sea,
Can ever dissever my soul from the soul
  Of the beautiful Annabel Lee.

For the moon never beams without bringing me dreams
  Of the beautiful Annabel Lee,
And the stars never rise but I feel the bright eyes
  Of the beautiful Annabel Lee.
And so, all the night-tide I lie down by the side
Of my darling, my darling, my life, and my bride,
  In her sepulchre there by the sea,
  In her tomb by the sounding sea.

For Annie

THANK Heaven! the crisis,—
  The danger is past,
And the lingering illness
  Is over at last,—
And the fever called "Living"
  Is conquered at last.

Sadly, I know,
  I am shorn of my strength,
And no muscle I move
  As I lie at full length,—
But no matter!—I feel
  I am better at length.

And I rest so composedly
  Now, in my bed,
That any beholder
  Might fancy me dead,—
Might start at beholding me,
  Thinking me dead.

The moaning and groaning,
  The sighing and sobbing,
Are quieted now,
  With that horrible throbbing
At heart,—ah, that horrible,
  Horrible throbbing!

The sickness, the nausea,
  The pitiless pain,
Have ceased, with the fever
  That maddened my brain,—
With the fever called "Living"
  That burned in my brain.

And O, of all tortures
  That torture the worst
Has abated,—the terrible
  Torture of thirst
For the naphthaline river
  Of Passion accurst!
I have drunk of a water
  That quenches all thirst.

Of a water that flows,
  With a lullaby sound,
From a spring but a very few
  Feet under ground,—
From a cavern not very far
  Down under ground.

And ah! let it never
  Be foolishly said
That my room it is gloomy
  And narrow my bed;
For man never slept
  In a different bed,—
And, to *sleep*, you must slumber
  In just such a bed.

My tantalized spirit
  Here blandly reposes,
Forgetting, or never
  Regretting, its roses,—
Its old agitations
  Of myrtles and roses:

For now, while so quietly
  Lying, it fancies
A holier odor
  About it, of pansies,—
A rosemary odor,
  Commingled with pansies,
With rue and the beautiful
  Puritan pansies.

And so it lies happily,
  Bathing in many
A dream of the truth
  And the beauty of Annie,—
Drowned in a bath
  Of the tresses of Annie.

She tenderly kissed me,
  She fondly caressed,
And then I fell gently
  To sleep on her breast,—
Deeply to sleep
  From the heaven of her breast.

When the light was extinguished,
  She covered me warm,
And she prayed to the angels
  To keep me from harm,—
To the queen of the angels
  To shield me from harm.

And I lie so composedly
  Now in my bed,
(Knowing her love,)
  That you fancy me dead,—
And I rest so contentedly

Now in my bed,
(With her love at my breast,)
That you fancy me dead,—
That you shudder to look at me,
Thinking me dead:

But my heart it is brighter
Than all of the many
Stars in the sky;
For it sparkles with Annie,—
It glows with the light
Of the love of my Annie,
With the thought of the light
Of the eyes of my Annie.

OLIVER WENDELL HOLMES

(1809–1894)

The Last Leaf

I SAW him once before,
As he passed by the door;
And again
The pavement-stones resound
As he totters o'er the ground
With his cane.

They say that in his prime,
Ere the pruning-knife of time
Cut him down,
Not a better man was found
By the crier on his round
Through the town.

But now he walks the streets,
And he looks at all he meets
So forlorn;
And he shakes his feeble head,
That it seems as if he said,
"They are gone."

The mossy marbles rest
On the lips that he has pressed
In their bloom;
And the names he loved to hear
Have been carved for many a year
On the tomb.

My grandmamma has said—
Poor old lady! she is dead
Long ago—
That he had a Roman nose,
And his cheek was like a rose
In the snow.

But now his nose is thin,
And it rests upon his chin
Like a staff;
And a crook is in his back,
And a melancholy crack
In his laugh.

I know it is a sin
For me to sit and grin
At him here,
But the old three-cornered hat,
And the breeches,—and all that,
Are so queer!

And if I should live to be
The last leaf upon the tree
In the spring,
Let them smile, as I do now,
At the old forsaken bough
Where I cling.

"Old Ironsides"

WRITTEN WITH REFERENCE TO THE PROPOSED BREAKING UP OF THE FAMOUS U. S. FRIGATE "CONSTITUTION."

AY, TEAR her tattered ensign down!
Long has it waved on high,
And many an eye has danced to see
That banner in the sky;
Beneath it rung the battle-shout,
And burst the cannon's roar:
The meteor of the ocean air
Shall sweep the clouds no more!

Her deck, once red with heroes' blood,
Where knelt the vanquished foe,
When winds were hurrying o'er the flood
And waves were white below,
No more shall feel the victor's tread,
Or know the conquered knee:
The harpies of the shore shall pluck
The eagle of the sea!

O better that her shattered hulk
Should sink beneath the wave!
Her thunders shook the mighty deep,
And there should be her grave:
Nail to the mast her holy flag,
Set every threadbare sail,
And give her to the god of storms,
The lightning and the gale!

ROBERT BROWNING
(1812–1889)

Porphyria's Lover

THE rain set early in to-night,
 The sullen wind was soon awake,
It tore the elm-tops down for spite,
 And did its worst to vex the lake:
 I listened with heart fit to break.
When glided in Porphyria; straight
 She shut the cold out and the storm,
And kneeled and made the cheerless grate
 Blaze up, and all the cottage warm;
 Which done, she rose, and from her form
Withdrew the dripping cloak and shawl,
 And laid her soiled gloves by, untied
Her hat and let the damp hair fall,
 And, last, she sat down by my side
 And called me. When no voice replied,
She put my arm about her waist,
 And made her smooth white shoulder bare,
And all her yellow hair displaced,
 And, stooping, made my cheek lie there,
 And spread, o'er all, her yellow hair,
Murmuring how she loved me—she
 Too weak, for all her heart's endeavor,
To set its struggling passion free
 From pride, and vainer ties dissever,
 And give herself to me for ever.
But passion sometimes would prevail,
 Nor could to-night's gay feast restrain
A sudden thought of one so pale
 For love of her, and all in vain:
 So, she was come through wind and rain.
Be sure I looked up at her eyes
 Happy and proud; at last I knew
Porphyria worshipped me; surprise

Made my heart swell, and still it grew
While I debated what to do.
That moment she was mine, mine, fair,
Perfectly pure and good: I found
A thing to do, and all her hair
In one long yellow string I wound
Three times her little throat around,
And strangled her. No pain felt she;
I am quite sure she felt no pain.
As a shut bud that holds the bee,
I warily oped her lids: again
Laughed the blue eyes without a stain.
And I untightened next the tress
About her neck; her cheek once more
Blushed bright beneath my burning kiss:
I propped her head up as before,
Only, this time my shoulder bore
Her head, which droops upon it still:
The smiling rosy little head,
So glad it has its utmost will,
That all it scorned at once is fled,
And I, its love, am gained instead!
Porphyria's love: she guessed not how
Her darling one wish would be heard.
And thus we sit together now,
And all night long we have not stirred,
And yet God has not said a word!

Heap Cassia, Sandal-buds and Stripes

HEAP cassia, sandal-buds and stripes
Of labdanum, and aloe-balls,
Smeared with dull nard an Indian wipes
From out her hair: such balsam falls
Down sea-side mountain pedestals,
From tree-tops where tired winds are fain,
Spent with the vast and howling main,
To treasure half their island-gain.

And strew faint sweetness from some old
    Egyptian's fine worm-eaten shroud
Which breaks to dust when once unrolled:
    Or shredded perfume, like a cloud
    From closet long to quiet vowed,
With mothed and dropping arras hung,
Mouldering her lute and books among,
As when a queen, long dead, was young.

The Year's at the Spring

THE year's at the spring
And day's at the morn;
Morning's at seven;
The hill-side's dew-pearled;
The lark's on the wing;
The snail's on the thorn:
God's in His heaven—
All's right with the world!

Meeting at Night

THE grey sea and the long black land;
And the yellow half-moon large and low;
And the startled little waves that leap
In fiery ringlets from their sleep,
As I gain the cove with pushing prow,
And quench its speed i' the slushy sand.

Then a mile of warm sea-scented beach
Three fields to cross till a farm appears;
A tap at the pane, the quick sharp scratch
And blue spurt of a lighted match,
And a voice less loud, thro' its joys and fears,
Than the two hearts beating each to each!

Parting at Morning

ROUND the cape of a sudden came the sea,
And the sun looked over the mountain's rim:
And straight was a path of gold for him,
And the need of a world of men for me.

Misconceptions

THIS is a spray the Bird clung to,
    Making it blossom with pleasure,
Ere the high tree-top she sprung to,
    Fit for her nest and her treasure.
    O, what a hope beyond measure
Was the poor spray's, which the flying feet hung to,—
So to be singled out, built in, and sung to!

This is a heart the Queen leant on,
    Thrilled in a minute erratic,
Ere the true bosom she bent on,
    Meet for love's regal dalmatic.
    O, what a fancy ecstatic
Was the poor heart's, ere the wanderer went on—
Love to be saved for it, proffered to, spent on!

Home-Thoughts, from Abroad

OH, TO be in England
Now that April's there,
And whoever wakes in England
Sees, some morning, unaware,
That the lowest boughs and the brushwood sheaf
Round the elm-tree bole are in tiny leaf,
While the chaffinch sings on the orchard bough
In England—now!

And after April, when May follows,
And the whitethroat builds, and all the swallows!
Hark, where my blossomed pear-tree in the hedge
Leans to the field and scatters on the clover
Blossoms and dewdrops—at the bent spray's edge—
That's the wise thrush; he sings each song twice over,
Lest you should think he never could recapture
The first fine careless rapture!
And though the fields look rough with hoary dew,
All will be gay when noontide wakes anew
The buttercups, the little children's dower
—Far brighter than this gaudy melon-flower!

The Lost Leader

Just for a handful of silver he left us,
Just for a riband to stick in his coat—
Found the one gift of which fortune bereft us,
Lost all the others she lets us devote;
They, with the gold to give, doled him out silver,
So much was theirs who so little allowed:
How all our copper had gone for his service!
Rags—were they purple, his heart had been proud!
We that had loved him so, followed him, honored him,
Lived in his mild and magnificent eye,
Learned his great language, caught his clear accents,
Made him our pattern to live and to die!
Shakespeare was of us, Milton was for us,
Burns, Shelley, were with us,—they watch from their graves!
He alone breaks from the van and the freemen,
He alone sinks to the rear and the slaves!

We shall march prospering,—not thro' his presence;
Songs may inspirit us,—not from his lyre;
Deeds will be done,—while he boasts his quiescence,
Still bidding crouch whom the rest bade aspire:

Blot out his name, then, record one lost soul more,
  One task more declined, one more footpath untrod,
One more devils'-triumph and sorrow for angels,
  One wrong more to man, one more insult to God!
Life's night begins: let him never come back to us!
  There would be doubt, hesitation, and pain,
Forced praise on our part—the glimmer of twilight,
  Never glad confident morning again!
Best fight on well, for we taught him,—strike gallantly,
  Menace our heart ere we master his own;
Then let him receive the new knowledge and wait us,
  Pardoned in heaven, the first by the throne!

Evelyn Hope

BEAUTIFUL Evelyn Hope is dead!
  Sit and watch by her side an hour.
That is her book-shelf, this her bed;
  She plucked that piece of geranium-flower,
Beginning to die too, in the glass.
  Little has yet been changed, I think;
The shutters are shut,—no light may pass
  Save two long rays through the hinge's chink.

Sixteen years old when she died!
  Perhaps she had scarcely heard my name,—
It was not her time to love; beside,
  Her life had many a hope and aim,
Duties enough and little cares;
  And now was quiet, now astir,—
Till God's hand beckoned unawares,
  And the sweet white brow is all of her.

Is it too late, then, Evelyn Hope?
  What! your soul was pure and true;
The good stars met in your horoscope,
  Made you of spirit, fire, and dew;

And just because I was thrice as old,
  And our paths in the world diverged so wide,
Each was naught to each, must I be told?
  We were fellow-mortals,—naught beside.

No, indeed! for God above
  Is great to grant as mighty to make,
And creates the love to reward the love;
  I claim you still, for my own love's sake!
Delayed, it may be, for more lives yet,
  Through worlds I shall traverse, not a few;
Much is to learn and much to forget
  Ere the time be come for taking you.

But the time will come—at last it will—
  When, Evelyn Hope, what meant, I shall say,
In the lower earth,—in the years long still,—
  That body and soul so pure and gay?
Why your hair was amber I shall divine,
  And your mouth of your own geranium's red,—
And what you would do with me, in fine,
  In the new life come in the old one's stead.

I have lived, I shall say, so much since then,
  Given up myself so many times,
Gained me the gains of various men,
  Ransacked the ages, spoiled the climes;
Yet one thing—one—in my soul's full scope,
  Either I missed or itself missed me,—
And I want and find you, Evelyn Hope!
  What is the issue? let us see!

I loved you, Evelyn, all the while;
  My heart seemed full as it could hold,—
There was place and to spare for the frank young smile,
  And the red young mouth, and the hair's young gold.
So, hush! I will give you this leaf to keep;
  See, I shut it inside the sweet, cold hand.
There, that is our secret! go to sleep;
  You will wake, and remember, and understand.

The Last Ride Together

I SAID—Then, dearest, since 'tis so,
Since now at length my fate I know,
Since nothing all my love avails,
Since all my life seemed meant for, fails,
  Since this was written and needs must be—
My whole heart rises up to bless
Your name in pride and thankfulness!
Take back the hope you gave,—I claim
Only a memory of the same,
—And this beside, if you will not blame,
  Your leave for one more last ride with me.

My mistress bent that brow of hers;
Those deep dark eyes where pride demurs
When pity would be softening through,
Fixed me a breathing-while or two
  With life or death in the balance: right!
The blood replenished me again;
My last thought was at least not vain:
I and my mistress, side by side
Shall be together, breathe and ride,
So, one day more am I deified.
  Who knows but the world may end to-night?

Hush! if you saw some western cloud
All billowy-bosomed, over-bowed
By many benedictions—sun's
And moon's and evening-star's at once—
  And so, you, looking and loving best,
Conscious grew, your passion drew
Cloud, sunset, moonrise, star-shine too,
Down on you, near and yet more near,
Till flesh must fade for heaven was here!—
Thus leant she and lingered—joy and fear!
  Thus lay she a moment on my breast.

Then we began to ride. My soul
Smoothed itself out, a long-cramped scroll

Freshening and fluttering in the wind.
Past hopes already lay behind.
  What need to strive with a life awry?
Had I said that, had I done this,
So might I gain, so might I miss.
Might she have loved me? just as well
She might have hated, who can tell!
Where had I been now if the worst befell?
  And here we are riding, she and I.

Fail I alone, in words and deeds?
Why, all men strive, and who succeeds?
We rode; it seemed my spirit flew,
Saw other regions, cities new,
  As the world rushed by on either side.
I thought,—All labor, yet no less
Bear up beneath their unsuccess.
Look at the end of work, contrast
The petty done, the undone vast,
This present of theirs with the hopeful past!
  I hoped she would love me; here we ride.

What hand and brain went ever paired?
What heart alike conceived and dared?
What act proved all its thought had been?
What will but felt the fleshly screen?
  We ride and I see her bosom heave.
There's many a crown for who can reach.
Ten lines, a statesman's life in each!
The flag stuck on a heap of bones,
A soldier's doing! what atones?
They scratch his name on the Abbey-stones.
  My riding is better, by their leave.

What does it all mean, poet? Well,
Your brains beat into rhythm, you tell
What we felt only; you expressed
You hold things beautiful the best,
  And pace them in rhyme so, side by side.
'Tis something, nay 'tis much: but then,

Have you yourself what's best for men?
Are you—poor, sick, old ere your time—
Nearer one whit your own sublime
Than we who have never turned a rhyme?
  Sing, riding's a joy! For me, I ride.

And you, great sculptor—so, you gave
A score of years to Art, her slave,
And that's your Venus, whence we turn
To yonder girl that fords the burn!
  You acquiesce, and shall I repine?
What, man of music, you grown gray
With notes and nothing else to say,
Is this your sole praise from a friend,
"Greatly his opera's strains intend,
But in music we know how fashions end!"
  I gave my youth; but we ride, in fine.

Who knows what's fit for us? Had fate
Proposed bliss here should sublimate
My being—had I signed the bond—
Still one must lead some life beyond,
  Have a bliss to die with, dim-descried.
This foot once planted on the goal,
This glory-garland round my soul,
Could I descry such? Try and test!
I sink back shuddering from the quest.
Earth being so good, would heaven seem best?
  Now, heaven and she are beyond this ride.

And yet—she has not spoke so long!
What if heaven be that, fair and strong
At life's best, with our eyes upturned
Whither life's flower is first discerned,
  We, fixed so, ever should so abide?
What if we still ride on, we two,
With life forever old yet new,
Changed not in kind but in degree,
The instant made eternity,—
And heaven just prove that I and she
  Ride, ride together, for ever ride?

Memorabilia

AH, DID you once see Shelley plain,
And did he stop and speak to you,
And did you speak to him again?
How strange it seems, and new!

But you were living before that,
And also you are living after;
And the memory I started at—
My starting moves your laughter!

I crossed a moor, with a name of its own
And a certain use in the world, no doubt,
Yet a hand's-breadth of it shines alone
'Mid the blank miles round about:

For there I picked up on the heather
And there I put inside my breast
A moulted feather, an eagle-feather!
Well, I forget the rest.

The Patriot

An Old Story

IT WAS roses, roses, all the way,
With myrtle mixed in my path like mad:
The house-roofs seemed to heave and sway,
The church-spires flamed, such flags they had,
A year ago on this very day.

The air broke into a mist with bells,
The old walls rocked with the crowd and cries.
Had I said, "Good folk, mere noise repels—
But give me your sun from yonder skies!"
They had answered, "And afterwards, what else?"

Alack, it was I who leaped at the sun
  To give it my loving friends to keep!
Naught man could do, have I left undone:
  And you see my harvest, what I reap
This very day, now a year is run.

There's nobody on the house-tops now—
  Just a palsied few at the windows set;
For the best of the sight is, all allow,
  At the Shambles' Gate—or, better yet,
By the very scaffold's foot, I trow.

I go in the rain, and, more than needs,
  A rope cuts both my wrists behind;
And I think, by the feel, my forehead bleeds,
  For they fling, whoever has a mind,
Stones at me for my year's misdeeds.

Thus I entered, and thus I go!
  In triumphs people have dropped down dead.
"Paid by the world, what dost thou owe
  Me?"—God might question; now instead,
'Tis God shall repay: I am safer so.

Rabbi Ben Ezra

Grow old along with me!
The best is yet to be,
The last of life, for which the first was made:
Our times are in his hand
Who saith, "A whole I planned,
Youth shows but half; trust God: see all, nor be afraid!"

Not that, amassing flowers,
Youth sighed, "Which rose make ours,
Which lily leave and then as best recall?"
Not that, admiring stars,
It yearned, "Nor Jove, nor Mars;
Mine be some figured flame which blends, transcends them all!"

Not for such hopes and fears
Annulling youth's brief years,
Do I remonstrate: folly wide the mark!
Rather I prize the doubt
Low kinds exist without,
Finished and finite clods, untroubled by a spark.

Poor vaunt of life indeed,
Were man but formed to feed
On joy, to solely seek and find and feast:
Such feasting ended, then
As sure an end to men;
Irks care the crop full bird? Frets doubt the maw-crammed beast?

Rejoice we are allied
To that which doth provide
And not partake, effect and not receive!
A spark disturbs our clod;
Nearer we hold of God
Who gives, than of his tribes that take, I must believe.

Then, welcome each rebuff
That turns earth's smoothness rough,
Each sting that bids nor sit nor stand but go!
Be our joys three-parts pain!
Strive, and hold cheap the strain;
Learn, nor account the pang; dare, never grudge the throe!

For thence,—a paradox
Which comforts while it mocks,—
Shall life succeed in that it seems to fail:
What I aspired to be,
And was not, comforts me:
A brute I might have been, but would not sink i' the scale.

What is he but a brute
Whose flesh has soul to suit,
Whose spirit works lest arms and legs want play?
To man, propose this test—
Thy body at its best,
How far can that project thy soul on its lone way?

Yet gifts should prove their use:
I own the Past profuse
Of power each side, perfection every turn:
Eyes, ears took in their dole,
Brain treasured up the whole;
Should not the heart beat once "How good to live and learn"?

Not once beat "Praise be thine!
I see the whole design,
I, who saw power, see now Love perfect too:
Perfect I call thy plan:
Thanks that I was a man!
Maker, remake, complete,—I trust what thou shalt do!"

For pleasant is this flesh;
Our soul, in its rose-mesh
Pulled ever to the earth, still yearns for rest:
Would we some prize might hold
To match those manifold
Possessions of the brute,—gain most as we did best!

Let us not always say,
"Spite of this flesh to-day
I strove, made head, gained ground upon the whole!"
As the bird wings and sings,
Let us cry, "All good things
Are ours, nor soul helps flesh more, now, than flesh helps soul!"

Therefore I summon age
To grant youth's heritage,
Life's struggle having so far reached its term:
Thence shall I pass, approved
A man, for aye removed
From the developed brute; a God though in the germ.

And I shall thereupon
Take rest, ere I be gone
Once more on my adventure brave and new:
Fearless and unperplexed,
When I wage battle next,
What weapons to select, what armor to indue.

Youth ended, I shall try
My gain or loss thereby;
Leave the fire ashes, what survives is gold:
And I shall weigh the same,
Give life its praise or blame:
Young, all lay in dispute; I shall know, being old.

For note, when evening shuts,
A certain moment cuts
The deed off, calls the glory from the gray:
A whisper from the west
Shoots—"Add this to the rest,
Take it and try its worth: here dies another day."

So, still within this life,
Though lifted o'er its strife,
Let me discern, compare, pronounce at last,
"This rage was right i' the main,
That acquiescence vain:
The Future I may face now I have proved the Past."

For more is not reserved
To man, with soul just nerved
To act to-morrow what he learns to-day:
Here, work enough to watch
The Master work, and catch
Hints of the proper craft, tricks of the tool's true play.

As it was better, youth
Should strive, through acts uncouth,
Toward making, than repose on aught found made:
So, better, age, exempt
From strife, should know, than tempt
Further. Thou waitedst age: wait death nor be afraid!

Enough now, if the Right
And Good and Infinite
Be named here, as thou callest thy hand thine own,
With knowledge absolute,
Subject to no dispute
From fools that crowded youth, nor let thee feel alone.

Be there, for once and all,
Severed great minds from small,
Announced to each his station in the Past!
Was I, the world arraigned,
Were they, my soul disdained,
Right? Let age speak the truth and give us peace at last!

Now, who shall arbitrate?
Ten men love what I hate,
Shun what I follow, slight what I receive;
Ten, who in ears and eyes
Match me: we all surmise,
They this thing, and I that: whom shall my soul believe?

Not on the vulgar mass
Called "work," must sentence pass,
Things done, that took the eye and had the price;
O'er which, from level stand,
The low world laid its hand,
Found straightway to its mind, could value in a trice:

But all, the world's coarse thumb
And finger failed to plumb,
So passed in making up the main account;
All instincts immature,
All purposes unsure,
That weighed not as his work, yet swelled the man's amount:

Thoughts hardly to be packed
Into a narrow act,
Fancies that broke through language and escaped;
All I could never be,
All, men ignored in me,
This, I was worth to God, whose wheel the pitcher shaped.

Ay, note that Potter's wheel,
That metaphor! and feel
Why time spins fast, why passive lies our clay,—
Thou, to whom fools propound,
When the wine makes its round,
"Since life fleets, all is change; the Past gone, seize to-day!"

Fool! All that is, at all,
Lasts ever, past recall;
Earth changes, but thy soul and God stand sure:
What entered into thee,
That was, is, and shall be:
Time's wheel runs back or stops: Potter and clay endure.

He fixed thee 'mid this dance
Of plastic circumstance,
This Present, thou, forsooth, would fain arrest:
Machinery just meant
To give thy soul its bent,
Try thee and turn thee forth, sufficiently impressed.

What though the earlier grooves,
Which ran the laughing loves
Around thy base, no longer pause and press;
What though, about thy rim,
Skull-things in order grim
Grow out, in graver mood, obey the sterner stress?

Look not thou down but up!
To uses of a cup,
The festal board, lamp's flash and trumpet's peal,
The new wine's foaming flow,
The Master's lips aglow!
Thou, heaven's consummate cup, what needst thou with earth's wheel?

But I need, now as then,
Thee, God, who moldest men;
And since, not even while the whirl was worst,
Did I—to the wheel of life
With shapes and colors rife,
Bound dizzily—mistake my end, to slake thy thirst:

So, take and use thy work:
Amend what flaws may lurk,
What strain o' the stuff, what warpings past the aim!
My times be in thy hand!
Perfect the cup as planned!
Let age approve of youth, and death complete the same!

Prospice

FEAR death?—to feel the fog in my throat,
The mist in my face,
When the snows begin, and the blasts denote
I am nearing the place,
The power of the night, the press of the storm,
The post of the foe;
Where he stands, the Arch Fear in a visible form,
Yet the strong man must go:
For the journey is done and the summit attained,
And the barriers fall,
Though a battle's to fight ere the guerdon be gained,
The reward of it all.
I was ever a fighter, so—one fight more,
The best and the last!

I would hate that death bandaged my eyes, and forbore,
And bade me creep past.
No! let me taste the whole of it, fare like my peers,
The heroes of old,
Bear the brunt, in a minute pay glad life's arrears
Of pain, darkness, and cold.
For sudden the worst turns the best to the brave,
The black minute's at end,
And the elements' rage, the fiend-voices that rave,
Shall dwindle, shall blend,
Shall change, shall become first a peace out of pain,
Then a light, then thy breast,
O thou soul of my soul! I shall clasp thee again,
And with God be the rest!

Epilogue from "Asolando"

AT THE midnight in the silence of the sleeptime,
When you set your fancies free,
Will they pass to where—by death, fools think, imprisoned—
Low he lies who once so loved you, whom you loved so,
—Pity me?

Oh to love so, be so loved, yet so mistaken!
What had I on earth to do
With the slothful, with the mawkish, the unmanly?
Like the aimless, helpless, hopeless, did I drivel
—Being—who?

One who never turned his back but marched breast forward,
Never doubted clouds would break,
Never dreamed, though right were worsted, wrong would triumph,
Held we fall to rise, are baffled to fight better,
Sleep to wake.

No, at noonday in the bustle of man's worktime
Greet the unseen with a cheer!
Bid him forward, breast and back as either should be,
"Strive and thrive!" cry "Speed,—fight on, fare ever
There as here!"

EDWARD LEAR

(1812–1888)

The Owl and the Pussy-Cat

THE Owl and the Pussy-cat went to sea
In a beautiful pea-green boat:
They took some honey, and plenty of money
Wrapped up in a five-pound note.
The Owl looked up to the stars above,
And sang to a small guitar,
"O lovely Pussy, O Pussy, my love,
What a beautiful Pussy you are,
You are,
You are!
What a beautiful Pussy you are!"

Pussy said to the Owl, "You elegant fowl,
  How charmingly sweet you sing!
Oh! let us be married; too long we have tarried:
  But what shall we do for a ring?"
They sailed away, for a year and a day,
  To the land where the bong-tree grows;
And there in a wood a Piggy-wig stood,
  With a ring at the end of his nose,
        His nose,
        His nose,
  With a ring at the end of his nose.

"Dear Pig, are you willing to sell for one shilling
  Your ring?" Said the Piggy, "I will."
So they took it away, and were married next day
  By the turkey who lives on the hill.
They dined on mince and slices of quince,
  Which they ate with a runcible spoon;
And hand in hand, on the edge of the sand,
  They danced by the light of the moon,
        The moon,
        The moon,
  They danced by the light of the moon.

The Pobble Who Has No Toes

THE Pobble who has no toes
  Had once as many as we;
When they said, "Some day you may lose them all;"
  He replied, "Fish fiddle-de-dee!"
And his Aunt Jobiska made him drink
Lavender water tinged with pink,
For she said, "The World in general knows
There's nothing so good for a Pobble's toes!"

The Pobble who has no toes
   Swam across the Bristol Channel;
But before he set out he wrapped his nose
   In a piece of scarlet flannel.
For his Aunt Jobiska said, "No harm
Can come to his toes if his nose is warm;
And it's perfectly known that a Pobble's toes
Are safe,—provided he minds his nose."

The Pobble swam fast and well,
   And when boats or ships came near him,
He tinkledy-blinkledy-winkled a bell,
   So that all the world could hear him.
And all the Sailors and Admirals cried,
When they saw him nearing the further side,—
"He has gone to fish, for his Aunt Jobiska's
Runcible Cat with crimson whiskers!"

But before he touched the shore,—
   The shore of the Bristol Channel,—
A sea-green Porpoise carried away
   His wrapper of scarlet flannel.
And when he came to observe his feet,
Formerly garnished with toes so neat,
His face at once became forlorn
On perceiving that all his toes were gone!

And nobody ever knew,
   From that dark day to the present,
Whoso had taken the Pobble's toes,
   In a manner so far from pleasant.
Whether the shrimps or crawfish gray,
Or crafty Mermaids stole them away—
Nobody knew; and nobody knows
How the Pobble was robbed of his twice five toes!

The Pobble who has no toes
   Was placed in a friendly Bark,
And they rowed him back, and carried him up
   To his Aunt Jobiska's Park.

And she made him a feast, at his earnest wish,
Of eggs and buttercups fried with fish;
And she said, "It's a fact the whole world knows,
That Pobbles are happier without their toes."

EPES SARGENT

(1813–1880)

A Life on the Ocean Wave

A LIFE on the ocean wave,
  A home on the rolling deep;
Where the scattered waters rave,
  And the winds their revels keep!
Like an eagle caged I pine
  On this dull, unchanging shore:
O, give me the flashing brine,
  The spray and the tempest's roar!

Once more on the deck I stand,
  Of my own swift-gliding craft:
Set sail! farewell to the land;
  The gale follows fair abaft.
We shoot through the sparkling foam,
  Like an ocean-bird set free,—
Like the ocean-bird, our home
  We 'll find far out on the sea.

The land is no longer in view,
  The clouds have begun to frown;
But with a stout vessel and crew,
  We'll say, Let the storm come down!
And the song of our hearts shall be,
  While the winds and the waters rave,
A home on the rolling sea!
  A life on the ocean wave!

HENRY DAVID THOREAU

(1817–1862)

Smoke

Light-wingèd Smoke! Icarian bird,
Melting thy pinions in thy upward flight;
Lark without song, and messenger of dawn,
Circling above the hamlets as thy nest;
Or else, departing dream, and shadowy form
Of midnight vision, gathering up thy skirts;
By night star-veiling, and by day
Darkening the light and blotting out the sun;
Go thou, my incense, upward from this hearth,
And ask the gods to pardon this clear flame.

My Prayer

Great God, I ask thee for no meaner pelf
Than that I may not disappoint myself;
That in my action I may soar as high
As I can now discern with this clear eye.

And next in value, which thy kindness lends,
That I may greatly disappoint my friends,
Howe'er they think or hope that it may be,
They may not dream how thou'st distinguished me.

That my weak hand may equal my firm faith,
And my life practise more than my tongue saith;
That my low conduct may not show,
Nor my relenting lines,
That I thy purpose did not know,
Or overrated thy designs.

EMILY BRONTË

(1818–1848)

The Old Stoic

RICHES I hold in light esteem,
And Love I laugh to scorn;
And lust of fame was but a dream,
That vanished with the morn:

And if I pray, the only prayer
That moves my lips for me
Is, "Leave the heart that now I bear
And give me liberty!"

Yes, as my swift days near their goal,
'Tis all that I implore;
In life and death a chainless soul,
With courage to endure.

Last Lines

NO COWARD soul is mine,
No trembler in the world's storm-troubled sphere:
I see Heaven's glories shine,
And faith shines equal, arming me from fear.

O God within my breast,
Almighty, ever-present Deity!
Life—that in me has rest,
As I—undying Life—have power in Thee.

Vain are the thousand creeds
That move men's hearts: unutterably vain;
Worthless as withered weeds,
Or idlest froth amid the boundless main,

To waken doubt in one
  Holding so fast by Thine infinity;
So surely anchored on
  The steadfast rock of immortality.

With wide-embracing love
  Thy Spirit animates eternal years,
Pervades and broods above,
  Changes, sustains, dissolves, creates, and rears.

Though earth and man were gone,
  And suns and universes cease to be,
And Thou were left alone,
  Every existence would exist in Thee.

There is not room for Death,
  Nor atom that his might could render void:
Thou—Thou art Being and Breath,
  And what Thou art may never be destroyed.

CECIL FRANCES ALEXANDER

(1818–1875)

Burial of Moses

"And he buried him in a valley in the land of Moab, over against Bethpeor; but no man knoweth of his sepulchre unto this day."—DEUT. XXXIV. 6.

BY NEBO's lonely mountain,
On this side Jordan's wave,
In a vale in the land of Moab,
There lies a lonely grave;
But no man built that sepulchre,
And no man saw it e'er;
For the angels of God upturned the sod,
And laid the dead man there.

That was the grandest funeral
That ever passed on earth;
Yet no man heard the trampling,
Or saw the train go forth:
Noiselessly as the daylight
Comes when the night is done,
And the crimson streak on ocean's cheek
Grows into the great sun;

Noiselessly as the spring-time
Her crown of verdure weaves,
And all the trees on all the hills
Unfold their thousand leaves:
So without sound of music
Or voice of them that wept,
Silently down from the mountain's crown
The great procession swept.

Perchance the bald old eagle
On gray Beth-peor's height
Out of his rocky eyry
Looked on the wondrous sight;
Perchance the lion stalking
Still shuns that hallowed spot;
For beast and bird have seen and heard
That which man knoweth not.

But, when the warrior dieth,
His comrades of the war,
With arms reversed and muffled drums,
Follow the funeral car:
They show the banners taken;
They tell his battles won;
And after him lead his masterless steed,
While peals the minute-gun.

Amid the noblest of the land
Men lay the sage to rest,

And give the bard an honored place,
With costly marbles drest,
In the great minster transept
Where lights like glories fall,
And the sweet choir sings, and the organ rings
Along the emblazoned hall.

This was the bravest warrior
That ever buckled sword;
This the most gifted poet
That ever breathed a word;
And never earth's philosopher
Traced with his golden pen
On the deathless page truths half so sage
As he wrote down for men.

And had he not high honor?—
The hillside for a pall!
To lie in state while angels wait,
With stars for tapers tall!
And the dark rock-pines, like tossing plumes,
Over his bier to wave,
And God's own hand, in that lonely land,
To lay him in his grave!—

In that strange grave without a name,
Whence his uncoffined clay
Shall break again—O wondrous thought!—
Before the judgment-day,
And stand, with glory wrapped around,
On the hills he never trod,
And speak of the strife that won our life
With the incarnate Son of God.

O lonely tomb in Moab's land!
O dark Beth-peor's hill!
Speak to these curious hearts of ours,
And teach them to be still:

God hath his mysteries of grace,
Ways that we cannot tell,
He hides them deep, like the secret sleep
Of him he loved so well.

CHARLES KINGSLEY

(1819–1875)

The Sands of Dee

"O MARY, go and call the cattle home,
And call the cattle home,
And call the cattle home
Across the sands of Dee;"
The western wind was wild and dank with foam,
And all alone went she.

The western tide crept up along the sand,
And o'er and o'er the sand,
And round and round the sand,
As far as eye could see.
The rolling mist came down and hid the land
And never home came she.

"Oh! is it weed, or fish, or floating hair—
A tress of golden hair,
A drownèd maiden's hair
Above the nets at sea?
Was never salmon yet that shone so fair
Among the stakes on Dee."

They rowed her in across the rolling foam,
The cruel crawling foam,
The cruel hungry foam,
To her grave beside the sea:
But still the boatmen hear her call the cattle home
Across the sands of Dee.

The Three Fishers

THREE fishers went sailing out into the west,—
  Out into the west as the sun went down;
Each thought of the woman who loved him the best,
  And the children stood watching them out of the town;
For men must work, and women must weep;
And there's little to earn, and many to keep,
    Though the harbor bar be moaning.

Three wives sat up in the light-house tower,
  And trimmed the lamps as the sun went down;
And they looked at the squall, and they looked at the shower,
  And the rack it came rolling up, ragged and brown;
But men must work, and women must weep,
Though storms be sudden, and waters deep,
    And the harbor bar be moaning.

Three corpses lay out on the shining sands
  In the morning gleam as the tide went down,
And the women are watching and wringing their hands,
  For those who will never come back to the town;
For men must work, and women must weep,—
And the sooner it 's over, the sooner to sleep,—
    And good-by to the bar and its moaning.

Young and Old

WHEN all the world is young, lad,
  And all the trees are green;
And every goose a swan, lad,
  And every lass a queen;
Then hey for boot and horse, lad,
  And round the world away;
Young blood must have its course, lad,
  And every dog his day.

When all the world is old, lad,
And all the trees are brown;
And all the sport is stale, lad,
And all the wheels run down;
Creep home, and take your place there,
The spent and maimed among:
God grant you find one face there,
You loved when all was young.

A Farewell

My fairest child, I have no song to give you;
No lark could pipe to skies so dull and gray;
Yet, ere we part, one lesson I can leave you
For every day.

Be good, sweet maid, and let who will be clever;
Do noble things, not dream them, all day long:
And so make life, death, and that vast forever
One grand, sweet song.

JAMES RUSSELL LOWELL

(1819–1891)

June

And what is so rare as a day in June?
Then, if ever, come perfect days;
Then Heaven tries the earth if it be in tune,
And over it softly her warm ear lays:

Whether we look, or whether we listen,
We hear life murmur, or see it glisten;
Every clod feels a stir of might,
   An instinct within it that reaches and towers,
And, groping blindly above it for light,
   Climbs to a soul in grass and flowers;
The flush of life may well be seen
   Thrilling back over hills and valleys;
The cowslip startles in meadows green,
   The buttercup catches the sun in its chalice,
And there's never a leaf nor a blade too mean
   To be some happy creature's palace;
The little bird sits at his door in the sun,
   Atilt like a blossom among the leaves,
And lets his illumined being o'errun
   With the deluge of summer it receives;
His mate feels the eggs beneath her wings,
And the heart in her dumb breast flutters and sings;
He sings to the wide world, and she to her nest,—
In the nice ear of Nature which song is the best?

Now is the high tide of the year,
   And whatever of life hath ebbed away
Comes flooding back, with a ripply cheer,
   Into every bare inlet and creek and bay;
Now the heart is so full that a drop overfills it,
We are happy now because God wills it;
No matter how barren the past may have been,
'T is enough for us now that the leaves are green;
We sit in the warm shade and feel right well
How the sap creeps up and the blossoms swell;
We may shut our eyes, but we cannot help knowing
That skies are clear and grass is growing;
The breeze comes whispering in our ear,
That dandelions are blossoming near,
   That maize has sprouted, that streams are flowing,
That the river is bluer than the sky,
That the robin is plastering his house hard by;
And if the breeze kept the good news back,
For other couriers we should not lack,

We could guess it all by yon heifer's lowing,—
And hark! how clear bold chanticleer,
Warmed with the new wine of the year,
Tells all in his lusty crowing!

GEORGE ELIOT (MARIAN EVANS CROSS)

(1819–1880)

O, May I Join the Choir Invisible!

O, MAY I join the choir invisible
Of those immortal dead who live again
In minds made better by their presence; live
In pulses stirred to generosity,
In deeds of daring rectitude, in scorn
Of miserable aims that end with self,
In thoughts sublime that pierce the night like stars,
And with their mild persistence urge men's minds
To vaster issues.
So to live is heaven:
To make undying music in the world,
Breathing a beauteous order, that controls
With growing sway the growing life of man.
So we inherit that sweet purity
For which we struggled, failed, and agonized
With widening retrospect that bred despair.
Rebellious flesh that would not be subdued,
A vicious parent shaming still its child,
Poor anxious penitence, is quick dissolved;
Its discords quenched by meeting harmonies,
Die in the large and charitable air.
And all our rarer, better, truer self,
That sobbed religiously in yearning song,
That watched to ease the burden of the world,
Laboriously tracing what must be,
And what may yet be better,—saw within

A worthier image for the sanctuary,
And shaped it forth before the multitude,
Divinely human, raising worship so
To higher reverence more mixed with love,
That better self shall live till human Time
Shall fold its eyelids, and the human sky
Be gathered like a scroll within the tomb,
Unread forever.
                    This is life to come,
Which martyred men have made more glorious
For us, who strive to follow.
                              May I reach
That purest heaven,—be to other souls
The cup of strength in some great agony,
Enkindle generous ardor, feed pure love,
Beget the smiles that have no cruelty,
Be the sweet presence of a good diffused,
And in diffusion ever more intense!
So shall I join the choir invisible,
Whose music is the gladness of the world.

ARTHUR HUGH CLOUGH

(1819–1861)

Qua Cursum Ventus

As SHIPS, becalmed at eve, that lay
   With canvas drooping, side by side,
Two towers of sail at dawn of day,
   Are scarce long leagues apart descried.

When fell the night, up sprang the breeze,
   And all the darkling hours they plied,
Nor dreamt but each the selfsame seas
   By each was cleaving, side by side.

E'en so,—but why the tale reveal
 Of those whom, year by year unchanged,
Brief absence, joined anew to feel,
 Astounded, soul from soul estranged?

At dead of night their sails were filled,
 And onward each rejoicing steered;—
Ah! neither blame, for neither willed
 Or wist what first with dawn appeared.

To veer, how vain! On, onward strain,
 Brave barks! In light, in darkness too,
Through winds and tides one compass guides:
 To that and your own selves be true.

But O blithe breeze! and O great seas!
 Though ne'er, that earliest parting past,
On your wide plain they join again,—
 Together lead them home at last.

One port, methought, alike they sought,—
 One purpose hold where'er they fare;
O bounding breeze, O rushing seas,
 At last, at last, unite them there!

Say Not the Struggle Naught Availeth

Say not the struggle naught availeth,
 The labor and the wounds are vain,
The enemy faints not, nor faileth,
 And as things have been they remain.

If hopes were dupes, fears may be liars;
 It may be, in yon smoke concealed,
Your comrades chase e'en now the fliers,
 And, but for you, possess the field.

For while the tired waves, vainly breaking,
Seem here no painful inch to gain,
Far back, through creeks and inlets making,
Comes silent, flooding in, the main.

And not by eastern windows only,
When the daylight comes, comes in the light,
In front, the sun climbs slow, how slowly,
But westward, look, the land is bright!

WALT WHITMAN

(1819–1892)

MEMORIES OF PRESIDENT LINCOLN

When Lilacs Last in the Dooryard Bloom'd

I

WHEN lilacs last in the dooryard bloom'd,
And the great star early droop'd in the western sky in the night,
I mourn'd, and yet shall mourn with ever-returning spring.

Ever-returning spring, trinity sure to me you bring,
Lilac blooming perennial and drooping star in the west,
And thought of him I love.

II

O powerful western fallen star!
O shades of night—O moody, tearful night!
O great star disappear'd—O the black murk that hides the star!
O cruel hands that hold me powerless—O helpless soul of me!
O harsh surrounding cloud that will not free my soul.

III

In the dooryard fronting an old farm-house near the white-wash'd palings,
Stands the lilac-bush tall-growing with heart-shaped leaves of rich green,
With many a pointed blossom rising delicate, with the perfume strong I love,
With every leaf a miracle—and from this bush in the dooryard,
With delicate-color'd blossoms and heart-shaped leaves of rich green,
A sprig with its flower I break.

IV

In the swamp in secluded recesses,
A shy and hidden bird is warbling a song.
Solitary the thrush,
The hermit withdrawn to himself, avoiding the settlements,
Sings by himself a song.

Song of the bleeding throat,
Death's outlet song of life, (for well dear brother I know,
If thou wast not granted to sing thou would'st surely die.)

V

Over the breast of the spring, the land, amid cities,
Amid lanes and through old woods, where lately the violets peep'd from the ground, spotting the gray débris,
Amid the grass in the fields each side of the lanes passing the endless grass,
Passing the yellow-spear'd wheat, every grain from its shroud in the dark-brown fields uprisen,
Passing the apple-tree blows of white and pink in the orchards,
Carrying a corpse to where it shall rest in the grave,
Night and day journeys a coffin.

VI

Coffin that passes through lanes and streets,
Through day and night with the great cloud darkening the land,
With the pomp of the inloop'd flags with the cities draped in black,
With the show of the States themselves as of crape-veil'd women standing,

With processions long and winding and the flambeaus of the night,
With the countless torches lit, with the silent sea of faces and the unbared heads
With the waiting depot, the arriving coffin, and the somber faces,
With dirges through the night, with the thousand voices rising strong and solemn,
With all the mournful voices of the dirges pour'd around the coffin,
The dim-lit churches and the shuddering organs—where amid these you journey,
With the tolling tolling bells' perpetual clang,
Here, coffin that slowly passes,
I give you my sprig of lilac.

VII

(Nor for you, for one alone,
Blossoms and branches green to coffins all I bring,
For fresh as the morning, thus would I chant a song for you O sane and sacred death.

All over bouquets of roses,
O death, I cover you over with roses and early lilies,
But mostly and now the lilac that blooms the first,
Copious I break, I break the sprigs from the bushes,
With loaded arms I come, pouring for you,
For you and the coffins all of you O death.)

VIII

O western orb sailing the heaven,
Now I know what you must have meant as a month since I walk'd,
As I walk'd in silence the transparent shadowy night,
As I saw you had something to tell as you bent to me night after night,
As you droop'd from the sky low down as if to my side, (while the other stars all look'd on,)
As we wander'd together the solemn night, (for something I know not what kept me from sleep,)
As the night advanced, and I saw on the rim of the west how full you were of woe,
As I stood on the rising ground in the breeze in the cool transparent night,

As I watch'd where you pass'd and was lost in the netherward black of the night,
As my soul in its trouble dissatisfied sank, as where you sad orb,
Concluded, dropt in the night, and was gone.

IX

Sing on there in the swamp,
O singer bashful and tender, I hear your notes, I hear your call,
I hear, I come presently, I understand you,
But a moment I linger, for the lustrous star has detain'd me,
The star my departing comrade holds and detains me.

X

O how shall I warble myself for the dead one there I loved?
And how shall I deck my song for the large sweet soul that has gone?
And what shall my perfume be for the grave of him I love?

Sea-winds blown from east and west,
Blown from the Eastern sea and blown from the Western sea, till there on the prairies meeting,
These and with these and the breath of my chant,
I'll perfume the grave of him I love.

XI

O what shall I hang on the chamber walls?
And what shall the pictures be that I hang on the walls,
To adorn the burial-house of him I love?

Pictures of growing spring and farms and homes,
With the Fourth-month eve at sundown, and the gray smoke lucid and bright,
With floods of the yellow gold of the gorgeous, indolent, sinking sun, burning, expanding the air,
With the fresh sweet herbage under foot, and the pale green leaves of the trees prolific,
In the distance the flowing glaze, the breast of the river, with a wind-dapple here and there,
With ranging hills on the banks, with many a line against the sky, and shadows,

And the city at hand with dwellings so dense, and stacks of chimneys,
And all the scenes of life and the workshops, and the workmen homeward returning.

XII

Lo, body and soul—this land,
My own Manhattan with spires, and the sparkling and hurrying tides, and the ships,
The varied and ample land, the South and the North in the light, Ohio's shores and flashing Missouri,
And ever the far-spreading prairies cover'd with grass and corn.

Lo, the most excellent sun so calm and haughty,
The violet and purple morn with just-felt breezes,
The gentle soft-born measureless light,
The miracle spreading bathing all, the fulfill'd noon,
The coming eve delicious, the welcome night and the stars,
Over my cities shining all, enveloping man and land.

XIII

Sing on, sing on you gray-brown bird,
Sing from the swamps, the recesses, pour your chant from the bushes,
Limitless out of the dusk, out of the cedars and pines.

Sing on dearest brother, warble your reedy song,
Loud human song, with voice of uttermost woe.

O liquid and free and tender!
O wild and loose to my soul—O wondrous singer!
You only I hear—yet the star holds me, (but will soon depart,)
Yet the lilac with mastering odor holds me.

XIV

Now while I sat in the day and look'd forth,
In the close of the day with its light and the fields of spring, and the farmers preparing their crops,
In the large unconscious scenery of my land with its lakes and forests,
In the heavenly aërial beauty, (after the perturb'd winds and the storms,)
Under the arching heavens of the afternoon swift passing, and the voices of children and women.

The many-moving sea-tides, and I saw the ships how they sail'd,
And the summer approaching with richness, and the fields all busy with labor,
And the infinite separate houses, how they all went on, each with its meals and minutia of daily usages,
And the streets how their throbbings throbb'd, and the cities pent—lo, then and there,
Falling upon them all and among them all, enveloping me with the rest,
Appear'd the cloud, appear'd the long black trail,
And I knew death, its thought, and the sacred knowledge of death.
Then with the knowledge of death as walking one side of me,
And the thought of death close-walking the other side of me,
And I in the middle as with companions, and as holding the hands of companions,
I fled forth to the hiding receiving night that talks not,
Down to the shores of the water, the path by the swamp in the dimness,
To the solemn shadowy cedars and ghostly pines so still.

And the singer so shy to the rest receiv'd me,
The gray-brown bird I know receiv'd us comrades three,
And he sang the carol of death, and a verse for him I love.

From deep secluded recesses,
From the fragrant cedars and the ghostly pines so still,
Came the carol of the bird.

And the charm of the carol rapt me,
As I held as if by their hands my comrades in the night,
And the voice of my spirit tallied the song of the bird.

Come lovely and soothing death,
Undulate round the world, serenely arriving, arriving,
In the day, in the night, to all, to each,
Sooner or later delicate death.

Prais'd be the fathomless universe,
For life and joy, and for objects and knowledge curious,
And for love, sweet love—but praise! praise! praise!
For the sure-enwinding arms of cool-enfolding death.

Dark mother always gliding near with soft feet,
Have none chanted for thee a chant of fullest welcome?
Then I chant it for thee, I glorify thee above all,
I bring thee a song that when thou must indeed come, come unfalteringly.

Approach strong deliveress,
When it is so, when thou hast taken them I joyously sing the dead,
Lost in the loving floating ocean of thee,
Laved in the flood of thy bliss O death.
From me to thee glad serenades,
Dances for thee I propose saluting thee, adornments and feastings for thee,
And the sights of the open landscape and the high-spread sky are fitting,
And life and the fields, and the huge and thoughtful night.

The night in silence under many a star,
The ocean shore and the husky whispering wave whose voice I know,
And the soul turning to thee O vast and well-veil'd death,
And the body gratefully nestling close to thee.

Over the tree-tops I float thee a song,
Over the rising and sinking waves, over the myriad fields and the prairies wide,
Over the dense-pack'd cities all and the teeming wharves and ways,
I float this carol with joy, with joy to thee O death.

XV

To the tally of my soul,
Loud and strong kept up the gray-brown bird,
With pure deliberate notes spreading filling the night.

Loud in the pines and cedars dim,
Clear in the freshness moist and the swamp-perfume,
And I with my comrades there in the night.

While my sight that was bound in my eyes unclosed,
As to long panoramas of visions.

And I saw askant the armies,
I saw as in noiseless dreams hundreds of battle-flags,

Borne through the smoke of the battles and pierc'd with missiles I saw them,
And carried hither and yon through the smoke, and torn and bloody,
And at last but a few shreds left on the staffs, (and all in silence,)
And the staffs all splinter'd and broken.

I saw battle-corpses, myriads of them,
And the white skeletons of young men, I saw them,
I saw the débris and débris of all the slain soldiers of the war,
But I saw they were not as was thought,
They themselves were fully at rest, they suffer'd not,
The living remain'd and suffer'd, the mother suffer'd,
And the wife and the child and the musing comrade suffer'd,
And the armies that remain'd suffer'd.

XVI

Passing the visions, passing the night,
Passing, unloosing the hold of my comrades' hands,
Passing the song of the hermit bird and the tallying song of my soul,
Victorious song, death's outlet song, yet varying ever-altering song,
As low and wailing, yet clear the notes, rising and falling, flooding the night,
Sadly sinking and fainting, as warning and warning, and yet again bursting with joy,
Covering the earth and filling the spread of the heaven,
As that powerful psalm in the night I heard from recesses,
Passing, I leave thee lilac with heart-shaped leaves,
I leave thee there in the door-yard, blooming, returning with spring.

I cease from my song for thee,
From my gaze on thee in the west, fronting the west, communing with thee,
O comrade lustrous with silver face in the night.

Yet each to keep and all, retrievements out of the night,
The song, the wondrous chant of the gray-brown bird,
And the tallying chant, the echo arous'd in my soul,
With the lustrous and drooping star with the countenance full of woe,
With the holders holding my hand nearing the call of the bird,
Comrades mine and I in the midst, and their memory ever to keep, for the dead I loved so well,

For the sweetest, wisest soul of all my days and lands—and this for his dear sake,
Lilac and star and bird twined with the chant of my soul,
There in the fragrant pines and the cedars dusk and dim.

O Captain! My Captain!

O CAPTAIN! my Captain! our fearful trip is done,
The ship has weather'd every rack, the prize we sought is won.
  The port is near, the bells I hear, the people all exulting,
  While follow eyes the steady keel, the vessel grim and daring;

      But O heart! heart! heart!
        O the bleeding drops of red,
      Where on the deck my Captain lies,
        Fallen cold and dead.

O Captain! my Captain! rise up and hear the bells;
Rise up—for you the flag is flung—for you the bugle trills,
  For you bouquets and ribbon'd wreaths—for you the shores a-crowding,
  For you they call, the swaying mass, their eager faces turning;

      Here, Captain! dear father!
        This arm beneath your head!
      It is some dream that on the deck,
        You've fallen cold and dead.

My Captain does not answer, his lips are pale and still,
My father does not feel my arm, he has no pulse nor will,
  The ship is anchor'd safe and sound, its voyage closed and done,
  From fearful trip the victor ship comes in with object won;

      Exult, O shores! and ring, O bells!
        But I with mournful tread,
      Walk the deck my Captain lies,
        Fallen cold and dead.

JEAN INGELOW
(1820–1897)

High-tide on the Coast of Lincolnshire

[*Time, 1571.*]

THE old mayor climbed the belfry tower,
  The ringers rang by two, by three;
"Pull! if ye never pulled before;
  Good ringers, pull your best," quoth he.
"Play uppe, play uppe, O Boston bells!
Ply all your changes, all your swells!
  Play uppe *The Brides of Enderby!*"

Men say it was a "stolen tyde,"—
  The Lord that sent it, he knows all,
But in myne ears doth still abide
  The message that the bells let fall;
And there was naught of strange, beside
The flights of mews and peewits pied,
  By millions crouched on the old sea-wall.

I sat and spun within the doore;
  My thread brake off, I raised myne eyes:
The level sun, like ruddy ore,
  Lay sinking in the barren skies;
And dark against day's golden death
She moved where Lindis wandereth,—
My sonne's faire wife, Elizabeth.

"Cusha! Cusha! Cusha!" calling,
Ere the early dews were falling,
Farre away I heard her song.
"Cusha! Cusha!" all along;
Where the reedy Lindis floweth,
    Floweth, floweth,
From the meads where melick groweth,
Faintly came her milking-song.

"Cusha! Cusha! Cusha!" calling,
"For the dews will soone be falling;
Leave your meadow grasses mellow,
        Mellow, mellow!
Quit your cowslips, cowslips yellow!
Come uppe, Whitefoot! come uppe, Lightfoot!
Quit the stalks of parsley hollow,
        Hollow, hollow!
Come uppe, Jetty! rise and follow;
From the clovers lift your head!
Come uppe, Whitefoot! come uppe, Lightfoot!
Come uppe, Jetty! rise and follow,
Jetty, to the milking-shed."

If it be long—ay, long ago—
  When I beginne to think howe long,
Againe I hear the Lindis flow,
  Swift as an arrowe, sharpe and strong;
And all the aire, it seemeth mee,
Bin full of floating bells (sayth shee),
That ring the tune of *Enderby*.

Alle fresh the level pasture lay,
  And not a shadowe mote be seene,
Save where, full fyve good miles away,
  The steeple towered from out the greene.
And lo! the great bell farre and wide
Was heard in all the country side
That Saturday at eventide.

The swannerds, where their sedges are,
  Moved on in sunset's golden breath;
The shepherde lads I heard afarre,
  And my sonne's wife, Elizabeth;
Till, floating o'er the grassy sea,
Came downe that kyndly message free,
The Brides of Mavis Enderby.

Then some looked uppe into the sky,
  And all along where Lindis flows
To where the goodly vessels lie,
  And where the lordly steeple shows.
They sayde, "And why should this thing be,
What danger lowers by land or sea?
They ring the tune of *Enderby*.

"For evil news from Mablethorpe,
  Of pyrate galleys, warping down,—
For shippes ashore beyond the scorpe,
  They have not spared to wake the towne;
But while the west bin red to see,
And storms be none, and pyrates flee,
Why ring *The Brides of Enderby?*"

I looked without, and lo! my sonne
  Came riding downe with might and main;
He raised a shout as he drew on,
  Till all the welkin rang again:
"Elizabeth! Elizabeth!"
(A sweeter woman ne'er drew breath
Than my sonne's wife, Elizabeth.)

"The olde sea-wall (he cryed) is downe!
  The rising tide comes on apace;
And boats adrift in yonder towne
  Go sailing uppe the market-place!"
He shook as one that looks on death:
"God save you, mother!" straight he sayth;
"Where is my wife, Elizabeth?"

"Good sonne, where Lindis winds away
  With her two bairns I marked her long;
And ere yon bells beganne to play,
  Afar I heard her milking-song."
He looked across the grassy sea,
To right, to left, *Ho, Enderby!*
They rang *The Brides of Enderby*.

With that he cried and beat his breast:
For lo! along the river's bed
A mighty eygre reared his crest,
And uppe the Lindis raging sped.
It swept with thunderous noises loud,—
Shaped like a curling snow-white cloud,
Or like a demon in a shroud.

And rearing Lindis, backward pressed,
Shook all her trembling bankes amaine;
Then madly at the eygre's breast
Flung uppe her weltering walls again.
Then bankes came downe with ruin and rout,—
Then beaten foam flew round about,—
Then all the mighty floods were out.

So farre, so fast, the eygre drave,
The heart had hardly time to beat
Before a shallow seething wave
Sobbed in the grasses at oure feet:
The feet had hardly time to flee
Before it brake against the knee,—
And all the world was in the sea.

Upon the roofe we sate that night;
The noise of bells went sweeping by;
I marked the lofty beacon light
Stream from the church-tower, red and high,—
A lurid mark, and dread to see;
And awsome bells they were to mee,
That in the dark rang *Enderby*.

They rang the sailor lads to guide,
From roofe to roofe who fearless rowed;
And I,—my sonne was at my side,
And yet the ruddy beacon glowed;
And yet he moaned beneath his breath,
"O, come in life, or come in death!
O lost! my love, Elizabeth!"

And didst thou visit him no more?
  Thou didst, thou didst, my daughter deare?
The waters laid thee at his doore
  Ere yet the early dawn was clear:
Thy pretty bairns in fast embrace,
The lifted sun shone on thy face,
Downe drifted to thy dwelling-place.

That flow strewed wrecks about the grass,
  That ebbe swept out the flocks to sea,—
A fatal ebbe and flow, alas!
  To manye more than myne and mee;
But each will mourne his own (she sayth)
And sweeter woman ne'er drew breath
Than my sonne's wife, Elizabeth.

I shall never hear her more
By the reedy Lindis shore,
"Cusha! Cusha! Cusha!" calling,
Ere the early dews be falling;
I shall never hear her song,
"Cusha! Cusha!" all along,
Where the sunny Lindis floweth,
    Goeth, floweth,
From the meads where melick groweth,
Where the water, winding down,
Onward floweth to the town.

I shall never see her more,
Where the reeds and rushes quiver,
    Shiver, quiver,
Stand beside the sobbing river,—
Sobbing, throbbing, in its falling,
To the sandy, lonesome shore;
I shall never hear her calling,
"Leave your meadow grasses mellow,
    Mellow, mellow!
Quit your cowslips, cowslips yellow!

Come uppe, Whitefoot! come uppe, Lightfoot!
Quit your pipes of parsley hollow,
 Hollow, hollow!
Come uppe, Lightfoot! rise and follow;
 Lightfoot! Whitefoot!
From your clovers lift the head;
Come uppe, Jetty! follow, follow,
Jetty, to the milking-shed!"

THEODORE O'HARA

(1820–1867)

The Bivouac of the Dead

THE muffled drum's sad roll has beat
 The soldier's last tattoo;
No more on Life's parade shall meet
 That brave and fallen few.
On Fame's eternal camping-ground
 Their silent tents are spread,
And Glory guards, with solemn round,
 The bivouac of the dead.

No rumor of the foe's advance
 Now swells upon the wind;
No troubled thought at midnight haunts
 Of loved ones left behind;
No vision of the morrow's strife
 The warrior's dream alarms;
No braying horn nor screaming fife
 At dawn shall call to arms.

Their shivered swords are red with rust,
 Their plumèd heads are bowed;
Their haughty banner, trailed in dust,
 Is now their martial shroud.

And plenteous funeral tears have washed
The red stains from each brow,
And the proud forms, by battle gashed,
Are free from anguish now.

The neighing troop, the flashing blade,
The bugle's stirring blast,
The charge, the dreadful cannonade,
The din and shout, are past;
Nor war's wild note nor glory's peal
Shall thrill with fierce delight
Those breasts that nevermore may feel
The rapture of the fight.

Like the fierce northern hurricane
That sweeps his great plateau,
Flushed with the triumph yet to gain,
Came down the serried foe.
Who heard the thunder of the fray
Break o'er the field beneath,
Knew well the watchword of that day
Was "Victory or Death."

Long had the doubtful conflict raged
O'er all that stricken plain,
For never fiercer fight had waged
The vengeful blood of Spain;
And still the storm of battle blew,
Still swelled the gory tide;
Not long, our stout old chieftain knew,
Such odds his strength could bide.

'Twas in that hour his stern command
Called to a martyr's grave
The flower of his belovèd land,
The nation's flag to save.
By rivers of their fathers' gore
His first-born laurels grew,
And well he deemed the sons would pour
Their lives for glory too.

Full many a norther's breath has swept
O'er Angostura's plain,
And long the pitying sky has wept
Above its mouldered slain.
The raven's scream, or eagle's flight,
Or shepherd's pensive lay
Alone awakes each sullen height
That frowned o'er that dread fray.

Sons of the Dark and Bloody Ground,
Ye must not slumber there,
Where stranger steps and tongues resound
Along the heedless air.
Your own proud land's heroic soil
Shall be your fitter grave;
She claims from war his richest spoil—
The ashes of her brave.

Thus 'neath their parent turf they rest,
Far from the gory field,
Borne to a Spartan mother's breast
On many a bloody shield;
The sunshine of their native sky
Smiles sadly on them here,
And kindred eyes and hearts watch by
The heroes' sepulchre.

Rest on, embalmed and sainted dead!
Dear as the blood ye gave;
No impious footstep here shall tread
The herbage of your grave;
Nor shall your story be forgot,
While Fame her record keeps,
Or Honor points the hallowed spot
Where Valor proudly sleeps.

Yon marble minstrel's voiceless stone
In deathless song shall tell,
When many a vanished age hath flown,
The story how ye fell;

Nor wreck, nor change, nor winter's blight,
Nor Time's remorseless doom,
Shall dim one ray of glory's light
That gilds your deathless tomb.

MATTHEW ARNOLD

(1822–1888)

The Forsaken Merman

COME, dear children, let us away;
Down and away below.
Now my brothers call from the bay;
Now the great winds shorewards blow;
Now the salt tides seaward flow;
Now the wild white horses play,
Champ and chafe and toss in the spray.
Children dear, let us away.
This way, this way.

Call her once before you go.
Call once yet,
In a voice that she will know:
"Margaret! Margaret!"
Children's voices should be dear
(Call once more) to a mother's ear:
Children's voices wild with pain,
Surely she will come again.
Call her once, and come away,
This way, this way.
"Mother dear, we cannot stay!
The wild white horses foam and fret,
Margaret! Margaret!"

Come, dear children, come away down.
    Call no more.
One last look at the white-walled town,
And the little gray church on the windy shore,
    Then come down.
She will not come, though you call all day.
    Come away, come away.

Children dear, was it yesterday
We heard the sweet bells over the bay?
    In the caverns where we lay,
    Through the surf and through the swell,
The far-off sound of a silver bell?
Sand-strewn caverns cool and deep,
Where the winds are all asleep;
Where the spent lights quiver and gleam;
Where the salt weed sways in the stream;
Where the sea-beasts, ranged all round,
Feed in the ooze of their pasture-ground;
Where the sea-snakes coil and twine,
Dry their mail and bask in the brine;
Where great whales come sailing by,
Sail and sail, with unshut eye,
Round the world forever and aye?
    When did music come this way?
    Children dear, was it yesterday?

Children dear, was it yesterday
(Call yet once) that she went away?
Once she sat with you and me,
  On a red gold throne in the heart of the sea.
  And the youngest sat on her knee.
She combed its bright hair, and she tended it well,
When down swung the sound of the far-off bell,
She sighed, she looked up through the clear green sea,
She said, "I must go, for my kinsfolk pray
In the little gray church on the shore to-day.
'T will be Easter-time in the world,—ah me!
And I lose my poor soul, Merman, here with thee."

I said: "Go up, dear heart, through the waves:
Say thy prayer, and come back to the kind sea-caves."
She smiled, she went up through the surf in the bay,
Children dear, was it yesterday?

Children dear, were we long alone?
"The sea grows stormy, the little ones moan;
Long prayers," I said, "in the world they say."
"Come," I said, and we rose through the surf in the bay.
We went up the beach in the sandy down
Where the sea-stocks bloom, to the white-walled town,
Through the narrow paved streets, where all was still,
To the little gray church on the windy hill.
From the church came a murmur of folk at their prayers,
But we stood without in the cold blowing airs.
We climbed on the graves, on the stones worn with rains,
And we gazed up the aisle through the small leaded panes,
She sat by the pillar; we saw her clear;
"Margaret, hist! come quick, ye are here.
Dear heart," I said, "we are here alone.
The sea grows stormy, the little ones moan."
But, ah, she gave me never a look,
For her eyes were sealed to the holy book.
"Loud prays the priest; shut stands the door."
Come away, children, call no more,
Come away, come down, call no more.

Down, down, down,
Down to the depths of the sea.
She sits at her wheel in the humming town,
Singing most joyfully.
Hark what she sings: "O joy, O joy,
From the humming street, and the child with its toy,
From the priest and the bell, and the holy well,
From the wheel where I spun,
And the blessed light of the sun."
And so she sings her fill,
Singing most joyfully,
Till the shuttle falls from her hand,
And the whizzing wheel stands still.

She steals to the window, and looks at the sand,
And over the sand at the sea;
And her eyes are set in a stare;
And anon there breaks a sigh,
And anon there drops a tear,
From a sorrow-clouded eye,
And a heart sorrow-laden,
A long, long sigh,
For the cold strange eyes of a little Mermaiden,
And the gleam of her golden hair.

Come away, away, children,
Come, children, come down.
The hoarse wind blows colder,
Lights shine in the town.
She will start from her slumber
When gusts shake the door;
She will hear the winds howling,
Will hear the waves roar.
We shall see, while above us
The waves roar and whirl,
A ceiling of amber,
A pavement of pearl,—
Singing, "Here came a mortal,
But faithless was she,
And alone dwell forever
The kings of the sea."

But, children, at midnight,
When soft the winds blow,
When clear falls the moonlight,
When spring-tides are low;
When sweet airs come seaward
From heaths starred with broom;
And high rocks throw mildly
On the blanched sands a gloom:
Up the still, glistening beaches,
Up the creeks we will hie;
Over banks of bright seaweed
The ebb-tide leaves dry.

We will gaze from the sand-hills,
At the white sleeping town;
At the church on the hillside—
And then come back, down.
Singing, "There dwells a loved one,
But cruel is she:
She left lonely forever
The kings of the sea."

Shakespeare

OTHERS abide our question. Thou art free.
We ask and ask—Thou smilest and art still,
Out-topping knowledge. For the loftiest hill,
Who to the stars uncrowns his majesty.

Planting his steadfast footsteps in the sea,
Making the heaven of heavens his dwelling-place,
Spares but the cloudy border of his base
To the foiled searching of mortality;

And thou, who didst the stars and sunbeams know,
Self-schooled, self-scanned, self-honored, self-secure,
Didst tread on earth unguessed at.—Better so!

All pains the immortal spirit must endure,
All weakness which impairs, all griefs which bow,
Find their sole speech in that victorious brow.

Requiescat

STREW on her roses, roses,
   And never a spray of yew!
In quiet she reposes;
   Ah! would that I did too.

Her mirth the world required;
  She bathed it in smiles of glee.
But her heart was tired, tired,
  And now they let her be.

Her life was turning, turning,
  In mazes of heat and sound;
But for peace her soul was yearning,
  And now peace laps her round.

Her cabined, ample spirit,
  It fluttered and failed for breath;
To-night it doth inherit
  The vasty hall of death.

Philomela

HARK! ah, the Nightingale!
The tawny-throated!
Hark! from that moonlit cedar what a burst!
What triumph! hark—what pain!

O wanderer from a Grecian shore,
Still, after many years, in distant lands,
Still nourishing in thy bewildered brain
That wild, unquenched, deep-sunken, old-world pain—
  Say, will it never heal?
And can this fragrant lawn
With its cool trees, and night,
And the sweet, tranquil Thames,
And moonshine, and the dew,
To thy racked heart and brain
  Afford no balm?

Dost thou to-night behold
Here, through the moonlight on this English grass,
The unfriendly palace in the Thracian wild?
  Dost thou again peruse

With hot cheeks and seared eyes
The too clear web, and thy dumb Sister's shame?
  Dost thou once more assay
Thy flight, and feel come over thee,
Poor Fugitive, the feathery change
Once more, and once more seem to make resound
With love and hate, triumph and agony,
Lone Daulis, and the high Cephissian vale?
  Listen, Eugenia—
How thick the bursts come crowding through the leaves!
  Again—thou hearest!
Eternal Passion!
Eternal Pain!

Dover Beach

THE sea is calm to-night.
The tide is full, the moon lies fair
Upon the straits:—on the French coast the light
Gleams and is gone; the cliffs of England stand,
Glimmering and vast, out in the tranquil bay.
Come to the window, sweet is the night air!
Only, from the long line of spray
Where the sea meets the moon-blanched land,
Listen! you hear the grating roar
Of pebbles which the waves draw back, and fling,
At their return, up the high strand,
Begin, and cease, and then again begin,
With tremulous cadence slow, and bring
The eternal note of sadness in.

Sophocles long ago
Heard it on the Ægæan, and it brought
Into his mind the turbid ebb and flow
Of human misery; we
Find also in the sound a thought,
Hearing it by this distant northern sea.

The Sea of Faith
Was once, too, at the full, and round earth's shore
Lay like the folds of a bright girdle furled.
But now I only hear
Its melancholy, long, withdrawing roar,
Retreating, to the breath
Of the night wind, down the vast edges near
And naked shingles of the world.
Ah, love, let us be true
To one another! for the world, which seems
To lie before us like a land of dreams,
So various, so beautiful, so new,
Hath really neither joy, nor love, nor light,
Nor certitude, nor peace, nor help for pain;
And we are here as on a darkling plain
Swept with confused alarms of struggle and flight
Where ignorant armies clash by night.

WILLIAM (JOHNSON) CORY
(1823–1892)

Heraclitus

THEY told me, Heraclitus, they told me you were dead,
They brought me bitter news to hear and bitter tears to shed.
I wept as I remember'd how often you and I
Had tired the sun with talking and sent him down the sky.

And now that thou art lying, my dear old Carian guest,
A handful of gray ashes, long, long ago at rest,
Still are thy pleasant voices, thy nightingales, awake;
For Death, he taketh all away, but them he cannot take.

COVENTRY PATMORE

(1823–1896)

Departure

IT WAS not like your great and gracious ways!
Do you, that have nought other to lament,
Never, my Love, repent
Of how, that July afternoon,
You went,
With sudden, unintelligible phrase,
And frighten'd eye,
Upon your journey of so many days,
Without a single kiss, or a good-bye?
I knew, indeed, that you were parting soon;
And so we sate, within the low sun's rays,
You whispering to me, for your voice was weak,
Your harrowing praise.
Well, it was well,
To hear you such things speak,
And I could tell
What made your eyes a glowing gloom of love,
As a warm South-wind sombres a March grove.
And it was like your great and gracious ways
To turn your talk on daily things, my Dear,
Lifting the luminous, pathetic lash
To let the laughter flash,
Whilst I drew near,
Because you spoke so low that I could scarcely hear.
But all at once to leave me at the last,
More at the wonder than the loss aghast,
With huddled, unintelligible phrase,
And frighten'd eye,
And go your journey of all days
With not one kiss, or a good-bye,
And the only loveless look the look with which you pass'd:
'Twas all unlike your great and gracious ways.

WILLIAM ALLINGHAM
(1824–1889)

The Fairy Folk

UP THE airy mountain,
  Down the rushy glen
We daren't go a-hunting,
  For fear of little men;
Wee folk, good folk,
  Trooping all together;
Green jacket, red cap,
  And white owl's feather.

Down along the rocky shore
  Some make their home,
They live on crispy pancakes
  Of yellow tide-foam;
Some in the reeds
  Of the black mountain-lake,
With frogs for their watch-dogs,
  All night awake.

High on the hill-top
  The old King sits;
He is now so old and gray
  He's nigh lost his wits.
With a bridge of white mist
  Columbkill he crosses,
On his stately journeys
  From Slieveleague to Rosses;
Or going up with music,
  On cold starry nights,
To sup with the Queen
  Of the gay Northern Lights.

They stole little Bridget
  For seven years long;
When she came down again

Her friends were all gone.
They took her lightly back,
Between the night and morrow;
They thought that she was fast asleep,
But she was dead with sorrow.
They have kept her ever since
Deep within the lakes,
On a bed of flag leaves,
Watching till she wakes.

By the craggy hillside,
Through the mosses bare,
They have planted thorn-trees
For pleasure here and there.
Is any man so daring
As dig one up in spite?
He shall find the thornies set
In his bed at night.

Up the airy mountain,
Down the rushy glen,
We daren't go a-hunting
For fear of little men;
Wee folk, good folk,
Trooping all together;
Green jacket, red cap,
And white owl's feather.

DINAH MARIA MULOCK CRAIK

(1826–1887)

Douglas, Douglas, Tender and True

COULD ye come back to me, Douglas, Douglas,
In the old likeness that I knew,
I would be so faithful, so loving, Douglas,
Douglas, Douglas, tender and true.

Never a scornful word should grieve ye,
  I'd smile on ye sweet as the angels do;—
Sweet as your smile on me shone ever,
  Douglas, Douglas, tender and true.

O, to call back the days that are not!
  My eyes were blinded, your words were few:
Do you know the truth now up in heaven,
  Douglas, Douglas, tender and true?

I never was worthy of you, Douglas;
  Not half worthy the like of you:
Now all men beside seem to me like shadows—
  I love *you,* Douglas, tender and true.

Stretch out your hand to me, Douglas, Douglas,
  Drop forgiveness from heaven like dew;
As I lay my heart on your dead heart, Douglas,
  Douglas, Douglas, tender and true.

DANTE GABRIEL ROSSETTI

(1828–1882)

The Blessed Damozel

THE blessed damozel leaned out
  From the golden bar of Heaven;
Her eyes were deeper than the depth
  Of waters stilled at even;
She had three lilies in her hand,
  And the stars in her hair were seven.

Her robe, ungirt from clasp to hem,
  No wrought flowers did adorn,
But a white rose of Mary's gift,
  For service meetly worn;
Her hair that lay along her back
  Was yellow like ripe corn.

Herseemed she scarce had been a day
  One of God's choristers;
The wonder was not yet quite gone
  From that still look of hers;
Albeit, to them she left, her day
  Had counted as ten years.

(To one, it is ten years of years.
  . . . Yet now, and in this place,
Surely she leaned o'er me—her hair
  Fell all about my face. . . .
Nothing: the autumn fall of leaves.
  The whole year sets apace.)

It was the rampart of God's house
  That she was standing on;
By God built over the sheer depth
  The which is Space begun;
So high, that looking downward thence
  She scarce could see the sun.

It lies in Heaven, across the flood
  Of ether, as a bridge.
Beneath, the tides of day and night
  With flame and darkness ridge
The void, as low as where this earth
  Spins like a fretful midge.

Around her, lovers, newly met
  'Mid deathless love's acclaims,
Spoke evermore among themselves
  Their heart-remembered names;
And the souls mounting up to God
  Went by her like thin flames.

And still she bowed herself and stooped
  Out of the circling charm;
Until her bosom must have made
  The bar she leaned on warm,
And the lilies lay as if asleep
  Along her bended arm.

From the fixed place of Heaven she saw
  Time like a pulse shake fierce
Through all the world. Her gaze still strove
  Within the gulf to pierce
Its path; and now she spoke as when
  The stars sang in their spheres.

The sun was gone now; the curled moon
  Was like a little feather
Fluttering far down the gulf; and now
  She spoke through the still weather.
Her voice was like the voice the stars
  Had when they sang together.

(Ah sweet! Even now, in that bird's song,
  Strove not her accents there,
Fain to be hearkened? When those bells
  Possessed the mid-day air,
Strove not her steps to reach my side
  Down all the echoing stair?)

"I wish that he were come to me,
  For he will come," she said.
"Have I not prayed in Heaven?—on earth,
  Lord, Lord, has he not pray'd?
Are not two prayers a perfect strength?
  And shall I feel afraid?

"When round his head the aureole clings,
  And he is clothed in white,
I'll take his hand and go with him
  To the deep wells of light;
As unto a stream we will step down,
  And bathe there in God's sight.

"We two will stand beside that shrine,
  Occult, withheld, untrod,
Whose lamps are stirred continually
  With prayer sent up to God;
And see our old prayers, granted, melt
  Each like a little cloud.

"We two will lie i' the shadow of
  That living mystic tree
Within whose secret growth the Dove
  Is sometimes felt to be,
While every leaf that His plumes touch
  Saith His Name audibly.

"And I myself will teach to him,
  I myself, lying so,
The songs I sing here; which his voice
  Shall pause in, hushed and slow,
And find some knowledge at each pause,
  Or some new thing to know."

(Alas! We two, we two, thou say'st!
  Yea, one wast thou with me
That once of old. But shall God lift
  To endless unity
The soul whose likeness with thy soul
  Was but its love for thee?)

"We two," she said, "will seek the groves
  Where the lady Mary is,
With her five handmaidens, whose names
  Are five sweet symphonies,
Cecily, Gertrude, Magdalen,
  Margaret and Rosalys.

"Circlewise sit they, with bound locks
  And foreheads garlanded;
Into the fine cloth white like flame
  Weaving the golden thread,
To fashion the birth-robes for them
  Who are just born, being dead.

"He shall fear, haply, and be dumb:
  Then will I lay my cheek
To his, and tell about our love,
  Not once abashed or weak:
And the dear Mother will approve
  My pride, and let me speak.

"Herself shall bring us, hand in hand,
To Him round whom all souls
Kneel, the clear-ranged unnumbered heads
Bowed with their aureoles:
And angels meeting us shall sing
To their citherns and citoles.

"There will I ask of Christ the Lord
Thus much for him and me:—
Only to live as once on earth
With Love, only to be,
As then awhile, forever now
Together, I and he."

She gazed and listened and then said,
Less sad of speech than mild,—
"All this is when he comes." She ceased.
The light thrilled towards her, fill'd
With angels in strong level flight.
Her eyes prayed, and she smil'd.

(I saw her smile.) But soon their path
Was vague in distant spheres:
And then she cast her arms along
The golden barriers,
And laid her face between her hands,
And wept. (I heard her tears.)

Lovesight

WHEN do I see thee most, beloved one?
When in the light the spirits of mine eyes
Before thy face, their altar, solemnize
The worship of that Love through thee made known?
Or when in the dusk hours (we two alone),
Close-kissed and eloquent of still replies
Thy twilight-hidden glimmering visage lies,
And my soul only sees thy soul it's own?

O love, my love! if I no more should see
Thyself, nor on the earth the shadow of thee,
  Nor image of thine eyes in any spring,—
How then should sound upon Life's darkening slope
The ground-whirl of the perished leaves of Hope,
  The wind of Death's imperishable wing?

The Choice

I

EAT thou and drink; to-morrow thou shalt die.
  Surely the earth, that's wise being very old,
  Needs not our help. Then loose me, love, and hold
Thy sultry hair up from my face; that I
May pour for thee this yellow wine, brim-high,
  Till round the glass thy fingers glow like gold.
  We'll drown all hours: thy song, while hours are toll'd,
Shall leap, as fountains veil the changing sky.
Now kiss, and think that there are really those,
  My own high-bosomed beauty, who increase
    Vain gold, vain lore, and yet might choose our way!
    Through many days they toil; then comes a day
  They die not,—never having lived,—but cease;
And round their narrow lips the mould falls close.

II

Watch thou and fear: to-morrow thou shalt die.
  Or art thou sure thou shalt have time for death?
  Is not the day which God's word promiseth
To come man knows not when? In yonder sky,
Now while we speak, the sun speeds forth: can I
  Or thou assure him of his goal? God's breath
  Even at the moment haply quickeneth
The air to a flame; till spirits, always nigh
Though screened and hid, shall walk the daylight here.

And dost thou prate of all that man shall do?
Canst thou, who hast but plagues, presume to be
Glad in his gladness that comes after thee?
Will *his* strength slay *thy* worm in Hell? Go to:
Cover thy countenance, and watch, and fear.

III

Think thou and act; to-morrow thou shalt die.
Outstretched in the sun's warmth upon the shore,
Thou say'st: "Man's measured path is all gone o'er:
Up all his years, steeply, with strain and sigh,
Man clomb until he touched the truth; and I,
Even I, am he whom it was destined for."
How should this be? Art thou then so much more
Than they who sowed, that thou shouldst reap thereby?
Nay, come up hither. From this wave-washed mound
Unto the furthest flood-brim look with me;
Then reach on with thy thought till it be drown'd.
Miles and miles distant though the last line be,
And though thy soul sail leagues and leagues beyond,—
Still, leagues beyond those leagues, there is more sea.

Lost on Both Sides

As WHEN two men have loved a woman well,
Each hating each, through Love's and Death's deceit;
Since not for either this stark marriage-sheet
And the long pauses of this wedding-bell;
Yet o'er her grave the night and day dispel
At last their feud forlorn, with cold and heat;
Nor other than dear friends to death may fleet
The two lives left that most of her can tell:—
So separate hopes, which in a soul had wooed
The one same Peace, strove with each other long,
And Peace before their faces perished since:
So through that soul, in restless brotherhood,
They roam together now, and wind among
Its bye-streets, knocking at the dusty inns.

A Superscription

Look in my face; my name is Might-have-been;
I am also called No-more, Too-late, Farewell;
Unto thine ear I hold the dead-sea shell
Cast up thy Life's foam-fretted feet between;
Unto thine eyes the glass where that is seen
Which had Life's form and Love's, but by my spell
Is now a shaken shadow intolerable,
Of ultimate things unuttered the frail screen.
Mark me, how still I am! But should there dart
One moment through my soul the soft surprise
Of that winged Peace which lulls the breath of sighs,—
Then shalt thou see me smile, and turn apart
Thy visage to mine ambush at thy heart
Sleepless with cold commemorative eyes.

The Woodspurge

The wind flapped loose, the wind was still,
Shaken out dead from tree and hill:
I had walked on at the wind's will,—
I sat now, for the wind was still.

Between my knees my forehead was,—
My lips, drawn in, said not Alas!
My hair was over in the grass,
My naked ears heard the day pass.

My eyes, wide open, had the run
Of some ten weeds to fix upon;
Among those few, out of the sun,
The woodspurge flowered, three cups in one.

From perfect grief there need not be
Wisdom or even memory:
One thing then learnt remains to me,—
The woodspurge has a cup of three.

GEORGE MEREDITH

(1828–1909)

From "Love in the Valley"

UNDER yonder beech-tree single on the green-sward,
Couched with her arms behind her golden head,
Knees and tresses folded to slip and ripple idly,
Lies my young love sleeping in the shade.
Had I the heart to slide an arm beneath her,
Press her parting lips as her waist I gather slow,
Waking in amazement she could not but embrace me:
Then would she hold me and never let me go?

Shy as the squirrel and wayward as the swallow,
Swift as the swallow along the river's light
Circleting the surface to meet his mirrored winglets,
Fleeter she seems in her stay than in her flight.
Shy as the squirrel that leaps among the pine-tops,
Wayward as the swallow overhead at set of sun,
She whom I love is hard to catch and conquer,
Hard, but O the glory of the winning were she won!

When her mother tends her before the laughing mirror,
Tying up her laces, looping up her hair,
Often she thinks, were this wild thing wedded,
More love should I have, and much less care.
When her mother tends her before the lighted mirror,
Loosening her laces, combing down her curls,
Often she thinks, were this wild thing wedded,
I should miss but one for many boys and girls.

HENRY TIMROD
(1829–1867)

Spring in Carolina

SPRING, with that nameless pathos in the air
Which dwells with all things fair,
Spring, with her golden suns and silver rain,
Is with us once again.

Out in the lonely woods the jasmine burns
Its fragrant lamps, and turns
Into a royal court with green festoons
The banks of dark lagoons.

In the deep heart of every forest tree
The blood is all aglee,
And there's a look about the leafless bowers
As if they dreamed of flowers.

Yet still on every side we trace the hand
Of Winter in the land,
Save where the maple reddens on the lawn,
Flushed by the season's dawn;

Or where, like those strange semblances we find
That age to childhood bind,
The elm puts on, as if in Nature's scorn,
The brown of autumn corn.

As yet the turf is dark, although you know
That, not a span below,
A thousand germs are groping through the gloom,
And soon will burst their tomb.

In gardens you may note amid the dearth,
The crocus breaking earth;
And near the snowdrop's tender white and green,
The violet in its screen.

But many gleams and shadows need must pass
Along the budding grass,
And weeks go by, before the enamored South
Shall kiss the rose's mouth.

Still there's a sense of blossoms yet unborn
In the sweet airs of morn;
One almost looks to see the very street
Grow purple at his feet.

At times a fragrant breeze comes floating by,
And brings, you know not why,
A feeling as when eager crowds await
Before a palace gate

Some wondrous pageant; and you scarce would start,
If from a beech's heart,
A blue-eyed Dryad, stepping forth, should say,
"Behold me! I am May!"

Ode

SUNG ON THE OCCASION OF DECORATING THE GRAVES OF THE CONFEDERATE DEAD, AT MAGNOLIA CEMETERY, CHARLESTON, S. C.

Sleep sweetly in your humble graves,—
  Sleep, martyrs of a fallen cause!
Though yet no marble column craves
  The pilgrim here to pause,

In seeds of laurel in the earth
  The blossom of your fame is blown,
And somewhere, waiting for its birth,
  The shaft is in the stone!

Meanwhile, behalf the tardy years
  Which keep in trust your storied tombs,
Behold! your sisters bring their tears,
  And these memorial blooms.

Small tributes! but your shades will smile
More proudly on these wreaths to-day,
Than when some cannon-moulded pile
Shall overlook this bay.

Stoop, angels, hither from the skies!
There is no holier spot of ground
Than where defeated valor lies,
By mourning beauty crowned!

THOMAS EDWARD BROWN

(1830–1897)

My Garden

A GARDEN is a lovesome thing, God wot!
Rose plot,
Fringed pool,
Ferned grot—
The veriest school
Of peace; and yet the fool
Contends that God is not—
Not God! in gardens! when the eve is cool?
Nay, but I have a sign;
'Tis very sure God walks in mine.

EMILY DICKINSON

(1830–1886)

The Soul Selects Her Own Society

THE soul selects her own society,
Then shuts the door;
On her divine majority
Obtrude no more.

Unmoved, she notes the chariot's pausing
At her low gate;
Unmoved, an emperor is kneeling
Upon her mat.

I've known her from an ample nation
Choose one;
Then close the valves of her attention
Like stone.

I'm Nobody! Who Are You?

I'M NOBODY! Who are you?
Are you nobody, too?
Then there's a pair of us—don't tell!
They'd banish us, you know.

How dreary to be somebody!
How public, like a frog
To tell your name the livelong day
To an admiring bog!

Chartless

I NEVER saw a moor,
I never saw the sea;
Yet know I how the heather looks,
And what a wave must be.

I never spoke with God,
Nor visited in heaven;
Yet certain am I of the spot
As if the chart were given.

CHRISTINA GEORGINA ROSSETTI

(1830–1894)

Song

WHEN I am dead, my dearest,
   Sing no sad songs for me;
Plant thou no roses at my head,
   Nor shady cypress-tree:
Be the green grass above me
   With showers and dewdrops wet;
And if thou wilt, remember,
   And if thou wilt, forget.

I shall not see the shadows,
   I shall not feel the rain;
I shall not hear the nightingale
   Sing on, as if in pain:
And dreaming through the twilight
   That doth not rise nor set,
Haply I may remember,
   And haply may forget.

Remember

REMEMBER me when I am gone away,
   Gone far away into the silent land;
   When you can no more hold me by the hand,
Nor I half turn to go, yet turning stay.
Remember me when no more, day by day,
   You tell me of our future that you planned:
   Only remember me; you understand
It will be late to counsel then or pray.
Yet if you should forget me for a while
   And afterwards remember, do not grieve:

For if the darkness and corruption leave
A vestige of the thoughts that once I had,
Better by far you should forget and smile
Than that you should remember and be sad.

Dream-Love

YOUNG Love lies sleeping
In May-time of the year,
Among the lilies,
Lapped in the tender light:
White lambs come grazing,
White doves come building there:
And round about him
The May-bushes are white.

Soft moss the pillow
For oh, a softer cheek;
Broad leaves cast shadow
Upon the heavy eyes:
There wind and waters
Grow lulled and scarcely speak;
There twilight lingers
The longest in the skies.

Young Love lies dreaming;
But who shall tell the dream?
A perfect sunlight
On rustling forest tips;
Or perfect moonlight
Upon a rippling stream;
Or perfect silence,
Or song of cherished lips.

Burn odours round him
To fill the drowsy air;
Weave silent dances
Around him to and fro;

For oh, in waking
  The sights are not so fair,
And song and silence
  Are not like these below.

Young Love lies dreaming
  Till summer days are gone,—
Dreaming and drowsing
  Away to perfect sleep:
He sees the beauty
  Sun hath not looked upon,
And tastes the fountain
  Unutterably deep.

Him perfect music
  Doth hush unto his rest,
And through the pauses
  The perfect silence calms:
Oh, poor the voices
  Of earth from east to west,
And poor earth's stillness
  Between her stately palms.

Young Love lies drowsing
  Away to poppied death;
Cool shadows deepen
  Across the sleeping face:
So fails the summer
  With warm, delicious breath;
And what hath autumn
  To give us in its place?

Draw close the curtains
  Of branched evergreen;
Change cannot touch them
  With fading fingers sere:
Here first the violets
  Perhaps will bud unseen,
And a dove, may be,
  Return to nestle here.

A Birthday

MY HEART is like a singing bird
  Whose nest is in a watered shoot;
My heart is like an apple-tree
  Whose boughs are bent with thick-set fruit;
My heart is like a rainbow shell
  That paddles in a halcyon sea;
My heart is gladder than all these
  Because my love is come to me.

Raise me a dais of silk and down;
  Hang it with vair and purple dyes;
Carve it in doves and pomegranates,
  And peacocks with a hundred eyes;
Work it in gold and silver grapes,
  In leaves and silver fleurs-de-lys;
Because the birthday of my life
  Is come, my love is come to me.

Up-Hill

DOES the road wind up-hill all the way?
  Yes, to the very end.
Will the day's journey take the whole long day?
  From morn to night, my friend.

But is there for the night a resting-place?
  A roof for when the slow dark hours begin.
May not the darkness hide it from my face?
  You cannot miss that inn.

Shall I meet other wayfarers at night?
  Those who have gone before.
Then must I knock, or call when just in sight?
  They will not keep you standing at that door.

Shall I find comfort, travel-sore and weak?
  Of labour you shall find the sum.
Will there be beds for me and all who seek?
  Yea, beds for all who come.

Twice

I TOOK my heart in my hand
  (O my love, O my love),
I said: Let me fall or stand,
  Let me live or die,
But this once hear me speak—
  (O my love, O my love)—
Yet a woman's words are weak;
  You should speak, not I.

You took my heart in your hand
  With a friendly smile,
With a critical eye you scanned,
  Then set it down,
And said: It is still unripe,
  Better wait awhile;
Wait while the skylarks pipe,
  Till the corn grows brown.

As you set it down it broke—
  Broke, but I did not wince;
I smiled at the speech you spoke,
  At your judgment that I heard:
But I have not often smiled
  Since then, nor questioned since,
Nor cared for corn-flowers wild,
  Nor sung with the singing bird.

I take my heart in my hand,
  O my God, O my God,
My broken heart in my hand:
  Thou hast seen, judge Thou.

My hope was written on sand,
  O my God, O my God:
Now let Thy judgment stand—
  Yea, judge me now.

This contemned of a man,
  This marred one heedless day,
This heart take Thou to scan
  Both within and without:
Refine with fire its gold,
  Purge Thou its dross away—
Yea, hold it in Thy hold,
  Whence none can pluck it out.

I take my heart in my hand—
  I shall not die, but live—
Before Thy face I stand;
  I, for Thou callest such:
All that I have I bring,
  All that I am I give,
Smile Thou and I shall sing,
  But shall not question much.

PAUL HAMILTON HAYNE

(1831–1886)

In Harbor

I THINK it is over, over,
  I think it is over at last;
Voices of foeman and lover,
  The sweet and the bitter, have passed:
Life, like a tempest of ocean,
Hath outblown its ultimate blast:
There's but a faint sobbing seaward
While the calm of the tide deepens leeward,
And behold! like the welcoming quiver
Of heart-pulses throbbed through the river,
  Those lights in the harbor at last,
  The heavenly harbor at last!

I feel it is over! over!
  For the winds and the waters surcease;
Ah, few were the days of the rover
  That smiled in the beauty of peace!
And distant and dim was the omen
That hinted redress or release:—
From the ravage of life, and its riot,
What marvel I yearn for the quiet
  Which bides in the harbor at last,—
For the lights, with their welcoming quiver,
That throb through the sanctified river,
  Which girdle the harbor at last,
  This heavenly harbor at last?

I know it is over, over,
  I know it is over at last!
Down sail! the sheathed anchor uncover,
  For the stress of the voyage has passed:
Life, like a tempest of ocean,
  Hath outbreathed its ultimate blast:
There's but a faint sobbing to seaward,
While the calm of the tide deepens leeward;
And behold! like the welcoming quiver
Of heart-pulses throbbed through the river,
  Those lights in the harbor at last,
  The heavenly harbor at last!

LEWIS CARROLL (CHARLES LUTWIDGE DODGSON)

(1832–1898)

Jabberwocky

'Twas brillig, and the slithy toves
  Did gyre and gimble in the wabe;
All mimsy were the borogoves,
  And the mome raths outgrabe.

"Beware the Jabberwock, my son!
  The jaws that bite, the claws that catch!
Beware the Jubjub bird, and shun
  The frumious Bandersnatch!"

He took his vorpal sword in hand:
  Long time the manxome foe he sought,—
So rested he by the Tumtum tree,
  And stood awhile in thought.

And as in uffish thought he stood,
  The Jabberwock, with eyes of flame,
Came whiffling through the tulgey wood,
  And burbled as it came!

One, two! One, two! And through and through
  The vorpal blade went snicker-snack!
He left it dead, and with his head
  He went galumphing back.

"And hast thou slain the Jabberwock?
  Come to my arms, my beamish boy!
O frabjous day! Callooh! Callay!"
  He chortled in his joy.

'Twas brillig, and the slithy toves
  Did gyre and gimble in the wabe;
All mimsy were the borogoves,
  And the mome raths outgrabe.

The Gardener's Song

He thought he saw an Elephant
  That practised on a fife:
He looked again, and found it was
  A letter from his wife.
"At length I realize," he said,
  "The bitterness of life!"

He thought he saw a Buffalo
  Upon the chimney-piece:
He looked again, and found it was
  His Sister's Husband's Niece.
"Unless you leave this house," he said,
  "I'll send for the Police!"

He thought he saw a Rattlesnake
  That questioned him in Greek:
He looked again, and found it was
  The Middle of Next Week.
"The one thing I regret," he said,
  "Is that it cannot speak!"

He thought he saw a Banker's Clerk
  Descending from the 'bus:
He looked again, and found it was
  A Hippopotamus.
"If this should stay to dine," he said,
  "There won't be much for us!"

He thought he saw a Kangaroo
  That worked a coffee-mill:
He looked again, and found it was
  A Vegetable -Pill.
"Were I to swallow this," he said,
  "I should be very ill!"

He thought he saw a Coach-and-Four
  That stood beside his bed:
He looked again, and found it was
  A Bear without a Head.
"Poor thing," he said, "poor silly thing!
  It's waiting to be fed!"

He thought he saw an Albatross
  That fluttered round the lamp:
He looked again, and found it was
  A penny-Postage-Stamp.
"You'd best be getting home," he said:
  "The nights are very damp!"

He thought he saw a Garden Door
  That opened with a key:
He looked again, and found it was
  A Double-Rule-of-Three:
"And all its mystery," he said,
  "Is clear as day to me."

The Walrus and the Carpenter

THE sun was shining on the sea,
  Shining with all his might:
He did his very best to make
  The billows smooth and bright—
And this was odd, because it was
  The middle of the night.

The moon was shining sulkily,
  Because she thought the sun
Had got no business to be there
  After the day was done—
"It's very rude of him," she said,
  "To come and spoil the fun!"

The sea was wet as wet could be,
  The sands were dry as dry.
You could not see a cloud, because
  No cloud was in the sky:
No birds were flying overhead—
  There were no birds to fly.

The Walrus and the Carpenter
  Were walking close at hand:
They wept like anything to see
  Such quantities of sand:
  "If this were only cleared away,"
  They said, "it *would* be grand!"

"If seven maids with seven mops
  Swept it for half a year,
Do you suppose," the Walrus said,
  "That they could get it clear?"
"I doubt it," said the Carpenter,
  And shed a bitter tear.

"O oysters, come and walk with us!"
  The Walrus did beseech.
"A pleasant walk, a pleasant talk,
  Along the briny beach:
We cannot do with more than four,
  To give a hand to each."

The eldest Oyster looked at him,
  But never a word he said:
The eldest Oyster winked his eye,
  And shook his heavy head—
Meaning to say he did not choose
  To leave the oyster-bed.

But four young Oysters hurried up,
  All eager for the treat:
Their coats were brushed, their faces washed,
  Their shoes were clean and neat—
And this was odd, because, you know,
  They hadn't any feet.

Four other Oysters followed them,
  And yet another four;
And thick and fast they came at last,
  And more, and more, and more—
All hopping through the frothy waves,
  And scrambling to the shore.

The Walrus and the Carpenter
  Walked on a mile or so,
And then they rested on a rock
  Conveniently low:
And all the little Oysters stood
  And waited in a row.

"The time has come," the Walrus said,
  "To talk of many things:
Of shoes—and ships—and sealing wax—
  Of cabbages—and kings—
And why the sea is boiling hot—
  And whether pigs have wings."

"But wait a bit," the Oysters cried,
  "Before we have our chat;
For some of us are out of breath,
  And all of us are fat!"
"No hurry!" said the Carpenter.
  They thanked him much for that.

"A loaf of bread," the Walrus said,
  "Is what we chiefly need:
Pepper and vinegar besides
  Are very good indeed—
Now, if you're ready, Oysters dear,
  We can begin to feed."

"But not on us!" the Oysters cried,
  Turning a little blue.
"After such kindness, that would be
  A dismal thing to do!"
"The night is fine," the Walrus said.
  "Do you admire the view?

"It was so kind of you to come!
  And you are very nice!"
The Carpenter said nothing but
  "Cut us another slice.
I wish you were not quite so deaf—
  I've had to ask you twice!"

"It seems a shame," the Walrus said,
  "To play them such a trick.
After we've brought them out so far,
  And made them trot so quick!"
The Carpenter said nothing but
  "The butter's spread too thick!"

"I weep for you," the Walrus said:
  "I deeply sympathize."
With sobs and tears he sorted out
  Those of the largest size,
Holding his pocket-handkerchief
  Before his streaming eyes.

"O Oysters," said the Carpenter,
  "You've had a pleasant run!
Shall we be trotting home again?"
  But answer came there none—
And this was scarcely odd, because
  They'd eaten every one.

The Whiting and the Snail

"WILL you walk a little faster?" said a whiting to a snail,
"There's a porpoise close behind us, and he's treading on my tail,
See how eagerly the lobsters and the turtles all advance!
They are waiting on the shingle—will you come and join the dance?
  Will you, won't you, will you, won't you, will you join the dance?
  Will you, won't you, will you, won't you, won't you join the dance?

"You can really have no notion how delightful it will be
When they take us up and throw us, with the lobsters, out to sea!"
But the snail replied, "Too far, too far!" and gave a look askance—
Said he thanked the whiting kindly, but he would not join the dance.
  Would not, could not, would not, could not, would not join the dance.
  Would not, could not, would not, could not, could not join the dance.

"What matters it how far we go?" his scaly friend replied.
"There is another shore, you know, upon the other side.
The further off from England the nearer is to France—
Then turn not pale, belovèd snail, but come and join the dance.
  Will you, won't you, will you, won't you, will you join the dance?
  Will you, won't you, will you, won't you, won't you join the dance?"

Father William

(AFTER SOUTHEY)

"You are old, Father William," the young man said,
"And your hair has become very white;
And yet you incessantly stand on your head—
Do you think, at your age, it is right?"

"In my youth," Father William replied to his son,
"I feared it might injure the brain;
But, now that I'm perfectly sure I have none,
Why, I do it again and again."

"You are old," said the youth, "as I mentioned before,
And have grown most uncommonly fat;
Yet you turned a back-somersault in at the door—
Pray, what is the reason of that?"

"In my youth," said the sage, as he shook his gray locks,
"I kept all my limbs very supple
By the use of this ointment—one shilling the box—
Allow me to sell you a couple?"

"You are old," said the youth, "and your jaws are too weak
For anything tougher than suet;
Yet you finished the goose, with the bones and the beak—
Pray, how did you manage to do it?"

"In my youth," said his father, "I took to the law,
And argued each case with my wife;
And the muscular strength which it gave to my jaw,
Has lasted the rest of my life."

"You are old," said the youth, "one would hardly suppose
  That your eye was as steady as ever;
Yet you balanced an eel on the end of your nose—
  What made you so awfully clever?"

"I have answered three questions, and that is enough,"
  Said his father; "don't give yourself airs!
Do you think I can listen all day to such stuff?
  Be off, or I'll kick you downstairs."

WILLIAM MORRIS

(1834–1896)

The Nymph's Song to Hylas

I KNOW a little garden close
  Set thick with lily and red rose,
Where I would wander if I might
From dewy dawn to dewy night,
And have one with me wandering.
  And though within it no birds sing,
And though no pillared house is there,
And though the apple boughs are bare
Of fruit and blossom, would to God,
Her feet upon the green grass trod,
And I beheld them as before.
  There comes a murmur from the shore,
And in the place two fair streams are,
Drawn from the purple hills afar,
Drawn down unto the restless sea;
The hills whose flowers ne'er fed the bee,
The shore no ship has ever seen,
Still beaten by the billows green,
Whose murmur comes unceasingly
Unto the place for which I cry.
  For which I cry both day and night,
For which I let slip all delight,

That maketh me both deaf and blind,
Careless to win, unskilled to find,
And quick to lose what all men seek.
  Yet tottering as I am, and weak,
Still have I left a little breath
To seek within the jaws of death
An entrance to that happy place,
To seek the unforgotten face
Once seen, once kissed, once reft from me
Anigh the murmuring of the sea.

March

Slayer of winter, art thou here again?
O welcome, thou that bring'st the summer nigh!
The bitter wind makes not thy victory vain,
Nor will we mock thee for thy faint blue sky.
Welcome, O March! whose kindly days and dry
Make April ready for the throstle's song,
Thou first redresser of the winter's wrong!

Yea, welcome, March! and though I die ere June,
Yet for the hope of life I give thee praise,
Striving to swell the burden of the tune
That even now I hear thy brown birds raise,
Unmindful of the past or coming days;
Who sing, "O joy! a new year is begun!
What happiness to look upon the sun!"

O, what begetteth all this storm of bliss,
But Death himself, who, crying solemnly,
Even from the heart of sweet Forgetfulness,
Bids us, "Rejoice! lest pleasureless ye die.
Within a little time must ye go by.
Stretch forth your open hands, and, while ye live,
Take all the gifts that Death and Life may give."

Love Is Enough

Love is enough: though the World be a-waning,
And the woods have no voice but the voice of complaining,
Though the sky be too dark for dim eyes to discover
The gold-cups and daisies fair blooming thereunder,
Though the hills be held shadows, and the sea a dark wonder,
And this day draw a veil over all deeds pass'd over,
Yet their hands shall not tremble, their feet shall not falter;
The void shall not weary, the fear shall not alter
These lips and these eyes of the loved and the lover.

An Apology

Of heaven or Hell I have no power to sing;
I cannot ease the burden of your fears,
Or make quick-coming death a little thing,
Or bring again the pleasure of past years,
Nor for my words shall ye forget your tears,
Or hope again for aught that I can say,—
The idle singer of an empty day.

But rather when, aweary of your mirth,
From full hearts still unsatisfied ye sigh,
And, feeling kindly unto all the earth,
Grudge every minute as it passes by,
Made the more mindful that the sweet days die:
Remember me a little then, I pray,—
The idle singer of an empty day.

The heavy trouble, the bewildering care
That weighs us down who live and earn our bread,
These idle verses have no power to bear;
So let me sing of names rememberèd,
Because they, living not, can ne'er be dead,
Or long time take their memory quite away
From us poor singers of an empty day.

Dreamer of dreams, born out of my due time,
Why should I strive to set the crooked straight?
Let it suffice me that my murmuring rhyme
Beats with light wing against the ivory gate,—
Telling a tale not too importunate
To those who in the sleepy region stay,
Lulled by the singer of an empty day.

Folk say, a wizard to a northern king
At Christmas-tide such wondrous things did show,
That through one window men beheld the spring,
And through another saw the summer glow,
And through a third the fruited vines a-row,—
While still, unheard, but in its wonted way,
Piped the drear wind of that December day.

So with this Earthly Paradise it is,
If ye will read aright, and pardon me,
Who strive to build a shadowy isle of bliss
Midmost the beating of the steely sea,
Where tossed about all hearts of men must be;
Whose ravening monsters mighty men shall slay—
Not the poor singer of an empty day.

THOMAS BAILEY ALDRICH

(1836–1907)

Memory

My mind lets go a thousand things,
Like dates of wars and deaths of kings,
And yet recalls the very hour—
'Twas noon by yonder village tower,
And on the last blue noon in May—
The wind came briskly up this way,
Crisping the brook beside the road;
Then, pausing here, set down its load
Of pine-scents, and shook listlessly
Two petals from that wild-rose tree.

SIR WILLIAM SCHWENCK GILBERT

(1836–1911)

Captain Reece

Of all the ships upon the blue,
No ship contained a better crew
Than that of worthy Captain Reece,
Commanding of *The Mantelpiece.*

He was adored by all his men,
For worthy Captain Reece, R. N.,
Did all that lay within him to
Promote the comfort of his crew.

If ever they were dull or sad,
Their captain danced to them like mad,
Or told, to make the time pass by,
Droll legends of his infancy.

A feather-bed had everyman,
Warm slippers and hot-water can,
Brown Windsor from the captain's store,
A valet, too, to every four.

Did they with thirst in summer burn,
Lo, seltzogenes at every turn,
And on all very sultry days
Cream ices handed round on trays.

Then currant wine and ginger-pops
Stood handily on all the "tops;"
And also, with amusement rife,
A "Zoetrope, or Wheel of Life."

New volumes came across the sea
From Mister Mudie's libraree;
The *Times* and *Saturday Review*
Beguiled the leisure of the crew.

Kind-hearted Captain Reece, R. N.,
Was quite devoted to his men;
In point of fact, good Captain Reece
Beatified *The Mantelpiece.*

One summer eve, at half-past ten,
He said (addressing all his men):
"Come, tell me, please, what I can do
To please and gratify my crew.

"By any reasonable plan
I'll make you happy if I can;
My own convenience count as *nil:*
It is my duty, and I will."

Then up and answered William Lee
(The kindly captain's coxswain he,
A nervous, shy, low-spoken man),
He cleared his throat and thus began:

"You have a daughter, Captain Reece,
Ten female cousins and a niece,
A ma, if what I'm told is true,
Six sisters, and an aunt or two.

"Now, somehow, sir, it seems to me,
More friendly like we all should be,
If you united of 'em to
Unmarried members of the crew.

"If you'd ameliorate our life,
Let each select from them a wife;
And as for nervous me, old pal,
Give me your own enchanting gal!"

Good Captain Reece, that worthy man.
Debated on his coxswain's plan:
"I quite agree," he said, "O Bill;
It is my duty, and I will.

"My daughter, that enchanting gurl,
Has just been promised to an Earl,
And all my other famillee
To peers of various degree.

"But what are dukes and viscounts to
The happiness of all my crew?
The word I gave you I'll fulfil;
It is my duty, and I will.

"As you desire it shall befall,
I'll settle thousands on you all,
And I shall be, despite my hoard,
The only bachelor on board."

The boatswain of *The Mantelpiece,*
He blushed and spoke to Captain Reece:
"I beg your honour's leave," he said;
"If you would wish to go and wed,

"I have a widowed mother who
Would be the very thing for you—
She long has loved you from afar;
She washes for you, Captain R."

The Captain saw the dame that day—
Addressed her in his playful way—
"And did it want a wedding ring?
It was a tempting ickle sing!

"Well, well, the chaplain I will seek,
We'll all be married this day week
At yonder church upon the hill;
It is my duty, and I will!"

The sisters, cousins, aunts, and niece,
And widowed ma of Captain Reece,
Attended there as they were bid;
It was their duty, and they did.

JOHN BURROUGHS

(1837–1921)

Waiting

SERENE, I fold my hands and wait,
Nor care for wind, nor tide, nor sea;
I rave no more 'gainst time or fate,
For lo! my own shall come to me.

I stay my haste, I make delays,
For what avails this eager pace?
I stand amid the eternal ways,
And what is mine shall know my face.

Asleep, awake, by night or day,
The friends I seek are seeking me;
No wind can drive my bark astray
Nor change the tide of destiny.

What matter if I stand alone?
I wait with joy the coming years;
My heart shall reap where it has sown,
And garner up its fruit of tears.

The law of love binds every heart
And knits it to its utmost kin,
Nor can our lives flow along apart
From souls our secret souls would win.

The stars come nightly to the sky,
The tidal wave comes to the sea;
Nor time, nor space, nor deep, nor high
Can keep my own away from me.

ALGERNON CHARLES SWINBURNE
(1837–1909)

The Sea

I WILL go back to the great sweet mother—
  Mother and lover of men, the Sea.
I will go down to her, I and none other,
  Close with her, kiss her, and mix her with me;
Cling to her, strive with her, hold her fast.
O fair white mother, in days long past
Born without sister, born without brother,
  Set free my soul as thy soul is free.

O fair green-girdled mother of mine,
  Sea, that art clothed with the sun and the rain,
Thy sweet hard kisses are strong like wine,
  Thy large embraces are keen like pain.
Save me and hide me with all thy waves,
Find me one grave of thy thousand graves,
Those pure cold populous graves of thine,—
  Wrought without hand in a world without stain.

I shall sleep, and move with the moving ships,
  Change as the winds change, veer in the tide;
My lips will feast on the foam of thy lips,
  I shall rise with thy rising, with thee subside;
Sleep, and not know if she be, if she were,—
Filled full with life to the eyes and hair,
As a rose is full filled to the rose-leaf tips
  With splendid summer and perfume and pride.

This woven raiment of nights and days,
  Were it once cast off and unwound from me,
Naked and glad would I walk in thy ways,
  Alive and aware of thy waves and thee;
Clear of the whole world, hidden at home,
Clothed with the green, and crowned with the foam,
A pulse of the life of thy straits and bays,
  A vein in the heart of the streams of the Sea.

A Match

If love were what the rose is,
  And I were like the leaf,
Our lives would grow together
In sad or singing weather,
Blown fields or flowerful closes,
  Green pleasure or gray grief;
If love were what the rose is,
  And I were like the leaf.

If I were what the words are,
  And love were like the tune,
With double sound and single
Delight our lips would mingle,
With kisses glad as birds are
  That get sweet rain at noon;
If I were what the words are,
  And love were like the tune.

If you were life, my darling,
  And I, your love, were death,
We'd shine and snow together
Ere March made sweet the weather
With daffodil and starling
  And hours of fruitful breath;
If you were life, my darling,
  And I, your love, were death.

If you were thrall to sorrow,
  And I were page to joy,
We'd play for lives and seasons,
With loving looks and treasons,
And tears of night and morrow,
  And laughs of maid and boy;
If you were thrall to sorrow,
  And I were page to joy.

If you were April's lady,
  And I were lord in May,
We 'd throw with leaves for hours,
And draw for days with flowers,
Till day like night were shady,
  And night were bright like day;
If you were April's lady,
  And I were lord in May.

If you were queen of pleasure,
  And I were king of pain,
We 'd hunt down love together,
Pluck out his flying-feather,
And teach his feet a measure,
  And find his mouth a rein;
If you were queen of pleasure,
  And I were king of pain.

Itylus

Swallow, my sister, O sister swallow,
  How can thine heart be full of the spring?
    A thousand summers are over and dead.
What hast thou found in the spring to follow?
  What hast thou found in thine heart to sing?
    What wilt thou do when the summer is shed?

O swallow, sister, O fair swift swallow,
  Why wilt thou fly after spring to the south,
    The soft south whither thine heart is set?
Shall not the grief of the old time follow?
  Shall not the song thereof cleave to thy mouth?
    Hast thou forgotten ere I forget?

Sister, my sister, O fleet sweet swallow,
  Thy way is long to the sun and the south;
    But I, fulfilled of my heart's desire,
Shedding my song upon height, upon hollow,
  From tawny body and sweet small mouth
    Feed the heart of the night with fire.

I the nightingale all spring through,
O swallow, sister, O changing swallow,
All spring through till the spring be done,
Clothed with the light of the night on the dew,
Sing, while the hours and the wild birds follow,
Take flight and follow and find the sun.

Sister, my sister, O soft light swallow,
Though all things feast in the spring's guest-chamber,
How hast thou heart to be glad thereof yet?
For where thou fliest I shall not follow,
Till life forget and death remember,
Till thou remember and I forget.

Swallow, my sister, O singing swallow,
I know not how thou hast heart to sing.
Hast thou the heart? is it all past over?
Thy lord the summer is good to follow,
And fair the feet of thy lover the spring:
But what wilt thou say to the spring thy lover?

O swallow, sister, O fleeting swallows,
My heart in me is a molten ember
And over my head the waves have met.
But thou wouldst tarry or I would follow,
Could I forget or thou remember,
Couldst thou remember and I forget.

O sweet stray sister, O shifting swallow,
The heart's division divideth us.
Thy heart is light as a leaf of a tree;
But mine goes forth among sea-gulfs hollow
To the place of the slaying of Itylus,
The feast of Daulis, the Thracian sea.

O swallow, sister, O rapid swallow,
I pray thee sing not a little space.
Are not the roofs and the lintels wet?
The woven web that was plain to follow,
The small slain body, the flower-like face,
Can I remember if thou forget?

O sister, sister, thy first-begotten!
The hands that cling and the feet that follow,
The voice of the child's blood crying yet
Who hath remembered me? who hath forgotten?
Thou hast forgotten, O summer swallow.
But the world shall end when I forget.

When the Hounds of Spring Are on Winter's Traces

WHEN the hounds of spring are on winter's traces,
The mother of months in meadow or plain
Fills the shadows and windy places
With lisp of leaves and ripple of rain;
And the brown bright nightingale amorous
Is half assuaged for Itylus,
For the Thracian ships and the foreign faces,
The tongueless vigil, and all the pain.

Come with bows bent and with emptying of quivers,
Maiden most perfect, lady of light,
With a noise of winds and many rivers,
With a clamour of waters, and with might;
Bind on thy sandals, O thou most fleet,
Over the splendour and speed of thy feet;
For the faint east quickens, the wan west shivers,
Round the feet of the day and the feet of the night.

Where shall we find her, how shall we sing to her,
Fold our hands round her knees, and cling?
O that man's heart were as fire and could spring to her,
Fire, or the strength of the streams that spring!
For the stars and the winds are unto her
As raiment, as songs of the harp-player;
For the risen stars and the fallen cling to her,
And the southwest-wind and the west-wind sing.

For winter's rains and ruins are over,
   And all the season of snows and sins;
The days dividing lover and lover,
   The light that loses, the night that wins;
And time remembered is grief forgotten,
And frosts are slain and flowers begotten,
And in green underwood and cover
   Blossom by blossom the spring begins.

The full streams feed on flower of rushes,
   Ripe grasses trammel a travelling foot,
The faint fresh flame of the young year flushes
   From leaf to flower and flower to fruit;
And fruit and leaf are as gold and fire,
And the oat is heard above the lyre,
And the hoofèd heel of a satyr crushes
   The chestnut-husk at the chestnut-root.

And Pan by noon and Bacchus by night,
   Fleeter of foot than the fleet-foot kid,
Follows with dancing and fills with delight
   The Mænad and the Bassarid;
And soft as lips that laugh and hide
The laughing leaves of the trees divide,
And screen from seeing and leave in sight
   The god pursuing, the maiden hid.

The ivy falls with the Bacchanal's hair
   Over her eyebrows hiding her eyes;
The wild vine slipping down leaves bare
   Her bright breast shortening into sighs;
The wild vine slips with the weight of its leaves,
But the berried ivy catches and cleaves
To the limbs that glitter, the feet that scare,
   The wolf that follows, the fawn that flies.

Hymn to Proserpine

(After the Proclamation in Rome of the Christian Faith)

Vicisti, Galilæe

I HAVE lived long enough, having seen one thing, that love hath an end;
Goddess and maiden and queen, be near me now and befriend.
Thou art more than the day or the morrow, the seasons that laugh or that weep;
For these give joy and sorrow; but thou, Proserpina, sleep.
Sweet is the treading of wine, and sweet the feet of the dove;
But a goodlier gift is thine than foam of the grapes or love.
Yea, is not even Apollo, with hair and harpstring of gold,
A bitter God to follow, a beautiful God to behold?
I am sick of singing: the bays burn deep and chafe: I am fain
To rest a little from praise and grievous pleasure and pain.
For the Gods we know not of, who give us our daily breath,
We know they are cruel as love or life, and lovely as death.
O Gods dethroned and deceased, cast forth, wiped out in a day!
From your wrath is the world released, redeemed from your chains, men say.
New Gods are crowned in the city; their flowers have broken your rods;
They are merciful, clothed with pity, the young compassionate Gods.
But for me their new device is barren, the days are bare;
Things long passed over suffice, and men forgotten that were.
Time and the Gods are at strife; ye dwell in the midst thereof,
Draining a little life from the barren breasts of love.
I say to you, cease, take rest; yea, I say to you all, be at peace,
Till the bitter milk of her breast and the barren bosom shall cease.
Wilt thou yet take all, Galilean? but these thou shalt not take,
The laurel, the palms and the pæan, the breasts of the nymphs in the brake;
Breasts more soft than a dove's, that tremble with tenderer breath;
And all the wings of the Loves, and all the joy before death;
All the feet of the hours that sound as a single lyre,
Dropped and deep in the flowers, with strings that flicker like fire.
More than these wilt thou give, things fairer than all these things?
Nay, for a little we live, and life hath mutable wings.
A little while and we die; shall life not thrive as it may?

For no man under the sky lives twice, outliving his day.
And grief is a grievous thing, and a man hath enough of his tears:
Why should he labour, and bring fresh grief to blacken his years?
Thou hast conquered, O pale Galilean; the world has grown gray from thy breath;
We have drunken of things Lethean, and fed on the fullness of death.
Laurel is green for a season, and love is sweet for a day;
But love grows bitter with treason, and laurel outlives not May.
Sleep, shall we sleep after all? for the world is not sweet in the end;
For the old faiths loosen and fall, the new years ruin and rend.
Fate is a sea without shore, and the soul is a rock that abides;
But her ears are vexed with the roar and her face with the foam of the tides.
O lips that the live blood faints in, the leavings of racks and rods!
O ghastly glories of saints, dead limbs of gibbeted Gods!
Though all men abase them before you in spirit, and all knees bend,
I kneel not neither adore you, but standing look to the end!
All delicate days and pleasant, all spirits and sorrows are cast
Far out with the foam of the present that sweeps to the surf of the past:
Where beyond the extreme sea-wall, and between the remote sea-gates,
Waste water washes, and tall ships founder, and deep death waits:
Where, mighty with deepening sides, clad about with the seas as with wings,
And impelled of invisible tides, and fulfilled of unspeakable things,
White-eyed and poisonous-finned, shark-toothed and serpentine-curled,
Rolls, under the whitening wind of the future, the wave of the world.
The depths stand naked in sunder behind it, the storms flee away;
In the hollow before it the thunder is taken and snared as a prey;
In its sides is the north-wind bound; and its salt is of all men's tears;
With light of ruin, and sound of changes, and pulse of years:
With travail of day after day, and with trouble of hour upon hour;
And bitter as blood is the spray; and the crests are as fangs that devour:
And its vapour and storm of its steam as the sighing of spirits to be;
And its noise as the noise in a dream; and its depth as the roots of the sea:
And the height of its heads as the height of the utmost stars of the air:
And the ends of the earth at the might thereof tremble, and time is made bare.
Will ye bridle the deep sea with reins, will ye chasten the high sea with rods?
Will ye take her to chain her with chains, who is older than all ye Gods?

All ye as a wind shall go by, as a fire shall ye pass and be past;
Ye are Gods, and behold, ye shall die, and the waves be upon you at last.
In the darkness of time, in the deeps of the years, in the changes of things,
Ye shall sleep as a slain man sleeps, and the world shall forget you for kings.
Though the feet of thine high priests tread where thy lords and our forefathers trod,
Though these that were Gods are dead, and thou being dead art a God,
Though before thee the throned Cytherean be fallen, and hidden her head,
Yet thy kingdom shall pass, Galilean, thy dead shall go down to thee dead.
Of the maiden thy mother men sing as a goddess with grace clad around;
Thou art throned where another was king; where another was queen she is crowned.
Yea, once we had sight of another: but now she is queen, say these.
Not as thine, not as thine was our mother, a blossom of flowering seas,
Clothed around with the world's desire as with raiment and fair as the foam,
And fleeter than kindled fire, and a goddess and mother of Rome.
For thine came pale and a maiden, and sister to sorrow; but ours,
Her deep hair heavily laden with odour and colour of flowers,
White rose of the rose-white water, a silver splendour, a flame,
Bent down unto us that besought her, and earth grew sweet with her name.
For thine came weeping, a slave among slaves, and rejected; but she
Came flushed from the full-flushed wave, and imperial, her foot on the sea.
And the wonderful waters knew her, the winds and the viewless ways,
And the roses grew rosier, and bluer the sea-blue stream of the bays.
Ye are fallen, our lords, by what token? we wist that ye should not fall.
Ye were all so fair that are broken; and one more fair than ye all.
But I turn to her still, having seen she shall surely abide in the end;
Goddess and maiden and queen, be near me now and befriend.
O daughter of earth, of my mother, her crown and blossom of birth,
I am also, I also, thy brother; I go as I came unto earth.

In the night where thine eyes are as moons are in heaven, the night where thou art,
Where the silence is more than all tunes, where sleep overflows from the heart,
Where the poppies are sweet as the rose in our world, and the red rose is white,
And the wind falls faint as it blows with the fume of the flowers of the night,
And the murmur of spirits that sleep in the shadow of Gods from afar
Grows dim in thine ears and deep as the deep dim soul of a star,
In the sweet low light of thy face, under heavens untrod by the sun,
Let thy soul with their souls find place, and forget what is done and undone.
Thou art more than the Gods who number the days of our temporal breath;
For these give labour and slumber, but thou, Proserpina, death.
Therefore now at thy feet I abide for a season in silence. I know
I shall die as my fathers died, and sleep as they sleep; even so.
For the glass of the years is brittle wherein we gaze for a span;
A little soul for a little bears up this corpse which is man.
So long I endure, no longer; and laugh not again, neither weep.
For there is no God found stronger than death; and death is a sleep.

WILFRID SCAWEN BLUNT

(1840–1922)

With Esther

HE WHO has once been happy is for aye
  Out of destruction's reach. His fortune then
Holds nothing secret; and Eternity,
  Which is a mystery to other men,
Has like a woman given him its joy.
  Time is his conquest. Life, if it should fret,
Has paid him tribute. He can bear to die,
  He who has once been happy! When I set

The world before me and survey its range,
  Its mean ambitions, its scant fantasies,
The shreds of pleasure which for lack of change
  Men wrap around them and call happiness,
The poor delights which are the tale and sum
Of the world's courage in its martyrdom;

When I hear laughter from a tavern door,
  When I see crowds agape and in the rain
Watching on tiptoe and with stifled roar
  To see a rocket fired or a bull slain,
When misers handle gold, when orators
  Touch strong men's hearts with glory till they weep,
When cities deck their streets for barren wars
  Which have laid waste their youth, and when I keep
Calmly the count of my own life and see
  On what poor stuff my manhood's dreams were fed
Till I too learn'd what dole of vanity
  Will serve a human soul for daily bread,
—Then I remember that I once was young
And lived with Esther the world's gods among.

To Manon, on His Fortune in Loving Her

I DID not choose thee, dearest. It was Love
That made the choice, not I. Mine eyes were blind
As a rude shepherd's who to some long grove
His offering brings and cares not at what shrine
He bends his knee. The gifts alone were mine;
The rest was Love's. He took me by the hand,
And fired the sacrifice, and poured the wine,
And spoke the words I might not understand.
I was unwise in all but the dear chance
Which was my fortune, and the blind desire
Which led my foolish steps to Love's abode,
And youth's sublime unreason'd prescience
Which raised an altar and inscribed in fire
Its dedication *To the Unknown God.*

(HENRY) AUSTIN DOBSON
(1840–1921)

Urceus Exit

Triolet

I INTENDED an Ode,
And it turn'd to a Sonnet.
It began *à la mode,*
I intended an Ode;
But Rose cross'd the road
  In her latest new bonnet;
I intended an Ode;
  And it turn'd to a Sonnet.

In After Days

IN AFTER days when grasses high
O'ertop the stone where I shall lie,
  Though ill or well the world adjust
  My slender claim to honored dust,
I shall not question or reply.

I shall not see the morning sky;
I shall not hear the night-wind sigh;
  I shall be mute, as all men must
    In after days!

But yet, now living, fain were I
That someone then should testify,
  Saying—"He held his pen in trust
  To Art, not serving shame or lust."
Will none?—Then let my memory die
    In after days!

Fame

FAME is a food that dead men eat,—
I have no stomach for such meat.
In little light and narrow room,
They eat it in the silent tomb,
With no kind voice of comrade near
To bid the feaster be of cheer.

But friendship is a nobler thing,—
Of Friendship it is good to sing.
For truly, when a man shall end,
He lives in memory of his friend,
Who doth his better part recall
And of his fault make funeral.

THOMAS HARDY

(1840–1928)

Weather

THIS is the weather the cuckoo likes,
        And so do I;
When showers benumble the chestnut spikes,
        And nestlings fly;
And the little brown nightingale bills his best,
And they sit outside the "Traveller's Rest,"
And maids come forth sprig-muslin drest,
And citizens dream of the South and West,
        And so do I.

This is the weather the shepherd shuns,
        And so do I:
When beeches drip in browns and duns,
        And thresh, and ply;

And hill-hid tides throb, throe on throe,
And meadow rivulets overflow,
And drops on gate-bars hang in a row,
And rooks in families homeward go,
And so do I.

The Oxen

CHRISTMAS EVE, and twelve of the clock.
"Now they are all on their knees,"
An elder said as we sat in a flock
By the embers in hearthside ease.

We pictured the meek mild creatures where
They dwelt in their strawy pen,
Nor did it occur to one of us there
To doubt they were kneeling then.

So fair a fancy few would weave
In these years! Yet, I feel,
If some one said on Christmas Eve,
"Come; see the oxen kneel

"In the lonely barton by yonder coomb
Our childhood used to know,"
I should go with him in the gloom,
Hoping it might be so.

EDWARD ROWLAND SILL

(1841–1887)

Opportunity

THIS I beheld, or dreamed it in a dream:—
There spread a cloud of dust along a plain;

And underneath the cloud, or in it, raged
A furious battle, and men yelled, and swords
Shocked upon swords and shields. A prince's banner
Wavered, then staggered backward, hemmed by foes.
A craven hung along the battle's edge,
And thought, "Had I a sword of keener steel—
That blue blade that the king's son bears,—but this
Blunt thing!" he snapt and flung it from his hand,
And lowering crept away and left the field.
Then came the king's son, wounded, sore bestead,
And weaponless, and saw the broken sword,
Hilt-buried in the dry and trodden sand,
And ran and snatched it, and with battle-shout
Lifted afresh he hewed his enemy down,
And saved a great cause that heroic day.

The Fool's Prayer

THE royal feast was done; the King
  Sought some new sport to banish care,
And to his jester cried: "Sir Fool,
  Kneel now, and make for us a prayer!"

The jester doffed his cap and bells,
  And stood the mocking court before;
They could not see the bitter smile
  Behind the painted grin he wore.

He bowed his head, and bent his knee
  Upon the monarch's silken stool;
His pleading voice arose: "O Lord,
  Be merciful to me, a fool!

" 'Tis not by guilt the onward sweep
  Of truth and right, O Lord, we stay;
'Tis by our follies that so long
  We hold the earth from heaven away.

"These clumsy feet, still in the mire,
  Go crushing blossoms without end;
These hard, well-meaning hands we thrust
  Among the heart-strings of a friend.

"The ill-timed truth we might have kept—
  Who knows how sharp it pierced and stung?
The word we had not sense to say—
  Who knows how grandly it had rung?

"Our faults no tenderness should ask,
  The chastening stripes must cleanse them all;
But for our blunders—oh, in shame
  Before the eyes of heaven we fall.

"Earth bears no balsam for mistakes;
  Men crown the knave, and scourge the tool
That did his will; but Thou, O Lord,
  Be merciful to me, a fool!"

The room was hushed; in silence rose
  The King, and sought his gardens cool,
And walked apart, and murmured low,
  "Be merciful to me, a fool!"

ROBERT BUCHANAN

(1841–1901)

The Ballad of Judas Iscariot

'Twas the body of Judas Iscariot
  Lay in the Field of Blood;
'Twas the soul of Judas Iscariot
  Beside the body stood.

Black was the earth by night,
  And black was the sky;
Black, black were the broken clouds,
  Though the red Moon went by.

'Twas the body of Judas Iscariot
  Strangled and dead lay there;
'Twas the soul of Judas Iscariot
  Looked on it in despair.

The breath of the World came and went
  Like a sick man's in rest;
Drop by drop on the World's eyes
  The dews fell cool and blest.

Then the soul of Judas Iscariot
  Did make a gentle moan—
"I will bury underneath the ground
  My flesh and blood and bone.

"I will bury deep beneath the soil,
  Lest mortals look thereon,
And when the wolf and raven come
  The body will be gone!

"The stones of the field are sharp as steel,
  And hard and bold, God wot;
And I must bear my body hence
  Until I find a spot!"

'Twas the soul of Judas Iscariot
  So grim, and gaunt, and gray,
Raised the body of Judas Iscariot,
  And carried it away.

And as he bare it from the field
  Its touch was cold as ice,
And the ivory teeth within the jaw
  Rattled aloud, like dice.

As the soul of Judas Iscariot
  Carried its load with pain,
The Eye of Heaven, like a lantern's eye
  Opened and shut again.

Half he walked, and half he seemed
  Lifted on the cold wind;
He did not turn, for chilly hands
  Were pushing from behind.

The first place that he came unto
  It was the open wold,
And underneath were prickly whins,
  And a wind that blew so cold.

The next place that he came unto
  It was a stagnant pool,
And when he threw the body in
  It floated light as wool.

He drew the body on his back,
  And it was dripping chill,
And the next place he came unto
  Was a Cross upon a hill.

A Cross upon the windy hill,
  And a Cross on either side,
Three skeletons that swing thereon,
  Who had been crucified.

And on the middle cross-bar sat
  A white Dove slumbering;
Dim it sat in the dim light,
  With its head beneath its wing.

And underneath the middle Cross
  A grave yawned wide and vast,
But the soul of Judas Iscariot
  Shivered, and glided past.

The fourth place that he came unto
  It was the Brig of Dread,
And the great torrents rushing down
  Were deep, and swift, and red.

He dared not fling the body in
  For fear of faces dim,
And arms were waved in the wild water
  To thrust it back to him.

'Twas the soul of Judas Iscariot
  Turned from the Brig of Dread,
And the dreadful foam of the wild water
  Had splashed the body red.

For days and nights he wandered on
  Upon an open plain,
And the days went by like blinding mist,
  And the nights like rushing rain.

For days and nights he wandered on,
  All through the Wood of Woe;
And the nights went by like moaning wind,
  And the days like drifting snow.

'Twas the soul of Judas Iscariot
  Came with a weary face—
Alone, alone, and all alone,
  Alone in a lonely place!

He wandered east, he wandered west,
  And heard no human sound;
For months and years, in grief and tears,
  He wandered round and round.

For months and years, in grief and tears,
  He walked the silent night;
Then the soul of Judas Iscariot
  Perceived a far-off light.

A far-off light across the waste,
As dim and dim might be,
That came and went like a lighthouse gleam
On a black night at sea.

'Twas the soul of Judas Iscariot
Crawled to the distant gleam;
And the rain came down, and the rain was blown
Against him with a scream.

For days and nights he wandered on,
Pushed on by hands behind;
And the days went by like black, black rain,
And the nights like rushing wind.

'Twas the soul of Judas Iscariot,
Strange, and sad, and tall,
Stood all alone at dead of night
Before a lighted hall.

And the wold was white with snow,
And his foot-marks black and damp,
And the ghost of the silver Moon arose,
Holding her yellow lamp.

And the icicles were on the eaves,
And the walls were deep with white,
And the shadows of the guests within
Passed on the window light.

The shadows of the wedding guests
Did strangers come and go,
And the body of Judas Iscariot
Lay stretched along the snow.

The body of Judas Iscariot
Lay stretched along the snow;
'Twas the soul of Judas Iscariot
Ran swiftly to and fro.

To and fro, and up and down,
He ran so swiftly there,
As round and round the frozen Pole
Glideth the lean white bear.

'Twas the Bridegroom sat at the table-head,
And the lights burned bright and clear—
"Oh, who is that?" the Bridegroom said,
"Whose weary feet I hear?"

'Twas one looked from the lighted hall,
And answered soft and low,
"It is a wolf runs up and down
With a black track in the snow."

The Bridegroom sat in his robe of white
Sat at the table-head—
"Oh, who is that who moans without?"
The blessed Bridegroom said.

'Twas one who looked from the lighted hall,
And answered fierce and low,
" 'Tis the soul of Judas Iscariot
Gliding to and fro."

'Twas the soul of Judas Iscariot
Did hush itself and stand,
And saw the Bridegroom at the door
With a light in his hand.

The Bridegroom stood in the open door,
And he was clad in white,
And far within the Lord's Supper
Was spread so long and bright.

The Bridegroom shaded his eyes and looked,
And his face was bright to see—
"What dost thou here at the Lord's Supper
With thy body's sins?" said he.

'Twas the soul of Judas Iscariot
  Stood black, and sad, and bare—
"I have wandered many nights and days;
  There is no light elsewhere."

'Twas the wedding guests cried out within,
  And their eyes were fierce and bright—
"Scourge the soul of Judas Iscariot
  Away into the night!"

The Bridegroom stood in the open door,
  And he waved his hands still and slow,
And the third time that he waved his hands
  The air was thick with snow.

And of every flake of falling snow,
  Before it touched the ground,
There came a dove, and a thousand doves
  Made sweet sound.

'Twas the body of Judas Iscariot
  Floated away full fleet,
And the wings of the doves that bare it off
  Were like its winding-sheet.

'Twas the Bridegroom stood at the open door,
  And beckoned, smiling sweet;
'Twas the soul of Judas Iscariot
  Stole in, and fell at his feet.

"The Holy supper is spread within,
  And the many candles shine,
And I have waited long for thee
  Before I poured the wine!"

The supper wine is poured at last,
  The lights burn bright and fair,
Iscariot washes the Bridegroom's feet,
  And dries them with his hair.

SIDNEY LANIER

(1842–1881)

The Marshes of Glynn

GLOOMS of the live-oaks, beautiful-braided and woven
With intricate shades of the vines that myriad-cloven
  Clamber the forks of the multiform boughs,—
      Emerald twilights,—
      Virginal shy lights,
Wrought of the leaves to allure to the whisper of vows,
When lovers pace timidly down through the green colonnades
Of the dim sweet woods, of the dear dark woods,
  Of the heavenly woods and glades,
That run to the radiant marginal sand-beach within
   The wide sea-marshes of Glynn;—

Beautiful glooms, soft dusks in the noon-day fire,—
Wildwood privacies, closets of lone desire,
Chamber from chamber parted with wavering arras of leaves,—
Cells for the passionate pleasure of prayer to the soul that grieves,
Pure with a sense of the passing of saints through the wood,
Cool for the dutiful weighing of ill with good;—
O braided dusks of the oak and woven shades of the vine,
While the riotous noon-day sun of the June-day long did shine
Ye held me fast in your heart and I held you fast in mine;
But now when the noon is no more, and riot is rest,
And the sun is a-wait at the ponderous gate of the West,
And the slant yellow beam down the wood-aisle doth seem
Like a lane into heaven that leads from a dream,—
Ay, now, when my soul all day hath drunken the soul of the oak,
And my heart is at ease from men, and the wearisome sound of the stroke
  Of the scythe of time and the trowel of trade is low,
  And belief overmasters doubt, and I know that I know,
  And my spirit is grown to a lordly great compass within,
That the length and the breadth and the sweep of the marshes of Glynn
Will work me no fear like the fear they have wrought me of yore
When length was fatigue, and when breadth was but bitterness sore,

And when terror and shrinking and dreary unnamable pain
Drew over me out of the merciless miles of the plain,—

Oh, now, unafraid, I am fain to face
The vast sweet visage of space.
To the edge of the wood I am drawn, I am drawn,
Where the gray beach glimmering runs, as a belt of the dawn,
For a mete and a mark
To the forest-dark:—
So:
Affable live-oak, leaning low,—
Thus—with your favor—soft, with a reverent hand
(Not lightly touching your person, Lord of the land!),
Bending your beauty aside, with a step I stand
On the firm-packed sand,
Free
By a world of marsh that borders a world of sea.
Sinuous southward and sinuous northward the shimmering band
Of the sand-beach fastens the fringe of the marsh to the folds of the land.
Inward and outward to northward and southward the beach-lines linger and curl
As a silver-wrought garment that clings to and follows the firm sweet limbs of a girl.
Vanishing, swerving, evermore curving again into sight,
Softly the sand-beach wavers away to a dim gray looping of light.
And what if behind me to westward the wall of the woods stands high?
The world lies east: how ample, the marsh and the sea and the sky!
A league and a league of marsh-grass, waist-high, broad in the blade,
Green, and all of a height, and unflecked with a light or a shade,
Stretch leisurely off, in a pleasant plain,
To the terminal blue of the main.

Oh, what is abroad in the marsh and the terminal sea?
Somehow my soul seems suddenly free
From the weighing of fate and the sad discussion of sin,
By the length and the breadth and the sweep of the marshes of Glynn.

Ye marshes, how candid and simple and nothing-withholding and free
Ye publish yourselves to the sky and offer yourselves to the sea!

Tolerant plains, that suffer the sea and the rains and the sun,
Ye spread and span like the catholic man who hath mightily won
God out of knowledge and good out of infinite pain
And sight out of blindness and purity out of a stain.

As the marsh-hen secretly builds on the watery sod,
Behold I will build me a nest on the greatness of God:
I will fly in the greatness of God as the marsh-hen flies
In the freedom that fills all the space 'twixt the marsh and the skies:
By so many roots as the marsh-grass sends in the sod
I will heartily lay me a-hold on the greatness of God:
Oh, like to the greatness of God is the greatness within
The range of the marshes, the liberal marshes of Glynn.

And the sea lends large, as the marsh: lo, out of his plenty the sea
Pours fast: full soon the time of the flood-tide must be:
Look how the grace of the sea doth go
About and about through the intricate channels that flow
Here and there,
Everywhere,
Till his waters have flooded the uttermost creeks and the low-lying lanes,
And the marsh is meshed with a million veins,
That like as with rosy and silvery essences flow
In the rose-and-silver evening glow.
Farewell, my lord Sun!
The creeks overflow: a thousand rivulets run
'Twixt the roots of the sod; the blades of the marsh-grass stir;
Passeth a hurrying sound of wings that westward whir;
Passeth, and all is still; and the currents cease to run;
And the sea and the marsh are one.

How still the plains of the waters be!
The tide is in his ecstasy.
The tide is at his highest height:
And it is night.

And now from the Vast of the Lord will the waters of sleep
Roll in on the souls of men,
But who will reveal to our waking ken
The forms that swim and the shapes that creep
Under the waters of sleep?

And I would I could know what swimmeth below when the tide comes in
On the length and the breadth of the marvelous marshes of Glynn.

A Ballad of Trees and the Master

INTO the woods my Master went,
Clean forspent, forspent.
Out of the woods my Master came,
Forspent with love and shame.
But the olives they were not blind to Him;
The little gray leaves were kind to Him;
The thorn-tree had a mind to Him
When into the woods He came.

Out of the woods my Master went,
And He was well content.
Out of the woods my Master came,
Content with death and shame.
When Death and Shame would woo Him last,
From under the trees they drew Him last:
'Twas on a tree they slew Him—last,
When out of the woods He came.

The Stirrup-Cup

DEATH, thou 'rt a cordial old and rare:
Look how compounded, with what care!
Time got his wrinkles reaping thee
Sweet herbs from all antiquity.

David to thy distillage went.
Keats, and Gotama excellent,
Omar Khayyám, and Chaucer bright,
And Shakespeare for a king-delight.

Then, Time, let not a drop be spilt:
Hand me the cup whene'er thou wilt;
'Tis thy rich stirrup-cup to me;
I'll drink it down right smilingly.

ROBERT BRIDGES

(1844–1930)

On a Dead Child

PERFECT little body, without fault or stain on thee,
With promise of strength and manhood full and fair!
Though cold and stark and bare,
The bloom and the charm of life doth awhile remain on thee.

Thy mother's treasure wert thou;—alas! no longer
To visit her heart with wondrous joy; to be
Thy father's pride;—ah, he
Must gather his faith together, and his strength make stronger.

To me, as I move thee now in the last duty,
Dost thou with a turn or gesture anon respond;
Startling my fancy fond
With a chance attitude of the head, a freak of beauty.

Thy hand clasps, as 'twas wont, my finger, and holds it:
But the grasp is the clasp of Death, heart-breaking and stiff;
Yet feels to my hand as if
'Twas still thy will, thy pleasure and trust that enfolds it.

So I lay thee there, thy sunken eyelids closing—
Go lie thou there in thy coffin, thy last little bed!—
Propping thy wise, sad head,
Thy firm, pale hands across thy chest disposing.

o quiet! doth the change content thee?—Death, whither hath he taken thee?
To a world, do I think, that rights the disaster of this?
The vision of which I miss,
Vho weep for the body, and wish but to warm thee and awaken thee?

.h! little at best can all our hopes avail us
To lift this sorrow, or cheer us, when in the dark,
Unwilling, alone we embark,
.nd the things we have seen and have known and have heard of, fail us.

Since to Be Loved Endures

SINCE to be loved endures,
To love is wise:
Earth hath no good but yours,
Brave, joyful eyes:

Earth hath no sin but thine,
Dull eye of scorn:
O'er thee the sun doth pine
And angels mourn.

My Delight and Thy Delight

MY DELIGHT and thy delight
Walking, like two angels white,
In the gardens of the night:

My desire and thy desire
Twining to a tongue of fire,
Leaping live, and laughing higher;

Thro' the everlasting strife
In the mystery of life.

Love, from whom the world begun,
Hath the secret of the sun.

Love can tell, and love alone,
Whence the million stars were strewn,
Why each atom knows its own,
How, in spite of woe and death,
Gay is life, and sweet is breath:

This he taught us, this we knew,
Happy in his science true,
Hand in hand as we stood
'Neath the shadows of the wood,
Heart to heart as we lay
In the dawning of the day.

ARTHUR WILLIAM EDGAR O'SHAUGHNESSY

(1844–1881)

The New Love and the Old

I MADE another garden, yea,
For my new Love:
I left the dead rose where it lay
And set the new above.
Why did my Summer not begin?
Why did my heart not haste?
My old Love came and walk'd therein,
And laid the garden waste.

She enter'd with her weary smile,
Just as of old;
She look'd around a little while
And shiver'd with the cold:

Her passing touch was death to all,
  Her passing look a blight;
She made the white rose-petals fall,
  And turn'd the red rose white.

Her pale robe clinging to the grass
  Seem'd like a snake
That bit the grass and ground, alas!
  And a sad trail did make.
She went up slowly to the gate,
  And then, just as of yore,
She turn'd back at the last to wait
  And say farewell once more.

From "Ode"

WE ARE the music-makers,
  And we are the dreamers of dreams,
Wandering by lone sea-breakers,
  And sitting by desolate streams;
World-losers and world-forsakers,
  On whom the pale moon gleams:
Yet we are the movers and shakers
  Of the world forever, it seems.

With wonderful deathless ditties
We build up the world's great cities,
  And out of a fabulous story
  We fashion an empire's glory:
One man with a dream, at pleasure,
  Shall go forth and conquer a crown;
And three with a new song's measure
  Can trample a kingdom down.

We, in the ages lying
  In the buried past of the earth,
Built Nineveh with our sighing,
  And Babel itself in our mirth;

And o'erthrew them with prophesying
  To the old of the new world's worth;
For each age is a dream that is dying,
  Or one that is coming to birth.

JOHN BOYLE O'REILLY

(1844–1890)

A White Rose

THE red rose whispers of passion,
  And the white rose breathes of love;
Oh, the red rose is a falcon,
  And the white rose is a dove.

But I send you a cream white rosebud
  With a flush on its petal tips;
For the love that is purest and sweetest
  Has a kiss of desire on the lips.

WILLIAM ERNEST HENLEY

(1849–1903)

Invictus

OUT of the night that covers me,
  Black as the Pit from pole to pole,
I thank whatever gods may be
  For my unconquerable soul.

In the fell clutch of circumstance
  I have not winced nor cried aloud.
Under the bludgeonings of chance
  My head is bloody, but unbowed.

Beyond this place of wrath and tears
  Looms but the Horror of the shade,
And yet the menace of the years
  Finds, and shall find me, unafraid.

It matters not how strait the gate,
  How charged with punishments the scroll,
I am the master of my fate:
  I am the captain of my soul.

Margaritæ Sorori

A LATE lark twitters from the quiet skies
And from the west,
Where the sun, his day's work ended,
Lingers as in content,
There falls on the old, gray city
An influence luminous and serene,
A shining peace.

The smoke ascends
In a rosy-and-golden haze. The spires
Shine, and are changed. In the valley
Shadows rise. The lark sings on. The sun,
Closing his benediction,
Sinks, and the darkening air
Thrills with a sense of the triumphing night—
Night with her train of stars
And her great gift of sleep.

So be my passing!
My task accomplished and the long day done,
My wages taken, and in my heart
Some late lark singing,
Let me be gathered to the quiet west,
The sundown splendid and serene,
Death.

EUGENE FIELD

(1850–1895)

A Dutch Lullaby

WYNKEN, Blynken, and Nod one night
  Sailed off in a wooden shoe,—
Sailed on a river of crystal light
  Into a sea of dew.
"Where are you going, and what do you wish?"
  The old moon asked the three.
"We have come to fish for the herring fish
  That live in this beautiful sea;
  Nets of silver and gold have we!"
          Said Wynken,
          Blynken,
          And Nod.

The old moon laughed and sang a song,
  As they rocked in the wooden shoe;
And the wind that sped them all night long
  Ruffled the waves of dew.
The little stars were the herring fish
  That lived in that beautiful sea—
"Now cast your nets wherever you wish,—
  Never afeard are we!"
  So cried the stars to the fishermen three,
          Wynken,
          Blynken,
          And Nod.

All night long their nets they threw
  To the stars in the twinkling foam,—
Then down from the skies came the wooden shoe,
  Bringing the fishermen home:
'Twas all so pretty a sail, it seemed
  As if it could not be;

And some folk thought 'twas a dream they'd dreamed
  Of sailing that beautiful sea;
  But I shall name you the fishermen three:
          Wynken,
          Blynken,
          And Nod.

Wynken and Blynken are two little eyes,
  And Nod is a little head,
And the wooden shoe that sailed the skies
  Is a wee one's trundle-bed;
So shut your eyes while Mother sings
  Of wonderful sights that be,
And you shall see the beautiful things
  As you rock in the misty sea
  Where the old shoe rocked the fishermen three:—
          Wynken,
          Blynken,
          And Nod.

Little Boy Blue

THE little toy dog is covered with dust,
  But sturdy and stanch it stands;
And the little toy soldier is red with rust,
  And his musket molds in his hands.
Time was when the little toy dog was new
  And the soldier was passing fair,
And that was the time when our Little Boy Blue
  Kissed them and put them there.

"Now, don't you go till I come," he said,
  "And don't you make any noise!"
So toddling off to his trundle-bed
  He dreamed of the pretty toys.
And as he was dreaming, an angel song
  Awakened our Little Boy Blue—
Oh, the years are many, the years are long,
  But the little toy friends are true.

Ay, faithful to Little Boy Blue they stand,
  Each in the same old place,
Awaiting the touch of a little hand,
  And the smile of a little face.
And they wonder, as waiting these long years through,
  In the dust of that little chair,
What has become of our Little Boy Blue
  Since he kissed them and put them there.

ALICE MEYNELL

(1850–1922)

The Lady Poverty

THE Lady Poverty was fair:
But she has lost her looks of late,
With change of times and change of air.
Ah, slattern, she neglects her hair,
Her gown, her shoes. She keeps no state
As once when her pure feet were bare.

Or—almost worse, if worse can be—
She scolds in parlors; dusts and trims,
Watches and counts. Oh, is this she
Whom Francis met, whose step was free,
Who with Obedience carolled hymns,
In Umbria walked with Chastity?

Where is her ladyhood? Not here,
Not among modern kinds of men;
But in the stony fields, where clear
Through the thin trees the skies appear;
In delicate spare soil and fen,
And slender landscape and austere.

The Lady of the Lambs

SHE walks—the lady of my delight—
  A shepherdess of sheep.
Her flocks are thoughts. She keeps them white;
  She guards them from the steep.
She feeds them on the fragrant height,
  And folds them in for sleep.

She roams maternal hills and bright,
  Dark valleys safe and deep.
Her dreams are innocent at night;
  The chastest stars may peep.
She walks—the lady of my delight—
  A shepherdess of sheep.

She holds her little thoughts in sight,
  Though gay they run and leap.
She is so circumspect and right;
  She has her soul to keep.
She walks—the lady of my delight—
  A shepherdess of sheep.

ROBERT LOUIS STEVENSON

(1850–1894)

Romance

I WILL make you brooches and toys for your delight
Of bird-song at morning and star-shine at night.
I will make a palace fit for you and me,
Of green days in forests and blue days at sea.

I will make my kitchen, and you shall keep your room,
Where white flows the river and bright blows the broom,

And you shall wash your linen and keep your body white
In rainfall at morning and dewfall at night.

And this shall be for music when no one else is near,
The fine song for singing, the rare song to hear!
That only I remember, that only you admire,
Of the broad road that stretches and the roadside fire.

Requiem

Under the wide and starry sky,
Dig the grave and let me lie.
Glad did I live and gladly die,
  And I laid me down with a will.

This be the verse you grave for me:
Here he lies where he longed to be,
Home is the sailor, home from sea,
  And the hunter home from the hill.

EDWIN MARKHAM

(1852–)

The Man with the Hoe

WRITTEN AFTER SEEING MILLET'S WORLD-FAMOUS PAINTING OF A BRUTALIZED TOILER IN THE DEEP ABYSS OF LABOR.

God made man in his own image:
in the image of God He made him.
—Genesis.

Bowed by the weight of centuries he leans
Upon his hoe and gazes on the ground,
The emptiness of ages in his face,
And on his back the burden of the world.

Who made him dead to rapture and despair,
A thing that grieves not and that never hopes,
Stolid and stunned, a brother to the ox?
Who loosened and let down this brutal jaw?
Whose was the hand that slanted back this brow?
Whose breath blew out the light within this brain?

Is this the Thing the Lord God made and gave
To have dominion over sea and land;
To trace the stars and search the heavens for power;
To feel the passion of Eternity?
Is this the dream He dreamed who shaped the suns
And markt their ways upon the ancient deep?
Down all the caverns of Hell to their last gulf
There is no shape more terrible than this——
More tongued with cries against the world's blind greed——
More filled with signs and portents for the soul—
More packt with danger to the universe.

What gulfs between him and the seraphim!
Slave of the wheel of labor, what to him
Are Plato and the swing of Pleiades?
What the long reaches of the peaks of song,
The rift of dawn, the reddening of the rose?
Thru this dread shape the suffering ages look;
Time's tragedy is in that aching stoop;
Thru this dread shape humanity betrayed,
Plundered, profaned and disinherited,
Cries protest to the Powers that made the world,
A protest that is also prophecy.

O masters, lords and rulers in all lands,
Is this the handiwork you give to God,
This monstrous thing distorted and soul-quencht?
How will you ever straighten up this shape;
Touch it again with immortality;
Give back the upward looking and the light;
Rebuild in it the music and the dream;
Make right the immemorial infamies,
Perfidious wrongs, immedicable woes?

O masters, lords and rulers in all lands,
How will the future reckon with this Man?
How answer his brute question in that hour
When whirlwinds of rebellion shake all shores?
How will it be with kingdoms and with kings—
With those who shaped him to the thing he is—
When this dumb Terror shall rise to judge the world,
After the silence of the centuries?

HENRY VAN DYKE

(1852–)

Four Things

FOUR things a man must learn to do
If he would make his record true:
To think without confusion clearly;
To love his fellow-men sincerely;
To act from honest motives purely;
To trust in God and Heaven securely.

FRANCIS WILLIAM BOURDILLON

(1852–1921)

Light

THE night has a thousand eyes,
    The day but one;
Yet the light of the bright world dies
    With the dying sun.

The mind has a thousand eyes,
    And the heart but one;
Yet the light of a whole life dies
    When its love is done.

JAMES WHITCOMB RILEY

(1853–1916)

When the Frost Is on the Punkin

When the frost is on the punkin and the fodder's in the shock,
And you hear the kyouck and gobble of the struttin' turkey-cock,
And the clackin' of the guineys, and the cluckin' of the hens,
And the rooster's hallylooyer as he tiptoes on the fence;
Oh, it's then's the times a feller is a-feelin' at his best,
With the risin' sun to greet him from a night of peaceful rest,
As he leaves the house, bareheaded, and goes out to feed the stock,
When the frost is on the punkin and the fodder's in the shock.

They's something kind o' harty-like about the atmusfere
When the heat of summer's over and the coolin' fall is here.—
Of course we miss the flowers, and the blossums on the trees,
And the mumble of the hummin'-birds and buzzin' of the bees;
But the air's so appetizin', and the landscape through the haze
Of a crisp and sunny morning of the airly autumn days
Is a pictur' that no painter has the colorin' to mock,—
When the frost is on the punkin and the fodder's in the shock.

The husky, rusty russel of the tossels of the corn,
And the raspin' of the tangled leaves, as golden as the morn;
The stubble in the furries—kind o' lonesome-like, but still
A-preachin' sermuns to us of the barns they growed to fill;
The straw-stack in the medder, and the reaper in the shed;
The hosses in theyr stalls below, the clover overhead,—
Oh, it sets my hart a-clickin' like the tickin' of a clock,
When the frost is on the punkin and the fodder's in the shock!

Then your apples all is gethered, and the ones a feller keeps
Is poured around the celler-floor in red and yeller heaps;
And your cider-makin' 's over, and your wimmern-folks is through
With their mince and apple butter, and theyr souse and saussage, too! . . .
I don't know how to tell it—but ef sich a thing could be
As the Angels wantin' boardin', and they'd call around on *me*—
I'd want to 'commodate 'em—all the whole-indurin' flock—
When the frost is on the punkin and the fodder's in the shock!

LIZETTE WOODWORTH REESE

(1856–)

Tears

WHEN I consider Life and its few years—
A wisp of fog betwixt us and the sun;
A call to battle, and the battle done
Ere the last echo dies within our ears;
A rose choked in the grass; an hour of fears;
The gusts that past a darkening shore do beat;
The burst of music down an unlistening street,—
I wonder at the idleness of tears.
Ye old, old dead, and ye of yesternight
Chieftains, and bards, and keepers of the sheep,
By every cup of sorrow that you had,
Loose me from tears, and make me see aright
How each hath back what once he stayed to weep:
Homer his sight, David his little lad!

OSCAR WILDE

(1856–1900)

The Harlot's House

WE CAUGHT the tread of dancing feet,
We loitered down the moonlit street,
And stopped beneath the harlot's house.

Inside, above the din and fray,
We heard the loud musicians play
The "Treues Liebes Herz" of Strauss.

Like strange mechanical grotesques,
Making fantastic arabesques,
The shadows raced across the blind.

We watched the ghostly dancers spin
To sound of horn and violin,
Like black leaves wheeling in the wind.

Like wire-pulled automatons,
Slim silhouetted skeletons
Went sidling through the slow quadrille.

They took each other by the hand,
And danced a stately saraband;
Their laughter echoed thin and shrill.

Sometimes a clockwork puppet pressed
A phantom lover to her breast,
Sometimes they seemed to try to sing.

Sometimes a horrible marionette
Came out, and smoked its cigarette
Upon the steps like a live thing.

Then, turning to my love, I said,
"The dead are dancing with the dead,
The dust is whirling with the dust."

But she—she heard the violin,
And left my side and entered in:
Love passed into the house of lust.

Then suddenly the tune went false,
The dancers wearied of the waltz,
The shadows ceased to wheel and whirl.

And down the long and silent street,
The dawn, with silver-sandaled feet,
Crept like a frightened girl.

The Ballad of Reading Gaol

He did not wear his scarlet coat,
  For blood and wine are red,
And blood and wine were on his hands
  When they found him with the dead,
The poor dead woman whom he loved,
  And murdered in her bed.

He walked amongst the Trial Men
  In a suit of shabby gray;
A cricket cap was on his head,
  And his step seemed light and gay;
But I never saw a man who looked
  So wistfully at the day.

I never saw a man who looked
  With such a wistful eye
Upon that little tent of blue
  Which prisoners call the sky,
And at every drifting cloud that went
  With sails of silver by.

I walked with other souls in pain,
  Within another ring,
And was wondering if the man had done
  A great or little thing,
When a voice behind me whispered low,
  "That fellow's got to swing."

Dear Christ! the very prison walls
  Suddenly seemed to reel,
And the sky above my head became
  Like a casque of scorching steel;
And, though I was a soul in pain,
  My pain I could not feel.

I only knew what hunted thought
  Quickened his step, and why
He looked upon the garish day
  With such a wistful eye;
The man had killed the thing he loved,
  And so he had to die.

Yet each man kills the thing he loves,
  By each let this be heard,
Some do it with a bitter look,
  Some with a flattering word,
The coward does it with a kiss,
  The brave man with a sword!

Some kill their love when they are young,
  And some when they are old;
Some strangle with the hands of Lust,
  Some with the hands of Gold:
The kindest use a knife, because
  The dead so soon grow cold.

Some love too little, some too long,
  Some sell, and others buy;
Some do the deed with many tears,
  And some without a sigh:
For each man kills the thing he loves,
  Yet each man does not die.

He does not die a death of shame
  On a day of dark disgrace,
Nor have a noose about his neck,
  Nor a cloth upon his face,
Nor drop feet foremost through the floor
  Into an empty space.

He does not sit with silent men
  Who watch him night and day;
Who watch him when he tries to weep,
  And when he tries to pray;
Who watch him lest himself should rob
  The prison of its prey.

He does not wake at dawn to see
  Dread figures throng his room,
The shivering Chaplain robed in white,
  The Sheriff stern with gloom,
And the Governor all in shiny black,
  With the yellow face of Doom.

He does not rise in piteous haste
  To put on convict-clothes,
While some coarse-mouthed Doctor gloats, and notes
  Each new and nerve-twitched pose,
Fingering a watch whose little ticks
  Are like horrible hammer-blows.

He does not know that sickening thirst
  That sands one's throat, before
The hangman with his gardener's gloves
  Slips through the padded door,
And binds one with three leathern thongs
  That the throat may thirst no more.

He does not bend his head to hear
  The Burial Office read,
Nor, while the terror of his soul
  Tells him he is not dead,
Cross his own coffin, as he moves
  Into the hideous shed.

He does not stare upon the air
  Through a little roof of glass:
He does not pray with lips of clay
  For his agony to pass;
Nor feel upon his shuddering cheek
  The kiss of Caiaphas.

II

Six weeks our guardsman walked the yard
  In the suit of shabby gray:
His cricket cap was on his head,
  And his step seemed light and gay,
But I never saw a man who looked
  So wistfully at the day.

I never saw a man who looked
  With such a wistful eye
Upon that little tent of blue
  Which prisoners call the sky.
And at every wandering cloud that trailed
  Its ravelled fleeces by.

He did not wring his hands, as do
  Those witless men who dare
To try to rear the changeling Hope
  In the cave of black Despair:
He only looked upon the sun,
  And drank the morning air.

He did not wring his hands nor weep,
  Nor did he peek or pine,
But he drank the air as though it held
  Some healthful anodyne;
With open mouth he drank the sun
  As though it had been wine!

And I and all the souls in pain,
  Who tramped the other ring,
Forgot if we ourselves had done
  A great or little thing,
And watched with gaze of dull amaze
  The man who had to swing.

And strange it was to see him pass
  With a step so light and gay,
And strange it was to see him look
  So wistfully at the day,
And strange it was to think that he
  Had such a debt to pay.

For oak and elm have pleasant leaves
  That in the spring-time shoot:
But grim to see is the gallows-tree,
  With its adder-bitten root,
And, green or dry, a man must die
  Before it bears its fruit

The loftiest place is that seat of grace
  For which all worldlings try:
But who would stand in hempen band
  Upon a scaffold high,
And through a murderer's collar take
  His last look at the sky?

It is sweet to dance to violins
  When Love and Life are fair:
To dance to flutes, to dance to lutes
  Is delicate and rare:
But it is not sweet with nimble feet
  To dance upon the air!

So with curious eyes and sick surmise
  We watched him day by day,
And wondered if each one of us
  Would end the self-same way,
For none can tell to what red Hell
  His sightless soul may stray.

At last the dead man walked no more
  Amongst the Trial Men,
And I knew that he was standing up
  In the black dock's dreadful pen,
And that never would I see his face
  In God's sweet world again.

Like two doomed ships that pass in storm
  We had crossed each other's way:
But we made no sign, we said no word,
  We had no word to say;
For we did not meet in the holy night,
  But in the shameful day.

A prison wall was round us both,
  Two outcast men we were:
The world had thrust us from its heart,
  And God from out His care:
And the iron gin that waits for Sin
  Had caught us in its snare.

III

In Debtors' Yard the stones are hard,
  And the dripping wall is high,
So it was there he took the air
  Beneath the leaden sky.
And by each side a Warder walked,
  For fear the man might die.

Or else he sat with those who watched
  His anguish night and day;
Who watched him when he rose to weep,
  And when he crouched to pray;
Who watched him lest himself should rob
  Their scaffold of its prey.

The Governor was strong upon
  The Regulations Act:
The Doctor said that Death was but
  A scientific fact:
And twice a day the Chaplain called,
  And left a little tract.

And twice a day he smoked his pipe,
  And drank his quart of beer:
His soul was resolute, and held
  No hiding-place for fear;
He often said that he was glad
  The hangman's hands were near.

But why he said so strange a thing
  No Warder dared to ask:
For he to whom a watcher's doom
  Is given as his task,
Must set a lock upon his lips,
  And make his face a mask.

Or else he might be moved, and try
  To comfort or console:
And what should Human Pity do
  Pent up in Murderers' Hole?
What word of grace in such a place
  Could help a brother's soul?

With slouch and swing around the ring
  We trod the Fools' Parade!
We did not care: we knew we were
  The Devil's Own Brigade:
And shaven head and feet of lead
  Make a merry masquerade.

We tore the tarry rope to shreds
  With blunt and bleeding nails;
We rubbed the doors, and scrubbed the floors,
  And cleaned the shining rails:
And, rank by rank, we soaped the plank,
  And clattered with the pails.

We sewed the sacks, we broke the stones.
  We turned the dusty drill:
We banged the tins, and bawled the hymns,
  And sweated on the mill:
But in the heart of every man
  Terror was lying still.

So still it lay that every day
  Crawled like a weed-clogged wave:
And we forgot the bitter lot
  That waits for fool and knave,
Till once, as we tramped in from work,
  We passed an open grave.

With yawning mouth the yellow hole
  Gaped for a living thing;
The very mud cried out for blood
  To the thirsty asphalt ring:
And we knew that ere one dawn grew fair
  Some prisoner had to swing.

Right in we went, with soul intent
  On Death and Dread and Doom:
The hangman, with his little bag,
  Went shuffling through the gloom:
And each man trembled as he crept
  Into his numbered tomb.

That night the empty corridors
 Were full of forms of Fear,
And up and down the iron town
 Stole feet we could not hear,
And through the bars that hide the stars
 White faces seemed to peer.

He lay as one who lies and dreams
 In a pleasant meadow-land,
The watchers watched him as he slept,
 And could not understand
How one could sleep so sweet a sleep
 With a hangman close at hand.

But there is no sleep when men must weep
 Who never yet have wept:
So we—the fool, the fraud, the knave—
 That endless vigil kept,
And through each brain on hands of pain
 Another's terror crept.

Alas! it is a fearful thing
 To feel another's guilt!
For, right within, the sword of Sin
 Pierced to its poisoned hilt,
And as molten lead were the tears we shed
 For the blood we had not spilt.

The Warders with their shoes of felt
 Crept by each padlocked door,
And peeped and saw, with eyes of awe,
 Gray figures on the floor,
And wondered why men knelt to pray
 Who never prayed before.

All through the night we knelt and prayed,
 Mad mourners of a corse!
The troubled plumes of midnight were
 The plumes upon a hearse:
And bitter wine upon a sponge
 Was the savor of Remorse.

The gray cock crew, the red cock crew,
But never came the day:
And crooked shapes of Terror crouched,
In the corners where we lay:
And each evil sprite that walks by night
Before us seemed to play.

They glided past, they glided fast,
Like travelers through a mist:
They mocked the moon in a rigadoon
Of delicate turn and twist,
And with formal pace and loathsome grace
The phantoms kept their tryst.

With mop and mow, we saw them go,
Slim shadows hand in hand:
About, about, in ghostly rout
They trod a saraband:
And the damned grotesques made arabesques,
Like the wind upon the sand!

With the pirouettes of marionettes,
They tripped on pointed tread:
But with flutes of Fear they filled the ear,
As their grisly masque they led,
And loud they sang, and long they sang,
For they sang to wake the dead.

"*Oho!*" they cried, "*The World is wide,*
But fettered limbs go lame!
And once, or twice, to throw the dice
Is a gentlemanly game;
But he does not win who plays with Sin
In the secret House of Shame."

No things of air these antics were,
That frolicked with such glee:
To men whose lives were held in gyves,
And whose feet might not go free,
Ah! wounds of Christ! they were living things,
Most terrible to see.

Around, around, they waltzed and wound;
  Some wheeled in smirking pairs;
With the mincing step of a demirep
  Some sidled up the stairs:
And with subtle sneer, and fawning leer,
  Each helped us at our prayers.

The morning wind began to moan,
  But still the night went on:
Through its giant loom the web of gloom
  Crept till each thread was spun:
And, as we prayed, we grew afraid
  Of the Justice of the Sun.

The moaning wind went wandering round
  The weeping prison-wall:
Till like a wheel of turning steel
  We felt the minutes crawl:
O moaning wind! what had we done
  To have such a seneschal?

At last I saw the shadowed bars,
  Like a lattice wrought in lead,
Move right across the whitewashed wall
  That faced my three-plank bed,
And I knew that somewhere in the world
  God's dreadful dawn was red.

At six o'clock we cleaned our cells,
  At seven all was still,
But the sough and swing of a mighty wing
  The prison seemed to fill,
For the Lord of Death with icy breath
  Had entered in to kill.

He did not pass in purple pomp,
  Nor ride a moon-white steed.
Three yards of cord and a sliding board
  Are all the gallows' need:
So with rope of shame the Herald came
  To do the secret deed.

We were as men who through a fen
  Of filthy darkness grope:
We did not dare to breathe a prayer,
  Or to give our anguish scope:
Something was dead in each of us,
  And what was dead was Hope.

For Man's grim Justice goes its way,
  And will not swerve aside:
It slays the weak, it slays the strong,
  It has a deadly stride:
With iron heel it slays the strong,
  The monstrous parricide!

We waited for the stroke of eight:
  Each tongue was thick with thirst:
For the stroke of eight is the stroke of Fate
  That makes a man accursed,
And Fate will use a running noose
  For the best man and the worst.

We had no other thing to do,
  Save to wait for the sign to come:
So, like things of stone in a valley lone,
  Quiet we sat and dumb:
But each man's heart beat thick and quick,
  Like a madman on a drum!

With sudden shock the prison clock
  Smote on the shivering air,
And from all the gaol rose up a wail
  Of impotent despair,
Like the sound that frightened marshes hear
  From some leper in his lair.

And as one sees most fearful things
  In the crystal of a dream,
We saw the greasy hempen rope
  Hooked to the blackened beam,
And heard the prayer the hangman's snare
  Strangled into a scream.

And all the woe that moved him so
  That he gave that bitter cry,
And the wild regrets, and the bloody sweats,
  None knew so well as I:
For he who lives more lives than one
More deaths than one must die.

IV

There is no chapel on the day
  On which they hang a man:
The Chaplain's heart is far too sick,
  Or his face is far too wan,
Or there is that written in his eyes
  Which none should look upon.

So they kept us close till nigh on noon,
  And then they rang the bell,
And the Warders with their jingling keys
  Opened each listening cell,
And down the iron stair we tramped,
  Each from his separate Hell.

Out into God's sweet air we went,
  But not in wonted way,
For this man's face was white with fear,
  And that man's face was gray,
And I never saw sad men who looked
  So wistfully at the day.

I never saw sad men who looked
  With such a wistful eye
Upon that little tent of blue
  We prisoners called the sky,
And at every careless cloud that passed
  In happy freedom by.

But there were those amongst us all
  Who walked with downcast head,
And knew that, had each got his due,
  They should have died instead:
He had but killed a thing that lived,
  Whilst they had killed the dead.

For he who sins a second time
  Wakes a dead soul to pain,
And draws it from its spotted shroud,
  And makes it bleed again,
And makes it bleed great gouts of blood,
  And makes it bleed in vain!

Like ape or clown, in monstrous garb
  With crooked arrows starred,
Silently we went round and round
  The slippery asphalt yard;
Silently we went round and round,
  And no man spoke a word.

Silently we went round and round,
  And through each hollow mind
The Memory of dreadful things
  Rushed like a dreadful wind,
And Horror stalked before each man,
  And Terror crept behind.

The Warders strutted up and down,
  And kept their herd of brutes,
Their uniforms were spick and span,
  And they wore their Sunday suits,
But we knew the work they had been at,
  By the quicklime on their boots.

For where a grave had opened wide,
  There was no grave at all:
Only a stretch of mud and sand
  By the hideous prison-wall,
And a little heap of burning lime,
  That the man should have his pall.

For he has a pall, this wretched man,
  Such as few men can claim:
Deep down below a prison-yard,
  Naked for greater shame,
He lies, with fetters on each foot,
  Wrapt in a sheet of flame!

And all the while the burning lime
  Eats flesh and bone away;
It eats the brittle bone by night,
  And the soft flesh by day,
It eats the flesh and bone by turns,
  But it eats the heart away.

For three long years they will not sow
  Or root or seedling there:
For three long years the unblessed spot
  Will sterile be and bare,
And look upon the wondering sky
  With unreproachful stare.

They think a murderer's heart would taint
  Each simple seed they sow.
It is not true! God's kindly earth
  Is kindlier than men know,
And the red rose would but blow more red,
  The white rose whiter blow.

Out of his mouth a red, red rose!
  Out of his heart a white!
For who can say by what strange way,
  Christ brings His will to light,
Since the barren staff the pilgrim bore
  Bloomed in the great Pope's sight?

But neither milk-white rose nor red
  May bloom in prison air;
The shard, the pebble, and the flint,
  Are what they give us there:
For flowers have been known to heal
  A common man's despair.

So never will wine-red rose or white,
  Petal by petal, fall
On that stretch of mud and sand that lies
  By the hideous prison-wall,
To tell the men who tramp the yard
  That God's Son died for all.

Yet though the hideous prison-wall
  Still hems him round and round,
And a spirit may not walk by night
  That is with fetters bound,
And a spirit may but weep that lies
  In such unholy ground.

He is at peace—this wretched man—
  At peace, or will be soon:
There is no thing to make him mad,
  Nor does Terror walk at noon,
For the lampless Earth in which he lies
  Has neither Sun nor Moon.

They hanged him as a beast is hanged:
  They did not even toll
A requiem that might have brought
  Rest to his startled soul,
But hurriedly they took him out,
  And hid him in a hole.

They stripped him of his canvas clothes,
  And gave him to the flies;
They mocked the swollen purple throat,
  And the stark and staring eyes;
And with laughter loud they heaped the shroud
  In which their convict lies.

The Chaplain would not kneel to pray
  By his dishonored grave:
Nor mark it with that blessed Cross
  That Christ for sinners gave,
Because the man was one of those
  Whom Christ came down to save.

Yet all is well; he has but passed,
  To Life's appointed bourne:
And alien tears will fill for him
  Pity's long-broken urn,
For his mourners will be outcast men,
  And outcasts always mourn.

V

I know not whether Laws be right,
Or whether Laws be wrong;
All that we know who lie in gaol
Is that the wall is strong;
And that each day is like a year,
A year whose days are long.

But this I know, that every Law
That men have made for Man,
Since first Man took his brother's life,
And the sad world began,
But straws the wheat and saves the chaff
With a most evil fan.

This too I know—and wise it were
If each could know the same—
That every prison that men build
Is built with bricks of shame,
And bound with bars lest Christ should see
How men their brothers maim.

With bars they blur the gracious moon,
And blind the goodly sun:
And they do well to hide their Hell,
For in it things are done
That Son of God nor Son of Man
Ever should look upon!

The vilest deeds like poison weeds
Bloom well in prison-air:
It is only what is good in Man
That wastes and withers there:
Pale Anguish keeps the heavy gate,
And the Warder is Despair.

For they starve the little frightened child
Till it weeps both night and day:
And they scourge the weak, and flog the fool,
And gibe the old and gray,
And some grow mad, and all grow bad,
And none a word may say.

Each narrow cell in which we dwell
Is a foul and dark latrine.
And the fetid breath of living Death
Chokes up each grated screen,
And all, but Lust, is turned to dust
In Humanity's machine.

The brackish water that we drink
Creeps with a loathsome slime,
And the bitter bread they weigh in scales
Is full of chalk and lime,
And Sleep will not lie down, but walks
Wild-eyed, and cries to Time.

But though lean Hunger and green Thirst
Like asp with adder fight,
We have little care of prison fare,
For what chills and kills outright
Is that every stone one lifts by day
Becomes one's heart by night.

With midnight always in one's heart,
And twilight in one's cell,
We turn the crank, or tear the rope,
Each in his separate Hell,
And the silence is more awful far
Than the sound of a brazen bell.

And never a human voice comes near
To speak a gentle word:
And the eye that watches through the door
Is pitiless and hard:
And by all forgot, we rot and rot,
With soul and body marred.

And thus we rust Life's iron chain
Degraded and alone:
And some men curse, and some men weep,
And some men make no moan:
But God's eternal Laws are kind
And break the heart of stone.

And every human heart that breaks,
  In prison-cell or yard,
Is as that broken box that gave
  Its treasure to the Lord,
And filled the unclean leper's house
  With the scent of costliest nard.

Ah! happy they whose hearts can break
  And peace of pardon win!
How else may man make straight his plan
  And cleanse his soul from Sin?
How else but through a broken heart
  May Lord Christ enter in?

And he of the swollen purple throat,
  And the stark and staring eyes
Waits for the holy hands that took
  The Thief to Paradise;
And a broken and a contrite heart
  The Lord will not despise.

The man in red who reads the Law
  Gave him three weeks of life,
Three little weeks in which to heal
  His soul of his soul's strife,
And cleanse from every blot of blood
  The hand that held the knife.

And with tears of blood he cleansed the hand,
  The hand that held the steel:
For only blood can wipe out blood,
  And only tears can heal:
And the crimson stain that was of Cain
  Became Christ's snow-white seal.

VI

In Reading gaol by Reading town
  There is a pit of shame,
And in it lies a wretched man
  Eaten by teeth of flame,
In a burning winding-sheet he lies,
  And his grave has got no name.

And there, till Christ call forth the dead,
In silence let him lie:
No need to waste the foolish tear,
Or heave the windy sigh:
The man had killed the thing he loved,
And so he had to die.

And all men kill the thing they love,
By all let this be heard,
Some do it with a bitter look,
Some with a flattering word,
The coward does it with a kiss,
The brave man with a sword!

JOHN DAVIDSON

(1857–1909)

A Runnable Stag

WHEN the pods went pop on the broom, green broom,
And apples began to be golden-skinn'd, 22
We harbour'd a stag in the Priory coomb,
And we feather'd his trail up-wind, up-wind,
We feather'd his trail up-wind—
A stag of warrant, a stag, a stag,
A runnable stag, a kingly crop,
Brow, bay and tray and three on top,
A stag, a runnable stag.

Then the huntsman's horn rang yap, yap, yap,
And "Forwards" we heard the harbourer shout;
But 'twas only a brocket that broke a gap
In the beechen underwood, driven out,
From the underwood antler'd out

By warrant and might of the stag, the stag,
The runnable stag, whose lordly mind
Was bent on sleep, though beam'd and tined
He stood, a runnable stag.

So we tufted the covert till afternoon
With Tinkerman's Pup and Bell-of-the-North;
And hunters were sulky and hounds out of tune
Before we tufted the right stag forth,
Before we tufted him forth,
The stag of warrant, the wily stag,
The runnable stag with his kingly crop,
Brow, bay and tray and three on top,
The royal and runnable stag.

It was Bell-of-the-North and Tinkerman's Pup
That stuck to the scent till the copse was drawn.
"Tally ho! tally ho!" and the hunt was up,
The tufters whipp'd and the pack laid on,
The resolute pack laid on,
And the stag of warrant away at last,
The runnable stag, the same, the same,
His hoofs on fire, his horns like flame,
A stag, a runnable stag.

"Let your gelding be: if you check or chide
He stumbles at once and you're out of the hunt;
For three hundred gentlemen, able to ride,
On hunters accustom'd to bear the brunt,
Accustom'd to bear the brunt,
Are after the runnable stag, the stag,
The runnable stag with his kingly crop,
Brow, bay and tray and three on top,
The right, the runnable stag."

By perilous paths in coomb and dell,
The heather, the rocks, and the river-bed,
The pace grew hot, for the scent lay well,
And a runnable stag goes right ahead,
The quarry went right ahead—

Ahead, ahead, and fast and far;
His antler'd crest, his cloven hoof,
Brow, bay and tray and three aloof,
The stag, the runnable stag.

For a matter of twenty miles and more,
By the densest hedge and the highest wall,
Through herds of bullocks he baffled the lore
Of harbourer, huntsman, hounds and all,
Of harbourer, hounds and all—
The stag of warrant, the wily stag,
For twenty miles, and five and five,
He ran, and he never was caught alive,
This stag, this runnable stag.

When he turn'd at bay in the leafy gloom,
In the emerald gloom where the brook ran deep
He heard in the distance the rollers boom,
And he saw in a vision of peaceful sleep,
In a wonderful vision of sleep,
A stag of warrant, a stag, a stag,
A runnable stag in a jewell'd bed,
Under the sheltering ocean dead,
A stag, a runnable stag.

So a fateful hope lit up his eye,
And he open'd his nostrils wide again,
And he toss'd his branching antlers high
As he headed the hunt down the Charlock glen
As he raced down the echoing glen—
For five miles more, the stag, the stag,
For twenty miles, and five and five,
Not to be caught now, dead or alive,
The stag, the runnable stag.

Three hundred gentlemen, able to ride,
Three hundred horses as gallant and free,
Beheld him escape on the evening tide,
Far out till he sank in the Severn Sea,
Till he sank in the depths of the sea—

The stag, the buoyant stag, the stag
That slept at last in a jewell'd bed
Under the sheltering ocean spread,
The stag, the runnable stag.

DOROTHY FRANCES GURNEY

(1858–1932)

God's Garden

THE Lord God planted a garden
  In the first white days of the world,
And He set there an Angel warden
  In a garment of light enfurled.

So near to the peace of Heaven
  The hawk might nest with the wren,
For there in the cool of the even
  God walked with the first of men.

And I dream that these garden closes
  With their shade and their sun-flecked sod,
And their lilies and bowers of roses
  Were laid by the hand of God.

The kiss of the sun for pardon,
  The song of the birds for mirth,
One is nearer God's heart in a garden
  Than anywhere else on earth.

For He broke it for us in a garden
  Under the olive-trees
Where the angel of strength was the warden
  And the soul of the world found ease.

KATHARINE LEE BATES

(1859-1929)

America the Beautiful

O BEAUTIFUL for spacious skies,
For amber waves of grain,
For purple mountain majesties
Above the fruited plain!
America! America!
God shed His grace on thee
And crown thy good with brotherhood
From sea to shining sea!

O beautiful for pilgrim feet,
Whose stern, impassioned stress
A thoroughfare for freedom beat
Across the wilderness!
America! America!
God mend thine every flaw,
Confirm thy soul in self-control,
Thy liberty in law!

O beautiful for heroes proved
In liberating strife,
Who more than self their country loved,
And mercy more than life!
America! America!
May God thy gold refine
Till all success be nobleness
And every gain divine!

O beautiful for patriot dream
That sees beyond the years
Thine alabaster cities gleam
Undimmed by human tears!
America! America!
God shed His grace on thee
And crown thy good with brotherhood
From sea to shining sea!

FRANCIS THOMPSON

(1859–1907)

The Hound of Heaven

I FLED Him, down the nights and down the days;
I fled Him, down the arches of the years;
I fled Him, down the labyrinthine ways
Of my own mind; and in the mist of tears
I hid from Him, and under running laughter.
Up vistaed hopes I sped;
And shot, precipitated
Adown Titanic glooms of chasmed fears,
From those strong Feet that followed, followed after.
But with unhurrying chase,
And unperturbèd pace,
Deliberate speed, majestic instancy,
They beat—and a Voice beat
More instant than the Feet—
"All things betray thee, who betrayest Me."

I pleaded, outlaw-wise,
By many a hearted casement, curtained red,
Trellised with intertwining charities;
(For, though I knew His Love Who followèd,
Yet was I sore adread
Lest, having Him, I must have naught beside);
But, if one little casement parted wide,
The gust of his approach would clash it to.
Fear wist not to evade, as Love wist to pursue.
Across the margent of the world I fled,
And troubled the gold gateways of the stars,
Smiting for shelter on their clangèd bars;
Fretted to dulcet jars
And silver chatter the pale ports o' the moon.
I said to dawn, Be sudden; to eve, Be soon;
With thy young skiey blossoms heap me over
From this tremendous Lover!
Float thy vague veil about me, lest He see!

I tempted all his servitors, but to find
My own betrayal in their constancy,
In faith to Him their fickleness to me,
Their traitorous trueness, and their loyal deceit.
To all swift things for swiftness did I sue;
Clung to the whistling mane of every wind.
But whether they swept, smoothly fleet,
The long savannahs of the blue;
Or whether, Thunder-driven,
They clanged his chariot 'thwart a heaven
Plashy with flying lightnings round the spurn o' their feet:—
Fear wist not to evade as Love wist to pursue.
Still with unhurrying chase,
And unperturbèd pace,
Deliberate speed, majestic instancy,
Came on the following Feet,
And a Voice above their beat—
"Naught shelters thee, who wilt not shelter Me."

I sought no more that after which I strayed
In face of man or maid;
But still within the little children's eyes
Seems something, something that replies;
They at least are for me, surely for me!
I turned me to them very wistfully;
But, just as their young eyes grew sudden fair
With dawning answers there,
Their angel plucked them from me by the hair.
"Come then, ye other children, Nature's—share
With me" (said I) "your delicate fellowship;
Let me greet you lip to lip,
Let me twine with you caresses,
Wantoning
With our Lady-Mother's vagrant tresses,
Banqueting
With her in her wind-walled palace,
Underneath her azured daïs,
Quaffing, as your taintless way is,
From a chalice
Lucent-weeping out of the dayspring."
So it was done:

I in their delicate fellowship was one—
Drew the bolt of Nature's secrecies.
I knew all the swift importings
On the wilful face of skies;
I knew how the clouds arise
Spumèd of the wild sea-snortings;
All that's born or dies
Rose and drooped with—made them shapers
Of mine own moods, or wailful or divine—
With them joyed and was bereaven.
I was heavy with the even,
When she lit her glimmering tapers
Round the day's dead sanctities.
I laughed in the morning's eyes.
I triumphed and I saddened with all weather,
Heaven and I wept together,
And its sweet tears were salt with mortal mine;
Against the red throb of its sunset-heart
I laid my own to beat,
And share commingling heat;
But not by that, by that, was eased my human smart.
In vain my tears were wet on Heaven's grey cheek.
For ah! we know not what each other says,
These things and I; in sound *I* speak—
Their sound is but their stir, they speak by silences.
Nature, poor stepdame, cannot slake my drouth;
Let her, if she would owe me,
Drop yon blue bosom-veil of sky, and show me
The breasts o' her tenderness:
Never did any milk of hers once bless
My thirsting mouth.
Nigh and nigh draws the chase,
With unperturbèd pace,
Deliberate speed, majestic instancy;
And past those noisèd Feet
A voice comes yet more fleet—
"Lo! naught contents thee, who content'st not Me."

Naked I wait Thy love's uplifted stroke!
My harness piece by piece Thou hast hewn from me,
And smitten me to my knee;

I am defenceless utterly.
I slept, methinks, and woke,
And, slowly gazing, find me stripped in sleep.
In the rash lustihead of my young powers,
I shook the pillaring hours
And pulled my life upon me; grimed with smears,
I stand amid the dust o' the mounded years—
My mangled youth lies dead beneath the heap.
My days have crackled and gone up in smoke,
Have puffed and burst as sun-starts on a stream.
Yea, faileth now even dream
The dreamer, and the lute the lutanist;
Even the linked fantasies, in whose blossomy twist
I swung the earth a trinket at my wrist,
Are yielding; cores of all too weak account
For earth with heavy griefs so overplussed.
Ah! is Thy love indeed
A weed, albeit an amaranthine weed,
Suffering no flowers except its own to mount?
Ah! must—
Designer infinite!—
Ah! must Thou char the wood ere Thou canst limn with it?
My freshness spent its wavering shower i' the dust;
And now my heart is as a broken fount,
Wherein tear-drippings stagnate, split down ever
From the dank thoughts that shiver
Upon the sighful branches of my mind.
Such is; what is to be?
The pulp so bitter, how shall taste the rind?
I dimly guess what Time in mists confounds;
Yet ever and anon a trumpet sounds
From the hid battlements of Eternity;
Those shaken mists a space unsettle, then
Round the half glimpsed turrets slowly wash again.
But not ere him who summoneth
I first have seen, enwound
With glooming robes purpureal, cypress-crowned;
His name I know, and what his trumpet saith.
Whether man's heart or life it be which yields
Thee harvest, must Thy harvest fields
Be dunged with rotten death?

Now of that long pursuit
Comes on at hand the bruit;
That Voice is round me like a bursting sea:
"And is thy earth so marred
Shattered in shard on shard?
Lo, all things fly thee, for thou fliest Me!
Strange, piteous, futile thing,
Wherefore should any set thee love apart?
Seeing none but I makes much of naught" (He said),
"And human love needs human meriting:
How hast thou merited—
Of all man's clotted clay the dingiest clot?
Alack, thou knowest not
How little worthy of any love thou art!
Whom wilt thou find to love ignoble thee
Save Me, save only Me?
All which I took from thee I did but take,
Not for thy harms,
But just that thou might'st seek it in My arms.
All which thy child's mistake
Fancies as lost, I have stored for thee at home:
Rise, clasp My hand, and come!"

Halts by me that footfall:
Is my gloom, after all,
Shade of His hand, outstretched caressingly?
"Ah, fondest, blindest, weakest,
I am He Whom thou seekest!
Thou dravest love from thee, who dravest Me."

CHARLOTTE PERKINS STETSON GILMAN

(1860–)

A Conservative

THE garden beds I wandered by
One bright and cheerful morn,

When I found a new-fledged butterfly,
  A-sitting on a thorn,
A black and crimson butterfly
  All doleful and forlorn.

I thought that life could have no sting
  To infant butterflies
So I gazed on this unhappy thing
  With wonder and surprise.
While sadly with his waving wing
  He wiped his weeping eyes.

Said I, "What can the matter be?
  Why weepest thou so sore?
With garden fair and sunlight free
  And flowers in goodly store,"—
But he only turned away from me
  And burst into a roar.

Cried he, "My legs are thin and few
  Where once I had a swarm!
Soft fuzzy fur—a joy to view—
  Once kept my body warm,
Before these flapping wing-things grew,
  To hamper and deform!"

At that outrageous bug I shot
  The fury of mine eye;
Said I, in scorn all burning hot,
  In rage and anger high,
"You ignominious idiot!
  Those wings are made to fly!"

"I do not want to fly," said he,
  "I only want to squirm!"
And he drooped his wings dejectedly,
  But still his voice was firm:
"I do not want to be a fly!
  I want to be a worm!"

O yesterday of unknown lack,
Today of unknown bliss!
I left my fool in red and black;
The last I saw was this,—
The creature madly climbing back
Into his chrysalis.

BLISS CARMAN
(1861–1929)

A Vagabond Song

THERE is something in the Autumn that is native to my blood—
Touch of manner, hint of mood;
And my heart is like a rhyme,
With the yellow and the purple and the crimson keeping time.

The scarlet of the maples can shake me like a cry
Of bugles going by.
And my lonely spirit thrills
To see the frosty asters like smoke upon the hills.

There is something in October sets the gipsy blood astir;
We must rise and follow her,
When from every hill of flame
She calls and calls each vagabond by name.

The Joys of the Road

Now the joys of the road are chiefly these:
A crimson touch on the hard-wood trees;

A vagrant's morning wide and blue,
In early fall, when the wind walks, too;

A shadowy highway cool and brown
Alluring up and enticing down

From rippled water to dappled swamp,
From purple glory to scarlet pomp;

The outward eye, the quiet will,
And the striding heart from hill to hill;

The tempter apple over the fence;
The cobweb bloom on the yellow quince;

The palish asters along the wood,—
A lyric touch of the solitude;

An open hand, an easy shoe,
And a hope to make the day go through,—

Another to sleep with, and a third
To wake me up at the voice of a bird;

The resonant far-listening morn,
And the hoarse whisper of the corn;

The crickets mourning their comrades lost,
In the night's retreat from the gathering frost;

(Or is it their slogan, plaintive and shrill,
As they beat on their corselets, valiant still?)

A hunger fit for the kings of the sea,
And a loaf of bread for Dickon and me;

A thirst like that of the Thirsty Sword,
And a jug of cider on the board;

An idle noon, a bubbling spring,
The sea in the pine-tops murmuring;

A scrap of gossip at the ferry;
A comrade neither glum nor merry,

Asking nothing, revealing naught,
But minting his words from a fund of thought.

A keeper of silence eloquent,
Needy, yet royally well content,

Of the mettled breed, yet abhorring strife,
And full of the mellow juice of life,

A taster of wine, with an eye for a maid,
Never too bold, and never afraid,

Never heart-whole, never heart-sick,
(These are the things I worship in Dick)

No fidget and no reformer, just
A calm observer of ought and must,

A lover of books, but a reader of man,
No cynic and no charlatan,

Who never defers and never demands,
But, smiling, takes the world in his hands,—

Seeing it good as when God first saw
And gave it the weight of his will for law.

And O the joy that is never won,
But follows and follows the journeying sun,

By marsh and tide, by meadow and stream,
A will-o'-the-wind, a light-o'-dream,

Delusion afar, delight anear,
From morrow to morrow, from year to year,

A jack-o'-lantern, a fairy fire,
A dare, a bliss, and a desire!

The racy smell of the forest loam,
When the stealthy, sad-heart leaves go home;

(O leaves, O leaves, I am one with you,
Of the mould and the sun and the wind and the dew!)

The broad gold wake of the afternoon;
The silent fleck of the cold new moon;

The sound of the hollow sea's release
From stormy tumult to starry peace;

With only another league to wend;
And two brown arms at the journey's end!

These are the joys of the open road—
For him who travels without a load.

LOUISE IMOGEN GUINEY

(1861–1920)

Out in the Fields with God

THE little cares that fretted me,
  I lost them yesterday
Among the fields above the sea,
  Among the winds at play;
Among the lowing of the herds,
  The rustling of the trees,
Among the singing of the birds,
  The humming of the bees.

The fears of what may come to pass,
  I cast them all away
Among the clover-scented grass,
  Among the new-mown hay;

Among the husking of the corn,
  Where drowsy poppies nod,
Where ill thoughts die and good are born,
  Out in the fields with God.

SIR HENRY NEWBOLT

(1862–)

Drake's Drum

DRAKE he's in his hammock an' a thousand mile away,
  (Capten, art tha sleepin' there below?)
Slung atween the round shot in Nombre Dios Bay,
  An' dreamin' arl the time o' Plymouth Hoe.
Yarnder lumes the Island, yarnder lie the ships,
  Wi' sailor lads a-dancin' heel-an'-toe,
An' the shore-lights flashin', an' the night-tide dashin',
  He sees et arl so plainly as he saw et long ago.

Drake he was a Devon man, an' rüled the Devon seas,
  (Capten, art tha sleepin' there below?)
Rovin' tho' his death fell, he went wi' heart at ease,
  An' dreamin' arl the time o' Plymouth Hoe.
"Take my drum to England, hang et by the shore,
  Strike et when your powder's runnin' low;
If the Dons sight Devon, I'll quit the port o' Heaven,
  An' drum them up the Channel as we drumm'd them long ago."

Drake he's in his hammock till the great Armadas come,
  (Capten, art tha sleepin' there below?)
Slung atween the round shot, listenin' for the drum,
  An' dreamin' arl the time o' Plymouth Hoe.
Call him on the deep sea, call him up the Sound,
  Call him when ye sail to meet the foe;
Where the old trade's plyin' an' the old flag flyin'
  They shall find him ware an' wakin', as they found him long ago!

GEORGE SANTAYANA
(1863–)

O World

O WORLD, thou choosest not the better part!
It is not wisdom to be only wise,
And on the inward vision close the eyes,
But it is wisdom to believe the heart.
Columbus found a world, and had no chart,
Save one that faith deciphered in the skies;
To trust the soul's invincible surmise
Was all his science and his only art.
Our knowledge is a torch of smoky pine
That lights the pathway but one step ahead
Across a void of mystery and dread.
Bid, then, the tender light of faith to shine
By which alone the mortal heart is led
Unto the thinking of the thought divine.

RICHARD HOVEY
(1864–1900)

A Stein Song

GIVE a rouse, then, in the Maytime
  For a life that knows no fear!
Turn night-time into daytime
  With the sunlight of good cheer!
    For it's always fair weather
    When good fellows get together,
With a stein on the table and a good song ringing clear

When the wind comes up from Cuba,
  And the birds are on the wing,
And our hearts are patting juba
  To the banjo of the spring,
    Then it's no wonder whether
    The boys will get together,
With a stein on the table and a cheer for everything.

For we're all frank-and-twenty
  When the spring is in the air;
And we've faith and hope a-plenty,
  And we've life and love to spare;
    And it's birds of a feather
    When we all get together,
With a stein on the table and heart without a care.

For we know the world is glorious,
  And the goal a golden thing,
And that God is not censorious
  When his children have their fling;
    And life slips its tether
    When the boys get together,
With a stein on the table in the fellowship of spring.

Unmanifest Destiny

To WHAT new fates, my country, far
  And unforseen of foe or friend,
Beneath what unexpected star
  Compelled to what unchosen end,

Across the sea that knows no beach,
  The Admiral of Nations guides
Thy blind obedient keels to reach
  The harbor where thy future rides!

The guns that spoke at Lexington
  Knew not that God was planning then
The trumpet word of Jefferson
  To bugle forth the rights of men.

To them that wept and cursed Bull Run,
  What was it but despair and shame?
Who saw behind the cloud the sun?
  Who knew that God was in the flame?

Had not defeat upon defeat,
  Disaster on disaster come,
The slave's emancipated feet
  Had never marched behind the drum.

There is a Hand that bends our deeds
  To mightier issues than we planned:
Each son that triumphs, each that bleeds,
  My country, serves Its dark command.

I do not know beneath what sky
  Nor on what seas shall be thy fate:
I only know it shall be high,
  I only know it shall be great.

ROBERT LOVEMAN

(1864–1923)

April Rain

It is not raining rain for me,
  It's raining daffodils;
In every dimpled drop I see
  Wild flowers on the hills.

The clouds of gray engulf the day
And overwhelm the town;
It is not raining rain to me,
It's raining roses down.

It is not raining rain to me,
But fields of clover bloom,
Where any buccaneering bee
Can find a bed and room.

A health unto the happy,
A fig for him who frets!
It is not raining rain to me,
It's raining violets.

RUDYARD KIPLING

(1865-)

Recessional

God of our fathers, known of old,—
Lord of our far-flung battle line,—
Beneath whose awful hand we hold
Dominion over palm and pine,—
Lord God of Hosts, be with us yet,
Lest we forget,—lest we forget!

The tumult and the shouting dies,
The captains and the kings depart:
Still stands thine ancient sacrifice,—
An humble and a contrite heart.
Lord God of Hosts, be with us yet,
Lest we forget,—lest we forget!

Far-called, our navies melt away;
  On dune and headland sinks the fire.
Lo! all our pomp of yesterday
  Is one with Nineveh and Tyre!
Judge of the nations, spare us yet,
Lest we forget,—lest we forget!

If drunk, with sight of power, we loose
  Wild tongues that have not thee in awe,
Such boasting as the Gentiles use
  Or lesser breeds without the law,—
Lord God of Hosts, be with us yet,
Lest we forget,—lest we forget!

For heathen heart that puts her trust
  In reeking tube and iron shard,
All valiant dust that builds on dust,
  And guarding calls not thee to guard
For frantic boast and foolish word,
Thy mercy on thy people, Lord!

ARTHUR SYMONS

(1865–   )

Amends to Nature

I HAVE loved colours, and not flowers;
Their motion, not the swallow's wings;
And wasted more than half my hours
Without the comradeship of things.

How is it, now, that I can see,
With love and wonder and delight,
The children of the hedge and tree,
The little lords of day and night?

How is it that I see the roads,
No longer with usurping eyes,
A twilight meeting-place for toads,
A mid-day mart for butterflies?

I feel, in every midge that hums,
Life, fugitive and infinite,
And suddenly the world becomes
A part of me and I of it.

WILLIAM BUTLER YEATS

(1865–)

The Lake Isle of Innisfree

I WILL arise and go now, and go to Innisfree,
And a small cabin build there, of clay and wattles made:
Nine bean rows will I have there, a hive for the honey bee,
And live alone in the bee-loud glade.

And I shall have some peace there, for peace comes dropping slow,
Dropping from the veils of the morning to where the cricket sings;
There midnight's all a glimmer, and noon a purple glow,
And evening full of the linnet's wings.

I will arise and go now, for always night and day
I hear lake water lapping with low sounds by the shore;
While I stand on the roadway, or on the pavements gray,
I hear it in the deep heart's core.

When You Are Old

WHEN you are old and grey and full of sleep,
And nodding by the fire, take down this book,
And slowly read, and dream of the soft look
Your eyes had once, and of their shadows deep:

How many loved your moments of glad grace,
And loved your beauty with love false or true;
But one man loved the pilgrim soul in you,
And loved the sorrows of your changing face.

And bending down beside the glowing bars
Murmur, a little sadly, how love fled
And paced upon the mountains overhead
And hid his face amid a crowd of stars.

GELETT BURGESS

(1866–)

The Purple Cow

Reflections on a Mythic Beast Who's Quite Remarkable, at Least.

I NEVER saw a Purple Cow,
I never hope to see one;
But I can tell you, anyhow,
I'd rather see than be one.

ERNEST DOWSON

(1867–1900)

Vitae Summa Brevis Spem Nos Vetat Incohare Longam

THEY are not long, the weeping and the laughter,
Love and desire and hate;
I think they have no portion in us after
We pass the gate.

They are not long, the days of wine and roses:
  Out of a misty dream
Our path emerges for a while, then closes
  Within a dream.

Non Sum Qualis Eram Bonæ Sub Regno Cynaræ

Last night, ah, yesternight, betwixt her lips and mine
There fell thy shadow, Cynara! Thy breath was shed
Upon my soul between the kisses and the wine;
And I was desolate and sick of an old passion,
  Yea, I was desolate and bowed my head.
I have been faithful to thee, Cynara! in my fashion.

All night upon mine heart I felt her warm heart beat,
Night-long within mine arms in love and sleep she lay;
Surely the kisses of her bought red mouth were sweet;
But I was desolate and sick of an old passion,
  When I awoke and found the dawn was gray:
I have been faithful to thee, Cynara! in my fashion.

I have forgot much, Cynara! Gone with the wind,
Flung roses, roses riotously with the throng,
Dancing, to put thy pale lost lilies out of mind;
But I was desolate and sick of an old passion,
  Yea, all the time, because the dance was long:
I have been faithful to thee, Cynara! in my fashion.

I cried for madder music and for stronger wine,
But when the feast is finished and the lamps expire,
Then falls thy shadow, Cynara! the night is thine,
And I am desolate and sick of an old passion,
  Yea, hungry for the lips of my desire:
I have been faithful to thee, Cynara! in my fashion.

LAURENCE BINYON

(1869–)

O World, Be Nobler

O WORLD, be nobler, for her sake!
If she but knew thee what thou art,
What wrongs are borne, what deeds are done
In thee, beneath thy daily sun,
Know'st thou not that her tender heart
For pain and very shame would break?
O World, be nobler, for her sake!

WILLIAM VAUGHN MOODY

(1869–1910)

Gloucester Moors

A MILE behind is Gloucester town
Where the fishing fleets put in,
A mile ahead the land dips down
And the woods and farms begin.
Here, where the moors stretch free
In the high blue afternoon,
Are the marching sun and talking sea,
And the racing winds that wheel and flee
On the flying heels of June.

Jill-o'er-the-ground is purple blue,
Blue is the quaker-maid,
The wild geranium holds its dew
Long in the boulder's shade.

Wax-red hangs the cup
From the huckleberry boughs,
In barberry bells the grey moths sup
Or where the choke-cherry lifts high up
Sweet bowls for their carouse.

Over the shelf of the sandy cove
Beach-peas blossom late.
By copse and cliff the swallows rove
Each calling to his mate.
Seaward the sea-gulls go,
And the land-birds all are here;
That green-gold flash was a vireo,
And yonder flame where the marsh-flags grow
Was a scarlet tanager.

This earth is not the steadfast place
We landsmen build upon;
From deep to deep she varies pace,
And while she comes is gone.
Beneath my feet I feel
Her smooth bulk heave and dip;
With velvet plunge and soft upreel
She swings and steadies to her keel
Like a gallant, gallant ship.

These summer clouds she sets for sail,
The sun is her masthead light,
She tows the moon like a pinnace frail
Where her phosphor wake churns bright.
Now hid, now looming clear,
On the face of the dangerous blue
The star fleets tack and wheel and veer,
But on, but on does the old earth steer
As if her port she knew.

God, dear God! Does she know her port,
Though she goes so far about?
Or blind astray, does she make her sport
To brazen and chance it out?

I watched when her captains passed:
She were better captainless.
Men in the cabin, before the mast,
But some were reckless and some aghast,
And some sat gorged at mess.

By her battened hatch I leaned and caught
Sounds from the noisome hold,—
Cursing and sighing of souls distraught
And cries too sad to be told.
Then I strove to go down and see;
But they said, "Thou art not of us!"
I turned to those on the deck with me
And cried, "Give help!" But they said, "Let be:
Our ship sails faster thus."

Jill-o'er-the-ground is purple blue,
Blue is the quaker-maid,
The alder-clump where the brook comes through
Breeds cresses in its shade.
To be out of the moiling street
With its swelter and its sin!
Who has given to me this sweet,
And given my brother dust to eat?
And when will his wage come in?

Scattering wide or blown in ranks,
Yellow and white and brown,
Boats and boats from the fishing banks
Come home to Gloucester town.
There is cash to purse and spend,
There are wives to be embraced,
Hearts to borrow and hearts to lend,
And hearts to take and keep to the end,—
O little sails, make haste!

But thou, vast outbound ship of souls,
What harbor town for thee?
What shapes, when thy arriving tolls,
Shall crowd the banks to see?

Shall all the happy shipmates then
Stand singing brotherly?
Or shall a haggard ruthless few
Warp her over and bring her to,
While the many broken souls of men
Fester down in the slaver's pen,
And nothing to say or do?

EDGAR LEE MASTERS

(1869–)

Herbert Marshall

ALL your sorrow, Louise, and hatred of me
Sprang from your delusion that it was wantonness
Of spirit and contempt of your soul's rights
Which made me turn to Annabelle and forsake you.
You really grew to hate me for love of me,
Because I was your soul's happiness,
Formed and tempered
To solve your life for you, and would not.
But you were my misery. If you had been
My happiness would I not have clung to you?
This is life's sorrow:
That one can be happy only where two are;
And that our hearts are drawn to stars
Which want us not.

EDWIN ARLINGTON ROBINSON

(1869–)

The Sheaves

WHERE long the shadows of the wind had rolled,
Green wheat was yielding to the change assigned;
And as by some vast magic undivined
The world was turning slowly into gold.

Like nothing that was ever bought or sold
It waited there, the body and the mind;
And with a mighty meaning of a kind
That tells the more the more it is not told.
So in a land where all days are not fair,
Fair days went on till on another day
A thousand golden sheaves were lying there,
Shining and still, but not for long to stay—
As if a thousand girls with golden hair
Might rise from where they slept and go away.

Richard Cory

WHENEVER Richard Cory went down town,
  We people on the pavement looked at him:
He was a gentleman from sole to crown,
  Clean favored, and imperially slim.

And he was always quietly arrayed,
  And he was always human when he talked;
But still he fluttered pulses when he said,
  "Good-morning," and he glittered when he walked.

And he was rich—yes, richer than a king—
  And admirably schooled in every grace:
In fine, we thought that he was everything
  To make us wish that we were in his place.

So on we worked, and waited for the light,
  And went without the meat, and cursed the bread;
And Richard Cory, one calm summer night,
  Went home and put a bullet through his head.

WILLIAM HENRY DAVIES

(1870–)

Leisure

WHAT is this life if, full of care,
We have no time to stand and stare.

No time to stand beneath the boughs
And stare as long as sheep or cows.

No time to see, when woods we pass,
Where squirrels hide their nuts in grass.

No time to see, in broad daylight,
Streams full of stars, like skies at night.

No time to turn at Beauty's glance,
And watch her feet, how they can dance.

No time to wait till her mouth can
Enrich that smile her eyes began.

A poor life this if, full of care,
We have not time to stand and stare.

STEPHEN CRANE

(1871–1900)

War Is Kind

DO NOT weep, maiden, for war is kind.
Because your lover threw wild hands toward the sky
And the affrighted steed ran on alone,
Do not weep.
War is kind.

Hoarse, booming drums of the regiment,
Little souls who thirst for fight—
These men were born to drill and die.
The unexplained glory flies above them;
Great is the battle-god, great—and his kingdom
A field where a thousand corpses lie.

Do not weep, babe, for war is kind.
Because your father tumbled in the yellow trenches,
Raged at his breast, gulped and died,
Do not weep.
War is kind.

Swift-blazing flag of the regiment,
Eagle with crest of red and gold,
These men were born to drill and die.
Point for them the virtue of slaughter,
Make plain to them the excellence of killing,
And a field where a thousand corpses lie.

Mother whose heart hung humble as a button
On the bright splendid shroud of your son,
Do not weep.
War is kind.

RALPH HODGSON

(1872–)

Time, You Old Gipsy Man

TIME, you old gipsy man,
Will you not stay,
Put up your caravan
Just for one day?

All things I'll give you
Will you be my guest,
Bells for your jennet
Of silver the best,

Goldsmiths shall beat you
A great golden ring,
Peacocks shall bow to you,
Little boys sing,
Oh, and sweet girls will
Festoon you with may.
Time, you old gipsy,
Why hasten away?

Last week in Babylon,
Last night in Rome,
Morning, and in the crush
Under Paul's dome;
Under Paul's dial
You tighten your rein—
Only a moment,
And off once again;
Off to some city
Now blind in the womb,
Off to another
Ere that's in the tomb.

Time, you old gipsy man,
Will you not stay,
Put up your caravan
Just for one day?

Eve

EVE, with her basket, was
Deep in the bells and grass,
Wading in bells and grass
Up to her knees,
Picking a dish of sweet
Berries and plums to eat,
Down in the bells and grass
Under the trees.

Mute as a mouse in a
Corner the cobra lay,
Curled round a bough of the
Cinnamon tall . . .
Now to get even and
Humble proud heaven and
Now was the moment or
Never at all.

"Eva!" Each syllable
Light as a flower fell,
"Eva!" he whispered the
Wondering maid,
Soft as a bubble sung
Out of a linnet's lung,
Soft and most silverly
"Eva!" he said.

Picture that orchard sprite,
Eve, with her body white,
Supple and smooth to her
Slim finger tips,
Wondering, listening,
Listening, wondering,
Eve with a berry
Half-way to her lips.

Oh had our simple Eve
Seen through the make-believe!
Had she but known the
Pretender he was!
Out of the boughs he came,
Whispering still her name,
Tumbling in twenty rings
Into the grass.

Here was the strangest pair
In the world anywhere,
Eve in the bells and grass
Kneeling, and he

Telling his story low . . .
Singing birds saw them go
Down the dark path to
The Blasphemous Tree.

Oh what a clatter when
Titmouse and Jenny Wren
Saw him successful and
Taking his leave!
How the birds rated him,
How they all hated him!
How they all pitied
Poor motherless Eve!

Picture her crying
Outside in the lane,
Eve, with no dish of sweet
Berries and plums to eat,
Haunting the gate of the
Orchard in vain . . .
Picture the lewd delight
Under the hill to-night—
"Eva!" the toast goes round,
"Eva!" again.

EVA GORE-BOOTH

(1872–1926)

The Waves of Breffny

THE grand road from the mountain goes shining to the sea,
 And there is traffic on it and many a horse and cart
But the little roads of Cloonagh are dearer far to me
 And the little roads of Cloonagh go rambling through my heart.

A great storm from the ocean goes shouting o'er the hill,
 And there is glory in it; and terror on the wind:
But the haunted air of twilight is very strange and still,
 And the little winds of twilight are dearer to my mind.

The great waves of the Atlantic sweep storming on their way,
  Shining green and silver with the hidden herring shoal;
But the little waves of Breffny have drenched my heart in spray,
  And the little waves of Breffny go stumbling through my soul.

JOHN McCRAE
(1872–1918)

In Flanders Fields

IN FLANDERS fields the poppies blow
Between the crosses, row on row,
  That mark our place, and in the sky,
  The larks, still bravely singing, fly,
Scarce heard amid the guns below.

We are the dead; short days ago
  We lived, felt dawn, saw sunset glow,
Loved and were loved, and now we lie
  In Flanders fields.

Take up our quarrel with the foe!
To you from failing hands we throw
  The torch; be yours to hold it high!
  If ye break faith with us who die,
We shall not sleep, though poppies grow
  In Flanders fields.

CALE YOUNG RICE
(1872–   )

New Dreams for Old

IS THERE no voice in the world to come crying,
    "New dreams for old!
    New for old!"?
Many have long in my heart been lying,
    Faded, weary, and cold.

All of them, all, would I give for a new one.
  (Is there no seeker
  Of dreams that were?)
Nor would I ask if the new were a true one:
  Only for new dreams!
  New for old!

For I am here, halfway of my journey,
  Here with the old!
  All so old!
And the best heart with death is at tourney,
  If naught new it is told.
Will there no voice, then, come—or a vision—
  Come with the beauty
  That ever blows
Out of the lands that are called Elysian?
  I must have new dreams!
  New for old!

WALTER DE LA MARE

(1873-)

The Listeners

"Is THERE anybody there?" said the Traveller,
  Knocking on the moonlit door;
And his horse in the silence champed the grasses
  Of the forest's ferny floor:
And a bird flew up out of the turret,
  Above the Traveller's head:
And he smote upon the door again a second time;
  "Is there anybody there?" he said.
But no one descended to the Traveller;
  No head from the leaf-fringed sill
Leaned over and looked into his grey eyes,
  Where he stood perplexed and still.

But only a host of phantom listeners
  That dwelt in the lone house then
Stood listening in the quiet of the moonlight
  To that voice from the world of men:
Stood thronging the faint moon beams on the dark stair,
  That goes down to the empty hall,
Hearkening in an air stirred and shaken
  By the lonely traveller's call.
And he felt in his heart their strangeness,
  Their stillness answering his cry,
While his horse moved, cropping the dark turf,
  'Neath the starred and leafy sky;
For he suddenly smote on the door, even
  Louder, and lifted his head:—
"Tell them I came, and no one answered,
  That I kept my word," he said.
Never the least stir made the listeners,
  Though every word he spake
Fell echoing through the shadowiness of the still house
  From the one man left awake:
Ay, they heard his foot upon the stirrup,
  And the sound of iron on stone
And how the silence surged softly backward
  When the plunging hoofs were gone.

JOHN MASEFIELD

(1874-   )

A Consecration

Not of the princes and prelates with periwigged charioteers
Riding triumphantly laurelled to lap the fat of the years,—
Rather the scorned—the rejected—the men hemmed in with the spears

The men of the tattered battalion which fights till it dies,
Dazed with the dust of the battle, the din and the cries,
The men with the broken heads and the blood running into their eyes.

Not the be-medalled Commander, beloved of the throne,
Riding cock-horse to parade when the bugles are blown,
But the lads who carried the koppie and cannot be known.

Not the ruler for me, but the ranker, the tramp of the road,
The slave with the sack on his shoulders pricked on with the goad,
The man with too weighty a burden, too weary a load.

The sailor, the stoker of steamers, the man with the clout,
The chantyman bent at the halliards putting a tune to the shout,
The drowsy man at the wheel and the tired look-out.

Others may sing of the wine and the wealth and the mirth,
The portly presence of potentates goodly in girth;—
Mine be the dirt and the dross, the dust and scum of the earth!

Theirs be the music, the colour, the glory, the gold;
Mine be a handful of ashes, a mouthful of mould.
Of the maimed, of the halt and the blind in the rain and the cold—
Of these shall my songs be fashioned, my tales be told.

Sea-Fever

I MUST down to the seas again, to the lonely sea and the sky,
And all I ask is a tall ship and a star to steer her by,
And the wheel's kick and the wind's song and the white sail's shaking,
And a grey mist on the sea's face and a grey dawn breaking.

I must down to the seas again, for the call of the running tide
Is a wild call and a clear call that may not be denied;
And all I ask is a windy day with the white clouds flying,
And the flung spray and the blown spume, and the sea-gulls crying.

I must down to the seas again to the vagrant gypsy life.
To the gull's way and the whale's way where the wind's like a whetted knife;
And all I ask is a merry yarn from a laughing fellow-rover,
And quiet sleep and a sweet dream when the long trick's over.

Roadways

ONE road leads to London,
One road runs to Wales,
My road leads me seawards
To the white dipping sails.

One road leads to the river,
As it goes singing slow;
My road leads to shipping,
Where the bronzed sailors go.

Leads me, lures me, calls me
To salt green tossing sea;
A road without earth's road-dust
Is the right road for me.

A wet road heaving, shining,
And wild with seagulls' cries,
A mad salt sea-wind blowing
The salt spray in my eyes.

My road calls me, lures me
West, east, south, and north;
Most roads lead men homewards,
My road leads me forth

To add more miles to the tally
Of grey miles left behind,
In quest of that one beauty
God put me here to find.

On Growing Old

BE WITH me, Beauty, for the fire is dying,
My dog and I are old, too old for roving,
Man, whose young passion sets the spindrift flying
Is soon too lame to march, too cold for loving.

I take the book and gather to the fire,
Turning old yellow leaves; minute by minute,
The clock ticks to my heart; a withered wire
Moves a thin ghost of music in the spinet.

I cannot sail your seas, I cannot wander,
Your cornland, nor your hill-land nor your valleys,
Ever again, nor share the battle yonder
Where the young knight the broken squadron rallies.

Only stay quiet while my mind remembers
The beauty of fire from the beauty of embers.

Beauty, have pity, for the strong have power,
The rich their wealth, the beautiful their grace,
Summer of man its sunlight and its flower,
Spring time of man all April in a face.

Only, as in the jostling in the Strand,
Where the mob thrusts or loiters or is loud,
The beggar with the saucer in his hand
Asks only a penny from the passing crowd,

So, from this glittering world with all its fashion,
Its fire and play of men, its stir, its march,
Let me have wisdom, Beauty, wisdom and passion,
Bread to the soul, rain where the summers parch.

Give me but these, and though the darkness close
Even the night will blossom as the rose.

AMY LOWELL

(1874–1925)

Madonna of the Evening Flowers

ALL day long I have been working
Now I am tired.
I call: "Where are you?"
But there is only the oak tree rustling in the wind.
The house is very quiet,
The sun shines in on your books,
On your scissors and thimble just put down,
But you are not there.
Suddenly I am lonely:
Where are you?
I go about searching.

Then I see you,
Standing under a spire of pale blue larkspur,
With a basket of roses on your arm.
You are cool, like silver,
And you smile.
I think the Canterbury bells are playing little tunes.

You tell me that the peonies need spraying,
That the columbines have overrun all bounds,
That the pyrus japonica should be cut back and rounded.
You tell me these things.
But I look at you, heart of silver,
White heart-flame of polished silver,
Burning beneath the blue steeples of the larkspur.
And I long to kneel instantly at your feet,
While all about us peal the loud, sweet Te Deums of the Canterbury bells

Patterns

I WALK down the garden-paths,
And all the daffodils
Are blowing, and the bright blue squills.
I walk down the patterned garden-paths
In my stiff, brocaded gown.
With my powdered hair and jewelled fan,
I too am a rare
Pattern. As I wander down
The garden-paths.

My dress is richly figured,
And the train
Makes a pink and silver stain
On the gravel, and the thrift
Of the borders.
Just a plate of current fashion,
Tripping by in high-heeled, ribboned shoes.
Not a softness anywhere about me,
Only whale-bone and brocade.
And I sink on a seat in the shade
Of a lime-tree. For my passion
Wars against the stiff brocade.
The daffodils and squills
Flutter in the breeze
As they please.
And I weep;
For the lime-tree is in blossom
And one small flower has dropped upon my bosom.

And the plashing of waterdrops
In the marble fountain
Comes down the garden-paths.
The dripping never stops.
Underneath my stiffened gown
Is the softness of a woman bathing in a marble basin,

A basin in the midst of hedges grown
So thick, she cannot see her lover hiding.
But she guesses he is near,
And the sliding of the water
Seems the stroking of a dear
Hand upon her.
What is Summer in a fine brocaded gown!
I should like to see it lying in a heap upon the ground.
All the pink and silver crumpled upon the ground.

I would be the pink and silver as I ran along the paths,
And he would stumble after,
Bewildered by my laughter.
I should see the sun flashing from his sword-hilt and the buckles on his shoes.
I would choose
To lead him in a maze along the patterned paths,
A bright and laughing maze for my heavy-booted lover,
Till he caught me in the shade,
And the buttons of his waistcoat bruised my body as he clasped me,
Aching, melting, unafraid.
With the shadows of the leaves and the sundrops,
And the plopping of the waterdrops,
All about us in the open afternoon—
I am very like to swoon
With the weight of this brocade
For the sun sifts through the shade.

Underneath the fallen blossom
In my bosom,
Is a letter I have hid.
It was brought to me this morning by a rider from the Duke.
"Madam, we regret to inform you that Lord Hartwell
Died in action Thursday se'nnight."
As I read it in the white, morning sunlight,
The letters squirmed like snakes.
"Any answer, Madam?" said my footman.
"No," I told him.
"See that the messenger takes some refreshment.

No, no answer."
And I walked into the garden,
Up and down the patterned paths,
In my stiff, correct brocade.
The blue and yellow flowers stood up proudly in the sun,
Each one.
I stood upright too,
Held rigid to the pattern
By the stiffness of my gown.
Up and down I walked,
Up and down.

In a month he would have been my husband.
In a month, here, underneath this lime,
We would have broke the pattern;
He for me, and I for him,
He as Colonel, I as Lady,
On this shady seat.
He had a whim
That sunlight carried blessing.
And I answered, "It shall be as you have said."
Now he is dead.

In Summer and in Winter I shall walk
Up and down
The patterned garden-paths
In my stiff, brocaded gown.
The squills and daffodils
Will give place to pillared roses, and to asters, and to snow.
I shall go
Up and down,
In my gown.
Gorgeously arrayed,
Boned and stayed.
And the softness of my body will be guarded from embrace
By each button, hook, and lace.
For the man who should loose me is dead,
Fighting with the Duke in Flanders,
In a pattern called a war.
Christ! What are patterns for?

ROBERT FROST

(1875–)

Mending Wall

SOMETHING there is that doesn't love a wall,
That sends the frozen-ground-swell under it,
And spills the upper boulders in the sun;
And makes gaps even two can pass abreast.
The work of hunters is another thing:
I have come after them and made repair
Where they have left not one stone on a stone,
But they would have the rabbit out of hiding,
To please the yelping dogs. The gaps I mean,
No one has seen them made or heard them made,
But at spring mending-time we find them there.
I let my neighbor know beyond the hill;
And on a day we meet to walk the line
And set the wall between us once again.
We keep the wall between us as we go.
To each the boulders that have fallen to each.
And some are loaves and some so nearly balls
We have to use a spell to make them balance:
"Stay where you are until our backs are turned!"
We wear our fingers rough with handling them.
Oh, just another kind of outdoor game,
One on a side. It comes to little more:
There where it is we do not need the wall:
He is all pine and I am apple-orchard.
My apple trees will never get across
And eat the cones under his pines, I tell him.
He only says, "Good fences make good neighbors."
Spring is the mischief in me, and I wonder
If I could put a notion in his head:
"*Why* do they make good neighbors? Isn't it
Where there are cows? But here there are no cows.
Before I built a wall I'd ask to know
What I was walling in or walling out,
And to whom I was like to give offence.

Something there is that doesn't love a wall,
That wants it down!" I could say "elves" to him,
But it's not elves exactly, and I'd rather
He said it for himself. I see him there,
Bringing a stone grasped firmly by the top
In each hand, like an old-stone savage armed.
He moves in darkness, as it seems to me,
Not of woods only and the shade of trees.
He will not go behind his father's saying,
And he likes having thought of it so well
He says again, "Good fences make good neighbors."

Stopping by Woods on a Snowy Evening

WHOSE woods these are I think I know.
His house is in the village though;
He will not see me stopping here
To watch his woods fill up with snow.

My little horse must think it queer
To stop without a farmhouse near
Between the woods and frozen lake
The darkest evening of the year.

He gives his harness bells a shake
To ask if there is some mistake.
The only other sound's the sweep
Of easy wind and downy flake.

The woods are lovely, dark and deep.
But I have promises to keep,
And miles to go before I sleep,
And miles to go before I sleep.

AMELIA JOSEPHINE BURR

(1878–)

A Song of Living

BECAUSE I have loved life, I shall have no sorrow to die.
I have sent up my gladness on wings, to be lost in the blue of the sky.
I have run and leaped with the rain, I have taken the wind to my breast.
My cheek like a drowsy child to the face of the earth I have pressed.
Because I have loved life, I shall have no sorrow to die.
I have kissed young Love on the lips, I have heard his song to the end
I have struck my hand like a seal in the loyal hand of a friend.
I have known the peace of heaven, the comfort of work done well.
I have longed for death in the darkness and risen alive out of hell.
Because I have loved life, I shall have no sorrow to die.
I give a share of my soul to the world where my course is run.
I know that another shall finish the task I must leave undone.
I know that no flower, no flint was in vain on the path I trod.
As one looks on a face through a window, through life I have looked on God.
Because I have loved life, I shall have no sorrow to die.

KARLE WILSON BAKER

(1878–)

Let Me Grow Lovely

LET me grow lovely, growing old—
So many fine things do:
Laces, and ivory, and gold,
And silks need not be new;

And there is healing in old trees,
Old streets a glamour hold;
Why may not I, as well as these,
Grow lovely, growing old?

ADELAIDE CRAPSEY

(1878–1914)

Song

I MAKE my shroud but no one knows,
So shimmering fine it is and fair,
With stitches set in even rows.
I make my shroud but no one knows.

In door-way where the lilac blows,
Humming a little wandering air,
I make my shroud and no one knows,
So shimmering fine it is and fair.

CARL SANDBURG

(1878–)

Fog

THE fog comes
on little cat feet.

It sits looking
over harbor and city
on silent haunches
and then, moves on.

Grass

PILE the bodies high at Austerlitz and Waterloo,
Shovel them under and let me work—
  I am the grass; I cover all.

And pile them high at Gettysburg
And pile them high at Ypres and Verdun.
Shovel them under and let me work.
Two years, ten years, and passengers ask the conductor:
  What place is this?
  Where are we now?

  I am the grass.
  Let me work.

(NICHOLAS) VACHEL LINDSAY

(1879–1931)

Abraham Lincoln Walks at Midnight

It is portentous, and a thing of state
  That here at midnight, in our little town
A mourning figure walks, and will not rest
  Near the old court-house pacing up and down.

Or by his homestead, or the shadowed yards
  He lingers where his children used to play,
Or through the market, on the well-worn stones
  He stalks until the dawn-stars burn away.

A bronzed, lank man! His suit of ancient black,
  A famous high top-hat and plain worn shawl
Make him the quaint great figure that men love,
  The prairie-lawyer, master of us all.

He cannot sleep upon his hillside now.
  He is among us, as in times before!
And we who toss and lie awake for long
  Breathe deep, and start, to see him pass the door.

His head is bowed. He thinks on men and kings.
Yea, when the sick world cries, how can he sleep?
Too many peasants fight, they know not why,
Too many homesteads in black terror weep.

The sins of all the war-lords burn his heart.
He sees the dreadnaughts scouring every main.
He carries on his shawl-wrapt shoulders now
The bitterness, the folly and the pain.

He cannot rest until a spirit-dawn
Shall come;—the shining hope of Europe free;
The league of sober folk, the Workers' Earth
Bringing long peace to Cornland, Alp and Sea.

It breaks his heart that kings must murder still,
That all his hours of travail here for men
Seem yet in vain. And who will bring white peace
That he may sleep upon his hill again?

WILFRID WILSON GIBSON

(1880–)

The Fear

I DO not fear to die
'Neath the open sky,
To meet death in the fight
Face to face, upright.

But when at last we creep
Into a hole to sleep,
I tremble, cold with dread,
Lest I wake up dead.

Back

THEY ask me where I've been,
And what I've done and seen.
And what can I reply
Who knows it wasn't I,
But someone just like me,
Who went across the sea
And with my head and hands
Killed men in foreign lands . . .
Though I must bear the blame
Because he bore my name.

Marriage

GOING my way of old
Contented more or less
I dreamt not life could hold
Such happiness.

I dreamt not that love's way
Could keep the golden height
Day after happy day,
Night after night.

ALFRED NOYES

(1880–)

The Barrel-Organ[1]

THERE'S a barrel-organ caroling across a golden street
In the City as the sun sinks low;
And the music's not immortal; but the world has made it sweet
And fulfilled it with the sunset glow;

[1] Reprinted by permission from *Collected Poems,* Vol. I, by Alfred Noyes. Copyright, 1906, Frederick A. Stokes Company.

And it pulses through the pleasures of the City and the pain
  That surround the singing organ like a large eternal light;
And they've given it a glory and a part to play again
  In the Symphony that rules the day and night.

And now it's marching onward through the realms of old romance,
  And trolling out a fond familiar tune,
And now it's roaring cannon down to fight the King of France,
  And now it's prattling softly to the moon,
And all around the organ there's a sea without a shore
  Of human joys and wonders and regrets;
To remember and to recompense the music evermore
  For what the cold machinery forgets. . . .

Yes; as the music changes,
  Like a prismatic glass,
It takes the light and ranges
  Through all the moods that pass;
Dissects the common carnival
  Of passions and regrets,
And gives the world a glimpse of all
  The colors it forgets.

And there *La Traviata* sighs
  Another sadder song;
And there *Il Trovatore* cries
  A tale of deeper wrong;
And bolder knights to battle go
  With sword and shield and lance,
Than ever here on earth below
  Have whirled into—*a dance!*—

Go down to Kew in lilac-time, in lilac-time, in lilac-time;
  Go down to Kew in lilac-time (it isn't far from London!)
And you shall wander hand in hand with love in summer's wonderland;
  Go down to Kew in lilac-time (it isn't far from London!)

The cherry-trees are seas of bloom and soft perfume and sweet perfume,
  The cherry-trees are seas of bloom (and oh, so near to London!)
And there they say, when dawn is high and all the world's a blaze of sky
  The cuckoo, though he's very shy, will sing a song for London.

The Dorian nightingale is rare and yet they say you'll hear him there
At Kew, at Kew in lilac-time (and oh, so near to London!)
The linnet and the throstle, too, and after dark the long halloo
And golden-eyed *tu-whit, tu-whoo* of owls that ogle London.

For Noah hardly knew a bird of any kind that isn't heard
At Kew, at Kew in lilac-time (and oh, so near to London!)
And when the rose begins to pout and all the chestnut spires are out
You'll hear the rest without a doubt, all chorusing for London:—

Come down to Kew in lilac-time, in lilac-time, in lilac-time;
Come down to Kew in lilac-time (it isn't far from London!)
And you shall wander hand in hand with love in summer's wonderland;
Come down to Kew in lilac-time (it isn't far from London!)

And then the troubadour begins to thrill the golden street,
In the City as the sun sinks low;
And in all the gaudy busses there are scores of weary feet
Marking time, sweet time, with a dull mechanic beat,
And a thousand hearts are plunging to a love they'll never meet,
Through the meadows of the sunset, through the poppies and the wheat,
In the land where the dead dreams go.

Verdi, Verdi, when you wrote *Il Trovatore* did you dream
Of the City when the sun sinks low,
Of the organ and the monkey and the many-colored stream
On the Piccadilly pavement, of the myriad eyes that seem
To be litten for a moment with a wild Italian gleam
As *A che la morte* parodies the world's eternal theme
And pulses with the sunset-glow?

There's a thief, perhaps, that listens with a face of frozen stone
In the City as the sun sinks low;
There's a portly man of business with a balance of his own,
There's a clerk and there's a butcher of a soft reposeful tone.
And they're all of them returning to the heavens they have known:
They are crammed and jammed in busses and—they're each of them alone
In the land where the dead dreams go.

There's a very modish woman and her smile is very bland
 In the City as the sun sinks low;
And her hansom jingles onward, but her little jeweled hand
Is clenched a little tighter and she cannot understand
What she wants or why she wanders to that undiscovered land,
For the parties there are not at all the sort of thing she planned,
 In the land where the dead dreams go.

There's a rowing man that listens and his heart is crying out
 In the City as the sun sinks low;
For the barge, the eight, the Isis, and the coach's whoop and shout,
For the minute-gun, the counting and the long dishevelled rout,
For the howl along the tow-path and a fate that's still in doubt,
For a roughened oar to handle and a race to think about
 In the land where the dead dreams go.

There's a laborer that listens to the voices of the dead
 In the City as the sun sinks low;
And his hand begins to tremble and his face to smoulder red
As he sees a loafer watching him and—there he turns his head
And stares into the sunset where his April love is fled,
For he hears her softly singing and his lonely soul is led
 Through the land where the dead dreams go.

There's an old and haggard demi-rep, it's ringing in her ears,
 In the City as the sun sinks low;
With the wild and empty sorrow of the love that blights and sears,
Oh, and if she hurries onward, then be sure, be sure she hears,
Hears and bears the bitter burden of the unforgotten years,
And her laugh's a little harsher and her eyes are brimmed with tears
 For the land where the dead dreams go.

There's a barrel-organ caroling across a golden street
 In the City as the sun sinks low;
Though the music's only Verdi there's a world to make it sweet
Just as yonder yellow sunset where the earth and heaven meet
Mellows all the sooty City! Hark, a hundred thousand feet
Are marching on to glory through the poppies and the wheat
 In the land where the dead dreams go.

So it's Jeremiah, Jeremiah,
What have you to say
When you meet the garland girls
Tripping on their way?

All around my gala hat
I wear a wreath of roses
(A long and lonely year it is
I've waited for the May!)
If any one should ask you,
The reason why I wear it is—
My own love, my true love
Is coming home to-day.

And it's buy a bunch of violets for the lady
(*It's lilac-time in London; it's lilac-time in London!*)
Buy a bunch of violets for the lady
While the sky burns blue above:

On the other side of the street you'll find it shady
(*It's lilac-time in London; it's lilac-time in London!*)
But buy a bunch of violets for the lady
And tell her she's your own true love.

There's a barrel-organ caroling across a golden street
In the City as the sun sinks glittering and slow;
And the music's not immortal; but the world has made it sweet
And enriched it with the harmonies that make a song complete
In the deeper heavens of music where the night and morning meet,
As it dies into the sunset-glow;
And it pulses through the pleasures of the City and the pain
That surround the singing organ like a large eternal light,
And they've given it a glory and a part to play again
In the Symphony that rules the day and night.

And there, as the music changes,
The song runs round again.
Once more it turns and ranges
Through all its joy and pain,

Dissects the common carnival
  Of passions and regrets;
And the wheeling world remembers all
  The wheeling song forgets.

Once more *La Traviata* sighs
  Another sadder song:
Once more *Il Trovatore* cries
  A tale of deeper wrong;
Once more the knights to battle go
  With sword and shield and lance
Till once, once more, the shattered foe
  Has whirled into—*a dance!*

Come down to Kew in lilac-time, in lilac-time, in lilac-time;
  Come down to Kew in lilac-time (it isn't far from London!)
And you shall wander hand in hand with love in summer's wonderland;
  Come down to Kew in lilac-time (it isn't far from London!)

The Highwayman[1]

PART ONE

THE wind was a torrent of darkness among the gusty trees,
The moon was a ghostly galleon tossed upon cloudy seas,
The road was a ribbon of moonlight over the purple moor,
And the highwayman came riding—
            Riding—riding—
The highwayman came riding, up to the old inn-door.

He'd a French cocked-hat on his forehead, a bunch of lace at his chin,
A coat of the claret velvet, and breeches of brown doe-skin;
They fitted with never a wrinkle: his boots were up to the thigh!
And he rode with a jewelled twinkle,
            His pistol butts a-twinkle,
His rapier hilt a-twinkle, under the jewelled sky.

[1] Reprinted by permission from *Collected Poems,* Vol. I, by Alfred Noyes. Copyright, 1906, by Frederick A. Stokes Company.

Over the cobbles he clattered and clashed in the dark inn-yard,
And he tapped with his whip on the shutters, but all was locked and barred;
He whistled a tune to the window, and who should be waiting there
But the landlord's black-eyed daughter,
Bess, the landlord's daughter,
Plaiting a dark red love-knot into her long black hair.

And dark in the dark old inn-yard a stable-wicket creaked
Where Tim, the ostler, listened; his face was white and peaked;
His eyes were hollows of madness, his hair like mouldy hay,
But he loved the landlord's daughter,
The landlord's red-lipped daughter;
Dumb as a dog he listened, and he heard the robber say—

"One kiss, my bonny sweetheart, I'm after a prize tonight,
But I shall be back with the yellow gold before the morning light;
Yet, if they press me sharply, and harry me through the day,
Then look for me by moonlight,
Watch for me by moonlight,
I'll come to thee by moonlight, though hell should bar the way."

He rose upright in the stirrups; he scarce could reach her hand,
But she loosened her hair i' the casement! His face burnt like a brand
As the black cascade of perfume came tumbling over his breast;
And he kissed its waves in the moonlight,
(Oh, sweet black waves in the moonlight!)
Then he tugged at his reins in the moonlight, and galloped away to the West.

PART TWO

He did not come in the dawning; he did not come at noon;
And out o' the tawny sunset, before the rise o' the moon,
When the road was a gipsy's ribbon, looping the purple moor,
A red-coat troop came marching—
Marching—marching—
King George's men came marching, up to the old inn-door.

They said no word to the landlord, they drank his ale instead,
But they gagged his daughter and bound her to the foot of her narrow bed;

Two of them knelt at her casement, with muskets at their side!
There was death at every window;
And hell at one dark window;
For Bess could see, through her casement, the road that *he* would ride.

They had tied her up to attention, with many a sniggering jest;
They had bound a musket beside her, with the barrel beneath her breast!
"Now keep good watch!" and they kissed her. She heard the dead man say—
Look for me by moonlight;
Watch for me by moonlight;
I'll come to thee by moonlight, though hell should bar the way!

She twisted her hands behind her; but all the knots held good!
She writhed her hands till her fingers were wet with sweat and blood!
They stretched and strained in the darkness, and the hours crawled by like years,
Till, now, on the stroke of midnight,
Cold on the stroke of midnight,
The tip of one finger touched it! The trigger at least was hers!

The tip of one finger touched it; she strove no more for the rest!
Up, she stood up to attention, with the barrel beneath her breast,
She would not risk their hearing; she would not strive again;
For the road lay bare in the moonlight;
Blank and bare in the moonlight;
And the blood of her veins in the moonlight throbbed to her love's refrain.

Tlot-tlot, tlot-tlot! Had they heard it? The horse-hoofs ringing clear;
Tlot-tlot, tlot-tlot, in the distance? Were they deaf that they did not hear?
Down the ribbon of moonlight, over the brow of the hill,
The highwayman came riding
Riding, riding!
The red-coats looked to their priming! She stood up straight and still!

Tlot-tlot, in the frosty silence! *Tlot-tlot* in the echoing night!
Nearer he came and nearer! Her face was like a light!

Her eyes grew wide for a moment; she drew one last deep breath,
Then her finger moved in the moonlight,
Her musket shattered the moonlight,
Shattered her breast in the moonlight and warned him—with her death.

He turned; he spurred him Westward; he did not know who stood
Bowed, with her head o'er the musket, drenched with her own red blood!
Not till the dawn he heard it, his face grew gray to hear
How Bess, the landlord's daughter,
The landlord's black-eyed daughter,
Had watched for her love in the moonlight, and died in the darkness there.

Back, he spurred like a madman, shrieking a curse to the sky,
With the white road smoking behind him, and his rapier brandished high!
Blood-red were his spurs in the golden noon; wine-red was his velvet coat,
When they shot him down on the highway,
Down like a dog on the highway,
And he lay in his blood on the highway, with a bunch of lace at his throat.

. . . .

And still of a winter's night, they say, when the wind is in the trees,
When the moon is a ghostly galleon tossed upon cloudy seas,
When the road is a ribbon of moonlight over the purple moor,
A highwayman comes riding—
Riding—riding—
A highwayman comes riding up to the old inn-door.

Over the cobbles he clatters and clangs in the dark inn-yard;
And taps with his whip on the shutters, but all is locked and barred;
He whistles a tune to the window, and who should be waiting there
But the landlord's black-eyed daughter,
Bess, the landlord's daughter,
Plaiting a dark red love-knot into her long black hair.

MOIRA O'NEILL

(Now living)

Corrymeela

OVER here in England I'm helpin' wi' the hay,
And I wisht I was in Ireland the livelong day;
Weary on the English hay, an' sorra take the wheat!
Och! Corrymeela, an' the blue sky over it.

There's a deep dumb river flowin' by beyont the heavy trees,
This livin' air is moithered wi' the hummin' o' the bees;
I wisht I'd hear the Claddagh burn go runnin' through the heat,
Past Corrymeela, wi' the blue sky over it.

The people that's in England is richer nor the Jews,
There's not the smallest young gossoon but thravels in his shoes!
I'd give the pipe between me teeth to see a barefut child,
Och! Corrymeela, an' the low south wind.

Here's hands so full o' money an' hearts so full o' care,
By the luck o' love! I'd still go light for all I did go bare.
"God save ye, colleen dhas," I said; the girl she thought me wild!
Fair Corrymeela, an' the low south wind.

D'ye mind me now, the song at night is mortal hard to raise,
The girls are heavy goin' here, the boys are ill to plase;
When ones't I'm out this workin' hive, 'tis I'll be back again—
Aye, Corrymeela, in the same soft rain.

The puff o' smoke from one ould roof before an English town!
For a shaugh wid Andy Feelan here I'd give a silver crown,
For a curl o' like Mollie's ye'll ask the like in vain,
Sweet Corrymeela, an' the same soft rain.

PADRAIC COLUM

(1881–)

An Old Woman of the Roads

O TO have a little house!
To own the hearth and stool and all!
The heaped up sods upon the fire,
The pile of turf against the wall!

To have a clock with weights and chains
And pendulum, swinging up and down!
A dresser filled with shining delph,
Speckled and white and blue and brown!

I could be busy all the day
Clearing and sweeping hearth and floor,
And fixing on their shelf again
My white and blue and speckled store!

I could be quiet there at night
Beside the fire and by myself,
Sure of a bed and loth to leave
The ticking clock and the shining delph!

Och! but I'm weary of mist and dark,
And roads where there's never a house nor bush,
And tired I am of bog and road
And the crying wind and the lonesome hush!

And I am praying to God on high,
And I am praying Him night and day,
For a little house—a house of my own—
Out of the wind's and the rain's way.

JOHN G. NEIHARDT

(1881–)

Let Me Live Out My Years

LET me live out my years in heat of blood!
Let me die drunken with the dreamer's wine!
Let me not see this soul-house built of mud
Go toppling to the dust—a vacant shrine.

Let me go quickly, like a candle light
Snuffed out just at the heydey of its glow.
Give me high noon—and let it then be night!
Thus would I go.

And grant that when I face the grisly Thing,
My song may trumpet down the gray Perhaps.
Let me be as a tune-swept fiddlestring
That feels the Master Melody—and snaps!

HERMANN HAGEDORN

(1882–)

Song Is So Old

SONG is so old,
Love is so new—
Let me be still
And kneel to you.

Let me be still
And breathe no word,
Save what my warm blood
Sings unheard.

Let my warm blood
Sing low of you—
Song is so fair,
Love is so new.

JAMES STEPHENS

(1882–)

Deirdre

Do NOT let any woman read this verse!
It is for men, and after them their sons,
And their sons' sons!

The time comes when our hearts sink utterly;
When we remember Deirdre, and her tale,
And that her lips are dust.

Once she did tread the earth: men took her hand;
They looked into her eyes and said their say,
And she replied to them.

More than two thousand years it is since she
Was beautiful: she trod the waving grass;
She saw the clouds.

Two thousand years! The grass is still the same;
The clouds as lovely as they were that time
When Deirdre was alive.

But there has been again no woman born
Who was so beautiful; not one so beautiful
Of all the women born.

Let all men go apart and mourn together!
No man can ever love her! Not a man
Can dream to be her lover!

No man can bend before her! No man say—
What could one say to her? There are no words
That one could say to her!

Now she is but a story that is told
Beside the fire! No man can ever be
The friend of that poor queen!

Little Things

LITTLE things that run and quail
And die in silence and despair;

Little things that fight and fail
And fall on earth and sea and air;

All trapped and frightened little things,
The mouse, the coney, hear our prayer.

As we forgive those done to us,
The lamb, the linnet, and the hare,

Forgive us all our trespasses,
Little creatures everywhere.

MAX EASTMAN

(1883–)

Diogenes

A HUT, and a tree,
And a hill for me,
And a piece of a weedy meadow.
I'll ask no thing,
Of God or King,
But to clear away his shadow.

JAMES ELROY FLECKER
(1884–1915)

To a Poet a Thousand Years Hence

I WHO am dead a thousand years,
  And wrote this sweet archaic song,
Send you my words for messengers
  The way I shall not pass along.

I care not if you bridge the seas,
  Or ride secure the cruel sky,
Or build consummate palaces
  Of metal or of masonry.

But have you wine and music still,
  And statues and bright-eyed love,
And foolish thoughts of good and ill,
  And prayers to them who sit above?

How shall we conquer? Like a wind
  That falls at eve our fancies blow,
And old Mæonides the blind
  Said it three thousand years ago.

O friend unseen, unborn, unknown,
  Student of our sweet English tongue,
Read out my words at night, alone:
  I was a poet, I was young.

Since I can never see your face,
  And never shake you by the hand,
I send my soul through time and space
  To greet you. You will understand.

The Old Ships

I HAVE seen old ships sail like swans asleep
Beyond the village which men still call Tyre,
With leaden age o'ercargoed, dipping deep
For Famagusta and the hidden sun
That rings black Cyprus with a lake of fire;
And all those ships were certainly so old
Who knows how oft with squat and noisy gun,
Questing brown slaves or Syrian oranges,
The pirate Genoese
Hell-raked them till they rolled
Blood, water, fruit, and corpses up the hold.
But now through friendly seas they softly run,
Painted the mid-sea blue or shore-sea green,
Still patterned with the vine and grapes in gold.
But I have seen,
Pointing her shapely shadows from the dawn
And image tumbled on a rose-swept bay,
A drowsy ship of some yet older day;
And, wonder's breath indrawn,
Thought I—who knows—who knows—but that same
(Fished up beyond Ææa, patched up new
—Stern painted brighter blue—)
That talkative, bald-headed seaman came
(Twelve patient comrades sweating at the oar)
From Troy's doom-crimson shore,
And with great lies about his wooden horse
Set the crew laughing, and forgot his course.

It was so old a ship—who knows—who knows?
—And yet so beautiful, I watched in vain
To see the mast burst open with a rose,
And the whole deck put on its leaves again.

SARA TEASDALE

(1884–)

The Solitary

My heart has grown rich with the passing of years,
I have less need now then when I was young
To share myself with every comer,
Or shape my thoughts into words with my tongue.

It is one to me that they come or go
If I have myself and the drive of my will,
And strength to climb on a summer night
And watch the stars swarm over the hill.

Let me think I love them more than I do,
Let them think I care, though I go alone,
If it lifts their pride, what is it to me,
Who am self-complete as a flower or a stone?

HUMBERT WOLFE

(1885–)

Love Is a Keeper of Swans

Love is a keeper of swans!
Helen, amid what dark wherries
are you steering the silver boat,
that for all the love of Paris,
and his lips against your throat,
passed out of Troy with windless vans?

And, fairest of Italians,
where do you glimmer, Beatrice?
what light of heaven stains your wings
with gold that were all fleur de lys?
And do you hear when Dante sings?
"Love is a keeper of swans."

Love is a keeper of swans.
Have you left the barren plain,
and stormed a gold-eagle's eyrie?
Queen-swan of the eagle strain,
what mountain has you, Mary?
and is its name, as ever, still romance?

And you, bright cygnet of immortal Hans,
you need not join your sisters yet.
You have all time. Why should you hasten?
What though the lake with reeds be set,
one reed is murmuring, oh, listen!
"Love is a keeper of swans."

LOUIS UNTERMEYER

(1885–)

Caliban in the Coal Mines

God, we don't like to complain;
  We know that the mine is no lark.
But—there's the pools from the rain;
  But—there's the cold and the dark.

God, You don't know what it is—
  You, in Your well-lighted sky—
Watching the meteors whizz;
  Warm, with a sun always by.

God, if You had but the moon
  Stuck in Your cap for a lamp,
Even You'd tire of it soon,
  Down in the dark and the damp.

Nothing but blackness above
  And nothing that moves but the cars. . . .
God, if You wish for our love,
  Fling us a handful of stars!

Prayer

God, though this life is but a wraith,
  Although we know not what we use,
Although we grope with little faith,
  Give me the heart to fight—and lose.

Ever insurgent let me be,
  Make me more daring than devout;
From sleek contentment keep me free,
  And fill me with a buoyant doubt.

Open my eyes to visions girt
  With beauty, and with wonder lit—
But let me always see the dirt,
  And all that spawn and die in it.

Open my ears to music; let
  Me thrill with Spring's first flutes and drums—
But never let me dare forget
  The bitter ballads of the slums.

From compromise and things half-done,
  Keep me, with stern and stubborn pride.
And when, at last, the fight is won,
  God, keep me still unsatisfied.

JOYCE KILMER
(1886–1918)

Trees

I THINK that I shall never see
A poem lovely as a tree.

A tree whose hungry mouth is prest
Against the earth's sweet flowing breast;

A tree that looks at God all day
And lifts her leafy arms to pray;

A tree that may in summer wear
A nest of robins in her hair;

Upon whose bosom snow has lain;
Who intimately lives with rain.

Poems are made by fools like me,
But only God can make a tree.

WILLIAM ROSE BENÉT
(1886–)

Merchants From Cathay

How that They Came.

THEIR heels slapped their bumping mules; their fat chaps
glowed.
Glory unto Mary, each seemed to wear a crown!
Like sunset their robes were on the wide, white road:
So we saw those mad merchants come dusting into
town!

Of their Beasts,

Two paunchy beasts they rode on and two they drov
before.
May the Saints all help us, the tiger-stripes they had!
And the panniers upon them swelled full of stuffs and ore
The square buzzed and jostled at a sight so mad.

And their Boast,

They bawled in their beards, and their turbans they wried
They stopped by the stalls with curvetting and clatter.
As bronze as the bracken their necks and faces dyed—
And a stave they sat singing, to tell us of the matter.

With its Burthen

"For your silks, to Sugarmago! For your dyes, to Isfahan
Weird fruits from the Isle o' Lamaree!
But for magic merchandise,
For treasure-trove and spice,
Here's a catch and a carol to the great, grand Chan,
The King of all the Kings across the sea!

And Chorus.

"Here's a catch and a carol to the great grand Chan;
For we won through the deserts to his sunset barbican;
And the mountains of his palace no Titan's reach may spa
Where he wields his seignorie!

A first Stave Fearsome,

"Red-as-blood skins of Panthers, so bright against the sun
On the walls of the halls where his pillared state is set
They daze with a blaze no man may look upon!
And with conduits of beverage those floors run wet!

And a second Right hard To stomach

"His wives stiff with riches, they sit before him there.
Bird and beast at his feast make song and clappin
cheer.
And jugglers and enchanters, all walking on the air,
Make fall eclipse and thunder—make moons and sun
appear!

And a third, Which is a Laughable Thing.

"Once the Chan, by his enemies sore-prest, and sorel
spent,
Lay, so they say, in a thicket 'neath a tree
Where the howl of an owl vexed his foes from thei
intent:
Then that fowl for an holy bird of reverence made he!

f the Chan's Hunting

"And when he will a-hunting go, four elephants of white
Draw his wheeling daïs of lignum aloes made;
And marquises and admirals and barons of delight
All courier his chariot, in orfrayes arrayed!

Ve gape to lear them end,

"A catch and a carol to the great, grand Chan!
Pastmasters of disasters, our desert caravan
Won through all peril to his sunset barbican,
Where he wields his seignorie!
And crowns he gave us! We end where we began:
A catch and a carol to the great, grand Chan,
The King of all the Kings across the sea!"

Ind are in 'error,

Those mad, antic Merchants! Their striped beasts did beat
The market-square suddenly with hooves of beaten gold!
The ground yawned gaping and flamed beneath our feet!
They plunged to Pits Abysmal with their wealth untold!

Ind dread : is Devil's Work!

And some say the Chan himself in anger dealt the stroke—
For sharing of his secrets with silly, common folk:
But Holy, Blessed Mary, preserve us as you may
Lest once more those mad Merchants come chanting from Cathay!

SHEAMUS O'SHEEL

(1886–)

He Whom a Dream Hath Possessed

He whom a dream hath possessed knoweth no more of doubting,
For mist and the blowing of winds and the mouthing of words he scorns;
No sinuous speech and smooth he hears, but a knightly shouting,
And never comes darkness down, yet he greeteth a million morns.

He whom a dream hath possessed knoweth no more of roaming.
All roads and the flowing of waves and the speediest flight he knows,
But wherever his feet are set his soul is forever homing,
And going he comes, and coming he heareth a call and goes.

He whom a dream hath possessed knoweth no more of sorrow.
At death and the dropping of leaves and the fading of sun he smiles,
For a dream remembers no past and takes no thought of a morrow,
And staunch amid seas of doom a dream sets the ultimate isles.

He whom a dream hath possessed treads the impalpable marches.
From the dust of the day's long road he leaps to a laughing star,
And the ruin of worlds that fall he views from eternal arches,
And rides God's battlefield in a flashing and golden car.

SIEGFRIED SASSOON

(1886–)

Everyone Sang

EVERYONE suddenly burst out singing;
And I was filled with such delight
As prisoned birds must find in freedom
Winging wildly across the white
Orchards and dark green fields; on; on; and out of sight.

Everyone's voice was suddenly lifted,
And beauty came like the setting sun.
My heart was shaken with tears, and horror
Drifted away . . . O but every one
Was a bird; and the song was wordless; the singing will never be done.

RUPERT BROOKE
(1887–1915)

The Soldier

If I should die, think only this of me:
  That there's some corner of a foreign field
That is for ever England. There shall be
  In that rich earth a richer dust concealed;
A dust whom England bore, shaped, made aware,
  Gave, once, her flowers to love, her ways to roam,
A body of England's, breathing English air,
  Washed by the rivers, blest by suns of home.

And think, this heart, all evil shed away,
  A pulse in the eternal mind, no less
    Gives somewhere back the thoughts by England given;
Her sights and sounds; dreams happy as her day;
  And laughter, learnt of friends; and gentleness,
    In hearts at peace, under an English heaven.

Day That I Have Loved

Tenderly, day that I have loved, I close your eyes,
  And smooth your quiet brow, and fold your thin dead hands.
The grey veils of the half-light deepen; colour dies.
  I bear you, a light burden, to the shrouded sands,

Where lies your waiting boat, by wreaths of the sea's making
  Mist-garlanded, with all grey weeds of the water crowned.
There you'll be laid, past fear of sleep or hope of waking;
  And over the unmoving sea, without a sound,

Faint hands will row you outward, out beyond our sight,
  Us with stretched arms and empty eyes on the far-gleaming
And marble sand. . . .
      Beyond the shifting cold twilight,
  Further than laughter goes, or tears, further than dreaming,

There'll be no port, no dawn-lit islands! But the drear
  Waste darkening, and, at length, flame ultimate on the deep.
Oh, the last fire—and you, unkissed, unfriended there!
  Oh, the lone way's red ending, and we not there to weep!

(We found you pale and quiet, and strangely crowned with flowers,
  Lovely and secret as a child. You came with us,
Came happily, hand in hand with the young dancing hours,
  High on the downs at dawn!) Void now and tenebrous,

The grey sands curve before me . . .
        From the inland meadows,
  Fragrant of June and clover, floats the dark, and fills
The hollow sea's dead face with little creeping shadows,
  And the white silence brims the hollow of the hills.

Close in the nest is folded every weary wing,
  Hushed all the joyful voices; and we, who held you dear,
Eastward we turn, and homeward, alone, remembering . . .
  Day that I loved, day that I loved, the Night is here!

ALAN SEEGER

(1888–1916)

I Have a Rendezvous with Death

I HAVE a rendezvous with Death
At some disputed barricade,
When Spring comes back with rustling shade
And apple-blossoms fill the air—
I have a rendezvous with Death
When Spring brings back blue days and fair.

It may be he shall take my hand
And lead me into his dark land
And close my eyes and quench my breath—
It may be I shall pass him still.
I have a rendezvous with Death
On some scarred slope of battered hill,
When Spring comes round again this year
And the first meadow-flowers appear.

God knows 'twere better to be deep
Pillowed in silk and scented down,
Where Love throbs out in blissful sleep,
Pulse nigh to pulse, and breath to breath,
When hushed awakenings are dear . . .
But I have a rendezvous with Death
At midnight in some flaming town,
When Spring trips north again this year,
And I to my pledged word am true,
I shall not fail that rendezvous.

CONRAD AIKEN

(1889–)

Bread and Music

MUSIC I heard with you was more than music,
And bread I broke with you was more than bread;
Now that I am without you, all is desolate;
All that was once so beautiful is dead.

Your hands once touched this table and this silver,
And I have seen your fingers hold this glass.
These things do not remember you, belovèd,
And yet your touch upon them will not pass.

For it was in my heart you moved among them,
And blessed them with your hands and with your eyes;
And in my heart they will remember always,—
They knew you once, O beautiful and wise.

This Is the Shape of the Leaf

THIS is the shape of the leaf, and this of the flower,
And this the pale bole of the tree
Which watches its bough in a pool of unwavering water
In a land we never shall see.

The thrush on the bough is silent, the dew falls softly,
In the evening is hardly a sound.
And the three beautiful pilgrims who come here together
Touch lightly the dust of the ground,

Touch it with feet that trouble the dust but as wings do,
Come shyly together, are still,
Like dancers who wait, in a pause of the music, for music
The exquisite silence to fill.

This is the thought of the first, and this of the second,
And this the grave thought of the third:
"Linger we thus for a moment, palely expectant,
And silence will end, and the bird

"Sing the pure phrase, sweet phrase, clear phrase in the twilight
To fill the blue bell of the world;
And we, who on music so leaflike have drifted together,
Leaflike apart shall be whirled

"Into what but the beauty of silence, silence forever?" . . .
. . . This is the shape of the tree,
And the flower, and the leaf, and the three pale beautiful pilgrims;
This is what you are to me.

CHRISTOPHER (DARLINGTON) MORLEY

(1890–)

Where More Is Meant

DAZZLED, how the brown moth flutters
(In my fingers prisoned tight)
Ere, through opened sash and shutters,
Loosed into the night.

Surely clutched but softly holden
(Least of struggling ticklish things)
Let him go . . .
My hand is golden,
Dusty from his wings.

The Secret

IT WAS the House of Quietness
To which I came at dusk;
The garth was lit with roses
And heavy with their musk.

The tremulous tall poplar trees
Stood whispering around,
The gentle flicker of their plumes
More quiet than no sound.

And as I wondered at the door
What magic might be there,
The Lady of Sweet Silences
Came softly down the stair.

EDNA ST. VINCENT MILLAY

(1892–)

God's World

O WORLD, I cannot hold thee close enough!
Thy winds, thy wide grey skies!
Thy mists, that roll and rise!
Thy woods, this autumn day, that ache and sag
And all but cry with colour! That gaunt crag
To crush! To lift the lean of that black bluff!
World, World, I cannot get thee close enough!

Long have I known a glory in it all,
But never knew I this;
Here such a passion is
As stretcheth me apart,—Lord, I do fear
Thou'st made the world too beautiful this year;
My soul is all but out of me,—let fall
No burning leaf; prithee, let no bird call.

RICHARD ALDINGTON

(1892–)

After Two Years

SHE is all so slight
And tender and white
As a May morning.
She walks without hood
At dusk. It is good
To hear her sing.

It is God's will
That I shall love her still
   As he loves Mary,
And night and day
I will go forth to pray
   That she love me.

She is as gold
Lovely, and far more cold.
   Do thou pray with me,
For if I win grace
To kiss twice her face
   God has done well to me.

V. (VICTORIA MARY) SACKVILLE WEST

(1892–)

Full Moon

SHE was wearing the coral taffeta trousers
Some one had brought her from Ispahan
And the little gold coat with pomegranate blossoms,
And the coral hafted feather fan:
As she ran down a Kentish lane in the moonlight,
And skipped in the pool of the moon as she ran.

She cared not a rap for all the big planets,
For Betelgeuse or Aldebaran
And all the big planets cared nothing for her
That small impertinent charlatan,
But she climbed on a Kentish stile in the moonlight
And laughed at the sky through the sticks of her fan.

INDEX OF AUTHORS

INDEX OF TITLES

INDEX OF FIRST LINES